DEVIANCY
AND THE FAMILY

DEVIANCY
AND THE FAMILY

Edited by

Clifton D. Bryant, Ph. D.

Professor and Head of Department of Sociology
Virginia Polytechnic Institute and State University
Blacksburg, Virginia

J. Gipson Wells, Ph. D.

Associate Professor, Department of Sociology
Western Kentucky University
Bowling Green, Kentucky

F. A. DAVIS COMPANY
PHILADELPHIA

Preface

The relationship between the family as an institution, and deviancy as a general mode of individual and group behavior, has, in our opinion, received inadequate attention. With the possible exception of a few specific forms of deviancy, such as juvenile delinquency and alcoholism, there is little in the way of a substantial body of empirical research data or comprehensive theory which links family structure and process with deviant behavior which might be concomitantly related to either. This volume attempts to assemble some appropriate materials which treat the relationship between family and deviant behavior, and, hopefully, makes some contribution toward conceptually integrating the existing literature on the subject.

There are several ways in which the concept of deviancy may be related to the family. One of the more obvious is that of the impact upon, or the reaction of, a family to a deviant act or pattern of behavior on the part of one of its members. A second linkage of deviancy and the family exists within the dynamics through which the family itself might act as a causative element or tend to precipitate deviant behavior on the part of one or more of its members. Here the family may be seen as the independent variable with respect to deviancy. A third manner in which deviancy and the family are related is in those situations in which the family itself or a family subgroup comes to be viewed as a deviant group or where certain configurations of family behavior are defined as deviant.

This collection examines deviancy and the family from all of these perspectives. The selections included in this volume represent a wide variety of disciplinary orientations and reflect an equally wide diversity of sources ranging from the more sophisticated professional journals to the popular family type periodicals. This diversity results from the fact that literature of sociological relevance, both professional and lay, concerning the topic of family deviancy is relatively limited and widely scattered, as well as our belief that the first step in developing an integrated literature is to assemble the best that is available from the various sources, and to try and organize it into some conceptually meaningful framework.

With this idea in mind, the basic organization of the book reflects a family perspective, but for those instructors who may undertake to use this volume for courses which primarily focus on deviancy, we have included an alternate contents with the articles arranged within a typological organization of deviant behavior. This alternate contents is found after the last selection in the book.

Finally, it is our hope that this volume will serve to initiate a wider interest in a somewhat neglected area, albeit one which we feel is of significant sociological import.

We are indebted to our clerical staffs at both institutions—Mrs. Katharine Van Eaton, and Mrs. Elashia Jennings, at Western Kentucky University, and Mrs. Karen Bass, Mrs. Linda Martin, and Miss Phyllis Tribble at Virginia Polytechnic Institute for their thoroughness and diligence in preparing the manuscript for publication.

CLIFTON D. BRYANT AND J. GIPSON WELLS

Contents

PART 1

INTRODUCTION

Deviancy and the Family:
A Theoretical Overview

J. GIPSON WELLS AND
CLIFTON D. BRYANT

" . . . *perhaps the best approach to criminal and antisocial behavior is not through the community and society but through the family where it is engendered.*"

F. R. Schreiber and M. Herman
Science Digest, Vol. 57, (March, 1965) p. 20.

Of all social configurations, none is more pervasive and all-embracing than the family. It is within the family that we are born, live much of our lives, and die. The family has been termed the natural matrix of personality. It provides us with our initial status, and not infrequently it is a most significant contributor, to our subsequent social statuses. Thus it is our major contact or link with the rest of society. The family affords us emotional succor, a societally legitimate channel of sexual gratification, opportunity for intense interpersonal interaction, and a shared life style. Our socialization experiences begin, and often partially continue throughout life in the family. In our sociopsychological make-up and accordingly in our behavior, we are very much a product of the family.

Just as conventional behavior on the part of an individual manifesting conformity to the norms of society may be viewed as significantly related to the family, so may deviant behavior be viewed. In this connection, the belief in such a relationship between family and deviancy has long been held as the common sense view. Furthermore, lay belief also suggests that this relationship is in fact a causal one in that the family life of the individual, if somehow socially or emotionally deficient, especially during the so-called formative years, is viewed as the foundation of subsequent emergent deviant behavior on the part of the individual. In short, citizenship, morality, and conformity

3

are nurtured in the bosom of the family. However, other relational possibilities between the family and the individual do exist, even though some of these have not been examined in the comprehensive manner which they deserve.

In recent decades the increased research activity of the social scientists in their investigations of both family life and deviant behavior has tended to enhance the popular beliefs in a strong relationship between deviant behavior and the family. Still, the weight of empirical data amassed to date is inconclusive and insufficient to fully support this belief or to adequately articulate and explain the nature of these relationships. Its strongest support exists in the observations of sociologists, psychologists, psychiatrists, social workers, and others in the various related fields, whose largely impressionistic and intuitive insights give considerable credence to the causal relationship between social deficiencies in the family and deviant activity on the part of the family member.

The aim of this introductory chapter, and subsequently the remainder of the book is to explore some of the relationships between family and deviant behavior as they manifest themselves in different configurations, and to examine these relationships in light of several theoretical perspectives which may be of use in their explanation and understanding.

While a number of core sociological concepts have acquired somewhat generalized and wide-ranging definitions which may vary with the particular context and the user of the term, this is not particularly the case with the concept of deviancy. Although considered by some to be a concept of relatively general applicability, its meaning is usually consistently specific. In most contexts, the term refers simply to norm violation, or more simply, it refers to a person or group doing what they are not supposed to be doing, or not doing what they are supposed to. A difficulty which arises in defining deviancy as norm violation is the inconsistency which sometimes appears in the definition of the term "norm." Here norms will be defined as those actions which are expected of an individual or group, given a particular role status, or situation. Thus, norms are standards of behavior or rules of conduct which exist in society as both formal laws and regulations and informal expectations. The deviant, then, is one who either openly or secretly violates society's expectations of what his behavior should be. The term "family" as used in this chapter and throughout the editorial commentary will refer mainly to the basic nuclear unit which usually consists of the adult male and female who are husband and wife, and to their children, if they have any. When additional extended kin are referred to as a part of the family, this will be specified. Additionally, our concern here is with this type of family unit rather than with the family as an institution in the broadest sense.

WAYS OF RELATING FAMILY AND DEVIANCY

There are essentially five ways in which deviancy and the family may be related; the organization of this book reflects these relationship patterns. Initially, there is deviancy which is specifically defined as the violation of norms directly related to family structure or activities. A significant portion of our societal normative structure does prescribe appropriate marital and family relationships and behavior. The resulting body of societal norms which is concerned with the regulation of the behavior of various individual family members as well as the regulation of the family as a group within the context of social life, possesses both quantity and complexity. Such norms are constituent to the family roles which dictate the expecetd behavior of the individual in his status role. Violations of these normative expectations are proscribed with legal as well as social sanctions. Because of the conflict between the restrictive and demanding nature of this normative structure and the urgency of social forces and circumstances mitigating and sometimes negating their observance, violations do occur, and with increasing frequency. Thus a family member, motivated by various social exigencies, may choose to simply abdicate his role, or he may elect to play it in an unacceptable manner, or in a manner which is disruptive to the family as well as to the surrounding community. In such instances, the individual might appropriately be termed a deviant and more specifically, a family deviant. Accordingly, a substantial amount of deviant behavior in our society takes the form of violation of familial expectation and behavioral prescription.

A second link between family and deviancy concerns the effect of an individual's deviant behavior upon his family. Whether the deviancy is intra-familial or extrafamilial, it often has some impact or influence upon the other members of the family. The family, in a sense, may become the collective victim of the errant member's behavior. The emphasis here is also on the collision of deviancy with family structure and the subsequent impetus of family disequilibrium. The systemic linkages of family and the symbiotic relationships of its constituent members may permit little slack in the absorption of deviancy and its attendant disruption and stigma. The deviancy of any one individual or set of individual members cannot help but impinge on the equilibrium of the family system itself and on the well being of the various members.

A third and opposite pattern of family deviancy involves deviant behavior on the part of one or more family members and the impact of such behavior, which, in this instance, falls primarily on one individual like the spouse or child. While it is valid to speak of a deviant person as partially the product of his family background, it is also valid to speak of an individual as the victim either directly or indirectly of deviant behavior occurring in the family or committed by family members. The victimized family member may suffer either the immediate circumstances or residual stigma and trauma resulting from such deviant acts. The family may in some instances deliberately undertake to perpetrate deviant acts upon a single member, for instance parents may jointly assault an infant or conspire to abandon a child.

An alternate view is that causative agents may be found within the family which allow for and give impetus to deviant behavior. The deviancy may not necessarily be caused by the family, but rather the meaning and motivations for deviant behavior such as problems, frustrations, and pressures, may often be identified in the family situation of the individual violator. This can be the case whether the deviancy is intrafamilial or extrafamilial. In some instances, the motivation for deviancy may extend to most, if not all, of the family members. A family may constitute a deviant social collective, with all members violating societal norms. Some accounts of criminal and deviant families are hoary with age. Stories about Gypsy families, for example, and their nefarious activities and social misdeeds are well embedded in our cultural folklore. A more relevant and topical illustration might be that of the "terrible Williamsons," an inbred clan of 2,000 related persons of Scots ancestry who travel about the country engaged in what the *New York Times* has termed "fleecing" people. As "gyp artists," they "blacktop" driveways with crankcase oil, sell inferior merchandise under misrepresented claims or conditions, and offer questionable services on a door-to-door basis.[1] Families may engage in a variety of deviant pursuits as a collective enterprise for fun, profit, or therapeutic reasons.

A fifth, and final, linkage pattern between the family and deviancy involves the various techniques and approaches which the family employs to adjust or adapt to the deviancy of one or more of its members. In some instances, the family, unable to successfully cope with the trauma of deviancy, may disintegrate. On the other hand, the family often displays considerable resilience in its reaction to the occurrence of deviancy, and also an extensive repertoire of social mechanisms and adaptive devices which allows it to cope with the disequilibrium created by the deviant behavior of its members. Such a capacity for adequate accommodation and for the reestablishment of family equilibrium following the crisis of deviancy suggests a relationship between family and deviancy as worthy of consideration as those previously mentioned.

USEFUL THEORETICAL ORIENTATIONS

In attempting to understand and explain the several relationships between deviancy and the family, a number of basic theoretical orientations have demonstrated their utility. At least one and sometimes several of the orientations to be discussed have relevancy for each of the various relationship patterns previously mentioned. Some of these theoretical orientations are relatively broad in application, while the others are more specifically derived from family sociology. They will be discussed in the following order: (1) role theory combined with systems theory; (2) conflict theory; (3) family functions theory; and (4) family crisis theory.

Role Theory and Systems Theory

Role theory attempts to explain individual and group behavior in terms of the various roles which individuals are called upon to play within group structures. A role is defined as that behavior or pattern of behavior expected of an individual who occupies a certain status or position in a group. Since each person is usually a member of several groups, he also holds several statuses and, therefore, plays multiple roles. Furthermore, statuses and their roles are always reciprocal or complimentary to other statuses and roles. It is this reciprocal nature of roles which, in fact, creates the structure of the group and binds the members to one another. Examples of reciprocal roles might be the husband and wife set, or the parent and child set.

As is readily seen, not only do individuals hold a number of statuses in a variety of groups, but one may also hold multiple statuses within a single group. As an example, the adult male may hold the statuses of father, husband, and perhaps that of son, while the child in the family might be a son, as well as a brother.[2]

It is at this point that systems theory may be introduced into the discussion, for the family may now be viewed as a system of interrelated roles and statuses in which each member is intimately and symbiotically bound to the others through the duties, rights, and obligations constituent to the various reciprocal roles.[3] Furthermore, it is theoretically worthwhile to view the family as operating in a state of relative balance or equilibrium in which each member is meeting his role requirements, thus effecting the smooth operation of the system.

These two theoretical conceptual frameworks, role analysis and systems analysis, are useful when dealing with deviancy as a problem of inappropriate or inadequate role performance. They are also useful in examining the impact of deviancy upon the family. In the latter case, when a family member is unable for one reason or another to fulfill his role obligations and responsibilities, the performance of the other members in their roles may be directly and adversely affected. Additionally, the entire system of interrelated roles is thrown into imbalance or disequilibrium which results in the erosion or breakdown of family organization and integration.

Conflict Theory

Although conflict theory, as a general analytical framework, does not share the same highly organized and developed state of some of the other theoretical orientations, various components of conflict analysis are useful in treating deviancy associated with the family. This is because such deviancy often results in, results from, or is a manifestation of conflict or violence. Furthermore, the conflict aspects of deviancy may take both an emotional and physical form, and may have at least two different effects upon family integration and family relationships. The conflict may have some impact upon the internal organization and cohesiveness of the family unit or it may have an effect upon the manner in which the family relates to its surrounding community and to society in general.

Several theoretical statements derived from the sociologist Georg Simmel who was active in the late nineteenth and early twentieth centuries are particularly useful in explaining the effects of deviancy on the family from the point of view of conflict. Some of his ideas have been explained and expanded upon more recently by Lewis Coser,[4] who, in paraphrasing Simmel with respect to internal group conflict, states that:

Conflict is more passionate and more radical when it arises out of close relationships. The coexistence of union and opposition in such relations makes for the peculiar sharpness of the conflict. Enmity calls forth deeper and more violent reactions, the greater the involvement of the parties among whom it originates.

In conflict within a close group, one side hates the other more intensely the more (the conflict) is felt to be a threat to the unity and the identity of the group.[5]

If the assumption may validly be made that deviancy by a family member may generate conflict within the group, then this proposition may be significant in explaining other behavior. This assumption is especially applicable if the deviant behavior is a specific violation of a family norm, for example, non-support or incest, because there will be a greater likelihood of one or more members of the family sustaining serious injury or trauma by the deviant act. The deeper emotional and psychological ties within the family, as well as the additional economic interdependence, are likely to be conducive to such injury and harm. Accordingly, this proposition is specially relevant to the analysis of deviancy in a family context.

Another possibility for deviancy-generated conflict involves conflict between the family and the surrounding community. Paraphrasing Simmel again, Coser suggests that:

Conflict serves to establish and maintain the identity and boundary lines of societies and groups.

Conflict with other groups contributes to the establishment and reaffirmation of the identity of the group and maintains its boundaries against the surrounding social world.[6]

Conflict with another group leads to the mobilization of the energies of group members and hence to increased cohesion of the group.

Social systems lacking social solidarity are likely to disintegrate in the face of outside conflict, although some unity may be despotically enforced.[7]

Most types of deviancy, especially those which result in the violation of formalized rules and statutes, bring the family into conflict with the outside community. Either the individual deviant family member or his family, who may attempt to protect the reputation of the deviant or the family, is likely to meet with some outside social opposition. It seems to follow from Coser's first three suggestions above that such conflict should lead to increased unity and integration on the part of the family members. However, this is more likely when the family is deviant as a collective unit rather than when only one of its members is deviant. There is a limit to the applicability to deviancy-induced conflict of these propositions, because, in these situations, there exists internal as well as external conflict. Conflict does not always lead to cohesion and solidarity.

On the other hand, the fourth proposition has considerable relevance, because there is ample evidence that the degree of family unity, prior to the deviancy-induced conflict, is closely related to the manner in which the family confronts the difficulty and the subsequent outcome of the situation. This situation will be discussed more fully under "Family Crisis Theory."

Family Functions Theory

Almost any textbook addressing itself to the topics of marriage and family will often have a lengthy section treating the functions of the family in society, both from the standpoint of universal functions and from the standpoint of particular functions within a particular culture. Included may be such functions as procreation, status placement, socialization, protection, companionship, and so forth. Of course, the fulfillment of these functions is critical for the maintenance and smooth operation of the family, and their fulfillment may well be eroded or impaired by deviant behavior. However, we are not concerned with such specific, concrete functions here. Rather, we are dealing with a more generalized and inclusive type of function in terms of a higher theoretical level of explanation. Specifically, we are concerned with two particular functions: the *mediating* function suggested by William J. Goode,[8] and the *adaptive* function as elucidated by Clark Vincent.[9]

Goode states that "the strategic significance of the family is to be found in its mediating function in the larger society. It links the individual to the larger social structure."[10] In other words, the family socializes the child and subsequently introduces him to the society, while at the same time it serves as a haven or place of refuge and safety from the larger society. As society's link to the individual, the family is able to motivate the individual to perform basic social roles as well as to conform to society's standards of behavior. When an individual, however, becomes a deviant, his family, by serving as a mediator, may perform a service for both the individual and the society. It can dilute the impact of the deviant's behavior upon the society by either punishing the deviant within the family or by undertaking restitution to the injured parties or to the community. The family's actions may also aid the deviant by serving as a cushion against a sometimes irate and vengeful society. The family can also serve to protect the individual by covering up for or concealing his deviancy.

Although similar to Goode's mediating function, Vincent's approach to family functions is couched in terms of an industrial or industrializing society. These types of societies are characterized by rapid social change which has an inevitable and sometimes urgent effect upon the family institution. He states that:

The rapid and pervasive social changes associated with industrialization necessitate a family system that both structurally and functionally is highly adaptive externally to the demands of other social institutions and internally to the demands of its own members.[11]

Thus, the family can be a haven of stability by insulating its members from some of the consequences of rapid social change such as deviant behavior. By being adaptive and able to adjust to social change, the family as a source of stability is functional to both the individual and the society.

Another aspect of this adaptive or absorptive quality of the family is its function of shouldering the blame for many of the major social and individual problems in a sort of scapegoat fashion. Vincent says:

Superficially, the adaptive function of the family has some sponge-like characteristics that are evidenced by the family's absorption of blame for most social problems (mental illness, delinquency, dropouts, alcoholism, suicide, crime, illegitimacy, etc.).[12]

This practice can also be dysfunctional since it obscures the genuine causes or sources of social ills.

Family Crisis Theory

There are a number of sound and well-developed theories which attempt to explain and predict family behavior in the face of a variety of crises which may confront the family or the community in which it resides. This final section will attempt to delineate some of the more utilitarian of such theories and demonstrate how deviant behavior in relation to the family may be analyzed employing these theories. That deviancy on the part of a family member often precipitates a crisis is obvious, especially if the deviancy is of a serious nature. Deviancy may result in the temporary or permanent loss of a family member, in the loss of income to the family, in the stigmatization of the family's reputation, or the erosion of its community influence, or it may engender a variety of social problems dysfunctional to the family in countless other ways. Thus, it is appropriate to rely upon family crisis theory to understand the ways in which deviancy is related to the family.

There are several types of theories dealing with family crises. Most prevalent are those theories which are concerned with the sources of familial stress or crisis. Critically speaking, these might more accurately be referred to as typologies rather than theories, since most of them simply delineate sources of stress in a variety of categories. However, such typologies do often prove useful for gaining an overview of the events which threaten family maintenance. One of the more extensive classifications of crises is that developed by Reuben Hill which relies upon three basic causal elements: (1) the loss of a member of the family (dismemberment), (2) the addition of an unwanted or unprepared-for member (accession), and (3) the loss of family morale and unity (demoralization).[13] Specific crisis events are listed under each of these three categories along with a fourth category in which demoralization is combined with one of the other two elements. For example, a crisis of dismemberment would be the death of a spouse or a war separation; an accession crisis might result from an unwanted pregnancy or a returning deserter; and demoralization might result from infidelity or alcoholism. Suicide or homocide would be examples of demoralization combined with dismemberment, and illegitimacy would be an example of demoralization combined with accession.[14] One prominent weakness in this typology, however, is that there is no attempt to specify which comes first. That is, does infidelity, for instance, cause demoralization, or is it the result?

In any event, it is not difficult to see how different varieties of deviancy can coincide with these categories. In some cases the deviant act would be the cause of the dismemberment, accession, or demoralization, and in others, it would be the result. Unfortunately, even though it is sufficient for classification, this theory cannot adequately explain the causes and effects involved in a deviancy crisis. It can, however, illustrate how the structure of family membership may be related to specific configurations of deviancy.

Another conceptual approach to the classification of family stress was suggested by Ernest W. Burgess. This classification was based upon sudden or drastic shifts in social status brought about by such events as prolonged unemployment or natural disasters.[15] It might also be assumed that certain types of deviancy would cause the family to decline in social status, with all of the attendant consequences.

A second major theory, developed by Donald Hansen and Reuben Hill, is concerned with the various reactions of the community or the society to family crises including deviancy.[16] The theory is designed to predict the nature of the community response to the family based upon the particular combination of two dichotomous variables. The initial variable concerns the source of the community response to the family. This response can come from the official agencies for dealing with family problems, a positional response, or it can come from the friends and neighbors of the family, a personal response. The second variable is whether these two sources of response react with acceptance, which is a positive or helpful response, or with rejection, which is a negative response. Thus, based upon the combination of sources and kinds of response, there are four community response types. In the *therapeutic response* both the positional and personal responses are positive. In the *social welfare response* the positional response is positive and the personal response negative. The *repressive response* contains a negative positional and positive personal response. In the *persecutive response* both positional and personal responses are negative.[17] The obvious implication is that the kind of recovery which the family makes during the crisis depends to a great extent upon the manner of the community response.

A third major type of family crisis theory deals with the response of the family to the crisis and its subsequent move toward either disintegration or recovery. In Hill's study of families separated by war, for example, it was found that the families who experienced greatest difficulty adjusting to the situation were those characterized by mobility, transiency, and isolation from relatives.[18] Thus, it was theorized that families with these characteristics would be more likely to have more problems in any kind of crisis situation. Hill went on to redefine the so-called "roller-coaster" profile of family recovery which suggests that there are periods of ups and downs through which the family moves in the course of recovering from a crisis. These ups and downs are expressed in four stages: stress, disorganization, recovery, and reorganization. This same approach is developed by Joan Jackson in Part 6 of this book.[19] In most instances, families' actions during the first two stages are quite similar. However, the nature of the particular family, in terms of its past experience with crises and its prior level of organization and integration, greatly affects the manner in which it moves through the third and fourth stages of recovery and reorganization.

Moreover, Hansen and Hill felt that it was not sufficient to simply state that a family's manner of dealing with a crisis is dependent upon prior integration and organization since these concepts are so very general in their meanings. They attempted to formulate a theory which might explain and predict family strengths and weaknesses in more specific terms.[20] The basic assumption of the theory is that there are two types of relationships within the family, each with its own attitudes, activities, and satisfactions. The first is the structural or positional relationship, and the other is the interpersonal relationship. In the case of the former type of relationship, Hansen and Hill conclude:

The family offers an individual certain status and power, and serves him with goods to consume, and, with his positional relationship, expects him to act in certain ways. But it may also offer him individual personalities to enjoy and to help, and these individuals also expect him to act in harmony with the expectations they hold for him . . . .

Theoretically, a family could exist without one or the other type of relationship, and in such a case every act of the individuals could be labelled either "positional" or "personal." But in real life families, pure relationships of either type seem highly improbable. Action is determined by a blend of interpersonal and structural expectations. The question is just "how much" force each relationship has on each member.[21]

Thus, there is within a family the possibility of either a strong or a weak positional relationship, and also the possibility of either a strong or a weak interpersonal relationship. Combining the possibilities of strong or weak in both types of relationships yields four logical family types: (1) strong in both relationships; (2) weak in positional but strong in personal relations (an empirical rarity); (3) strong in positional but weak in personal; and (4) weak in both relations.[22] Obviously, the first type of family is the most capable of withstanding stress, the second and third types somewhat less capable, and the fourth the least capable since it is already at the point of disintegration.

In applying any of the several family crisis theories mentioned here, it is necessary only to substitute any particular type of deviant behavior in the place of the stressor or crisis-causing event to make the theory applicable.

SUMMARY

While folk belief bolstered by inconclusive scientific research has suggested that socially deficient or inadequate family life may, in some instances, be a significant contributory factor in individual criminality, delinquency, or antisocial behavior, the broader configurations of family-deviancy linkages have been neglected by social scientists, at least in terms of any comprehensive or extensive treatment. This volume seeks to provide such a comprehensive overview through the organization of the various illustrative selections included, which articulate differential patterns of family-related deviancy and demonstrate the pervasiveness of the linkages.

The functional significance of the family in society tends to subject its members to a complex system of normative expectations and proscriptions. In the face of social exigencies and pressures, violations of this restrictive and demanding normative structure appear inevitable with resulting disruptive and deteriorative effect on the family. Accordingly, the violation of family norms constitutes a significant and prominent variety of deviant behavior in our society.

An individual may exhibit deviancy partially due to his familial background and experiences, but he may also be victimized directly or indirectly as the object of deviant acts committed within the family. On the other hand, the family as a social entity or various individuals within the family may also individually or jointly suffer the residual effects of any other member's deviancy. The family also provides the context within which the meaning and motivation of much deviancy may be sought. Families may collectively violate societal norms or various groupings within it may engage in a variety of deviant pursuits for fun, profit, or therapeutic reasons. Finally, the family and its adaptive patterns in reestablishing internal social equilibrium, after it experiences the impact of deviant behavior, represent an additional linkage pattern worthy of examination. The range of family-related deviancy patterns may be usefully viewed through several theoretical perspectives including role and systems theory, conflict theory, family function theory, and family crisis theory.

The various statuses and roles that make up the individual's position within the family are defined by societally sanctioned expectations. The various status and role sets of different family members operate reciprocally and thus symbiotically, establishing an equilibrium in the family system. Violation of the normative expectations can lead to family disequilibrium thus constituting deviant behavior.

The intimate relationships inherent in primary groups like the family tend to encourage an emotional intensity which is often manifested in conflict. Deviant behavior within the family and the resultant trauma to other members may be viewed as a conflict situation. Similarly, hostile community response to family deviancy, with the attendant defensive increase in family cohesion, may also represent a conflict situation.

The family fulfills a number of social functions, like protecting a deviant member from a wrathful society as well as protecting society from its own deviant members by sanction or by making restitution. The family by being adaptive may also protect the individual member from deviant practices operative in society or from conditions and pressures which might promote deviancy. It may additionally shoulder the blame for individual deviancy.

Deviancy may be viewed as a crisis which confronts the family through dismemberment, accession, or demoralization. Thus, the structure of family membership may be related to specific configurations of deviancy. The crisis of deviancy will also effect the relationship of the family and the larger community. The source of society's response may be personal or positional and the quality of acceptance may be positive or negative. Thus, four combinations of community response are possible: *therapeutic, social welfare, repressive,* and *persecutive.* Family crisis theory also examines the family response to deviancy and the types of internal family relationships which might predispose the particular response pattern of the family.

Deviant behavior is significantly related to and often concomitant to the family as a social institution, primary group, and system of interpersonal relationships. Such a linkage deserves increased attention by sociologists.

NOTES AND REFERENCES

1. Vecsey, George: "Cincinnati Merchants Await Annual Visit of Terrible Williamsons, a Clan of Wandering Gyp Artists." *The New York Times,* Sunday, May 16, 1971, p. 43.
2. For a detailed discussion of role analysis, but with a more elaborate differentiation of the role concept, see Bates, Frederick L.: "Position, Role and Status: A Reformulation of Concepts." *Social Forces* 34:313–321, May, 1956.
3. Nadel, Siegfried F.: "On Role Systems," in Katz, Fred E. (ed.): *Contemporary Sociological Theory.* New York: Random House, Inc., 1971, pp. 128–131.
4. Coser, Lewis: *The Functions of Social Conflict.* New York: The Free Press, 1956.
5. *Ibid.,* p. 71.
6. *Ibid.,* p. 38.
7. *Ibid.,* p. 95.
8. Goode, William J.: *The Family.* Englewood Cliffs, N. J.: Prentice-Hall, Inc., 1964, pp. 2–3.

9. Vincent, Clark E.: "Familia Spongia: The Adaptive Function." *Journal of Marriage and the Family* 28:29–36, Feb., 1966.

10. Goode, *op. cit.,* p. 2.

11. Vincent, *op. cit.,* p. 29.

12. *Ibid.,* p. 32.

13. Hill, Reuben: *Families Under Stress.* New York: Harper & Row, Publishers, 1949, pp. 9–11.

14. *Ibid.*

15. Burgess, Ernest W.: "The Family and Sociological Research." *Social Forces* 26:1–6, Oct., 1947.

16. Hansen, Donald A.; and Hill, Reuben: "Families Under Stress," in Christensen, Harold T. (ed.): *Handbook of Marriage and the Family.* Chicago: Rand McNally & Co., 1964, pp. 798–800.

17. *Ibid.,* p. 799.

18. Hill, *op. cit.,* pp. 323–329.

19. Jackson, Joan K.: "The Adjustment of the Family to Alcoholism." *Marriage and Family Living* 18:361–369, Nov., 1956.

20. Hansen and Hill, *op. cit.,* pp. 811–815.

21. *Ibid.,* p. 812.

22. *Ibid.,* p. 812.

PART 2

INAPPROPRIATE FAMILY ROLE BEHAVIOR

Group behavior as collective effort is necessarily coordinated behavior, and to insure this coordination some measure of behavioral structuring is usually present. Such structuring permits the interaction of group members and ongoing group activities to proceed according to certain social rules. These rules may include the designation of specific members of the group to behave in particular ways, the manner in which members of the group should relate to each other or to outsiders, and the appropriate mode and circumstances by which group tasks are to be performed. Structured group behavior is compartmentalized in a fashion that permits ease of learning as well as of performance. This compartmentalization articulates the group structure into a number of individual statuses and accompanying social roles which delineate the expected behavioral requirements of those individuals who come to occupy the various statuses. The expectations of role are thus integral to the status. Furthermore, role expectations exist in a given situation even in the absence of specific others; that is, generalized concepts of role expectations are held by members of a society and these concepts influence the behavior of the actor. There are rewards for compliance and often negative sanctions for violation of role expectations. Such role violation constitutes socially deviant behavior. The compartmentalization of group structure and process into individual statuses and roles contributes to both the performance of group activity and to the monitoring and evaluation of the efficacy and appropriateness of this activity by members of the larger community.

Many social groups, for example, casual friendship groups, have limited significance for the needs of society. They are often loosely structured, with minimal articulation of group statuses and with relatively vague definitions of role requirements. Other social groups, such as those ancillary to basic social institutions, have far more significant import for the larger society and are, accordingly, subject to the more precise control afforded by rigid structuring. The family, among all basic institutional groups, is perhaps the most fundamental, the most universal, and the most durable. As such, it encompasses an expansive range of activities and behaviors. Furthermore, while individuals may participate in other basic institutional groups erratically or for limited periods of time, involvement in family activities tends to be more pervasive and demanding. There is a totality of involvement by individuals in families not usually observed in educational, religious, political, or economic groups. The entire life cycle transpires within the context of family, and for most people a substantial proportion of the cyclical daily routine also occurs within a family setting.

The family discharges a number of significant societal functions, including reproduction and the care and maintenance of the young, the regularization and channeling of sexual behavior, and the provision of basic foundation units in religious, educational, economic, and political endeavors. Finally, the family group engages its members in a degree of intimacy—spatial, physical, and emotional—unparalleled in other social groups. In view of the functions of the family, its importance to the social enterprise, and the pervasiveness of the presence and intimacy which it imposes on its members, it is not surprising that of all human social groupings none is more subject to narrowly prescribed and proscribed behavioral requirements, more rigidly structured, or more closely monitored and sanctioned by the larger society than is the family.

Since the family is such an important group in our society, its structure and functions are girded by the most rigid set of norms applied to any grouping in the society. The rigidity of these norms insures that the family maintains its structure and performs its functions. Initially, these norms are embodied in the roles which various family members are expected, even required, to play. They are further embodied formally in the legal codes and statutes of the society, usually under the label of "domestic relations" laws. These norms and laws both define and regulate the duties required of each role and status within the family by the larger social system.

In addition to the norms and statutes which address themselves to the qualifications and circumstances requisite to the creation and dissolution of marriage, there are those dealing with the obligations of married life, the extension of these obligations to offspring and kin, and conditions and limits with respect to special alterations in the family's structure. A significant part of our legal apparatus is concerned directly or indirectly with the enforcement of family statutes, and with the reintegration of residual family members should the family unit be dissolved.

There are a number of situations in which the violation of family norms and statutes also constitutes what we have previously defined as deviance. The norms being violated are essentially those which define the roles within the family. Thus, these situations might be termed as inappropriate or illegal role behavior. This section is concerned with just such deviant behavior, which may be seen as inappropriate role behavior from the standpoint of the society as well as the family itself.

Four types of inappropriate role behavior are described: the abdication of family responsibility, the violation of conjugal trust, pathological family role configurations, and addictive impediments to family role performance.

THE ABDICATION OF FAMILY RESPONSIBILITY

Basic to the concept of marriage and family are the reciprocal obligations between the spouses and between parents and children. William Stephens stated that the "family is a social arrangement, based on . . . reciprocal economic obligations between husband and wife," along with various other types of obligations.[1] Thus, the family may be seen as an economic unit. In fact, with respect to the division of labor in society, it is probably the most basic unit.

The family is almost always involved in a cooperative economic venture, and the individual roles involving economic behavior as well as the economic responsibilities of the members are usually implicitly articulated and sanctioned by the marriage contract. Economic role behavior specified may include appropriate work and division of labor for age and sex categories, a particular pattern of property ownership, and the legitimate authority to dictate the domicile or nature of family business. In our society, for example, the husband may obtain employment in another part of the country and if his wife does not elect to move with him, she may be guilty of desertion for divorce purposes. By the same token, role behavior specified by custom or law may assign economic responsibility for care and support of particular family members to other family members, for example, the support of children or aged parents to adults or support of wife to husband. In this way society can be assured that all members obtain care and subsistence and that the family functions adequately as a component of the larger societal economic structure.

The discharge of appropriate financial responsibility to spouse and offsprings has long been considered a significant marital obligation binding on the husband/father. Both historically and today, the husband's family role as sanctioned by law affords him economic privileges and prerogatives often denied the wife. As the legal and economic authority in the family, the husband may be the principal agent in making economic decisions, even far-reaching decisions, concerning the family. The greater economic privileges of the husband are accordingly counterbalanced by his greater economic responsibilities. Since the wife and children have been legally handicapped in economic matters, failure of the husband to provide support might render them financially destitute. In this eventuality the family might (and often does) become a public charge requiring financial relief through public welfare. The family unit may fail to function properly and may partially or completely disintegrate with accompanying individual trauma to all members.

The husband who does not support his family deviates from the role expectations of marriage, violates the legally established financial responsibility to wife and children, and violates the equilibrium of family order as well as social order. Non-support may occur through the process of the husband physically absenting himself and his income from his family, through willful failure to support his family, by maintenance of irregular work habits, or by drunkenness. In these situations, the husband's actions are legally defined as either "desertion," "abandonment," or both. However, desertion is not always an attempt to evade family financial obligations, as there are many other reasons why men leave their wives and children. Investigators have pointed out that men often desert because of marital strains, in-law problems, unsatisfactory sexual adjustments, incompatibility with the spouse, or feelings of rejection or inadequacy. In general, desertion represents an immature reaction to an unpleasant marital situation.[2]

Whatever the reason for the desertion, the result may well be the same, with the wife and children left without a provider and head of the household. In most states such action by the husband is a criminal offense, often even a felony.

Desertion is not a phenomenon randomly distributed throughout the population. Rather, the incidence of desertion appears to be biased in regard to particular subgroupings in society.[3] Catholics, for example, have tended to be overrepresented in desertions and Jews and Protestants conversely underrepresented. Inasmuch as the Catholic church does not recognize divorce, and Catholics are underrepresented in divorce actions, desertion may constitute an efficacious alternative. Furthermore, Catholics are generally of lower socioeconomic status than Jews and Protestants.

Although desertion continues to be associated with lower socioeconomic groups, it is not necessarily the so-called "poor man's divorce" that many believe it to be. Divorce is an expensive legal procedure and post-divorce financial support arrangements may simply be intolerable to many low income men. However, desertion does occur at all levels of the socioeconomic continuum, albeit to a lesser degree among higher status groups.

Negroes are also much overrepresented in desertion cases as compared to whites. This pattern perhaps can be traced to the erratic family life of slavery days and the post-slavery economic plight of Negro males. As lower socioeconomic persons, Negroes are likely motivated to desert for the same reasons as whites. Finally, and perhaps most important among Negroes and lower socioeconomic whites, there is frequently no appropriate role model of husband/father/provider for them to emulate. These persons simply never learn the normative patterns of conjugal and familial behavior which our society supports and sanctions. The middle and upper middle-class white patterns are the "normative" ones, and our mechanisms of social control operate to enforce conformity to these. Failure to conform constitutes deviancy, both social and legal, and for some disadvantaged the pattern of deviancy repeats itself generation after generation, as evidenced by the fact that in some instances several generations of one family may have been recipients of welfare, relief, or Aid to Dependent Children.

In the initial reading in this section, W. J. Brockelbank surveys the problem of family deviancy both historically and nationally. He points out that present day family responsibility laws and support and desertion statutes have their origins in both English Common Law and the Elizabethan Poor Laws. Desertion and non-support constitute a major social problem in this country both in terms of the wives and children who are left destitute when husbands desert, and in the staggering cost of welfare and public assistance which the taxpayers must assume. Most of our states have some type of statute requiring support by the husband of his wife and minor children. Curiously, many of these same laws also make provision for other destitute relatives to be supported by various members of their family such as spouses, parents, grandparents, children, or siblings. Unfortunately, as Brockelbank also demonstrates, there is considerable variation from state to state in support laws, and more importantly, until recently the violation of a non-support law in one state might be nonprosecutable in another state, making it possible for a deserting husband to seek legal refuge outside of the state where he left his family. Seeing the need for reform, the Uniform Desertion and Non-Support Act of 1910 was enacted by 22 states, followed in the late 1940s by the Uniform Support of Dependents Act, passed in New York. Ten other states passed similar laws that same year. Other legal devices such as the two-state suit offered new avenues of enforcement for family support. In the 1950s the Uniform Reciprocal Enforcement of Support Act appeared as a model for state legislatures, all of whom passed a similar act by 1957. A Revised Uniform Reciprocal Enforcement of Support Act appeared in 1968 and is being enacted by a number of state legislatures at this time. This new legislation appears to close most of the remaining loopholes and will permit enforcement of the support laws and prosecution of desertion cases even where flight to another state has occurred. As Brockelbank observes, such legislation will save millions of taxpayer's dollars. Inasmuch as desertion appears to be far more prevalent than divorce in our society, there is a pressing need to place the responsibility for family support where it belongs rather than permitting it to be allocated to the public at large.

The husband's responsibility to financially support his family in our society is a particularly serious one, especially in view of the relatively acute financial dependence of the wife and children on the husband and the reluctance of the public to permit the wife and children to live in destitution where the husband has deserted them. This responsibility continues throughout marriage and extends after marriage in the form of court-ordered alimony and child support payments. (It is interesting to note that courts occasionally order the wife to support her husband or ex-husband. In two recent cases a judge ordered a wife to pay support to her husband and the children in his custody. In the first case each parent had custody of two children, but the wife's income exceeded her husband's. In the other case, the employed wife supported her unemployed estranged husband and their two children, who were in his care.) The important element is that the children are to be cared for by the family unit. The public will provide support if necessary, but would rather sanction the father's discharging of his financial obligations. A husband's abrogation of family financial responsibility is in violation of religious, social, and legal norms, and is generally considered a particularly reprehensible form of deviant behavior. Furthermore, it violates the popularly held image of the masculine provider, husband, father, protector of the weak and helpless.

Although the sanctions for violation of family responsibility are theoretically severe, invoking both civil and criminal processes and providing for both fines and imprisonment, it appears that legal sanctions are not always involved in the instance of non-support offenses, nor are they uniformly applied where invoked. The next selection, "Deviance, Visibility, and Legal Action: The Duty to Support," provides data on child non-support offenses from a metropolitan county in Wisconsin for a ten-year period. The data represent a sample of fathers who had been ordered by the court at the time of their divorce to make support payments for their minor children. Support payments were made through the family court clerk who maintained records of the payments or non-payments. In spite of the "visibility" of non-support deviancy afforded by the public record, and the professed policy of authorities to enforce court support orders with criminal prosecution if necessary, enforcement appeared to be lax and selective. Most fathers failed to make support payments either in full or in part. During the first year, for example, more than 40 percent of the fathers made no payment and another 20 percent made only partial support payments. By the end of four years, more than 66 percent of the fathers made no payments and of those who had been under court order for 10 years, 79 percent contributed no support. Only 13 percent were in full conformity with the court order. Overall, a substantial majority of the fathers were deviant in their court-ordered financial responsibility, but only a minority ever had legal action initiated against them. During the first year, 62 percent of the fathers were eligible for prosecution but only 19 percent had legal action initiated against them; by the fifth the figures were 81 and 9 percent, respectively; and by the tenth year only 1 percent had legal action initiated aginst them although 86 percent were eligible for prosecution.

Apparently the initiation of legal action was selective and related to social class. Of the white-collar fathers, 92 percent were deviant in their compliance with court orders, but only 21 percent were subjected to legal action. On the other hand, 83 percent of blue-collar fathers were in violation of support orders, but 45 percent had legal action initiated against them. It also appears that the application of sanctions for the violation of support orders is selectively related to prior legal records. In this sample, 100 percent of all fathers with prior legal records had legal action initiated against them and all of them were subsequently sent to the county jail. The majority of them were later charged with the felony of non-support and six were ultimately sent to prison on this charge. Of the non-supporting fathers with no prior legal record, only a relatively small percentage ever had legal action initiated against them and the great majority of these actions were dismissed. According to Eckhardt, it appears that "the charge of non-support was the vehicle for the imprisonment of defendants who ran afoul of the law through other violations."

Thus it appears that the strong public sentiment and elaborate legal mechanisms which sanction the economic obligations of the father to his children are somewhat incongruous with the facts of marital instability in our society and with "society's general acceptance of divorce and especially the right of remarriage." In short, there is a kind of cultural lag between society's attempt to preserve the family unit and the father's economic responsibility to it and the reality of the father, especially the remarried father, cut off from the family unit. This cultural lag and the difficulty faced by the father in conforming to society's expectations tends to promote deviance in the form of evasion. Authorities who recognize the social dysfunctions of the legal sanctions against non-support frequently do not enforce the laws, and a pattern of official "covert tolerance" results. Non-support then is a kind of residual deviancy resulting from the impact of social change on marital stability. Traditional mechanisms for enforcing marital role conformity and preserving the family unit are both ineffective and dysfunctional. In the face of this dysfunction, officials become derelict in applying the existing sanctions and in a sense become deviant themselves in the process of tolerating deviancy.

The unbroken, relatively self-sufficient family unit has long been an historical and cultural ideal in Western society. To insure the continuity and completeness of the family unit and its economic independence, strong norms, buttressed by severe social, religious, and legal sanction, have evolved. These norms dictate, among other things, the presence of the father and the fullest discharge of his economic obligations for financial support of his wife and children. Willful failure to discharge this responsibility represents a violation of conjugal and familial role expectations and constitutes social deviancy of an officially labeled and serious nature. It calls for the application of severe sanctions to the offender. Traditionally a number of means existed for resisting, escaping, or evading these sanctions, such as fleeing to another state where legal enforcement was difficult. Such loopholes and patterned evasions have largely been eliminated through the standardization of statutory sanctions from state to state and the enactment of various interstate legal devices for enforcement of desertion and non-support laws.

With the accelerating tempo of social change in our society and the breakdown or erosion of traditional values concerning marriage and family, the problem of desertion and non-support increasingly endemic to today's marital instability and "serial monogamy" may well compound itself. The existing devices for enforcing conformity to traditional patterns of role expectations on the husband and father may become increasingly ineffective and dysfunctional for all concerned. Desertion and non-support, as persistent varieties of family deviancy today, may well call for reexamination of our traditional conceptualization of family roles.

THE VIOLATION OF CONJUGAL TRUST

The reciprocal obligations contained implicitly, if not stated explicitly, in the marriage contract concern themselves not only with economic requirements, but also with others such as the sexual obligation. In fact, as Stephens points out, marriage is a "socially legitimate sexual union."[4] Marriage, in short, "sanctions intercourse between the mates" and further relieves them of the necessity to be implicitly "discreet about the fact that they are having sexual intercourse." As a functional device for channeling, regularizing, and legitimating sexual behavior, marriage in a sense is built on a sexual foundation. Indeed sexual intercourse in our society is considered so fundamental and essential to marriage that in many states physical impediments or willful abstention from intercourse may be grounds for divorce. Included among such grounds are impotence, malformation preventing sexual intercourse, and refusal of sexual relations with the spouse. Furthermore, the privileges of sexual gratification are bound up in the other reciprocal obligations of the marriage contract, or as Stephens puts it, "it [marriage] imposes obligations in return for sexual gratifications." Along with the reciprocal sexual obligations goes an obligation of sexual exclusiveness. Adultery has traditionally been a serious breach of social norms in our society and has on occasion precipitated religious, social, and legal sanctions. As part of the so-called "double standard," adultery by the wife has been considered especially serious. This may result from concern in times past that a wife might be impregnated by another man, especially a rival or enemy. This adultery might go undetected and the offspring might ultimately inherit part or all of the husband's lands, property, or title. The rival or enemy would thus have "infiltrated" and acquired part of the individual's holdings through adulterous sex.

Inasmuch as marriage in Western society has traditionally been based on romantic love, adultery would suggest or imply a disillusionment, rejection, or dilution of the love and would thus be particularly traumatic and reprehensible to the spouse since it would violate the marriage vows as well as love-based conjugal trust. There has also been a strong tradition of "possession" with respect to marital sexuality in our culture, so that adultery suggests the loss or theft of one's property. Furthermore, one's ego-identity or self-image is bound up with one's perception of his desirability and performance as a sex partner. In this respect, adultery would imply undesirability or inability on the part of the so-called injured spouse.

Thus, adultery has emotional, psychological, and social consequences for those involved. The injured party is hurt by feelings of betrayal and being unloved, and probably feels incapable of satisfying the partner physically and emotionally. This leads to feelings of both inadequacy and rejection, which are particularly ego-damaging and make adultery a threatening experience and thus a reprehensible act. Furthermore, should adulterous behavior become public knowledge, the injured spouse might be held up to public ridicule as inadequate and unable to hold or control his spouse. Adultery also suggests divided loyalties and raises the problems of jealousy and rivalry, all of which lead to the weakening or disintegration of the family unit. Adultery then is destructive and dysfunctional to marriage and the family unit, the individual spouses, and to society at large.

Inasmuch as a sexually monogamous marital role is prescribed by customs and values and supported by social and legal sanction, adultery is a grave violation of conjugal trust and a critical deviation from expected marital role behavior. Thus even in modern society, a public disclosure of adultery produces such social repercussions as ridicule, ostracism, loss of job, or strain in relations with kinsmen and friends, especially with those of the "innocent" spouse. Adultery is grounds for divorce in most states, and the "guilty" spouse may stand to sustain considerable economic loss in a divorce action, not to mention the possibility of an inequitable custody arrangement concerning children. Religious sanctions may include expulsion, a demand for penance, or a public confrontation complete with accusations and ridicule. In some instances adultery may evoke legal sanctions.

In spite of the social, religious, and legal sanctions attendant to adultery, it is apparently widespread and perhaps on the increase.[5] Many observers have suggested that extramarital coitus represents symptoms of a troubled marriage more than urges for sexual pleasure. Apparently the husband is more often guilty of infidelity than the wife, and when she has engaged in extramarital coitus, it is sometimes retaliation against an errant husband. Some researchers have found little positive relationship between infidelity and income or education, although Kinsey asserts that both men and women at the higher educational levels are more likely to commit adultery after several years of marriage. For the most part, adultery in our society appears to be largely a neurotic response to strains in the marriage, or possibly to a poor image of self, precipitated by the onset of middle age or apathy on the part of the spouse.[6] In any event, sex outside of marriage can have an erosive if not disintegrative effect on the marital relationship.

In the third selection in Part 2, Ralph E. Johnson examines "Some Correlates of Extramarital Coitus." Drawing on data obtained from 100 middle-class middle-aged couples, the author concludes that husbands who had committed infidelity tend to express a significantly lower degree of sexual satisfaction from their marriage than do faithful husbands. (The same relationship does not appear to be as significant for wives.) He also finds basic differences between husband and wife in variables such as potential involvement (positive inclination to interact with a person of the opposite sex when the spouse is away) and justification of extramarital involvement. Most importantly perhaps, Johnson suggests that "opportunity for extramarital involvement is a critical factor in infidelity." His data indicate that opportunity is a significant element in adultery, but that research into the opportunity structure of infidelity is needed. For example, do certain occupations or occupational situations provide opportunity for infidelity or do unfaithful spouses "make their own opportunity"?

Infidelity is apparently a widespread phenomenon in our society. Some years ago, Kinsey estimated that one half of married men and one quarter of all married women by age 40 had sexual intercourse, while married, with a partner other than their spouse. The percentage involved in infidelity may well be greater today.[7] There is probably more permissiveness today than formerly, both on the part of spouses as well as the public.[8] It is interesting to note that at least one Western country, Denmark, has removed adultery from its list of legal divorce grounds, and with the advent of "no-fault" divorce laws in such states as California and Florida, adultery has been, for all practical purposes, removed from the list of grounds for divorce.

Whether or not there is more acceptance of the unfaithful spouse, infidelity is still a deviant departure from the marital role prescribed by custom and law. Adultery violates religious and civil mandate and breaks the bond of conjugal trust. It is deviant behavior by the standards of spouse or society, or both.

Another violation of conjugal trust is desertion by one of the spouses, which has already been discussed at length. Although the term desertion is usually applied to runaway husbands or husbands who willfully fail to support their wives and children, the label may also be used to describe the wife who flees from her husband, children, and family responsibilities. Such an action on the part of a wife does not consititute a felonious violation of legal statute, as would similar behavior on the part of the husband, inasmuch as the wife generally is not legally charged with the financial support of the family unit. It does, however, represent a deviation from the normative expectation of appropriate role behavior for a wife and mother traditionally sanctioned by social and religious custom and belief. It also constitutes legal grounds for divorce in most states. The wife's desertion deprives her husband of sexual gratification and companionship, as well as such household conjugal and maternal services as she may have rendered to both husband and children. In many ways it resembles adultery in its impact because it suggests a disenchantment with spouse, a rejection or disillusionment, or an assessment of inadequacy on the part of the mate. Like adultery it is a violation of conjugal trust.

In the reading by Max Gunther, the author explores the reasons why there are "Wives who Run Away." According to Gunther, there are an estimated 30,000 women who run away each year in America. Furthermore, there has been a significant increase in runaway wives in recent years. In the 1930s the runaway wife was practically non-existent, but by the time of World War II, there were 4 missing wives for every 100 missing husbands. Today almost 15 percent of missing spouses are women. The author suggests that wives often run away because they are bored, frustrated, or feel trapped in their domestic routine. This is particularly the case where, because of rapid social mobility, the husband and perhaps even the children have, in a sense, intellectually "outgrown" the wife. The husband is absorbed in his work, the children are engrossed in extrafamilial activities, and the wife is alienated from her own family and the mainstream of life. The author contends that there is a pattern to runaway wives. Most are between 35 and 50 years of age, with 79.6 percent of runaway wives in one statistical study between the ages of 35 and 45. The great majority are mothers, but they do not run away while their children are young; they leave only after the children are gone from home to college or work, or at least are teen-agers. Occasionally a wife and another man, perhaps someone else's husband, will run away together, but this is the exception rather than the rule, according to Gunther's data.

Gunther's research reveals that there are two distinct types of runaway wives: the childish, immature woman who in her insecurity has always run away from problems and continues to do so after marriage, and the woman who finds herself in "the untenable position in which our society has placed her." Here the wife becomes stranded or cut off from her family and a stimulating life because of circumstances beyond her control. Her running away represents a "profound search for meaning," and she is often mature and intelligent.

No matter what her personality type, it is often difficult for the runaway wife to stay hidden. In today's complex society, it is difficult to falsify an identity and almost impossible to operate without records and licenses which reveal one's past identity. As a result, it is relatively easy for missing persons detectives and tracers to find the wives. Sometimes, however, the husbands or families make no effort to look. Many wives become disenchanted with their new life and, according to Gunther, about half of all runaway wives return to their husbands and families within a few weeks or months or a year or so.

The runaway wife has physically deserted her husband and deprived him of her contribution to the conjugal unit. She has in a sense been unfaithful to him, although in this instance the rival may have been a new, different, and perhaps more stimulating life, rather than another man. In any event she has violated conjugal trust, and failed to conform to social and religious mandates of the marriage, becoming in the process a prominent type of family deviant.

PATHOLOGICAL FAMILY ROLE CONFIGURATIONS

In addition to questions of reciprocal economic and sexual obligations and trusts, the structured dimensions of conjugal role behavior frequently include some attempt at delineation of the power and privilege relationship between spouses. Some form of superiority-subordination relationship usually emerges from marital role interaction as prescribed by existing cultural norms. In speaking of this, Stephens observes that:

The power relationship between husband and wife has to do with who dominates and who submits; who makes the family decisions—husband, wife, or both jointly; who gets his (or her) way in case of disagreements; who is catered to; who commands; who obeys; and so forth.[9]

The allocation of marital privileges and prerogatives is normally attendant to the conjugal power pattern. Such prerogatives may even include the physical abuse of the subordinate spouse or offspring, inasmuch as physical force may be the culturally defined sanction for enforcing the power relationship and insuring conformity to the subordinate conjugal or filial role. Many societies such as our own permit and at times even encourage corporal punishment for children who misbehave. By the same token, many societies may sanction wife beating as an appropriate prerogative of the dominant husband role. Traditionally among the Ukranian peasants (as among many peasant peoples), wife beating was apparently something of a normative pattern, to the extent that "a wife whose husband never beats her feels that she is being neglected and that he no longer loves her."[10]

In our own society, habitual wifebeating (as opposed to isolated incidences or sporadic domestic battles) is not part of the normative pattern even though legally the husband is vested with the authority in the conjugal unit and enjoys a wide range of prerogatives under the law. Physical cruelty in the form of wifebeating is legal grounds for divorce in many states (in some cases "spanking" is not grounds), and many states have statutes over and above those generally prosecuting assault which specifically prohibit wifebeating. (Some of the older statutes prescribed the size rod which was permissible to use on the wife). However, wifebeating does occurs, and often with the tacit consent of the victimized wife. From time to time, letters to the editor of the various marital advice columns, as well as letters to the editors of the so-called men's magazines, bring up the subject of wife spanking or beating. Apparently many wives accept this arrangement as appropriate and relate to the husband as a kind of disciplinarian-father image. It is interesting to note that editors of the marital advice columns (usually female) react most vehemently to such letters and frequently accuse the wives of being masochistic or simply lacking intelligence. The husbands who perpetrated the beatings are naturally labeled sadists. In any event, contemporary marital norms do not include license to inflict physical violence on the other spouse. Wifebeating (or husbandbeating, for that matter) generally occurs among the less educated and the lower socioeconomic groups. The wifebeater is often intoxicated at the time of the assault, and this suggests his inability to maintain control of his role behavior, or his poor conceptualization of appropriate conjugal role behavior. In short, wifebeating is inappropriate role behavior by today's standards and deviates sufficiently from the commonly accepted norm to be considered a pathological familial pattern.

In "The Wifebeater's Wife," Snell, Rosenwalt, and Robey probe the personalities of both wifebeaters and their spouses, and more importantly, explore the situational concommitants which precipitate the wife's seeking legal intervention. In this study 37 men, charged by their wives with assault and battery, were referred to a psychiatric clinic serving the court. Both the husbands and their wives were interviewed in depth, in some instances over a period of time. Special attention was given to the respective marital roles of the spouses. In all of the cases, it was the first marriage for the wife. The wives averaged 37 years in age, and had been married for an average of over 13 years. All of the wives admitted that the fighting and physical abuse had existed throughout the marriage. The wives simply had never previously taken steps to seek help. Presumably the husband and wife had been able to complement each other's needs through the beatings.

The wives, according to the psychiatric team, were "aggressive, efficient, masculine, and sexually frigid," while the husbands on the whole were "shy, sexually ineffectual, reasonably hard-working 'mother's boys,' with a ten-

dency to drink excessively." The wife assertively controlled the marital relationship and this tended to complement the husband's dependency needs
and his subsequent subservient role. Even though the roles which the spouses
played were inappropriate, a kind of dyadic equilibrium was achieved.
From time to time, however, both husband and wife sought a change in
their role relationship. Usually this "role alteration" would take place
during one of the husband's heavy drinking bouts, the alcohol being used as
an aid to role alteration. The husband would become aggressive and beat
his wife. This served to "release him momentarily from his anxiety about
his ineffectiveness as a man." Many of the fights arose over the wife's
rejection of the husband's sexual advances. The resulting beatings gave
"his wife apparent masochistic gratification and helped probably to deal
with the guilt arising from the intense hostility expressed in her controlling,
castrating behavior."

With such periodic role reversals, the couples had maintained a kind
of marital balance for as long as 20 years in some cases. This equilibrium
was usually disturbed by children, usually the oldest boy. As the boy grew
older, he would take sides in the family fights, often attempting to protect
the mother. The intervention of the son was disturbing to the wife, who
feared either for the husband or the boy, or both. Basically, however, it was
the disturbance of the marital role equilibrium which prompted the wives
to seek legal recourse. Interestingly enough, almost all of the wives regretted
having called for legal help and in some instances, the couples eventually
drifted back into their former volatile pattern, playing marital roles pathologically deviant to the expected norms.

There is perhaps no social norm pertaining to marital role behavior
more universally encountered, rigidly delineated, or severely sanctioned than
the norm of sexual exogamy, with its incest taboo. The incest taboo prohibits marriage or sexual intercourse between close kinsmen. Invariably the
incest taboo is extended to kin more distant than the nuclear family. The
rationale for the incest taboo is open to controversy from both psychiatric
and anthropologic points of view.[11] Any biological rationale, however,
would almost have to be rejected, inasmuch as among preliterate peoples,
where the incest taboo is particularly strong, it is difficult, if not impossible,
to conceptualize any significant degree of sophistication concerning genetics
and possible adverse effects of close inbreeding. Furthermore, incest taboos,
even in our own society, frequently articulate forbidden kinsmen who are
only related by marriage rather than blood. Freud contended that incest
taboos are "a rejection of the frightening childhood sexual attraction toward
the opposite-sex parent." Such an explanation offers some insight concerning
the revulsion with which incest is normally viewed. At an operational level,
incest taboos apparently serve to "prevent disruptive sexual rivalry," or

"role confusion within the nuclear family," or both, depending on the view of the theorist involved.

Whatever the rationale, incest stands as one of the most reprehensible forms of deviancy in our society. It is severely sanctioned by social, religious, and legal norms, and conviction of incest carries a heavy sentence of imprisonment in most states. (Convicts, it is said, can always spot a "fish," or new inmate who has been incarcerated for incest, because he invariably carries a Bible with him, suggestive of considerable religious guilt.) In spite of the strong public sentiments against incest and the severe formal and informal punishments for violation, it does occur and with significant frequency. Some estimates have placed the number of incest cases in our country at more than 800,000 over a 15 year period.[12] More than a quarter of these were father-daughter incest, the "most commonly detected type, and probably the most socially detestible form." Lay response to the incidence of incest suggests a belief that the perpetrator, if not the victim-participant, is mentally disturbed or deficient. When incest is portrayed in fictional literature, invariably it occurs in a remote rural or mountainous area among "degenerate" peoples.

Scientific case study accounts of incest behavior usually assign a psychiatrically and sociologically pathological flavor to it.[13] Incest on the part of the father, for example, represents the violation of a variety of norms, both legal and informal. He would be guilty of adultery, fornication, incest, and probably statutory rape, all of which are illegal acts. He would also be violating his role as the protector of the wife and children, and would probably be labeled as a sexual exploiter of children and a sexual degenerate as well. It is certainly no accident that some of the most derisive profanity in our language makes reference to incest participants.

Cormier, Kennedy, and Sangowicz, in their article "Psychodynamics of Father Daughter Incest," examine the incidence of incest and the concommitant patterns of family role behavior. This study is based upon case materials from 27 offenders, 21 in prison and 6 in a court-referred clinic, who were guilty of having committed incest with their daughters. The men studied were, on the whole, of normal intelligence, and had made "an acceptable occupational and social adjustment," prior to the incest. They had been good workers, had shown no prior history of adult sexual perversion, and were not, as a group, "conspicuously promiscuous." The authors suggest that an important factor in incest is age. Father-daughter incest appears to most often occur when the father is in his late thirties and forties. It is during this period when his own marriage is subject to the most stress and also when his daughters are reaching adolescence. A variety of disruptive family factors such as the death of the wife, alcoholism, marital disturbances, and so forth may precipitate a situation where the daughter may have to assume the mother's family role in her absence, or in the event of the mother's role dereliction. In other instances, particularly where the wife is sexually frigid or hostile and unloving, the husband may turn to the daughter for response and support. Sometimes the father, as he reaches middle age, comes to see the daughter as the image of the wife at a younger age and thus through the daughter attempts to recapture his own youth. The daughter is substituted for the wife, who has disappointed him both in terms of aging and lack of sexual response, as well as in discharging her family role. The father becomes the sexual partner of the daughter and becomes extremely jealous and possessive of her, often restricting her contact with young men. The daughter originally may have been an assenting participant in the incest because she enjoyed succeeding in a rivalry with her mother or was flattered by the attention of her father. The daughter may also submit simply because he is her father and thus seemingly omnipotent. In any event the daughter may ultimately rebel and expose the incest as a means of achieving independence or freedom from her father's overly possessive actions. The wife, in the meanwhile, is transformed by the husband into the image of the menacing, severe mother who will punish him for his sexual transgressions if discovered. During the commission of incest, the father avoids feelings of guilt by rationalizing that it is a logical consequence of his wife's frigidity or lack of emotional support, or that it is an attempt to protect the daughter from the sexual advances of other men. Not infrequently the offender attempts to deny or minimize his guilt. Aside from such elaborate psychoanalytic explanations, father-daughter incestuous situations may also be viewed in terms of inappropriate role behavior. The wife is inadequate or deficient in discharging her marital and familial role responsibilities, and the husband experiences anxieties concerning his approaching middle age and his stressful marital situation. As his daughter reaches adolescence and develops a youthful attractiveness, the father may vicariously "court" the daughter symbolically seeking his lost youth. In his frustration he may seek a sexual affair with a young woman outside of marriage. Unable to cope with his frustration the father assumes pathological role configurations toward the daughter, actually initiating a sexual relationship with her. In the course of the incestuous relationship the father may waver between an adolescent-like suitor role and that of an overly protective father. The girl may have assumed a seductive or provocative and thus inappropriate role stance toward the father as well as taken on a rivalry role in regard to the mother. The mother in some instances may be indifferent or may conceal the fact of the incestuous interaction from others and even from herself, refusing to accept the fact of her replacement. The incestuous situation, then, represents an inappropriate system of triadic role interaction that is dysfunctional to the family, and pathological in configuration, and represents social deviancy of a most reprehensible nature.

ADDICTIVE IMPEDIMENTS TO FAMILY ROLE PERFORMANCE

Familial roles are usually quite demanding in the multiplicity of their requirements and the attendant efforts to meet those requirements. To successfully play the role of wife-mother or husband-father necessitates the fullest commitment of the individual. Any type of preoccupation will usually serve to hinder or impede the discharge of family obligations and be disruptive to the ongoing family processes. Such preoccupations may include a wide variety of distracting and engrossing deviant activities, such as gambling, drinking, narcotic addiction, or an illicit sexual affair. Even avocational activities such as hobbies may be preoccupying to the point of disrupting normal interaction between parent and children.

The habitual gambler disrupts family life through his absence when actively engaged in gambling, and through his preoccupation with matters pertaining to the races or games and their odds. More importantly, the money spent by the gambler deprives the family and in that sense dilutes the ability of the father to play the role of breadwinner and provider. Likewise, the mother cannot successfully function as household manager if she spends the weekly grocery money at the $2.00 window of the local race track. In a similar vein, the husband or wife lavishing money, time, and affection on an illicit mistress or paramour is not fully complying with role requirements in the family group. Having put so much of themselves into their lover role, they usually have few individual resources left for playing family roles. The restraints of time and finances alone present a formidable obstacle to successfully palying the role of husband-father or wife-mother.

The chemical impediments to family role performance are particularly insidious because they often totally dilute or destroy family loyalties and responsibilities. Narcotic addicts have been known to steal from spouses and children, and to neglect and ignore children even in the face of imminent illness or injury. If desperate enough for a "fix," an addict might even be driven to physical violence against a spouse or child. The alcoholic, under the influence of liquor, exhibits a similar apathy toward family members, and this apathy may turn into hostility if he is thwarted in his efforts to obtain a supply of alcohol. The alcoholic in a drunken rage or stupor may be negligent, indifferent, or belligerent to family members. Homes have burned down, killing the family occupants, including children, on occassions when a drunken parent has set a bed on fire with a cigarette, or let a fire start by other negligence. The alcoholic or addict may act inappropriately in public and thus stigmatize the family. In some instances, an alcoholic or addicted spouse may become promiscuous and may prostitute herself (or himself) to support a habit or satisfy distorted psychological needs.

The financial burden of alcoholism or addiction is such that many victims turn to larceny or other crimes to sustain their habit. While it is true that some alcoholics and addicts manage to control their habits to some degree and live a relatively conventional life (albeit with considerable allowances on the part of family members), most are not able to play the requisite family roles in a tolerable, much less socially acceptable, manner. Alcohol and narcotics, as addictive impediments to family role performance, also precipitate the abdication of family responsibility, represent the violation of conjugal trust, and often contribute to the evolution of normal family behavior into pathological configurations. The wives of alcoholics, for example, frequently manifest neurotic tendencies themselves, both as a result of the husbands' alcoholism, and as a complementary pattern to the husbands' drunkenness. The wife, in a sense, feeds her own neurotic needs from the drunken helplessness and abusiveness of the husband. Alcoholism is both conducive to and thrives in a family situation of pathological relationships and interaction.[14]

In the next article Joan Gage details the poignant account of the "Diary of an Alcoholic Wife." Pauline K., the protagonist, came from an upper middle-class family where the mother did not drink and the father drank only moderately. Like many young people she fell into a pattern of heavy social drinking starting in high school, continuing in college, and carrying over into her adult life after college. Her fiancé and subsequent husband also enjoyed heavy social drinking. Although she was able to maintain this pattern of drinking for a number of years without experiencing difficulty in discharging her family responsibility, after a time some problem signs appeared. The alcohol became more important than the social activity or occassion. Drinking became an imperative and integrated part of the daily household routine, like preparing meals. Pauline became accident prone, had blackouts, developed morning-after tremors and "alcoholic arthritis." She became increasingly embroiled in arguments with her husband concerning her drinking. As drinking began to interfere more and more with her appropriately playing her various family roles, she became self conscious, developed severe guilt feelings, and began to try to hide her drinking. By this time Pauline's alcoholism had become severely disruptive to family interaction and solidarity. She had automobile wrecks, even when the children were in the car. The children were apprehensive and started making excuses for her behavior, and small arguments with her husband became serious fights.

Ultimately, the limit of toleration for inadequate role performance was reached, and the family could no longer continue with the member. Pauline's husband announced his intention to take the children and leave her. Finally, faced with the inevitable, Pauline comes to grips with the full extent of her deviance, seeks treatment, and ultimately manages to stop her drinking. Even the period of sobriety, however, created problems of family routine and adjustment. The husband had to stop drinking around the house lest he tempt his wife, and liquor was kept locked in the trunk of the car, only to be brought out when a visitor wanted a drink. There are still problems of family interaction, but compared to the former situation, Pauline's sobriety permits her to contribute her share to family equilibrium. As she puts it, ". . . my husband and family and my life . . . it's just so peaceful."

Addictive impediments to family role performance are not only a factor in the inadequate behavior of husband-fathers and wife-mothers, they may also prevent a son or daughter from discharging the responsibilities of a dutiful offspring. As a general rule, alcohol may provide a temporary hindrance to family role playing. The teenager with too much to drink may willingly or unwillingly disobey his parents and stay out all night. He may create a disturbance in public and bring notoriety to the family or he may have an automobile wreck, injuring others and creating a financial liability for his parents. Alcohol may well constitute a diversion that preoccupies his free time rather than more constructive or productive activities, but it is not likely to permanently impede his ability to play the appropriate family roles.

While it is true that young people drink heavily, even before their teens, and that there are occassionally teen-age habitual drunks, as a general rule true addictive alcoholism among young people is rare. Narcotic addiction, however, is not so rare and is apparently becoming increasingly more common. Traditionally, drug usage was an addictive habit of the adult, and especially the middle-aged adult. Today the average age of drug users is going down and at an alarming rate. There have been cases of children ten years old mainlining heroin and some have died of overdoses. A nationwide survey conducted in 1969 showed that among college students, one in five admitted having tried marijuana. The number is likely higher today as marijuana becomes endemic to the college culture. Young people are also turning in increasing numbers to hard drugs such as heroin and cocaine which are physically addictive, as well as to other dangerous drugs such as LSD and psilocybin which may be both physically and psychologically damaging. Even the child under ten who develops a compulsion for glue-sniffing suffers an addictive impediment to role performance, for the youngster high on glue is usually unable to play, study, or relate to friends, parents, or siblings appropriately. Narcotic addiction, much more so than alcohol dependence, can divert the young person from the normative patterns of youth and family involvement. In some instances young addicts have been forced to become pushers themselves, to shoplift and steal, and to prostitute themselves to obtain the necessary funds to finance their addiction. Some young people, after using drugs, have rejected their families, both the members and its orientations, and have run away to join communes, traveling addict groups or hippie cultures in slum areas. Drugs are perhaps unrivaled in their ability to totally subvert conformity to family roles, expectations, and normative patterns.

In the final article in this part, Ira Mothner describes what it is like to have "A Junkie in the House." The family described had a son, Bobby, who at 13 began to drink beer and smoke marijuana. By 15 he was on "acid" and subsequently turned to barbiturates and finally heroin to counter the hallucinatory effects. Bobby swiftly progressed from "snorting" heroin to mainlining it. To raise the money for his habit, Bobby stole and became a pusher himself. The parents were suspicious of his behavior, but Bobby was clever in his deceptions. His parents ultimately made him seek treatment, but he returned to heroin and to a life of larceny and pushing. He was arrested and jailed on numerous occassions. He was conning other addicts and even his parents for money. As a last resort, the parents refused to provide bail and left him in jail for seven months after he was arrested for purse-snatching. After his release, Bobby entered a Phoenix House rehabilitation program and ultimately learned to control his addiction. But the threat always exists that Bobby, like other addicts, may once again be tempted by drugs.

The constellation of conjugal familial role behavior expected and sanctioned in our society is elaborate, pervasive, and demanding. The situational setting in which it occurs often renders compliance with the behavioral demands difficult and confusing. The accelerating pace of technological and social change has tended to intensify the challenge of conformity, and the tempting illusions of the mass media have increased and strengthened the distractions and diversions which often encourage role deviance. The extensive role requirements attendant to family are rooted in cultural and religious tradition, supported by public sentiment, and sanctioned by social and legal norms, but may themselves be anachronistic in contemporary society. In any event, violations and exceptions to normative family patterns in the form of role inadequacy and role inappropriateness constitute significant forms of deviant family behavior.

NOTES AND REFERENCES

1. Stephens, William N.: *The Family in Cross-Cultural Perspective.* New York: Holt, Rinehart & Winston, Inc., 1963, esp. pp. 5–10.
2. Abramson, Martin: "Why Men Up and Leave." *Cosmopolitan* 159: 42-45, No. 2, Aug., 1965.
3. Our remarks here are drawn largely from the discussion in Kephart, William M.: *The Family, Society, and the Individual.* Boston: Houghton Mifflin Co., 1961, esp. pp. 541–556.
4. Stephens, *op. cit.,* pp. 5–7.
5. See, for example, Callwood, J.: "Infidelity." *Ladies Home Journal* 82:76, No. 4, April, 1965.

6. For an intensive casework treatment of adultery see Weisberg, Miriam I.: "Early Treatment of Infidelity in the Neurotic Man." *Social Casework* 51:358-367, No. 1, June, 1970.

7. For a contemporary overview of infidelity in our society see Hunt, Morton: *The Affair.* New York: World Publishing Co., 1969; also see Boylan, Brian Richard: *Infidelity.* Englewood Cliffs, N. J.: Prentice-Hall, Inc., 1971.

8. For an interesting treatment on contemporary permissiveness, see Lipton, Lawrence: *The Erotic Revolution: An Affirmative View of the New Morality.* Los Angeles: Sherbourne Press, 1965.

9. Stephens, *op. cit.,* p. 296.

10. Quoted in *ibid.,* p. 269.

11. See *ibid.,* pp. 259–265, for a detailed discussion of the incest taboo. Our remarks here are drawn largely from this material.

12. See Formes, Yvonne M.: *Child Victims of Incest.* Denver: The American Humane Association Children's Division, n. d., p. 5.

13. See, for example, Cormier, Bruno M.; Kennedy, Miriam; and Sangowicz, Jadwiga: "Psychodynamics of Father Daughter Incest." *Canadian Psychiatric Association Journal* 7:203-217, No. 5, Oct., 1962; also Lustig, Noel; Dresser, John W.; Spellman, Seth W.; and Murray, Thomas B.; "Incest: A Family Group Survival Pattern." *Archives of General Psychiatry* 14:31-40, No. 1, Jan., 1966; Weiner, Irving B.: "Father-Daughter Incest: A Clinical Report." *Psychiatric Quarterly* 36:607-632, 1962; and Cavallin, Hector: "Incestuous Fathers: A Clinical Report." *American Journal of Psychiatry* 122:1132-1138, No. 10, 1966.

14. For a detailed account of a housewife's neurotic response to an alcoholic husband, see Jones, Barbara L.: "My Husband Was an Alcoholic." *Redbook* 131:13 No. 1, May, 1968. For a more authoritative view of this phenomena, see MacDonald, D. E.: "Mental Disorders in Wives of Alcoholics." *Quarterly Journal of Studies on Alcohol* 17:282-287, No. 1, June, 1956; and Futterman, S.: "Personality Trends in Wives of Alcoholics." *Journal of Psychiatric Social Work* 23:37-41, 1953.

The Family Desertion Problem Across State Lines

W. J. BROCKELBANK

In the year 1900, Joe and Mary Doakes and their four children, and Joe's father, eighty years old, lived in Central City, Oklahoma. They were an average American family. Joe earned enough for necessities, and Mary looked after the house and the children and Joe's father. If they quarrelled sometimes, their little rifts seemed no more than normal. When the youngest child was ten, Joe got the idea that Mary should get a job so that they could afford a few luxuries and start a savings account. At this idea, Mary exploded. On one week-end, the argument became more heated, and on Sunday afternoon, Joe packed his bags and, with them, disappeared. Later, when Mary found that Joe had taken all their money from the bank, she consulted her neighbors, and, on their advice, consulted a lawyer. She had no idea of getting a divorce. She only wanted to know how she could get money to support the family.

This was the first time that Mary had ever talked to a lawyer. She had always thought law and lawyers were only for criminals. She was surprised to find the lawyer sympathetic. The lawyer told her many things, but he stressed that it was all-important to find Joe Doakes and to find out how much money he had and whether he had a job. If he could be found in Oklahoma, things might be difficult, but at least Joe could be prosecuted for nonsupport and sent to the workhouse. What little he would earn there would be applied to the support of the family. That might teach him a lesson. But Joe had a brother in California and a sister in New York, and had always wanted to visit an uncle in Louisiana. So it was likely that he had left the state. What, then, could be done?

The lawyer had to explain at this point that action against Joe, although theoretically possible, was practically out of the question. Mary would have

From *Annals of the American Academy of Political and Social Science* 383:23–33, No. 1, May, 1969. Reprinted by permission of the author and The American Academy of Political and Social Science.

to find him, and follow him, in order to prosecute him. The lawyer disclosed what, to Mary, were some startling facts: that this was not just one country with one law, but a country of many states with different laws in each, and that the commands of the courts in one were not automatically effective in the others. Mary had her first practical lesson in civics. She learned further that the American Constitution created the federal government with powers to make and enforce laws only in certain specific fields; that the subject of family support is one in which the federal government has not been given power to legislate: that a citizen must depend on the laws of the states, which differ one from the other; and most important of all, that the power of the officials of each state stops at the state border. Mary had heard in high school about the states, but she had always thought of this as a bit of history which one could safely lay to one side as soon as the course was over. Now she was brought up with a start. What could she do? There was little public relief in 1900, and so Mary was forced to fall back on her own relatives or some form of private relief like her church.

This little story of Mary's plight is only one of thousands that the public-spirited men in the legislatures, the courts, and the bar associations faced in 1900. This article is an effort to describe what they and many others have done about it. One can hardly say that the problem of family support has been solved, but the proponents of reform have gone a long way.

Before *reform*, one has to see what it is that needs reforming. Like Mary, the reader will have to start with the fact that in the field of family support it is *state* law with which we have to deal. Keeping details to a minimum, the following is a short outline.

BRIEF SURVEY OF STATE LAW OF SUPPORT

(1) *Husband and wife:* Much of the American law of family support is of English origin. First, we may be somewhat startled to find that, at the common law of England, the wife could not sue her husband. This was thought to be too much of a strain on marital harmony. But if a tradesman supplied her with goods, he might recover the price from the husband if he could prove that the wife had acted as her husband's agent, and even without proof of agency, he might recover if the goods were "necessaries" (that is, suitable to the station and condition of life of the husband). This is still the law both in England and in most states. But the law of neither country says anything about how the wife is to persuade the tradesman to supply the goods when, as a practical matter, he could collect only through the courts. It really meant that the tradesman would not supply the goods unless he knew the husband was willing to pay.

(2) *Parent and child:* The duty of the father to support his children, at

the common law of England, was only moral. As late as 1868, an English judge said:

It is now well established that, except under the operation of the poor law, there is no legal obligation on the part of the father to maintain his child, unless, indeed, the neglect to do so should bring the case within the criminal law. Civilly there is no such obligation.[1]

The child could not sue the parent directly, and neither could the tradesman who had supplied the necessaries for the child.

The early American law differs only slightly. Chancellor Kent of New York does say that "the father is liable to support his minor children" but then adds that "he is not bound by the contracts or debts of his son even for articles suitable or necessary, unless an actual authority (to contract) be proved....What is necessary is left to his discretion."[2]

Thought of as a method for the civil enforcement of the duties of family support, this whole system was quite ineffective in both England and the United States. The difficulties and the legal entanglements of the system marked it as inadequate and, by modern standards, rather ridiculous.[3]

(3) *Elizabethan Poor Laws and American Family-Responsibility Laws:* A congeries of English statutes, first consolidated in 1601 (by 43 Eliz. 1, c. 1), provided that begging was forbidden, that the able-bodied who refused to work were to be sent to houses of correction, that hospitals and alms-houses were to be provided, and that *relatives were to be made responsible for their destitute kinsmen.* These statutes provided for no direct civil enforcement of the duties of support among relatives *inter se,* but merely that the state, which had given support to the poor, could then collect from their relatives. The relatives to be held liable in 1601 included grandparents, parents, and children. This was indeed a broadened solidarity among members of an enlarged family group.

These English Poor Laws were repealed in 1948 by the National Assistance Act, which provided that "the National Assistance Board has the duty to assist all persons in Great Britain who are without resources . . . from moneys provided from Parliament." The state may still recoup itself from the relatives.[4]

Forty of the American states have so-called Family-Responsibility Laws that are copied from or are inspired by the English example.[5] Some were adopted before 1776. All provide for a civil action by the state (or a public assistance agency) to collect for the poor relief supplied. But a few, unlike the English example, provide for direct action among relatives *inter se.* Most, however, bear the stamp of their English origin in providing that the one receiving relief must be *poor* and that collection can be made only after relief has been supplied by the state.

BASIC DUTIES OF SUPPORT IMPOSED BY STATE LAW

Code

A—Husband liable for support of wife.
B—Wife liable for support of husband unable to support himself.
C—Both mother and father liable for support of minor legitimate children.
D—Father alone liable for support of minor legitimate children.
E—Both mother and father liable for support of minor illegitimate children.
F—Father alone liable for support of minor illegitimate children.
G—Mother alone liable for support of minor illegitimate children.
H—Children liable for support of needy parent or parents.
 I—Brother liable for support of needy brother or sister.
 J—Sister liable for support of needy brother or sister.
K—Grandparent liable for support of needy grandchild.
L—Grandchild liable for support of needy grandparent.
M—Other support liability (such as guardians, etc.).

State	Duties of Support Imposed by Law
Alabama	A, C, E, H, I, J, K, L
Alaska	A, B, C, E (under 16), F, H, I, J, K, L, M
Arizona	A, B, C, E
Arkansas	A, B, C, E
California	A, B, C, E, H
Colorado	A, D (under 16), F (under 16), I, J, K, L
Connecticut	A, B, C, E, H
Delaware	A, B, C, E, H
District of Columbia	A, B, C, E (only to age 16), H (or mentally ill)
Florida	A, C (mother's liability is subsidiary), E, M
Georgia	A, C, E (C & E mother's liability is subsidiary), H (qualified), M
Guam	A, B, C, E, H (parent is liable to a child of any age if a pauper)
Hawaii	A, C (under 20), E (under 20), H
Idaho	A, B, C, E, H, M
Illinois	A, B, C, E, H, I (qualified), J (qualified)
Indiana	A, C, E, H
Iowa	A, C, E, H, K, L
Kansas	A, B, C, E
Kentucky	A, C (parents, primarily the father, liable for support of both minor child and an adult child wholly dependent because of permanent physical or mental disability), E, H (adult child residing in Kentucky liable for support of indigent parents residing in Kentucky).
Louisiana	A, B, C, E, H, K, L
Maine	A, B, C, G, H
Maryland	A, C, E, H
Massachusetts	A, C (mother liable to age 16), E, H, I, J (H, I & J only if receiving public assistance), M
Michigan	A, B, C, E, H
Minnesota	A, B, C, E, F, H, I, J, K, L
Mississippi	A, C, F
Missouri	A, C, G
Montana	A, B, D (under 16), H, I, J, K
Nebraska	A, B, C, E
Nevada	A, B, C, E, H, I, J, M

State	Duties of Support Imposed by Law
New Hampshire	A, B, C, G, H, M
New Jersey	A, B, C, E, H, K, L
New Mexico	A, B, C (mother liable only for children under 10), E
New York	A, B, C (mother's liability is subsidiary), E, H, K, M
North Carolina	A, B, C, F, H
North Dakota	A, B, C, E, H
Ohio	A, C, E, H
Oklahoma	A, B, C, E
Oregon	A, B, C, E, H (qualified)
Pennsylvania	A, B, C, E, H (qualified)
Puerto Rico	A, B, C, E, H, I, J, L
Rhode Island	A (qualified) C, D, F, H, K
South Carolina	A, C (primary liability on father), F, H
South Dakota	A, B, C, E, H
Tennessee	A, C, G
Texas	A, C
Utah	A, B, C, E, H, I, J, K, L (K & L if guardian and able to pay)
Vermont	A, B, C, E, H
Virginia	A, C, E, G, H, M (qualified)
Virgin Islands	A, B, C, E, H, I, J (I & J and disabled), K, M
Washington	A, B, C, E
West Virginia	A, B, C, E, H, I, J
Wisconsin	A, B, C, E, G, M
Wyoming	A, C, G

The American Family-Responsibility Laws differ from the English Poor Laws in extending the obligation to support to a wider group of relatives. In former centuries, a family group often included grandparents, parents, and children. It was not too much to expect, therefore, that the obligation to support should extend to all members of this group. In the United States, under conditions of modern urbanization, the family group usually includes only parents and children. Yet, over one third of American statutes still extend the obligation to grandparents; some extend it to grandchildren, and a few to brothers and sisters.[6] The institution of Medicare will solve most cases for the elderly. But if a younger person receives extended treatment in a state hospital, may the state shift the ultimate obligation to pay to the shoulders of a grandparent, a brother, or a sister? The whole family-responsibility situation has come under criticism in recent years; some courts have construed the statutes narrowly, and a California court, faced with the problem whether money from the estate of a daughter should be taken to pay for treatment of her mother in a state hospital, as permitted by a California statute, held the statute unconstitutional.[7]

What has been written about the American Family-Responsibility Laws would seem to indicate that the whole matter needs overhauling. Family conditions have changed since 1601.

(4) *Criminal enforcement:* English law has linked its criminal enforcement of the duties of family support to the Poor Laws. Many of these laws,

issued by a court, provided for criminal penalties for violations of certain orders of support and for probation or suspension of penalties if the violator complied with a support order. In the United States, all states have statutes, of one kind or another, making failure to support a crime. Twenty-five states have passed the Uniform Desertion and Nonsupport Act. Typically, punishment is by a fine or imprisonment, and the court may require periodic payments to wife and children.

Uncluttered by many details and qualifications written into the statutes of this and that state, the following table attempts to list, in capsule form, the duties of support as they now exist in all American jurisdictions.

From the above survey of the basic duties of family support, and the accompanying table, one has to conclude that it is all a disorderly tangle of "scissors and snails and puppy-dog tails." Indeed, one who has read no law, and little history, might well ask why the American people do not put their houses in order.

Coming back to the story of Joe and Mary Doakes with which we began this essay, it is certainly true that Mary's plight is, in large part, the result of this disorder.

Mary's immediate difficulty is that she has been deserted, has no job, has four children and her husband's father on her hands, and is now about to run out of groceries. But she has a husband, who has departed with all the money in the bank, who, doubtless, will soon be earning money at another job, and who, under the law of every state, has a duty to support both his wife and their children. Why has the legal machinery been so slow to supply a simple and inexpensive solution to Mary's difficulty?

Mary is hardly aware of it, but the fact is that her beloved United States has supplied her with, not just one, but 54 governments. The Congress makes the law for the District of Columbia, Guam, and the Virgin Islands; the legislature of Puerto Rico, for that Common-wealth; and fifty state legislatures, for the fifty states. Up to a point, these 54 laws are similar and sometimes identical. But when Joe leaves Oklahoma and goes to any one of the other 53 jurisdictions, his wife's lawyer has to deal with two very technical and knotty areas of the law called, among lawyers, "conflicts of laws" and "extradition." Competent work in either field requires top-level ability and many hours of hard work. Any tangible results are pretty sure to require more money than the deserted family can afford.

At first blush, the political philosopher, seeing that Mary's difficulties stem chiefly from the diversity of laws in 54 jurisdictions, might suggest that we create one and the same law in all of them. But if he has any knowledge of American history, he will soon discard the suggestion.

Under the United States Constitution, Congress has no power to legislate on family law. To turn the problem over to Congress would require a constitutional amendment. There is a strong feeling against centralization of government in general, and the states consider family law to be one of their last holdouts for state control. As a practical matter, any such constitutional amendment would meet massive resistance, and, as a practical matter, is out of the question.

UNIFORMITY OF LAW

Is there another road to uniformity of law? Yes, there is. It is the National Conference of Commissioners on Uniform State Laws.[8]

It is interesting to note that this body was first created to rectify the very defect of the Constitution which we have just discussed—the lack of power in the Congress to legislate in the field of family law. As early as 1879, the American Bar Association asked one of their committees to study, and to recommend some expedient for bringing about more uniformity in the laws of the several states in our laws of marriage and divorce. It took several years to get this matter going. Suffice it to say here that the committee which made recommendations was organized as the National Conference of Commissioners on Uniform State Laws in 1892. Today, a statute in every state requires the governor to appoint commissioners (usually three to six) to study and recommend laws in subjects in which uniformity is necessary or desirable. The Commissioners do their work through seven sections which, in turn, are divided into a number of specialized committees. The Commissioners meet in conference once a year to go over the work of the committees and either to approve or to reject drafts they have made of proposed uniform laws. When the conference approves a draft, it is then submitted to the American Bar Association. If that body approves the draft, it is then sent to the legislatures of all the states and recommended for enactment.[9] Today, over fifty acts have been thus approved, and have either been enacted by most of the states or are being actively recommended for enactment. The Uniform Commercial Code is the most important. The conference has done and is doing much recent work in a Consumers Credit and Probate Code.

In the field of family law, it cannot be said that the National Conference of Commissioners on Uniform State Laws forgot the plight of Mary Doakes. But they were slow in coming to grips, in any imaginative way, with her real difficulties.

The first act approved in this field was the Uniform Desertion and Nonsupport Act of 1910. It simply made family desertion a crime and imposed a number of penalties. It was enacted by only twenty-two states and was, by general consent, considered to be ineffective for solving the problem of family desertion.

Nothing further happened until 1942, when the Executive Committee of the NCCUSL appointed a committee to "study and report." The study committee, preoccupied by war conditions and other things, made little substantial progress between 1942 and 1949. When the war was over in 1945, the courts were flooded by cases asking for support for children. Word seems to have gotten around, among the runaway fathers, that, as a practical matter, a haven of legal immunity from liability for support payments existed just on the other side of the nearest state line. It was not financially feasible for the wife to follow and sue the deserter.

At this point, the New York Joint Legislative Committee on Interstate Cooperation drafted what is called the Uniform Support of Dependents Act. In the same year, ten other states passed similar laws. The act may have had many defects, but it had one great virtue. It created the *two-state suit*. A two-state suit is one which is begun in one state and terminated in another. The plaintiff wife files her complaint in the courts of her home state. That court sends it *by mail* to the court of another state which, it believes, can obtain jurisdiction over the defendant's husband, and the case will there proceed as justice may require.

With the two-state suit, the men of the law, draftsmen in legislative halls, judges, lawyers, and law teachers seem suddenly to have discovered the United States Post Office.

Now the legal haven across the state line was no longer so safe. The destitute wife in the home state no longer needed money to follow and sue the deserter. Instead she could send her complaint *by mail*.

The two-state suit is really an imaginative and revolutionary device. When the suggestion was made at the annual meeting of NCCUSL in 1949, there were shouts of "who ever heard of such a thing?" and the meeting ended in what might be called a state of shock. However, the Conference did not reject it completely. The statutes of ten states were already employing it, and admittedly without dire results! The Conference merely wanted to think it over for a year.

THE UNIFORM RECIPROCAL ENFORCEMENT
OF SUPPORT ACT

The Desertion and Nonsupport Committee of the NCCUSL became increasingly aware of the interstate aspects of family-desertion, and in 1950, they approved the Uniform Reciprocal Enforcement of Support Act. This act did not attempt to make the duties of support uniform, but from the New York Uniform Support of Dependents Act, it copied the *two-state unit*. The act was then approved by the American Bar Association.

The act was then reviewed by the Draft Committee of the Council of

State Governments[10] and was approved for incorporation in the 1951 program of suggested state legislation which was given wide distribution through the Commissions on Interstate Cooperation in the several states.

The act caught on. Popular magazines published articles with eye-catching titles, and technical articles appeared in the many law reviews.[11]

By the end of 1950, the legislatures of thirty states had passed the act.

By the end of the year 1957, it, or a substantially similar act, had been passed in all states and territories and the District of Columbia. A number of amendments to the act were approved by the NCCUSL and the American Bar Association in 1952 and 1958.

In 1968, the Committee, after a wealth of suggestions from many sources, drafted a Revised Uniform Reciprocal Enforcement of Support Act, which has received like approval, and is now being offered by the NCCUSL to the legislatures of the several states for enactment.

SOME DETAILS

We shall refer to the Uniform Reciprocal Enforcement of Support Act by its abbreviation URESA.

The following are essential points about URESA.

First, URESA does not attempt to change existing duties of support. The diverse duties of support still stand. It is the method of enforcement of these duties that has been improved.

Secondly, while we have often used the terms "fleeing fathers," the act itself does not mention them by that name. The act applies to "obligors"— those who owe a duty of support. So the term "obligor" includes, not just the runaway father, but all persons who have a duty to support under the applicable law, and this may include: wives, grandparents, children, brothers, and sisters. It will include Joe Doakes' father, who was mentioned at the beginning of this essay.

Thirdly, URESA enforces *all* duties of support, regardless of origin. A duty of support originates most frequently in a statute, but it may exist under the common law, as inherited from the law of England. It may even owe its existence to a support order issued by a court.

Fourthly, it must not be supposed that URESA functions only for the poor or for those receiving public relief. True, the poor have the advantage of free legal services, when these have been requested by the court (or, in some states, by the state department of public welfare or some other official agency), but URESA is designed to enforce support obligations regardless of the wealth of the person to whom the duty is owed.

EARLY DIFFICULTIES

Like every new device, URESA experienced difficulties. The constitutionality of the act was challenged in several early cases. But suffice it to say that the act has now been held constitutional everywhere.[12]

Many other difficulties appeared. Often, complaints did not include sufficient detail to enable the court or any official to find the obligor in the state to which he had fled. Did the plaintiff in the initiating state have to send a filing fee along with the complaint to the court in the responding state? Sometimes the amount of the filing fee varied from county to county. Then, anyway, how could a destitute Doakes family afford to pay the filing fee?

Most of such frustrating difficulties have been solved by the excellent work of the Council of State Governments. When a few states discovered that reimbursement for relief money paid out locally to destitute families might be had from obligors in other states, sizable administrative offices were created to look after the details. The Council of State Governments then began to lend a hand. As early as 1952, it organized a Reciprocal Support Conference in New York. This was followed by other conferences in other cities. Today a National Conference on Reciprocal Support and several regional conferences are held each year. Judges, directors of state welfare offices, lawyers, social workers, and a few uniform-law commissioners meet at these conferences to discuss and work out solutions. The letter of the law comes face to face with experience from the field. Practically, all the amendments to the act in 1952, 1958, and 1968 were created, discussed, and polished before finding their way into the act. Thus, more details in the complaint were required by a 1952 amendment to the act. In addition, a state information agency was created for each state for the purpose of channeling the complaints into the proper courts and supplying other services. For years, the Council of State Governments kept up a campaign to do away with filing fees, and, today, neither the court in the initiating state nor the court in the responding state can require a filing fee from the person seeking relief, but the responding court may require a fee to be paid by the obligor. In addition, the Council has put out a *Manual of Procedure* and a set of forms which have been very useful.

REGISTRATION OF SUPPORT ORDERS

One of the great improvements of the act came with an amendment in 1958 which was further elaborated in the Revised Act of 1968. This amendment provided that support orders, once obtained from the court of one state, may be registered in the court of any other state and may be enforced there directly, without the necessity of a new trial. The obligor is given notice, and if he does not appear and object to the legality of the registration, his property may be seized in execution and he may be in contempt of court for defaulting on his payments. The destitute can thus get relief quickly in any state to which the obligor may flee.

CONCLUSION

What has been the value of the reciprocal-support movement? As to monetary results, there are no complete statistics. The following statements are taken from the October 1966 report of the Council of State Governments:

Connecticut and Massachusetts reported collections of over $2.5 million each during the year. Florida reported almost $3 million although only a little more than half of its judicial districts reported. The city of New York collected over $5.5 million dollars . . . . The fact that almost every jurisdiction reported an increase indicates that there has been a sizable rise in total collections throughout the United States. . . The figures . . . presented indicate its value and make clear that state and local governments and citizens have much to gain by full enforcement of the reciprocal support laws.

In regard to nonmonetary value, the same source reports:

Aside from the economic value of the act, it should be noted that persons familiar with abandonment problems feel that the act serves as a tool for restoring family relationships. When the father is located and begins to fulfill his support obligations again, it is possible for him to maintain some contact with his children. Many obligors, who deserted because of psychological pressures, are anxious to renew this part of their relationship. Thus, some of the psychological and sociological results of abandonment are mitigated.

A comparison of the plight of Mary Doakes, as it existed in 1900, with what she might experience under the Revised Uniform Reciprocal Enforcement of Support Act of 1968 will show these remarkable changes:

In 1900 Mary Doakes' lawyer had to abandon all help for Mary, as a practical matter, if he knew that Joe had gone to another state and Mary was without funds to enable her to follow him and sue him. Now Mary will get relief from the state welfare department, which can conduct all proceedings for her and can help her to find Joe through the state information agents or location offices in the state to which Joe may have fled. When Joe is found, a complaint will be forwarded, by mail, to the state where he is found, and there, in a forum convenient to him, he may have his "day in court," and present his defenses. If the court finds he has a duty to support his family under the law of the state where he is, the court will render judgment against him, both for arrearages of support already supplied by Mary's welfare agency and for continuing support. The judgment may be enforced by seizure of his property or garnishment of his wages, and, if he gets behind in his payments, by the procedure of contempt of court. He may even be brought back to Oklahoma by extradition and there have to stand trial on a criminal charge of nonsupport.

The act is now being extended by reciprocal arrangements with the provinces of Canada, so that Joe will soon not be able to use Canada as a haven of immunity.

Hundreds of people have participated in the elaboration of the Revised Reciprocal Enforcement of Support Act of 1968. Those who have attended the conferences on reciprocal support and the National Conference of Commissioners on Uniform State Laws, law men, welfare administrators, public officials, social workers—all have spoken, and what they have said has been weighed in the balance of experience. The act has not brought uniformity in the obligations of support. But its enforcement will keep faith with the mosaic of the obligations of support as they exist on the statute books of the fifty states and, in doing so, will save the American taxpayer millions of dollars.

NOTES AND REFERENCES

1. *Bayely v. Forder* [1868], 3 Q.B. 559 at 565 (Cockburn, C. J., dissenting).
2. Kent: *Commentaries* 192 (13th ed.).
3. The best sources for more detailed information on this part of the law are: Brown: The Duties of the Huband to Support the Wife. 18 *W. Va. L. Rev.* 823 (1932); Crozier: Marital Support. 15 *Boston L. Rev.* 28 (1935). Both articles may also be found in *Selected Essays on Family Law* at 810 and 831, respectively.
4. The above summary is based on 9 *Halsbury, Laws of England,* 859 *et seq.* (2nd ed., 1949) and 27 *supra* (3rd ed., 1959), in which a new chapter on national assistance appears.
5. All states except Arkansas, Kansas, Kentucky, New Mexico, North Carolina, Tennessee, Texas, Washington, and Wyoming.
6. This statement is taken from Mandaker: Family Responsibility under the American Poor Laws. 54 *Mich. L. Rev.* 497 and 607 (1956). This is a very important eighty-page study. Another important study is Jacobus tenBroek: California's Dual System of Law. 16 *Stanford L. Rev.* 614 (1965), a 209–page article.
7. *Department of Mental Hygiene v. Kirchner,* 60 Cal. App. 2nd 716, 388 P. 2d 720 (1964). The Supreme Court of the United States refused to allow

an appeal because no federal question was involved in 380 U.S. 194 (1965). The case in the California court has been widely criticized in law review notes.

8. This long name will hereafter be referred to by its abbreviation NCCUSL.

9. Dunham: History of the National Conference of Commissioners on Uniform State Laws. *Law and Contemp. Prob.* (Spring 1965).

10. The Council of State Governments is a joint governmental agency of all the states, created by the states, entirely supported by the states, and directed by the states. It is an agency for co-operation among the states in solving interstate problems.

11. A list of both kinds of articles may be found in Brockelbank: *Interstate Enforcement of Family Support* 7 (1960).

12. For detailed treatment, see Brockelbank: Is the Uniform Reciprocal Enforcement of Support Act Unconstitutional? 17 *Mo. L. Rev.* 1 (1952) and 31 *Oregon L. Rev.* 17 (1952).

Deviance, Visibility, and Legal Action: The Duty to Support

KENNETH W. ECKHARDT

This paper analyzes the reaction of the legal community to a type of deviance which resists classification under the typologies generally employed by sociologists.[1] The offense under examination is the failure of a parent to support his minor children. The peculiar characteristics of the deviancy are such that the act is both a civil and criminal offense, appears to violate common public sentiments,[2] is perpetrated by a large segment of American society,[3] and yet the deviant and act are highly visible to the legal community.

In nucleated family systems, the economic dependence of the family unit on the father is especially acute. Under conditions of marital instability, this relationship becomes a significant societal problem. Figures released by the United States Bureau of Public Assistance indicate that continued absence of the father by separation, divorce, or desertion is a major reason for the deprivation of parental support in families receiving public assistance funds.[4] The bulk of the Aid to Families of Dependent Children caseload is accounted for through the failure of the father to support for the above reasons.[5] The extent of child nonsupport among family units not seeking public assistance is unknown since no agency is charged with the collection and distribution of this data.

From a legal perspective, however, the problem of child nonsupport has been of sufficient magnitude to result in both state and federal legislation.[6] The major intent of this legislation is to provide legal remedies for the (ex)-wife or guardian such that the errant father is compelled to assume his support obligations.

In Wisconsin, for example, the site of empirical research discussed later in the paper, the (ex)wife or guardian has recourse to either civil or criminal remedies for purposes of securing child support funds. Civil enforcement

From *Social Problems* 15:470–477, No. 4, Spring, 1968. Reprinted by permission of the author and The Society for the Study of Social Problems. The research reported here was made possible through a support grant from the Russell Sage Foundation.

55

requires only a demonstration that the father, if of sufficient ability, has failed to provide for the support of his children without lawful excuse. In a series of cases, the Wisconsin Supreme Court has carefully delimited the range of exemption from legal responsibility.[7] (The status of unemployment, for example, does not by itself relieve the father of his legal responsibility.)

To strengthen legal remedies, criminal proceedings may be initiated by the state under two statues. The first statute construes failure to support as a felony while the second defines the offense as a misdemeanor.

Wisconsin Code, Statute 52.05. Abandonment. . . . Any person who without just cause, deserts or willfully neglects or refuses to provide for the support and maintenance of his wife or child under 18 years (legitimate or born out of wedlock) in destitute or necessitous circumstances shall be fined not more than $500, or imprisoned not more than 2 years, or both . . .

Wisconsin Code, Statute 52.055. Failure to Support. . . . Any parent who intentionally neglects or refuses to provide the necessary and adequate support of his child under 18 years (legitimate or born out of wedlock), or any person who without just cause, intentionally neglects or refuses to provide the necessary and adequate maintenance of his wife, shall be guilty of a misdemeanor and may be fined not more than $100, or imprisoned not more than 3 months in the county jail, or both. . . .

A careful reading discloses that the primary difference between these statutes lies in the phrase "destitute and necessitous circumstances." The Wisconsin Supreme Court, however, virtually ruled this phrase meaningless in *Brandel v. State*[8] when it took the position that a wife need not descend to the lowest socioeconomic status to be classed as in "destitute or necessitous circumstances."

From this perspective, there is little substantive difference between child support as a misdemeanor, felony, or civil offense. It would appear that whatever variables are involved in defining the act are external to the offense of nonsupport itself. There is no *a priori* reason why nonsupport should be considered civil in one set of circumstances and criminal (misdemeanor or felony) in another.

The remainder of this paper is devoted to an analysis of the processes of enforcement and a discussion of their significance for deviancy and social control.

NATURE OF THE DATA

The data presented are based on a sample of fathers placed under court order at the time of divorce to support their minor children in a metropolitan county in the state of Wisconsin during the year 1955. Cases involving only alimony were excluded from the sample.

In Wisconsin, as in most states, fathers are required to make payments to the family court clerk who notes the record of payment, provides a receipt, and issues a check to the mother or guardian of the child or children. This practice is designed to insure conformity to the court order, the violation of which is contempt of court, and provides a legal record of payment for the litigants' lawyers, public assistance personnel, the court, and the county prosecutor. High visibility of deviance is therefore characteristic of this offense, and in cases of nonconformity the prosecuting attorney may automatically instigate legal action against nonsupporting fathers.

Because in most cases the age of the children is young at the time of the divorce and the legal obligation extends to their maturity (age 18), the duty of the fathers is extensive. Of the 163 fathers in our sample, 91 percent were obligated for child payments for a minimum of 10 years while 76 percent incurred a 15 year or longer obligation. (It should be noted that remarriage of the mother without legal action by the stepfather for adoption does *not* preclude the father's obligation to support his children.)

To examine the interaction between defendants and law enforcement agencies, patterns of child support payments and legal actions were observed through records for the sample from 1955 to 1964—a 10 year interval. Data were obtained from the divorce files, family and criminal court records, the county sheriff's office, the central file of the Wisconsin State Bureau of Corrections and the Bureau of Vital Statistics.

The sample appears representative of the population of family units dissolved in the county under study and is similar to the data released by the National Office of Vital Statistics. Modal duration of the marriage prior to divorce was less than five years with a majority being married less than ten years. Median age for husbands at divorce was 33.5 while the median for wives was 31.8 years. Socioeconomic status also appears representative in that 64 percent of the defendants held manual occupations. The only characteristic in which the sample is unique is in the virtual absence of nonwhites. Only two of the defendants were Negroes but this corresponds to the proportion in the general community. According to the United States Census Bureau (1960), only two percent of the general community in the county under study is nonwhite. In many respects, the lack of a nonwhite population is a research asset since the presence of racial differences might otherwise have masked other relationships in the law enforcement processes.

FINDINGS

In this sample, the court has clearly established the child support obligations of the father and has determined the "reasonable" financial contribution he is expected to pay.[9] As the defendants were placed under court order at the time of divorce, nonconformity with child support obligations furnished sufficient basis for the instigation of legal action. As previously noted, child support payments or their absence were a matter of public record thus creating a situation of high visibility of deviance or conformity.

Rates of conformity and nonconformity to the court order are presented in Table 1. As can be observed, 42 percent of the defendants made no payment during the *first* year and an additional 20 percent were in defiance of the court order through failure to pay the full amount. The initial rate of conformity is therefore only 38 percent and can be observed to decline steadily over the ten year period to a low of 13 percent. In general, the data indicate that fathers are unlikely to contribute to the support of their children immediately following the divorce and are even less likely to do so with the passage of time, much less to the time of maturity.[10]

How does the legal system respond to high rates of deviancy where the act of deviance is visible, where legal grounds for action are established, and where the deviance is publicly disapproved?

From the perspective of the *law on the books,* a highly effective threat system is offered fathers who fail to comply with the law. Alternatives entail contempt of court, civil action, and prosecution for a misdemeanor or

TABLE 1. RATES OF CONFORMITY TO, AND DEVIANCE FROM, COURT ORDERED CHILD SUPPORT PAYMENT IN PERCENTAGES BY YEARS FOLLOWING DIVORCE ACTION

Number of Years Since Date of Court Order	N^a	Full Conformity	Partial Conformity[b]	No Conformity	Total
One	163	38%	20	42	100%
Two	163	28%	20	52	100%
Three	161	26%	14	60	100%
Four	161	22%	11	67	100%
Five	160	19%	14	67	100%
Six	158	17%	12	71	100%
Seven	157	17%	12	71	100%
Eight	155	17%	8	75	100%
Nine	155	17%	8	75	100%
Ten	149	13%	8	79	100%

[a]N is adjusted for those fathers who were relieved of the court order to support. The general conditions under which this occurred were: (1) decease of the father, (2) termination of parental rights, or (3) maturity of the children. Remarriage of the mother without *adoption* of the children by the stepfather does not relieve the natural father of his legal obligations to support.

[b]Partial conformity indicates that *some* money was contributed by the father during the year for the support of his children although it was less than the court order and in some cases constituted a single payment.

felony. In addition, a continuous theme of rigorous law enforcement is directed at the public and at potentially errant fathers through the press. The following statements are representative of this theme and were selected from local newspapers.

The county prosecutor advised, "We have reached to other states to bring back fathers to face court, we have hauled them off railroad trains, sidewalks and out of taverns . . ."; a family court commissioner stated, "Retribution should be swift and immediate for a man who can afford to make his payments and becomes delinquent"; the chairman of a legal advisory committee favored "immediate jail terms for fathers who willfully refuse to support their divorced families"; the director of the county welfare department declared "errant fathers will go to jail"; and a county judge reported he has tightened his policy and "any nonpaying father will be sent to jail."

The message of these statements is clear: fathers who fail to support will be subject to swift and exacting legal sanctions. An examination of empirical data, however, quickly reveals a disparity between the law on the books, threatened sanctions, and the *law in action*.

Of the 163 defendants in the sample, 84 percent were in defiance of the court order at some time during the ten year interval but only 36 percent of those *eligible* for prosecution had legal action initiated against them.

In addition to the relationship between high visible deviance and low enforcement, there is also evidence of a steadily decreasing interest in securing compliance with the law following the second year of payments. It should be noted, however, that the first four years are high as a category relative to the remaining period. In Table 2, the proportion of defendants eligible for prosecution per year over the ten year interval is presented.

TABLE 2. DISTRIBUTION OF DEFENDANTS BY YEAR, VIOLATION, AND LEGAL ACTION

Year	N	Number and Percent of Sample Eligible for Legal Action		Number and Percent of Those Eligible Against Whom Legal Action Was Initiated	
		N	*Percent*	*N*	*Percent*
First	163	101	62	19	19
Second	163	117	72	37	32
Third	161	119	74	25	21
Fourth	161	126	78	23	18
Fifth	160	130	81	12	9
Sixth	158	131	83	8	6
Seventh	157	131	83	5	4
Eighth	155	129	83	3	2
Ninth	155	129	83	0	–
Tenth	149	128	86	1	1

The table confines itself to recording contempt proceedings since this is the usual first stage in law enforcement for defendants already under court order. During this period, a total of 116 contempt actions were initiated but these were confined to a select group of defendants. Of 137 defendants ever eligible for legal action, 92 defendants had no formal contact with the courts despite high visibility of deviance and clear grounds for legal action.

Of the 45 defendants charged with contempt, 31 defendants or 69 percent had more than one contempt action initiated against them. This is indicative of the lack of effectiveness of legal sanctions since a majority of defendants remained in defiance of the court order despite legal pressure. Even those defendants who experienced only one court appearance were in arrears within 12 months. Many of the defendants had stopped child support payments altogether.

Given the relative immunity of defendants to legal action, what were the characteristics of the subsample of fathers who were confronted with court pressure? Three variables appear to be most significant: social class, family's need for public assistance, and prior legal history of the defendant.

While social class was unrelated to deviance, it was significantly related to court action. As shown in Table 3, approximately 90 percent of the fathers in white collar and 80 percent in blue collar occupations were in defiance of the court order at some time during the 10-year interval. In contrast to the relatively equal proportions of deviance in these two categories, 44 percent of the blue collar as opposed to only 21 percent the of white collar defendants experienced court action.

From an economic point of view, one might have expected more intense legal action against white collar defendants since it is those fathers in upper socioeconomic positions from whom one might secure financial support for children. Of the variables which might explain the apparent lack of effort to secure financial support, family need appears to be relevant.

Since federal legislation requires notification to law enforcement officials of parental failure to support when public assistance funds are sought,[11] a review of public assistance grants and correlated legal actions, if any, was

TABLE 3. CONFORMITY, VIOLATION, AND LEGAL ACTION BY SOCIAL CLASS

	N	In Violation of Court Order		Legal Action Initiated	
		N	Percent	N	Percent
White Collar	48	44	92	9	21
Blue Collar	105	83	79	37	45
Total	153*	127	83	46	36

*N less than 163 since ten files did not contain sufficient information for identification of social class.

undertaken. It should be noted, however, that legal action is not required by federal legislation but remains a discretionary act of local officials. Of the 18 family units which sought public assistance grants, 89 percent of the corresponding defendant-fathers had contempt actions filed. This is in sharp contrast to those family units not seeking public funds in which only 24 percent of these defendant-fathers were involved in court action. The desire by the state to protect public funds is therefore significantly related to the decision to undertake legal action.

Finally we come to the variable of the defendant's prior legal history. Legal action by itself, of course, does not necessarily result in the application of legal sanctions. Following the initiation of action, the case may be withdrawn or dismissed. In addition, the defendant may be found not guilty or, if guilty, sanctions may be withheld.

The decision to apply legal sanctions is related to the defendant's possession of a prior legal record. Table 4 clearly demonstrates that the possession of a prior legal record has a significant bearing on (1) the decision of the court to undertake legal action and (2) the decision to apply or withhold legal sanctions.

Only 16 percent of the defendants without prior legal records had legal action initiated against them, and in all cases the action was withdrawn or dismissed. Of the 23 cases with prior legal records, all 23 had legal actions initiated and sanctions applied.

The legal history of these 23 defendants presents an interesting picture. All 23 defendants were sent to the county jail for nonsupport. Sixteen of the 23 defendants were later charged with the felony of nonsupport and placed on state probation. Six of the sixteen defendants were eventually sent to prison for nonsupport.

Further examination of the defendants who were sent to prison, however, leads one to suspect that nonsupport is *not* the basis for their confinement. All of the defendants had prior legal offenses of a felony character and at the

TABLE 4. VIOLATION, LEGAL ACTION, AND PRIOR LEGAL RECORDS

| | | Defendants Eligible for Prosecution | | | | | | |
| | | Legal Action Initiated But Dismissed | | Legal Action Initiated and Sanctions Applied | | No Legal Action Initiated | | Total |
	N	N	Percent	N	Percent	N	Percent	
Prior Legal Record[a]	23	0	—	23	100	0	—	100%
No Prior Legal Record	114	18	16	4	4	92	80	100%
	137	18	13	27	20	92	67	100%

[a]Prior legal record means conviction of a previous legal offense of a felony character, e.g., auto theft, armed robbery, larceny, etc.

time of commitment were *involved* in legal violations. Their legal involvement, for example, possession of stolen goods, during their probation for nonsupport resulted in revocation of probation and *formal commitment to prison for nonsupport*. Nonsupport, per se, was not the reason for commitment. An unsystematic but random analysis of some 20 other cases of men imprisoned for nonsupport led to similar evidence. The charge of nonsupport was the vehicle for the imprisonment of defendants who ran afoul of the law through other violations. This is in contrast to the picture presented by Wisconsin penitentiary statistics which indicates that approximately 20 percent of all inmates are confined for child nonsupport.

DISCUSSION

In this research we have examined an offense not commonly studied by sociologists. The offense of child nonsupport contains both civil and criminal elements, violates public sentiments, and yet is perpetrated by an apparently large segment of American society under conditions of high visibility.

The instability of marriages has produced a large number of family units dependent for support upon a father who is formally separated from the unit.[12] A system of laws designed to preserve the family unit and to protect society has resulted in a continuing obligation of the father to support his family. Society's general acceptance of divorce and especially the right of remarriage has created a situation highly productive of deviance.

Public sentiments concerning the obligation of the father and the right of children to parental support, however, is in opposition to the fact of divorce and its consequence. High deviance coupled with the economic character of the offense has created a dilemma for law enforcement. Legal actions frequently result in increased economic costs which is the obverse of the law's intent. Fathers who have remarried find it difficult if not impossible to support two family units. To require the father to attempt support of both units results in economic distress for both. Imprisonment as a legal sanction is further dysfunctional as it not only removes the father from the labor force but requires the state to support the defendant and the family unit. The result is a situation of covert tolerance on the part of law enforcement officials.

The cultural lag between the current nature of the family system in American society and the development of laws oriented toward preserving a "one-marriage" monogamous system has resulted in a situation of legal sanctions dysfunctional for effective social control.[13]

From the perspective of social policy, it is difficult to avoid the conclusion that important changes are necessary if we are to reduce the discrepancy between the law on the books and the law in action. Further analyses of the relationship between the agents of social control and the applicability of social sanctions may also prove useful for the development of social theory which relates the act of deviancy to the social structure and takes into account the consequences of sanctions as an important element in the societal reaction to behavior.[14]

NOTES AND REFERENCES

1. For a general discussion of typologies see Gibbs, J. P.: "Needed: Analytical Typologies in Criminology." *Southwestern Social Science Quarterly* 40:321–329, March, 1960.
2. Several surveys have indicated public support for the continuing obligation of the father. See, e.g., Robson, R.: Cohen, J.; and Bates, A.: *Parental Authority: The Community and the Law.* New Brunswick: Rutgers Univ. Press, 1958.
3. This observation is an inference based on the number of family units seeking public assistance as a result of parental failure to support. See Lynch, John M.: "Trends in AFDC Recipients, 1961–65." *Welfare in Review* 5:7–13, May, 1967.
4. *Ibid.,* p. 9.
5. An excellent discussion of the problem is contained in McKeany, M.: *The Absent Father and Public Policy in the Program of Aid to Dependent Children.* Berkeley: Univ. of California Press, 1960.
6. For a review of legislative action see *ibid.,* pp. 41–68.
7. For a review of these cases see Ottusch, J. J.: "Nonsupport Laws in Wisconsin." *Wisconsin Law Review,* May, 1952.
8. *Brandel v. State,* 161 Wisconsin 532 (1965).
9. A discussion of variations in policy for determining the ability of the father to support is contained in McKeany, *op. cit.,* pp. 94 ff. An extended analysis of judicial norms is also contained in Eckhardt, K.: *Social Change, Legal Controls and Child Support.* Unpublished Ph. D. dissertation, Univ. of Wisconsin, 1965.
10. Within the five year period following divorce, 30 percent of the men and 40 percent of the women had remarried. This figure understimates the proportion of actual remarried as data was available only for remarriages occurring in Wisconsin. In his survey of 33 states, Glick points out that approximately two-thirds of the women and three-fourths of the men remarry sometime during the post-divorce period. Glick, Paul: *American Families.* New York: John Wiley & Sons, Inc., 1957, p. 142.
11. See McKeany, *op. cit.*
12. For an insightful analysis of the problem see W. Goode: *After Divorce.* Glencoe: Free Press, 1956.

13. The problem of the relationship between sanctions and offenses is aptly reviewed in Ball, H.; and Friedman, L.: "The Use of Criminal Sanctions in the Enforcement of Economic Legislation: A Sociological View." *Stanford Law Review* 17, Jan., 1965.
14. The necessity for including social sanctions and societal reactions in any theory of deviancy is fully discussed by Lemert, E.: "Social Structure, Social Control, and Deviation," in Clinard, M. (ed.): *Anomie and Deviant Behavior*. Glencoe: Free Press, 1964, pp. 57–97.

AFFILIATIONS AND ACKNOWLEDGMENTS

1. I would like to thank Professors H. Ball and R. Middleton for their encouragement of the initial research.

Some Correlates of Extramarital Coitus

RALPH E. JOHNSON

The Kinsey research estimates that by the age of 40, approximately half of all married men (Kinsey *et al.,* 1948:583–594) and more than a quarter of all married women (Kinsey *et al.,* 1953:440) have sexual intercourse, during the course of their married life, with a partner other than their spouse. This estimate, of course, does not account for sexual contacts short of coitus that occur at cocktail parties, dances or other social gatherings where there is a certain degree of permissiveness regarding the extent of physical contact between the sexes. While extramarital sexual intercourse[1] is one of the most frequently cited sources of difficulty in couples undergoing divorce, nonetheless, relatively little research has been conducted toward assessing the actual impact of extramarital sexual relations on the marital relationship.

Traditionally, acts of adultery have been considered as repugnant by the larger society. In fact, in the early New England colonies, adulterers were at times put to death. Most commonly, however, they were punished by whipping, branding or physical disfigurement. While there has been considerable modification of the laws since early colonial times, nevertheless, today in every state in the United States and all Western European nations which permit divorce, adultery is given as grounds for divorce (Udry, 1966:433).

While there has been widespread interest in the phenomenon of extramarital coitus, the topic has received scant attention and either has been omitted from family analyses, treated as a pathologically based anomaly or only polemically discussed. Curiously, the dearth of information in this highly ego-involved area implies that research scholars and counselors have been content with the Kinsey data.

In order to provide empirical data on this most crucial aspect of the marriage relationship, a comparative analysis of respondents who admit to an EMI(s) with those who deny such an experience was undertaken. The

From *Journal of Marriage and the Family* 32:449–456, No. 3, Aug., 1970. Reprinted by permission of the author and the National Council on Family Relations. This study was financially supported in part by Community Studies Inc., Kansas City, Missouri and the Graduate School, University of Minnesota.

following independent variables were utilized as a basis for this comparison: (1) opportunity for involvement; (2) perceived desire of others for involvement; (3) potential or projective involvement; (4) justification of involvement; (5) marital sexual satisfaction, marital adjustment and involvement.

METHOD

In order to extract meaningful data on EMI, the study focused on three types of extramarital sexual involvement; namely, projective, fantasized and actual involvement. This paper will be confined to the substantive aspects of the study. The methodological implications have been published previously (Johnson, 1970).

Since sexually oriented data derived from interview schedules or questionnaires are likely to yield information which largely is reflective of the normative prescriptions or conventional response patterns of the respondents, techniques of item style were implemented in order to account for possible social desirability distortion (Straus, 1964:383–384). For example, the measurement of projective involvement was derived from responses concerning a hypothetical situation in which infidelity could presumably occur. The hypothetical situation was as follows: "Suppose that you were very close friends with several married couples in the Minneapolis-St. Paul area. As it happened, your husband (wife) had gone on an extended trip leaving you home alone. A similar thing happened to some of your close friends. That is, the wife (husband) of one of these acquaintances left the state of Minnesota to visit relatives leaving her husband (his wife) home alone. How would you feel about (1) spending an evening or evenings with him (her) in your or his (her) living room; (2) going out to dinner with him (her) at a secluded place; (3) dancing with him (her) to the stereo; (4) going to the movie or theatre together; (5) spending a couple of days in a secluded cabin with him (her) near a beautiful lake where no one would find out; (6) harmless necking or petting; and (7) becoming sexually involved? The fixed alternative responses developed included varying degrees of intimacy with a non-spouse person.

Two phases of projective involvement (the basic idea of projective involvement is not new, see Neubeck and Schletzer, 1962) were included; first, the subject responded to the hypothetical situation as an "average person," given the express situation. The second phase required the subject to respond personally to the same set of questions. The response categories involved four possible choices that were dichotomized into positive and negative involvement. Since most reponses to questions concerning sexual activity tend to be answered conventionally, this method was designed to provide the individual with a rationalization for having been involved if he needs such assurance. Moreover, the above technique places the respondent in a position where he is comparing himself with the "average person." The basic assumption underlying the above method assumes that individuals who participate in extramarital sexual affairs tend to "rationalize" their behavior by attributing to others (an average person) the tendency to also become involved.

The measure of fantasized involvement was represented by statements which were designed specifically to ascertain whether or not the respondent felt there were certain conditions under which extramarital coitus was justified. The statements were extracted from 60 case histories involving extramarital sexual relations from the files of a Family Service Agency. A content analysis resulted in nine indicators that were mentioned most frequently as reasons why either the husband, wife, or both participated in a sexual relationship outside of wedlock. Responses were taken at face value as the subjective rationale for sexual involvement. The nine indicators are as follows: (1) the spouse was unable to have sex because of a physical handicap; (2) the spouse was having an affair with someone else; (3) the spouse was unaffectionate or sexually frigid; (4) the spouse was extremely obese or "too fat"; (5) the spouse did not keep herself (himself) physically clean; (6) there was a separation because of the armed services, extended business trips, imprisonment; (7) the spouse was incapable of satisfying one sexually; (8) the spouse was convinced that the only time to have sexual intercourse was when having children; (9) the spouse looked at sex with contempt. The responses to each of the indicators were dichotomized into either affirmative (yes or perhaps) or negative (no) categories. After subjecting the fantasized index to Green's method of scalogram analysis (Green, 1956), the coefficients of reproducibility for husbands and wives were 95 and 98 respectively. The order of items did not vary between the husbands and wives.

Questions about actual extramarital sexual intercourse followed the section on projective and fantasized involvements. Thus, before the questions regarding actual extramarital coitus are posed, the respondent has been prepared to accept the legitimacy of reporting such involvements. In organizing the questions pertaining to sexual involvement, it was hoped that sufficient rationale could be given for responding affirmatively if that indeed was the case.

One of the methodological concerns in a study of this nature is to obtain independent responses from each spouse, that is, to insure that each marital partner is assured that his or her response would not be divulged to their respective mate. To encourage this feature, after completion of the interview schedule, the respondents were asked to fill out a questionnaire in different rooms of their home after which they were requested to place the completed questionnaire in a manila envelope to be handed directly to the interviewer.

During the study, no special problems occurred which detracted from the objectivity of this arrangement.

SAMPLE

The respondents in the study consisted of 100 middle class, middle-aged couples. The sample selection rationale was based on the fact that Kinsey (1948:581) discovered that both men and women at the higher educational levels were more likely to become involved in EMI after several years of marriage. The sample couples were systematically selected from two middle class suburbs in a large metropolitan city in the mid-west.

The middle-aged couples were initially contacted by an introductory letter. It was explained in the letter that there would be a telephone call within a few days for the purpose of setting up an interview. Of the 129 respondents that were contacted over the telephone, 29 refused to cooperate, thus resulting in an over-all refusal of 22 percent.

FINDINGS

Opportunity for Extramarital Coitus

The Kinsey (1948:587) studies reflect the importance of considering the opportunity of sexual expression as an essential intervening variable whenever the extent of premarital or extramarital coitus is examined. For example, Kinsey (1953:332), in assessing the extent of premarital sexual relations, found that many virgins desired coitus but had not yet experienced the proper opportunity. Among female virgins, he found about 22 percent, and among males, 35–52 percent, who said lack of opportunity had kept them virginal.

Katz and Hill (1958) have also illustrated the importance of considering intervening opportunities as an explanatory variable in their generalized theory of residential propinquity in mate selection. Their basic assumptions are that: (a) marriage is normative; (b) within a normative field of eligibles, the probability of marriage varies directly with the probability of interaction; and (c) the probability of interaction is proportional to the ratio of opportunities for interaction at a given distance over the intervening opportunities for interaction.

As in theories of mate selection and premarital sexual relations, there is little reason to dispute the importance of considering actual opportunity for EMI as an essential explanatory variable. Without careful consideration of this variable, it is difficult to place EMI in proper perspective.

As might be expected, Table 1 illustrates that husbands admit to having a significantly higher proportion of perceived opportunities for EMI than do their respective spouses. The question used to obtain responses pertaining to opportunity for EMI was "Have you ever been in a position where you could easily have had sexual relations with someone other than your spouse?" Furthermore, when employment and education of the wife were used as control variables, no significant differences emerged. That is, specific opportunities for an illicit relationship developing is a multifaceted phenomenon not directly attributable to a college education nor contingent upon whether or not the wife was employed.

The above data raises an issue that has been approached polemically by many scholars, namely, is a monogamous marriage in which there is presumably love, respect, trust and mutual satisfaction sufficient to guarantee that adultery will not take place. While the investigator does not purport to have the solution to this perplexing problem, nevertheless the above findings do have some interesting implications in this direction. For example, 28 percent of the marriages included in the sample were affected by at least one EMI. However, when the above intervening variable, perceived opportunities for EMI, was used as a control variable, 40 percent of the marriages where either wife, husband, or both had experienced an opportunity for EMI, had been affected by extramarital coitus.[2]

Additionally, when respondents who claimed that they had not experienced an opportunity for intercourse outside the conjugal bond were asked the question, "Would you like to have such an experience?", 48 percent of the husbands responded affirmatively, whereas only five percent of the wives were so inclined. If the EMI husbands are combined with the non-EMI husbands who would like to experience extramarital coitus, then between 50 and 60 percent of the husbands in the sample have a "positive inclination" toward becoming involved sexually with a woman other than their spouse.

It could be argued that the crucial variable in explaining the positive inclination toward EMI is marital adjustment and that if this was taken into

TABLE 1. RESPONDENTS WHO HAVE HAD AN OPPORTUNITY FOR EMI*

| Opportunity | Spouse | | | |
| | Wife | | Husband | |
	Number	Percent	Number	Percent
Yes	(28)	29	(68)	72
No	(67)	71	(27)	28
Total	(95)		(95)	

$x^2 = 32.06$, P $<$ .001 C = .54

*The total number of respondents will vary slightly from table to table because of refusal to answer specific questions. This, however, did not exceed five percent of the sample.

account a disproportionate number of those who are "positively inclined" toward EMI would be dissatisfied with their marriage. However, an analysis of the data did not bear this out as high marital adjustment was evenly distributed across the two groups (those positively inclined toward EMI and those who were not). Marital adjustment was measured by the Nye and MacDougall (1959) scale. The analysis indicated that the marital adjustment scale was unidimensional, as the coefficient of reproducibility ranged from .90 to .96.

It appears from the above data that the intervening variable, namely "perceived opportunity for EMI" is extremely important in any analysis of the extent of extramarital coitus.

A more subtle way of obtaining information regarding one's desire for EMI was attempted by asking the following projective question: "Do you feel that *most* women (men), even though they are happily married, would like to experience sexual intercourse with another man (woman)?" It is interesting to note that 78 percent of the men and 41 percent of the women who had denied an extramarital sexual affair responded affirmatively. It appears from these findings that extracting relevant data regarding desire for EMI is more promising through the utilization of projective questions than are "direct measures," especially for wives. For example, when comparing the above findings with data obtained from the direct question under the heading "opportunity for EMI" only five percent of the wives who had not had an "opportunity for EMI" indicated that they would "like to have such an experience."

The data also suggests that the so-called "seven-year itch" phenomenon of the man in the middle years (that is, the inclination or desire for a sexual object other than one's spouse), may indeed be characteristic of this middle class, middle-aged group. Neubeck (1968) in a discussion of this subject has stated the following:

The "seven-year itch" phenomenon or the middle-age adventure refers to a yet different aspect of extramarital activities. Linked to the age of the marriage, it is implied that periodically sexual appetites arise which have as their target a person outside of the marriage . . . (However, since these) sexual appetites really encompass a variety of other motivations, these "itchings" should then be understood as the arising of new needs over the life span of the marriage which, if not met by the spouse—and a good deal of testing may go with the partner inside the marriage first—are pursued in outside relationships.

While the husbands indicated a definite propensity to become involved in an extramarital affair, it does not necessarily follow that the middle-aged husband has more of an inclination to become involved than do husbands in earlier periods of the family life cycle. Only further research can clarify this issue.

Projective Involvement

Another possible way of assessing EMI is through a projective technique which was designed specifically to ascertain the potential for involvement with a non-spouse person. It might be recalled that the respondent was first presented with a hypothetical situation in which he or she was asked to predict how the average person would respond to questions representing varying degrees of intimacy—given the specific situation. Then, the same set of questions were directed toward the respondent in an attempt to obtain an estimate of his potential for involvement in an extramarital relationship.

It is interesting to note in Table 2 that 69 percent of the husbands and 56 percent of the wives indicated a positive inclination to interact with a person of the opposite sex when their spouse was out of town. Of the couples interviewed, 91 (or 91 percent) of the families (that is either husband, wife or both) indicated a positive propensity to interact with a person of the opposite sex while their spouse was out of town. This, of course, does not necessarily mean that coitus would result from such interaction, but it does indicate the possible potential for an affair developing—given the opportunity.

Neubeck (1968) in a discussion of extramarital coitus maintains that:

Opportunities which bring one together alone with a nonspouse are almost expected to produce an extramarital sexual involvement. Partial opportunities of this sort are built into our social life. Party ritual calls for a degree of flirtation. There are seductive moves, first tentative "dares," then more pronounced invitations that end up in full fledged sexual episodes. Our culture, while explicitly "puritan," promotes social affairs which in fact are institutionalizing men-women opportunities. There is the case of social dancing, for instance, where close body contact is "allowed," leading not infrequently to sexual relations as a matter of course.

TABLE 2. HUSBANDS' AND WIVES' POTENTIAL FOR INVOLVEMENT IN AN EXTRAMARITAL RELATIONSHIP BY DEGREE OF SEXUAL INVOLVEMENT

Potential Involvement	Husbands		Wives	
	Number	Percent	Number	Percent
High	(68)	69	(53)	56
Low	(30)	31	(42)	44
Total	(98)		(95)	

$x^2 = 2.90, .10 > P > .05$

If, as Professor Neubeck suggests, opportunities which bring one together with a non-spouse are "almost expected to produce an EMI," then projective methods which tap the respondents potential for extramarital sexual involvement should be considered essential in any assessment of extramarital sexuality.

Fantasized Sexual Involvement

The measure of fantasized involvement was represented by nine indicators which were designed specifically to ascertain whether or not the respondent felt there were certain conditions under which extramarital coitus was justified. Table 3 illustrates a highly significant association between respondents when controlling for EMI.

It is interesting to note that 90 percent of both husbands and wives who had experienced an EMI felt that there were definite conditions under which extramarital sexual intercourse was justified. On the other hand, only 21 percent of the wives as compared with 53 percent of the husbands who had not experienced an EMI claimed that there was justification for EMI. Justification of EMI included acceptance, on the part of the respondent, of one or more of the nine statements. Of those respondents who justified an illicit relationship, the mean number of statements sanctioning EMI for wives and husbands were 4.87 and 5.28 respectively.

The above findings suggest that it may be possible to develop an instrument which could assess the extent of EMI among middle-aged couples without direct questions that elicit socially desirable answers. For example, since the preponderance of respondents in the study involved in EMI had similar response patterns on the two projective indicators (potential involvement and fantasized involvement) when compared to those who had not experienced EMI, further replicative studies may produce indirect instruments that could discriminate between non-EMI and EMI respondents. It may be that an

TABLE 3. JUSTIFICATION OF EXTRAMARITAL COITUS BY DEGREE OF SEXUAL INVOLVEMENT

Justification of Extramarital Intercourse	Extramarital Involvement							
	Husbands				Wives			
	Yes		No		Yes		No	
	Number	Percent	Number	Percent	Number	Percent	Number	Percent
Justified	(18)	90	(40)	53	(9)	90	(18)	21
Not Justified	(2)	10	(36)	47	(1)	10	(68)	79
Totals	(20)		(76)		(10)		(86)	
		$x^2 = 7.22$ P $< .01$				$x^2 = 18.44$ P $< .001$		
		C $= .37$				C $= .57$		

index comprised of opportunity for EMI, potential involvement and fantasized involvement indicators would be a good starting point.

Sexual Satisfaction and Extramarital Involvements

One of the foremost explanations for EMI is found in terms of an unsatisfactory sex life or general dissatisfaction with the marriage. A common sense proposition would assert that a lower degree of marital sexual satisfaction is found among marriage partners who had coitus outside the conjugal bond, than those who had not experienced an extramarital sexual affair.

The findings indicate that husbands who had experienced EMI derived a significantly lower degree of sexual satisfaction from their marriages than did husbands who had not experienced coitus outside of their marriage—thus supporting the "common sense proposition" (see Table 4).

It appears that sexual satisfaction on the part of the wife is not as significantly associated with EMI as it is for the husbands. Landis and Bolles (1940:172) provide some evidence in this regard in their study of 153 normal women and 142 female psychiatric patients. For example, they maintain that:

. . . *although there were only 12 cases out of the 85 married women studied who had had extramarital sex relations, their attitudes and affective reactions to the affairs and toward their husbands are of interest. Since behavior of this type carries with it strong social disapproval, it is legitimate to expect that it might have a high emotional tone and that the affair would occur only if the general adjustment of sex adjustment in marriage were unsatisfactory. Yet almost all of those women who had extramarital experiences reported that*

TABLE 4. SEXUAL SATISFACTION OF HUSBANDS AND WIVES BY DEGREE OF SEXUAL INVOLVEMENT*

	Sexual Involvement							
	Husbands				Wives			
Sexual	EMI		Non-EMI		EMI		Non-EMI	
Satisfaction	Number	Percent	Number	Percent	Number	Percent	Number	Percent
High	(10)	50	(61)	80	(5)	50	(62)	63
Low	(10)	50	(15)	20	(5)	50	(27)	37
Total	(20)		(76)		(10)		(89)	
	$x^2 = 6.04$ .02 $>$ P $>$ .01 NS							
	C = .34							

*High sexual satisfaction included response in either the "extremely enjoyable," or "very enjoyable" categories. Other possible response categories were "somewhat enjoyable,' "not too enjoyable," "dissatisfying," and "extremely dissatisfying."

they had fairly adequate sexual experience with their husbands. That is, the extramarital affair was rarely the result of lack of opportunity to obtain sexual satisfaction from their spouse.

It is difficult to generalize from the data regarding sexual satisfaction as the study did not attempt to assess the many facets of sexual satisfaction, i.e., orgasm frequency of marital coitus, attitude toward sex, level of sexual desire between partners, frequency of marital coitus, etc. The study does not assert that sexual dissatisfaction in marriage is a cause of EMI[3]. However, it does appear clear that non-EMI spouses have been able to maintain a significantly higher degree of marital sexual satisfaction than did EMI spouses. A logical explanation could be that both sexual satisfaction and EMI are but symptomatic of low marital adjustment between the spouses. While family researchers have stressed the importance of the sexual relationship (sexual satisfaction) in maintaining an adequate marital adjustment, nevertheless, the impact of EMI on the family role complex has been largely ignored. In fact no studies to date have attempted to examine the relationship of marital adjustment. and EMI with respect to couples in the middle years. However, upon analyzing the data, no significant associations were found between EMI and non-EMI husbands and wives with respect to marital adjustment. It is interesting to note, however, that only 30 percent of the EMI husbands had high marital adjustment whereas 60 percent of the EMI wives had high marital adjustment.

Kinsey (1948:436) implies that there is a possible relationship between marital instability and extramarital relations. The data support this general contention for husbands, but it does not appear to be equally applicable for the wives. Furthermore, the data tend to lend support to the earlier contention, namely, that general dissatisfaction in the marriage or dissatisfaction over the sexual relationship is not as frequently associated with EMI for the wives as it is for the husbands.

The above findings are probably attributable to basic sex differences between husband and wife. It has been observed in several studies that the female comes into the marriage with a lower "sexual drive" than does her husband. Since the woman is presumably still sexually conditionable, the experiences that she obtains within the marriage may "increase her interest in sex," but by and large do not tend to reduce the difference appreciably between husband and wife. For example, Kephart (1961:457–58) points out that only "a minority of women—perhaps 10 or 15 percent—are aroused by sexual stimuli; think in sexual terms; or may suffei more or less serious hardships if they do not obtain regular sexual gratification." Because of this, the husband may find this sex life less satisfactory than he expected.

On the other hand, as the marriage continues, the wife's increasing sexual enjoyment may result in the husband's lowering of his basic expectations.

It is then possible that there will be some type of convergence of sexual expectations. If, however, this concurrence is not realized, the husband (or wife for that matter) may well seek additional sexual objects outside the marital relationship.

Udry (1966:415) maintains that:

For each sex, there is the same correlation between marital adjustment and sexual adjustment, but the main direction of causation is opposite for the two sexes. For a man, the level of sexual adjustment has a causal effect on his marital adjustment with little reciprocal effect of general marital adjustment on his sex life; for a woman, the level of general marital satisfaction has an effect on the sexual adjustment with little reciprocal effect of the sexual adjustment on her general satisfaction with the marriage.

Whether there is an actual cause and effect relationship remains to be seen. Only additional research will help clarify this issue.

CONCLUSION

This study was designed to provide an understanding of marital and extramarital sexual involvements through a comparative analysis of respondents who admit to an extramarital sexual experience and those who deny such an experience. Three major findings emerged from the data. First, it was found that husbands who had experienced EMI had a lower degree of sexual satisfaction and marital adjustment in their marriage than did non-EMI husbands. This finding suggests a common sense proposition relating EMI to a basic discontentment with the conjugal relationship. The data were, however, fairly inconclusive for the wives, notwithstanding the fact that they had the same general pattern as their husbands.

Secondly, there appears to be basic sex differences between husband and wife across all five independent variables used in the study, namely: (1) opportunity for involvement; (2) perceived desire of others for involvement; (3) potential involvement; (4) justification of involvement; (5) marital sexual satisfaction, marital adjustment and involvement.

Finally, when examining "opportunity for EMI," some interesting findings emerged. For example, it might be recalled, in 28 percent of the marriages there was an admission of one or more extramarital sexual experiences. However, when the perceived opportunity for an affair developing was taken into account, 40 percent of the marriages where either wife, husband, or both had experienced an opportunity for EMI, had been affected by extramarital coitus. It appears that the intervening variable, namely "opportunity for EMI," is quite crucial in the analysis of extramarital sexuality and suggests that future studies may be directed toward explicating the following issues: (1) To what extent is the "opporutnity for EMI" overt and straight-forward or intuitive and "wishful thinking"? For example, to what extent does projection (the process of ascribing to others ones own ideas or desires) enter into estimates of the "opportunity a person has for EMI"? (2) Do certain occupations have a higher propensity for EMI and "opportunity for EMI"? (3) Do EMI participants "make their own opportunity for EMI" (such as seeking out call girls, etc.) or is it the result of repeated exposure to EMI opportunities (such as secretary-boss, intern-nurse relationships)? and (4) To what extent are EMI petting and EMI intercourse interrelated?

NOTES AND REFERENCES

1. In the pages that follow, extramartial sexual involvement(s) will be designated as EMI.
2. Twenty percent of the husbands and 10 percent of the wives admitted experiencing extramarital coitus. For a discussion of the methodological problems involved in extracting data on EMI, see Johnson's "Extramarital Sexual Intercourse: A Methodological Note." *Journal of Marriage and the Family, May,* 1970.
3. An inherent weakness in the study was that the investigator obtained only responses pertaining to "enjoyment of sexual intercourse," and not "actual satisfaction with coitus." There is a difference in as much as it is entirely possible that an individual could find intercourse "distasteful" (thus rating it low as far as enjoyment is concerned) but be satisfied because of the low degree of actual coitus—in terms of frequency—within the marriage. Moreover, it could be argued that the sexual satisfaction response could be a consequence rather than antecedent to the husband's involvement in EMI, thus justifying EMI on the basis of low sexual satisfaction at home.
4. Green, B. F.: "A Method of Scalogram Analysis Using Summary Statistics." *Psychometrika* 21: 79–88, March 1956.
5. Johnson, R. E.: "Extramarital Sexual Intercourse: A Methodological Note." *Journal of Marriage and the Family* 32:279–282. May, 1970.
6. Katz, Alvin M., and Hill, Reuben: "Residential Propinquity and Marital Selection: A Review of Theory, Method, and Fact." *Marriage and Family Living* 20:27–35, Feb. 1958.
7. Kephart, William M.: *The Family, Society and the Individual.* Boston: Houghton Mifflin Company, 1961.
8. Kinsey, Alfred C., *et al.: Sexual Behavior in the Human Male.* Philadelphia: W. B. Saunders Company, 1948.

9. Kinsey, Alfred C., *et al.*: *Sexual Behavior in the Human Female*. Philadelphia: W. B. Saunders Company, 1953.
10. Landis, Agnes T., and Bolles, Marjorie M.: *Sex in Development*. New York: Paul B. Hoeber, Inc. 1940.
11. Neubeck, Gerhard: "The Dimensions of the 'Extra' in Extramarital Relations." Unpublished manuscript, Family Study Center, University of Minnesota, 1968.
12. Neubeck, Gerhard, and Schletzer, Vera M.: "A Study of Extramarital Relationships." *Journal of Marriage and Family Living* 24:279–281, Aug. 1962.
13. Nye, Ivan F., and MacDougall, Evelyn: "The Dependent Variable in Marital Research." *Pacific Sociological Review* 67–70, Fall, 1959.
14. Straus, Murray A.: "Measuring Families," in Christensen, Harold T. (ed.): *Handbook of Marriage and the Family*. Chicago: Rand-McNally and Company, 1964, pp. 335–400.
15. Suchman, E. A.: "The Scalogram Board Technique for Scale Analysis," and "The Utility of Scalogram Analysis," in Stouffer S. A. *et al.* (eds.): *Measurement and Prediction*. Princeton, New Jersey: Princeton University Press, 1950, pp. 91–171.
16. Udry, Richard J.: *The Social Context of Marriage*. Philadelphia: J. B. Lippincott Company, 1966.

AFFILIATIONS AND ACKNOWLEDGMENTS

1. Ralph E. Johnson, Ph. D., is associate professor in the Graduate School of Social Work, Sacramento State College, Sacramento, California.

Wives Who Run Away

MAX GUNTHER

She is an attractive woman in her early forties. Five years ago she was a suburban housewife. Today she is a runaway wife.

"Don't tell what color hair or eyes I have or how tall I am or what my name was or is now," she pleaded. I promised I wouldn't. Those terms agreed on, she began to tell me her story as we sat in the bar of the Statler-Hilton Hotel in Boston.

In 1966, shortly after she saw her only daughter off to college, the woman gathered a little money and a few clothes, boarded an eastbound jet and ran away to a new life. Her husband and daughter do not know where (or who) she is—nor does anyone else who was part of her life before 1966. She now works in an administrative office of a Boston university. Her friends in Boston don't know her real name or where she comes from, but they do know the basic outline of her story. Casual acquaintances probably assume she is a widow or a divorcee because she still wears her wedding ring.

Millions of tired, bored housewives have dreamed at one time or another of chucking it all, or running away to a new, exciting life in a new, exciting city. But for most, it's been only a dream. In the past decade, however, increasing numbers of women have acted upon that dream. Today, an estimated 30,000 American women a year run away from home and toward new lives.

Precise statistics are not available. No federal or state government agency makes a regular or formal study of the phenomenon. But two large private agencies do. One is the Family Location Service, a national nonprofit sociolegal organization that specializes in hunting missing spouses, parents and children. The other is Tracers Company of America, a private detective agency with investigators in 350 cities.

Solomon Weiss, the lawyer-psychologist who now heads FLS, says

From *Ladies Home Journal* 88:65–66, No. 2, Feb., 1971. © 1971 Downe Publishing, Inc. Reprinted by Special Permission of the *Ladies' Home Journal*.

it is hard to be precise about how many husbands and wives disappear. "When a spouse runs away," he says, "shame and embarrassment and other problems may keep the deserted partner from doing or saying anything about it. The only cases we know about are the ones where the deserted spouse takes some action. How many cases are there that we don't see—that nobody sees? We have no way of knowing." What Weiss does know is that, according to his files, the percentage of runaway wives has been increasing. Since the early 1950s, the percentage of missing wives has risen from about 5 percent to nearly 15 percent of the total number of missing spouses. Tracers tells the same story. In the 1930s there were so few runaway wives that Tracers didn't even give them a separate statistical category. In the 1940s, partly because of the social disruption caused by World War II, the company found itself handling four missing wives for every 100 missing husbands. Today the percentage of missing wives has tripled.

Why? In Boston, our runaway wife suggested part of the answer. "I think many women these days are troubled by too much education and too little chance to use it," she said, gazing into her martini. "There's a huge gap between what you feel you can do and what society *lets* you do. Especially if you're a housewife. I was stuck out there in a suburb, stuck with dirty dishes and TV soap operas, while a big, exciting world kind of whirled around me—out of reach. My husband was out in his business world, meeting interesting people, using his brain. He was growing intellectually while I was stagnating. I know he was losing interest in me. My daughter was growing past me, too. She'd try to explain her feelings about sex or civil rights or something and finally say, 'Oh, Mother, you just don't *understand!*' I thought, 'I've got to go somewhere and be somebody before it's too late.'"

She had once visited Boston as a young single woman, and had found it exhilarating. The frustrated wife found herself thinking more and more about how pleasant it would be to go back there, to vanish into its depths. One afternoon, seized by a sudden whim, she stepped into a telephone booth in a drugstore and from long-distance information obtained the phone numbers of colleges in and around Boston. Over the next few weeks—always using the same phone booth ("It got to feel homelike, cozy")—she phoned and found that secretarial jobs were available.

DEADLY BORE

For several months she did nothing. She simply nursed the information in her mind—"the delicious but scary thought that I could go if I really wanted to." Then, one night, she had an argument with her husband. "He'd been invited to a party with some business friends and didn't want me along. He told me, 'I don't think you'd enjoy it, you wouldn't have much in common with these people. They're kind of swinging types.' Well, that did it. He'd put me in a category: I was a deadly bore. A week later, when he took off on a business trip, I packed up, typed him a note and left."

I asked, "Are you glad you did?"

She smiled: "Sometimes. Sometimes not." She has a wide and apparently fascinating circle of friends in and around the university—faculty members and others. She has tried to shed "the shackles of my middle-class, suburban background"—shackles that she feels contributed to the dissatisfactions of her former life. She has experimented with new styles of living and new modes of thought; she has smoked marijuana a few times, has had a few sexual adventures, has attended hippie parties and blue movies and odd political gatherings. Her life is not boring.

But is it what she hoped it would be?

"The thing that bothers me sometimes," she said quietly, as we were preparing to leave, "is that I haven't tried to cover my tracks well. My husband could find me if he wanted to."

When I told this story to Tracers' vice president Ed Goldfader, he called it typical. "You can see why more women are vanishing from home," he said. "Women aren't bound to their husbands economically, socially or psychologically the way their grandmothers were. There are plenty of jobs for women, and more are opening up every year as sex discrimination in industry slowly breaks down. Thus a women has the *opportunity* to run away if she wants to.

"At the same time the *desire* to run seems to have been growing, too. There's this crazy situation of highly educated women washing dishes and sorting diapers; it's hellishly frustrating for some of them. This general discontent has been made more painful in our society by the expansion of mass media like TV. A discontented woman watches TV, finds that there are all kinds of glamorous worlds out there and thinks, 'Why can't I get out of my trap?' "

Most runaway wives, says Goldfader, are between 35 and 50 years old. Tracers once made a statistical study and found that 79.6 percent of the wives it had hunted were in the 35–45 age bracket. Fewer than 3 percent were under 30, and fewer than 7 percent were over 50.

About 75 percent of runaway wives are mothers. "With few exceptions," says Goldfader, "women do not run away from home while their children are young—which is why we see this clustering in the 35–45 age group. The typical runaway mother waits until her kids are at least teen-agers. Often she waits until they are gone from home, at college or at work."

In fact, the growing up of children is often among the key factors in a woman's decision to run away. "As her children grow," Goldfader says, "they need her less. So she runs, hoping to find a life where she can feel useful again."

Before she leaves, she chooses a destination. "The romantic notion of simply getting on any train and going in any direction," says Goldfader, "crops up more often in fiction than in real life. The runaway wife almost always goes to something—often to a prepicked or at least prescouted job, usually to a city or region she has known and liked before, sometimes to a distant, trusted friend."

She may run with, or to, a man. In FLS's case files is the story of two neighboring couples on a suburban block; the man of one house and the woman of the other disappeared together and have never been found. "But this cliche of 'running away with another man' is also more common in fiction than in fact," says Goldfader. "Divorces and separations are so easy to get these days that there's usually no need for an affair to end in a vanishing act. No, when a woman disappears, she most often goes alone, wishing to escape a life where things have been going wrong."

DISTINCT TYPES

What kind of woman is the runaway wife? Psychiatrists and psychologists talk about two distinct types, so unlike that at first glance it's hard to believe they both end up taking the same escape route.

One kind of runaway wife is childish and immature. She is the kind of woman who all her life has run away from problems. Mrs. Irene Blickstein, staff associate at the Community Service Society of New York, tells of one such woman. "She had had a difficult, insecure childhood and had come out of it as an adult without much backbone. She had married in her teens, probably romanticizing the idea of marriage too much, expecting it to be a situation in which she could receive without having to give. She expected her husband to be the whole support of the family. When children came, she couldn't face the reality of motherhood, the hard work, the long hours. She would stay in bed, complaining about how tired she was, letting her husband run the household. Understandably, he complained. The marriage deteriorated. She felt overwhelmed by cares and responsibilities. Finally she disappeared, leaving her children behind." A few years later, apparently feeling lonely and dissatisfied with her new life, the woman got in touch with her husband again. She had been working as a cocktail waitress in the Midwest. When her husband showed no inclination to patch up the marriage, she disappeared from view again and has not been heard from since.

A psychiatrist in New Mexico has studied another kind of runaway wife —one whose problems spring not so much from within herself as from what he calls "the untenable position in which our society has placed her."

Among the psychiatrist's current patients is a woman in her early forties who, three years ago, vanished from a Chicago suburb and headed for

New Mexico. "She had all the upper-middle-class goodies. Big house. Maid. Two cars. Country club. The whole scene. But she was desperately unhappy." She felt her family was a group of strangers living in the same house for no good reason. Her husband was clawing his way uphill in a mighty corporation. He traveled a lot. When home he was tense, tired, irritable. On weekends he invariably got drunk to ease his tensions and flirted with neighbors' wives. The teen-age youngsters barely knew their father. They saw him only as a weary grouch and periodic drunk. They wondered what thing of value, if any, he contributed to the world. Searching for meaning in their own way, they experimented with radical political movements ("a rejection of the materialism their father symbolized") and sex ("a yearning for closeness with any human being, on any terms"). The mother, meanwhile, felt stranded in an alien world. She was alone in the house most of the time, bored, frustrated, useless.

So she ran away. "Immature?" asks the psychiatrist. "I wouldn't say so. In this case as in many others, the act of running away seems to represent a profound search for meaning. It is often the act of a highly mature, intelligent woman."

Mature or immature, the woman who means to stay hidden must solve some difficult problems. "In this highly documented age," says New York private detective Bill Herman, "this age of Social Security cards and driver's licenses and birth certificates, it is not easy to forge a new identity and make it stick. Most missing persons are easy to find."

Many don't care if they are found. FLS's records show that about half of all runaway wives eventually return of their own accord—sometimes in a few weeks, sometimes in a year or two. "The act of disappearing may only have been intended to punish the husband or teach him a lesson," says Solomon Weiss. "In other cases, the runaway finds life out there isn't as free and glamorous as she'd hoped, so she comes home."

Others go with a firm intent to stay gone, and no posse of lawmen ever sets out after them. Contrary to popular myth, police missing-persons bureaus won't hunt a missing wife (or husband) as long as there is evidence that he or she is "voluntarily absent, alive and well." Technically, it is illegal in most states to desert children under 21, but in practice the law is seldom invoked unless the children become wards of the state. Courts and district attorneys' offices are simply too overworked to bother with what is considered essentially a private marital problem.

Thus a vanished wife need only evade private hunters such as Bill Herman, Tracers or FLS—if her husband chooses to hire them. He may not. "We had one case," Ed Goldfader recalls wryly, "where a woman disappeared and her mother hired us to make a search. Couple of days later, the husband phoned and said he'd pay us even more to quit." (A hunt usually costs $250 to $1,500.)

NEW IDENTITY

If a woman's husband or family elects to track her down, her chances of staying hidden are only one in five. Documents are her main problem. You can't make a major move without producing documents that show who you are and who you used to be. To leave the country you need a passport, and to get one you must produce a birth certificate. To drive a car you must have a license, and to get one you must produce identification. To get a job you must outline your past employment and educational history, and your history won't stand up under checking if you've given a fictitious name.

Another problem comes from personal characteristics. "Women in hiding often dye their hair, change their makeup and style of dress," says Ed Goldfader. "But this isn't enough. To disappear successfully, you must escape from your former self entirely. I mean change your hobbies, your food preferences, your work skills, everything."

Tracers found one woman, when she made the mistake of subscribing to a favorite hobby magazine. "We knew what city she'd probably gone to so we phoned the magazine and asked for a list of new women subscribers in that city. There were only three." Bill Herman found another missing wife because she was a food faddist. He showed her photograph in California health food shops until somebody recognized her as a new customer.

But it is possible to escape, given enough determination and planning. Goldfader speaks admiringly of Carol, a woman who vanished seven years ago from her San Francisco home and could not be found. Learning that her husband had divorced her *in absentia,* she eventually returned—smiling and triumphant—and told her story.

Carol's marriage had not been working well for some time. She asked her husband for a divorce, but he angrily refused. Carol then began to plan her disappearance. For a long time she thought about the problem of documents. She knew she would have to change her name and characteristics, but how? She decided to borrow someone else's.

She needed to find a woman about her own age who had fairly common maiden and married names, a college degree and an interesting job history. Finally she met one: call her Jane Smith, *nee* Parker. Under the guise of ordinary social interest, Carol drew from Jane Parker Smith a number of important details of her life.

Jane Smith, before marriage, had worked as an editorial researcher at a news magazine. Carol read books on newspaper and magazine work, learned the jargon and studied the structure of news stories. Meanwhile she applied for a new Social Security card under the name of Jane Parker Smith. Where the application form asked, "Have you ever before applied . . . ?" she checked the "No" box. She gave Jane Smith's address in care of her own. The card, bearing a brand-new number, eventually arrived in the mail.

Carol burned all her own identification, packed a suitcase, drew all the money out of her personal savings account, boarded a bus and disappeared.

She took up life again in the Southeast as Jane Parker Smith and immediately applied for a newspaper job. When the paper's personnel director checked her history, he found that a Jane Parker had indeed graduated from a certain college in a certain year and had worked at a certain news magazine. Jane Parker's Social Security number had been different back in those days, but Carol explained in advance, "I lost my card and forgot the number after I got married, so I applied for a new one."

She was hired. For six years she worked at the paper and became one of its ace women reporters. Then one summer she asked for a leave of absence and took a trip back to San Francisco to see her husband and her old social set. But she did not stay long. In September she dropped from sight again. Presumably, she is back on the job as a newswoman.

Before she left, she confided to a friend: "I wouldn't advise anybody to do what I've done. It takes a lot out of you. But I will say one thing. It has been a grand adventure."

The Wifebeater's Wife:
A Study of Family Interaction

JOHN E. SNELL, RICHARD J. ROSENWALD AND
AMES ROBEY

When a man beats his wife, why does she take him to court? This question appears to answer itself, but our experience with the wives of wifebeaters in a court psychiatric clinic has led us to believe that this decision to seek legal assistance is not a simple reaction but rather a result of complex familial interaction. This paper will share some of our observations from our work with these women and will suggest some explanations for what we have seen.

Our experience with wifebeaters' wives was gained in one of the psychiatric clinics which have been established under the Massachusetts Division of Legal Medicine to serve various district courts of the Commonwealth. The court to which our clinic is attached is in Framingham and serves a predominantly middle-class suburban area. In the five years of the clinic's operation (1957–1962) 37 men charged by their wives with assault and battery were referred to the clinic for psychiatric evaluation and possible treatment. This number represented the most frequent single type of assault and battery offender to be referred to the clinic and far exceeded the proportion of wifebeaters to all assault and battery offenders handled by the court. The judges and probation officers tended to refer these offenders frequently, apparently reflecting a general community feeling that "There must be something wrong with a man who would beat his wife," especially when he has a good job, a nice home, children, and an outwardly stable family.

In making these requested evaluations we began routinely interviewing both the husbands and the wives and quickly found that the latter tended to be much more willing to talk to a psychiatrist to give "My side of the story." The men were usually resistive to psychiatric contact, tending to deny that problems existed in their marriages which required outside help.

From *Archives of General Psychiatry* 11:107–113, Aug., 1964. Reprinted by permission of the publisher.

The interviewing of the wives, which was first seen as an expedient to supplement the husbands' reluctantly given history, moved into direct interest in exploring the wives' roles in the marital strife and, in some cases, to long-term therapeutic effort. We were able to study 12 of these families in detail, both husbands and wives being seen for three or more interviews. Four of the wives have been worked with in long-term individual dynamically oriented therapy, each being seen more than 18 months. In addition, group therapy with some of the wives and couple therapy has been attempted, and these efforts are continuing.

There were two distinct pieces of behavior necessary for each of these couples to be in court: the husband must presumably have made some form of assault, and the wife must have made a decision to call for help from the court with a formal complaint. That the second is not an invariable result of the first seems intuitively obvious, as there are undoubtedly many episodes of marital discord with some violence which are never reported to the courts. All of the attention of court, community, and social agencies has tended to focus on the motivations for the husband's behavior. As we became acquainted with the wives of these men, we began to be equally interested in the specific motivations for the wife's behavior. Each wife's decision to bring her husband to court constituted, in a sense, the *definition* of his offense, for it is only when this decision is made that the court (and, therefore, the community) formally sees the husband's behavior as a social offense requiring judicial notice rather than a purely intrafamilial disagreement which can be handled by the persons directly concerned. How and when she makes this decision to define her husband's behavior in this manner became the focus for our study of the wifebeater's wife.

Some of the considerations which led us to this focus can be made clear by a few simple observations about the group of women we studied. In each case the marriage was the wife's first, and the assault and battery complaint was also the first. The average age of the wives was 37 years, and they had been married for an average of over 13 years. One sees, therefore, that these women were not young brides in the throes of early marital adjustment, but tended rather to be women of mature years whose marriages had shown considerable stability. There was little spread from these average figures, only two women being under 35 or having been married less than 12 years. In no case was the husband's violence of recent onset. Each wife admitted readily that fighting had existed throughout her marriage. The decision of the wife to call for help was, then, the significant change in behavior, rather than the husband's assault. The central question became: why, after 12 to 20 years of marriage marked by frequent physical abuse from their husbands, had these women chosen this particular time to appeal for help outside their families, to bring their marital difficulties to the community for arbitration?

The wives' first answers to this question almost invariably involved the children in some way, directing our attention to the offspring of the marriages for examination of their roles in the decision to come to court. All but one of the marriages had produced children, the one childless wife describing a series of intense mothering relationships between herself and several teenage youngsters. All but the two younger wives mentioned had a child over ten years of age. In each of these cases the oldest child was male. These eldest children figured prominently in the description of the specific episode of violence which had triggered the court appearances. In some cases, the eldest boy had participated actively in the strife, defending his mother and physically attacking his father. Even where this activity was not described, this child was given as a major reason for requesting outside help and control. Typical reasons given by these wives for their action emphasized the male child's increasing age and strength: "He is growing old enough now for his father's behavior to affect him," or "he is big enough now to really hurt his father."

The husbands, for their part, had much complaint about their sons and about the relationships between their sons and wives. The relationship between father and son was reported to be distant and/or troubled in each of the nine families with eldest sons over ten years of age, and the sons' sympathies were universally reported by both parents to be with their mothers. The consistency of these observations throughout the group studied gave rise to our speculation that a common significant factor in determining the timing of the court appearance may be the presence in the family of an adolescent child (commonly male) whose intervention in the parents' struggle acts to disturb a marital equilibrium which had been working more or less satisfactorily.

The characteristics common to this type of family structure and the operation of such an equilibrium may best be described by a brief sketch of one of the therapy cases which illustrates much that we found to be typical in our experience.

CASE PRERENTATION

The patient is a 44-year-old Irish Catholic mother of six children who had been married for 20 years at the time of her complaint against her husband. She is a small red-haired woman with considerable intelligence and great energy. Her husband is a shy-appearing man with thick glasses, who has a record of 22 years of work with the railroad. His employment record is good despite heavy drinking throughout his adult life. Both described recurrent fights during their entire marriage, usually occurring when the husband was drunk. When not drinking, the husband is apparently shy, aloof, and passive. He admitted his drinking but denied that he is an alcoholic. He is very close to his elderly mother, who has lived with the couple during most of their married years. The wife complained particularly about her husband's very aggressive sexual demands when drunk, and much of the fighting seems to start with such demands. The wife noted that her children are now old enough to "know what is going on" when the parents fight about sex. The eldest child is a boy, 19, conceived out of wedlock in what the wife freely admitted was a conscious manipulation on her part to force the marriage against the stern disapproval of her mother-in-law.

In the year prior to our contact the relationship between father and oldest son had gradually deteriorated, and the son was open in his anger toward his drunken father and his sympathy for his mother. On the night of the fight which brought the husband to court, the son for the first time stepped between his arguing parents and physically restrained his father. At this point the wife called the police. She said later that the sight of her boy hitting his father was terrifying to her, and she acted in panic. She later felt a strong sense of guilt and swore she would never again turn her husband in.

In every aspect of this family's life, the wife seemed in control. This efficient, hard-working, aggressive woman had assumed all responsibility for handling the money, paying the bills, and disciplining the children.

Their sexual life, as might be expected, was not entirely satisfactory to either. The wife said "I really would not care if I never had relations again in my life." She doubted if she had ever experienced orgasm.

The husband complained bitterly about his wife's "coldness," but he admitted to rarely seeking relations except after drinking. His wife was perfectly aware that her husband had trouble initiating sexual activity when sober, but her firm decision to "never have relations with a drunken man" seemed to effectively preclude any mutually satisfactory sexual meeting ground.

The wife was offered individual psychotherapy, because of her intelligence, her apparently real concern about her marriage, and her motivation for help. Her husband was very hostile to any suggestion that he enter psychiatric tratment, but the wife entered treatment eagerly. She was seen for one hour weekly for more than two years. Initially she dealt mainly with her anger toward her husband but expressed the idea that she might be at fault in some way too.

The husband stopped drinking shortly after his wife began treatment, and the violent arguments practically stopped. This improvement, while not lasting, was impressive to him and his wife, and they both felt, for different reasons, that it was due to her treatment. He took it as confirmation that she had been the "cause" of his behavior; she felt that it was because she was learning how to "handle" his behavior. We felt that the initial improvement was due to the venting of the wife's hostility and manipulative behavior out of the marriage, taking pressure off the husband.

Later, the wife began dealing in treatment with her frigidity and the sexual repulsion she felt toward her husband. The husband resumed some drinking, but in a more controlled manner, and with less violence at home. One year after beginning treatment the wife became pregnant for the seventh time. Her husband's behavior and mood improved markedly at this event. This was striking to compare with his wife's depression and anger about her pregnancy. After delivery, the couple again assumed their more accustomed roles; he drinking and aloof; she aggressively in control at home.

It was about this time that the wife began dealing in treatment with her great hostility toward her husband, alocoholic brothers, and men in general. She talked more about her alcoholic father and his pattern of violence in the home, but it remained difficult for her to translate the hostility she so clearly felt toward other men into terms of her feelings toward her father.

The role of the eldest son as a rival for her affection came into treatment at this point, and she was able to accept quite direct interpretation of this relationship.

During the second year of treatment the oldest son finally made a decision to move out of the house and live with a friend while working and going to school. The husband's relationship with his son improved steadily after this move, and the wife, though depressed at first, expressed relief, and said that the marriage once again felt secure to her, although arguments and drinking continued in a subdued manner.

COMMENT

Wifebeating as a specific offense or type of behavior has not received much attention in the psychiatric literature. Schultz[1] described a group of men whose assaults had taken the character of attempts to kill their wives. These assaults, apparently often isolated events, may be considerably different in dynamic background from the less dangerous chronic assaults complained of by our group of wives. In none of the cases we studied did the husband express any intent to kill his wife, although some of the beatings were quite severe.

There have been some attempts to describe the families of alcoholics[2-4] and these families seem to resemble those of our wifebeaters in many respects. This is not suprising, as most of our men have been heavy drinkers; and, conversely, wifebeating has been mentioned as frequent behavior among alcoholic men. Therefore, although we are studying the structure of families defined by a single aspect of behavior (the bringing of charges of assault and battery by the wife) and others have defined their families by the alcoholic behavior of the husband, we may each be dealing with dynamically similar families. We have not been able to find a report of work focusing on wives of wifebeaters, but there have been several reports dealing with wives of alcoholics. (Again, this may be a similar group.) Price[3] in 1945 studied the wives of 20 alcoholics and pointed to the importance of the marital interaction, emphasizing that the husband's drinking may be of real use to the wife in helping fill her need to prove him inadequate. Futterman[4] also focused on the wife's role in her husband's alcoholism and saw a trend toward domineering and masochism in these women. MacDonald[5] pointed to the frequency of depression in these wives. Efforts to work with wives of alcoholics in group therapy have been made (Gleidman, 1956,[6] Ewing, et al. 1961[7]). These authors agreed that there was improvement in the husband's alcoholism when the wife was being seen in a group, which is similar to our observation that the husband's drinking and violence was diminished when the wife was in treatment. Ewing's findings corroborate those of Lewis (1954)[8] who saw wives of alcoholics as emotionally deprived people with particular emphasis on unsatisfied oral needs. Ewing stresses that these wives need to keep their husbands drinking while protesting their need for a sober husband. He sees the "husbanb's sobriety as a threat to his wife's emotional homeostasis." In a similar way, we see the husband's aggressive behavior as filling masochistic needs of the wife and to be necessary for the wife's (and the couple's) equilibrium.

Whether or not these studies can be applied to the wives of wifebeaters they do make clear the concept that a husband's behavior may serve to fill a wife's needs even though she protests it. This seemed the salient concept in our understanding of the behavior of the wives we studied.

Such wives as the one we have described in the case above, aggressive, efficient, masculine, and sexually frigid, were the rule in our group. And husbands of this husband's stamp—shy, sexually ineffectual, reasonably hard working "mother's boys" with a tendency to drink excessively—were their common counterparts. The couple's story is typical in many ways, including the association of the violence with drunkenness and the oldest son's intervention being coincident with, and perhaps the signal for, the wife's call for help. (Regret over taking legal action was expressed by all the wives with the exception of one—the most masculine of all—who felt she had done the proper thing and stated she would do it again. Her husband was seen as the most clasically passive, castrated male of them all. It was he who asked the doctor if he could have his testicles surgically removed so his sexual desires and their resultant rejection by his wife would not cause further trouble in his marriage.)

The masochism shown by this wife is typical of that seen in the other wives. Her need to control the marital relationship was evident and served to meet her husband's strong dependent needs. We felt that with this couple and others there was an alternation of roles involved in the equilibrium which existed. Both husband and wife seemed to need a frequent change from their accustomed roles in the marriage. The periods of violent behavior by the husband served to release him momentarily from his anxiety about his ineffectiveness as a man, while, at the same time, giving his wife apparent masochistic gratification and helping probably to deal with the guilt arising from the intense hostility expressed in her controlling, castrating behavior. This alternation of roles worked well enough for both partners to preserve the family unit without the need of outside support for 20 years. It seemed very likely that the intervention of the eldest son threatened to destroy the working of this delicately balanced system and necessitated outside intervention. It seems probable that treatment of this wife made it possible for her to allow this son to leave, thus re-establishing the working relationship. The likelihood of the second son becoming as potent a threat seemed small, in view of this wife's improved insight into some of the meanings of her behavior.

Our observations of the workings of these families have caused us to see this view of the dynamics as a promising one for understanding the substrate of the offense. The essential ingredient seems to us to be the need both husband and wife feel for periodic reversal of roles; she to be punished for her castrating activity; he to re-establish his masculine identity. So long as the opportunity exists for both to indulge with considerable freedom both sides of their conflicting desires, no need for help is perceived by either. The intervention of the child becomes a threat when the combination of physical size and a reactivated oedipal position in adolescence makes such intervention potentially dangerous. It may be at the point that this threat is first clearly perceived that the wife calls for outside help to change a situation which she has fostered but which now appears out of her control.

SUMMARY

We have described a family structure which we found to be fairly common among the families of men whose wives brought against them complaints of assault and battery. This structure is characterized by the husband's passivity, indecisiveness, sexual inadequacy; the wife's aggressiveness, masculinity, frigidity, and masochism; and a relationship between the two in which a frequent alternation of passive and aggressive roles serves to achieve a working equilibrium. The husband's drinking is often used as an aid to role alternation. The presence of an adolescent son who begins to tamper seriously with the equilibrium may be a threat to this structure. Strikingly characteristic of this type of family is the considerable stability of employment and of marriage, suggesting that this type of family equilibrium may be a more or less effective solution to mutual needs, although vulnerable to specific kinds of stress.

It is evident that many more families of wifebeaters must be studied before the speculations suggested here can be accepted or abandoned with some degree of confidence. We are, of course, continuing our interest in our study of this area. At present we are expanding our experience and our patient population. Some of the original group is still in treatment. Whatever the eventual fate of most of the ideas expressed here, we would suggest that the general approach of studying the families of offenders of various kinds is a promising one. There is a need for more facilities which will make possible this kind of study. It would not be surprising to find that many types of socially unacceptable behavioral manifestations have a situational dynamic substrate in the family. If this is shown to be so, it would open not only new avenues to understanding the "why" and "why now" of crime and misbehavior, but also new approaches to therapeutic intervention through the family. We have come to feel that the offender cannot be adequately understood, and treatment and correctional measures appropriate to him devised, until one knows whom he has offended, how, and why. One cannot hope to understand the offender and his offense without having some understanding of the people with whom he has to deal.

NOTES AND REFERENCES

1. Schultz, L. G.: "Wife Assaulter." *J. Soc. Ther.* 6:2, 1960.
2. Ullman, A. D.: "Sociocultural Backgrounds of Alcoholism." *The Annals of the American Academy of Political and Social Science* 315:48–51, 1958.
3. Price, G. M.: "Study of the Wives of 20 Alcoholics." *Quart. J. Stud. Alcohol.* 5:620–627, 1945.
4. Futterman, S.: "Personality Trends in Wives of Alcoholics." *J. Psychiat. Soc. Wk.* 23:37–41, 1953.
5. MacDonald, D. E.: "Mental Disorders in Wives of Alcoholics." *Quart. J. Stud. Alcohol.* 17: 282–287, 1956.
6. Gleidman, L. H. et al.: "Group Therapy of Alcoholics with Concurrent Group Meetings of Their Wives." *Quart. J. Stud. Alcohol.* 17:655–670, 1956.
7. Ewing, J. A. et al.: "Concurrent Group Psychotherapy of Alcoholic Patients and Their Wives." *Int. J. Group. Psychother.* 11:329–338, 1961.
8. Lewis, M. L.: "Initial Contact With Wives of Alcoholics." *Soc. Casework* 35:8–14, 1954.

AFFILIATIONS AND ACKNOWLEDGMENTS

1. Submitted for publication March 27, 1964.
2. Read before the meeting of the Massachusetts Chapter, Association for the Psychiatric Treatment of Offenders, Framingham, Mass., March 1, 1963.
3. Assistant Professor (Dr. Snell), Department of Psychiatry, Emory University, formerly Staff Psychiatrist, Framingham Court Clinic, Framingham, Mass; Director (Dr. Rosenwald), Framingham Court Clinic; Medical Director, Bridgewater State Hospital, Bridgewater, Mass. (Dr. Robey), Chelsea Court Clinic Chelsea, Mass., formerly Staff Psychiatrist, Framingham Court Clinic.

Psychodynamics of Father Daughter Incest

BRUNO M. CORMIER, MIRIAM KENNEDY, JADWIGA SANGOWICZ

Among human practices, incest is the one most enveloped in myth and mystery. This applies to some extent even to present times, and may partly explain why many age-long beliefs still prevail and tend to be accepted without examination. Thus, the incestuous father is generally described as a degenerate, intellectually inferior individual, living in poverty, with gross overcrowding; or an alcoholic with a low standard of morals and marked sexual pathology. Incest is likewise described as occurring mainly in remote rural areas, among backward, primitive people. Though it has been recognised that statistics on discovered incest are unreliable, and that the practice is more prevalent than would appear from police records, the feeling persists that incest is confined to the most debased, perverted elements in our society, or the relics of more archaic, primitive modes of behaviour.

More recent studies, however, give us a broader view of the subject and throw doubt on some earlier preconceived ideas about the incidence of incest, as well as the personality of the incestuous participants. It has been established, for instance, that incest is found as frequently in cities as in the countryside; overcrowding as a contributing factor appears to have been exaggerated, as incest is known to occur where this does not exist; incest may be committed by men who cannot be called otherwise criminal, nor degenerate, nor sexually psychopathic.

One of the most valuable recent contributions on the subject is the sociological study by Dr. S. K. Weinberg.[1] He differentiates male incest into three main types: (a) an indiscriminate promiscuity where the incest is part of a pattern of sexual psychopathology; (b) intense craving for young children, pedophilia, which also includes the daughter as a sexual object; and (c) the endogamic or intra-familial oriented incest. An incestuous participant

From the *Canadian Psychiatric Association Journal* 7:203–217, 1962. Reprinted by permission of the Association.

of this type is defined by Weinberg as "the adult . . . who confines his sexual objects to family members, resorts to incest with a daughter or sister because he does not cultivate and does not crave social or sexual contacts with women outside the family." It is with this type of incest offender that we are concerned.

The present paper on the subject of the incestuous father developed from research on offences which occur within the framework of the family, or are closely related to conflicts within the family.[2,3] The fathers described in this study are, apart from incest with a daughter, non-criminal and show no history of adult sexual perversion, including pedophilia. They are not, as a group, conspicuously promiscuous, and it was noted that some who had extra-marital affairs before the incest occurred discontinued once incest was established. The majority of the men are of normal intelligence or above; a few of low average. We have excluded those of defective intelligence, or with primitive personalities. We have, therefore, a group of men who have, until the commitment of incest, made on the whole an acceptable occupational and social adjustment. They are generally good workers, some skilled. Our findings, therefore, may differ from surveys which include all incest offenders, those who are intellectually sub-normal, or show overt sexual perversion and other pathology as well as incest. We have studied 27 cases: 21 were seen in prison, sometimes many years after the event, and six were seen in the clinic at the request of the court, social agency, or psychiatrist. Twenty-two of the men had committed incest, and five had confined themselves to sexual caresses or given evidence of abnormal sexual interest in the daughters.

In studying this group of men, we asked ourselves what problems of personal, social, or marital maladjustment led to incest. There are a few sociological and psychiatric investigations which give us data and suggest causes.

Among factors mentioned by sociologists as predisposing to incest is the prolonged absence of the father from the home. Cases are reported in the literature, among them Mannheim,[4] Nurnberger[5] and Greenland,[6] of men who, after many years of separation from the family, return to find a changed and aging wife and a young daughter who seems almost a stranger and becomes a temptation. The loss of the wife by divorce, separation, or death, leaving a father alone with an adolescent daughter, may, according to Holder[7] and Rennert,[8] precipitate incest. Gross overcrowding, physical proximity and alcoholism are analysed by many writers, including Riemer[9] and Szabo.[10] The inability to establish normal social and emotional contacts outside the family, created by extreme poverty and the remoteness of some rural areas which may draw the father to seek satisfaction within the immediate kinship group, is stressed by many, including Riemer,[9] Mannheim[4] and Scherer.[11] Intellectual and constitutional inferiority, as well as hereditary factors, are mentioned as predisposing to incest by von Hentig[12] and Holder,[7] who also describes the apparent lack of guilt in some incestuous fathers.

The important factor of age is mentioned by most authors. Incest generally occurs in a specific age span, the father being in the late thirties and forties. In these decades, the marital relationship is more subject to change through death, separation and divorce than in the earlier years of the marriage. Marital stress is also more likely to develop during this period. With time, a marriage may become increasingly frustrating, and where there is the presence of a daughter who has reached puberty and become appealing, incest may occur.

All these sociological factors, while significant, do not, however, in themselves explain incest. Many husbands are faced with similar problems, and find other solutions. They may accept the frustration of an unhappy family situation and find satisfaction elsewhere, in work or in outside interests, or they may indulge in affairs outside the marriage. In the psychoanalytic literature there is a scarcity of material on the psychogenesis of incest itself in contrast to unconscious and repressed strivings. The oedipal stage in particular has been well studied and documented. Psychiatric studies tend to be descriptive and most are concerned with the effects of incest on the daughter.

In the early psychoanalytic literature Abraham[13] describes "neurotic endogamy", referring to individuals who have been unable to establish object relationships outside the kinship group; therefore they tend to marry cousins or other relatives.

Bender and Blau[14] in their study of the reaction of children to sex experiences with adults make the observation that the child was often either a passive or active partner, and in some instances the initiator or seducer. This is borne out by other investigators, including Barry and Johnson,[15] who have noted that there is little anxiety in a father-daughter incest relationship in the case of young children and where the mother accepts the fact of incest. Friedlander[16] observes the presence of a desire for sexual relationship with the father in the young girl, and stresses the significance of the stage of emotional development at which incest occurs. In her view, a very early occurrence may impede the resolution of the oedipal complex and be the source of many later disturbances. On the other hand there may be no problems. She includes the case illustration of a girl of 12 who had incest relations with the father which affected her relationship to men afterwards. Her emotional development, however, was not eventually disturbed. Sloane and Karpinski,[17] in their study of a group of incestuous daughters, find that there appears to be more emotional damage where the incest occurs in adolescence than when it takes place during the latency period. Incest during adolescence is generally followed by promiscuous and unstable behaviour. Kinberg,[18] on the other hand, does not report psychic trauma in the daughters, and describes them as generally mentally inferior. The inability of the mother to protect her daughters is also discussed. Kaufman[19] made a study of daughters seen shortly after disclosure of incest and found that they were depressed, guilty and anxious. Guilt seemed related rather to the breakup of the home than to the act of incest itself. Vestergaard,[20] who had a contact with 16 daughters ten years after the event, claims that the incestuous relationship and the reaction of the family to it, had been almost invariably damaging. It sometimes resulted in acting out of an anti-social nature, though most of the daughters had overcome this in later life, and were no longer behaviour problems. There were feelings of intense anger and bitterness against the father. They tended to be anxious, depressed and over-fearful. There was evidence of sexual conflict in marital histories. Gordon,[21] in her study of the case of an incestuous girl, considers that rivalry against the mother originates not in the oedipal situation but in the oral phase. The seduction of the father is seen by the daughter as revenge against the mother for abandoning her, and the unresolved conflict is carried on in later life in incest, seduction of males, promiscuity, etc. Rascovsky and Rascovsky[22] report a psychoanalytical investigation of a case of consummated incest of a young woman, married and separated, with nymphomaniac compulsion and many somatic symptoms. The history revealed a very frustrating relationship with the mother and a precocious transition to the father. Incest did not actually occur till the twenties, though the father acted as a kind of seducer and pander. Sociological and psychiatric studies on incest and on the structure of the incestuous family, while giving us valuable information, have left unsolved the question of why incest occurs only in some cases, indeed in relatively few considering the prevalence of the problems described as favouring incest. The answer can be found only in the study of the individual psychology of the people concerned, and this study will deal mainly with the psychopathology of the father.

LATENT INCESTUOUS RELATIONSHIPS BETWEEN PARENTS AND ADOLESCENT CHILDREN

To understand how an abnormal relationship may develop between a father and a daughter, it is relevant to describe phenomena developing normally within a family in the course of time, as husband and wife meet inevitable changes in the children and in themselves. The adolescence of children is a period of change for parents as well as for children, which may bring problems, but also provides compensating satisfaction. While remaining the adult, parents, guiding their children's adolescence enables them to recall to some extent their own youth. Mothers become preoccupied with the success of their sons and vicariously relive their own girlhood and courtship, while fathers appreciate the beauty and charm of their daughters, and their success with young men. However, things do not always go so smoothly for the parents. It is during the children's adolescence that marriages often become shaky, or parents previously faithful go astray for the first time. On the part of adolescent children also there is a certain amount of playing at growing up, of experimenting in new kinds of relationships. For many of them, the first person on whom they test their growing powers to attract is the parent. We can say that both parents in their thirties and forties and adolescent children are in a somewhat special psychological position.

Normally, parents and children work through this situation safely as they are psychologically well protected. However, some fathers become very sensitive and aware of an adolescent daughter. They are tempted, and while they do not go so far as to court their own daughter, they may displace this temptation by having an affair outside the marriage with a young girl; or they may respond to the danger by being overly severe towards the daughter, refusing to grant her normal independence. They are sometimes extremely possessive, under the guise of shielding her from harm. In a few exceptional cases, the conflict about the daughter is neither unconscious, suppressed, nor displaced, but is acted out in an incestuous relationship.

To summarize, external reality such as the death or absence of the wife, disturbances in the marital relationship, the return of the father after a long absence, physical overcrowding, alcoholism, a relatively young father living close to an adolescent daughter, all these precipitating factors which are put forward are commonly found without leading to incest. In some predisposed fathers, however, they can reawaken concealed and suppressed incestuous temptation which is eventually acted out.

THE PARTICIPANTS

What characterises the incestuous father is that while fully exploiting his position as the authoritarian head of the home, he also acts in many ways like a caricature of an adolescent. Whether he uses threats, force, or black-mail, or offers rewards and bribes to gain his daughter, he behaves not so much as a grown man wooing a woman, but rather a maladroit adolescent attempting to win a young girl in his first love affair. The conduct of the incestuous father also resembles sexual play between brother and sister. He is like an older brother who forces his little sister to misbehave, threatens her with punishment if she tells the mother, and at the same time blackmails her by saying that if she complains about him, or the mother finds out, she, too, will be punished for wrongdoing. Mother will also be angry with her.

In the course of the incestuous relationship, the father becomes exceedingly jealous of the daughter, often refusing to permit her any social contact. He is afraid that she will tell, but even more afraid that he will lose her to others. He attemps to attach her to him by bribes and presents, and he sometimes shows great affection and tenderness. Conversely, however, he may seek to gain the same ends through the use of force and threats, and the exercise of his parental power. He thus moves from the adolescent to the all-powerful father who has absolute rights over his daughter, believing that one of his privileges is to initiate her sexually. As the father he even deceives himself into thinking that his conduct is virtuous; he sees himself as her protector, guarding her from the sexual advances of other men.

What is quite striking is the contradiction between the accounts made by the fathers and those elicited by the police from the daughters after disclosure. The fathers almost invariably claim that the daughters were provocative, or in any event willing. The daughters usually state that they were forced, threatened and ill-treated physically. The impression is that the latter statement is not invariably true and that in many cases there is at least a certain degree of assent. This is not as surprising as may appear at first sight. In very young girls, the father's conduct may be acceptable, simply because he is the father. Sometimes rivalry with the mother plays a part, and the daughter may consciously or otherwise enjoy her new status of supplanting the mother.

The role of the wife must here be considered. In studying the wives of incestuous fathers, we found that a certain number were not only frigid, but hostile and unloving women. Some never denied their husband and were described by them as good wives, but the relationship was ungratifying because of the inability of the wives to respond. Others were passive and submissive women to the point where they were unable to stand up against the husband, even in a known incestuous situation. The question may well be asked how incest could go on, often for years, without the wife finding out. In some cases, there is overt concealment of the fact of incest, but sometimes the wife does not know because she does not wish to know. Whether she is genuinely unaware, is concealing, or refusing to see, the mother is no longer able to fulfill her function in the family and protect the daughter.

Where there is an incestuous relationship with two or three of the daughters, rivalry often develops among the sisters, which may result eventually in disclosure. It would seem, however, that no matter what the precipitating circumstances of incest are, the daughter eventually rebels at this exclusive possessiveness and seeks her freedom. She either runs away, makes another attachment, or she reveals the fact of incest.

The sons are also involved, if indirectly. The incestuous father tends to over-value the daughters at the expense of the sons. He either ignores or is hostile to them.

GUILT AND DENIAL IN INCESTUOUS RELATIONSHIPS

It has been frequently pointed out that sex offenders as a group tend to deny their offences. Of all sex offenders, the one who denies the most is the man who commits incest. Even when confrontee with facts, and after confession, he will later deny or minimize greatly. A common explanation is that denial follows from the universal taboo against incest and the shame and humiliation resulting from the discovery. This denial is evidently necessary to preserve self-esteem in the face of the extreme feeling about incest, but it is also related to guilt. Some writers have noted what appears an absence of guilt in incest offenders. These observations seem mainly to apply to incestuous fathers who are physical degenerates, severe mental defectives or chronic alcoholics in whom not only is the feeling of guilt impaired but judgment and capacity to function at a normal social level. There are also fathers with abnormal personalities where incest is only one manifestation of many other sexual problems, and the incapacity to feel guilt is an aspect of the personality. The cases we have selected are of individuals much more within normal standards with regard to social and moral values, intellectual achievement, work adaptation, etc. In these men, guilt was obviously present throughout, though it was often repressed and denied. It manifested itself, however, in different ways in the period of the incestuous relationship, at the time of disclosure, and during the serving of the sentence. The guilt of the father was also, so to say, differently distributed among the family members involved, the wife, the victim and the other children.

With regard to the wife, guilt may be avoided during the period of incest by a process of rationalization. The incestuous father views his behaviour as a logical consequence of the wife's frigidity, or denial, or absence. The need for gratification suppresses his normal feeling of guilt. However, he fears the wife and the punishment that may follow should the incest come to light, and in this very realistic fear guilt is swallowed up. After incest has been discovered, there is almost invariably an invasion of deep guilt and remorse about the wife. It results from therealisation of having injured her and substituted another in her place, with irreparable damage to the relationship, and a resulting anxiety that he can never return to his wife, and as a consequence may lose his family. There is a great need to be forgiven, as if he were a child who must be reconciled to his mother. In some cases, a state of depression can only be alleviated when there is forgiveness and a satisfactory relationship can again be achieved.

In the type of incest we are discussing here, created by ingrown, intrafamilial relationships, a great deal of guilt exisis towards the daughter. Sometimes guilt does not appear present during the incest period, and if it is felt it does not stop the act. One of the reasons guilt is not dominant relates to the father's complex, many-faceted relationship to the daughter. His feelings towards her are sexual, but the giving and receiving of love and affection is often felt as the main need, and fatherly and sexual love are mingled. Some fathers up to disclosure deceive themselves about the nature of their relationship. They cannot see the expression of their love as harmful, and thus guilt is suppressed.

There are some fathers, however, who feel intense guilt throughout the whole incestuous relationship; which they try to cope with by various means. For example, they may resort to prayer, go to confession, and urge their daughters to do likewise; but so strong is the temptation that guilt, however present, is bypassed.

Once incest is discovered, guilt may be dealt with by a number of mechanisms. One is to admit the fact but find many excuses, such as the frigidity of the wife. There is also the need to implicate the daughter and make her equally responsible. The father thus accuses her of being provocative and seductive, or he says that she was a willing accomplice. He may claim that she was already not a virgin and had been with other men, or that all he did was to prevent her from misconduct outside the home. The father may, on the other hand, accuse both wife and daughter of laying false charges against him in order to put him into prison. All these manoeuvres serve to preserve a self-image, to deny the reality of the fact, and to avoid guilt by placing responsibility outside himself.

There is also eventually much guilt in relation to the other children, the daughters who have not been victimized and the sons. This results from the realization by the father that he has been a bad parent. When the father acted as an adolescent with his daughter, it inevitably created a confusion in his parental role. The consequent guilt was dealt with either by isolating or disregarding the other children, or acting like the all-powerful, over-harsh father.

CASE HISTORIES

Following are case summaries of two incestuous fathers, describing briefly the childhood, early history, marriage, and inter-personal relationship which led eventually to incest.

Case 1

B., a man in his late thirties, a skilled worker of at least average intelligence. In his childhood there was a certain amount of poverty and dislocation, as the father was invalided and the mother worked to support the family. This created a confusion of roles, the father in effect taking over the management of the home. B. was sent away to school when he was 10 and he missed his home very much. He recalls his father, an old Army man, as over-strict; the mother was warmer and more loved.

He remembers his adolescence as a quite happy one. He became a skilled worker, was a good looking lad, led quite an enjoyable life, had a number of sexual contacts, but no serious involvement till he met his future wife when he was in his twenties. He describes her as resembling him to the point that they could be taken for brother and sister. He fell deeply in love and claims he has continued to love her.

For the first five years, the marriage went fairly well from accounts of both husband and wife. He complains, however, that she was never sufficient-ly responsive sexually, and that she grew more frigid with the years, though she did not at any time deny him. Five children were born, the eldest a girl. In many ways it was a good marriage, as B. worked hard, was a faithful husband and very fond of his children. He had few interests outside the family; lack of money was a problem; the home was small and rather crowded for their rapidly growing family.

B.'s first evident failure was shown in increased drinking, which impaired the marital relationship. He was not an alcoholic and he never deprived his family in order to drink, but even a little alcohol, taken to relieve tension, affected him badly. He grew irritable, lost his temper, and became depressed. When depressed under the influence of alcohol, he was sexually very de-manding; along with compulsive sexuality, he became partially impotent. The marital relationship deteriorated, but it had never at any time occurred to B. that it could be dissolved.

About a year prior to the occurrence of incest, B. became involved for the first time in his married life with the wife of a friend, and this affair con-tinued for a few months. He described the relationship as satisfying, but there was guilt on the part of both. Nevertheless, when the mistress broke off the affair, he felt unhappy and at a loss. He tried to find the same kind of physical satisfaction with his wife, but failed.

In the summer of that year, his wife went to visit her family. She left the home in charge of the 14-year-old daughter. At this point, B. found himself deprived in every way. He was also worried about money and suffered from severe depression. In his account of what took place, he states that he be-came confused, and "lost" two or three weeks. In this crisis, he turned to his 14-year-old daughter. The girl accepted his advances, but after a few days ran away and told a neighbour. The mother was recalled and a charge was laid.

The daughter was admittedly the best-loved child, a very attractive girl named after his own mother. He has confused his daughter with many important female figures in his life. She resembles both himself and his wife, who, according to him could be taken for brother and sister. He has identified his daughter as the young wife he courted, as a sister, and also with his own mother, whose name she bears. Though feeling very guilty, he finds it hard to believe that she did not accept him willingly. He described how pretty she was, and how provocative she appeared to him. He said that he was jealous because she would make some man very happy, happier than he was with his own wife. It was not too difficult a step to act as if he were that young man instead of the father.

With exposure and sentence came severe depression, to the point where he made some suicide attempts in prison. As he recovered, he saw himself unrealistically re-establishing the old familial pattern, without of course the incest. The wife would not forgive him and he therefore oscillated between the hope that he could restore the marriage, and depression when he felt she would never pardon him and he could not return.

Case 2

F., now in his fifties, is nearing the end of a twelve-year sentence for incest, which he committed over a three year period with three of his four daughters. When first interviewed, F. was extremely puzzled himself by his behaviour and the only explanation he could give was that he was a heavy drinker, and that he was invariably at least a little drunk when the act occurred. He saw readily that this could not be the basic explanation, as this pattern of drinking was long-standing since early in his marriage. The alcohol could, therefore, be only one causative factor.

F. is a French Canadian, coming from a rural background, the father being a carpenter and woodworker as well as a farmer. He has one brother, considerably older, who left the home early. There is a younger sister, who married very young, leaving F. for many years alone with his parents. He got on well enough with his father, who taught him his trade. F. is a very good worker, who has never had trouble getting and keeping a job. The relationship to the mother was far closer than to the father. She was the stronger, a woman of considerable force, dominant but very warm. F. describes her as gay and high-spirited, with a temper. As he grew up, she permitted him a good deal of liberty, did not object to his love affairs, but he remained very much under her control. He gave her most of his money, but more important, when at age 19 he fell in love with a young girl and wanted to marry, the mother broke off the match. She said he was too young, and she did not like the girl. As a result, he continued to live at home until his mother's death when he was 36, and then he drifted into a marriage with a neighbour's daughter.

The marriage was conspicuously poor from the start. He seems to have found in the wife the controlling dominating mother, without her gaiety and warmth. He claims that she has always been a frigid and denying woman, and fanatically devout. She was also bad-tempered and a scold. He responded by withdrawing from her dominance; he worked in Montreal and came home to the farm for weekends. He began to drink quite early in the marriage. Though generally a good-natured, easy-going man, under drink he grew quarrelsome. Also, when on rather extended alcoholic bouts, he had casual relationships with women who meant little to him.

F. had four daughters, followed by three sons. His favourite child was his oldest daughter, who at a very early age acted as a substitute mother for the younger children. He found her bright and sharp, resembling his own mother, but as a daughter she was also obedient. He was always more interested in his daughters, and paid little attention to his sons.

The marriage continued its comfortless and unsatisfying way until the oldest daughter was 15. One night, when the wife was away, and he was in a state of intoxication, he initiated sexual relations. The girl was sleeping in the same room with him, as she was minding the baby in her mother's absence. He claims that she did not object, that she knew more than he suspected. After this, the relationship continued regularly. About a year later, he began to commit incest with the second daughter, and this in turn was followed with the third. The first daughter continued, however, to be his favourite. He bought her pretty things and gave her money, partly because she blackmailed him mildly, but also because he wanted to. When the fourth daughter reached puberty, he attempted relations with her, but she was unwilling. He did not persist.

This situation continued for almost three years without discovery. From the time incest started, F. stopped going out with other women. At age 18, the eldest daughter suddenly decided to leave the home to take a job in Montreal. The second daughter replaced her to some degree. A few weeks later, the eldest daughter, during a visit home, unexpectedly and apparently impulsively disclosed the situation. This was followed by police inquiry, resulting in a confession on the part of F. His wife was vindictive in her accusations, and according to him did her best to have him heavily punished. He was given a severe sentence. Since his imprisonment, he has had no word from his daughters, and contact with his wife only around farm business. Otherwise, she has neither visited nor written. F. understands that his daughters are lost to him, but he is now very anxious to have news about his sons, with whom he is at last concerned. With regard to the wife, after many ambivalent feelings he has now decided to relinquish any attempt to return to the marriage.

One fact that emerges is that the eldest daughter, in spite of her acceptance, eventually turned against her father. She not only left home, putting herself out of his power, but she accused him. The younger daughters followed suit, and in their turn confessed the relationship. They united to denounce the father. In doing this they appear to have been motivated as much by a desire for independence as for punishment of the father. Young as they are, they have all left the home and are working in Montreal.

We have had a contact of over two years with F. and he has himself thought out some of his motivations. He thinks that the main problem lay in his poor marriage and that he chose badly. For a number of years, he forgot his griefs and his needs in drink and in casual sexual affairs. When his oldest daughter, however, became adolescent, she reminded him not so much of his wife, but of the girl he loved when he was 19 and whom he was not permitted to marry. He found his mother's warmth and acceptance in this first love and looked for it again in his daughter. He also felt that in his daughters his youth was restored.

DISCUSSION

In the light of these two clinical examples, and from material from our other cases, we will describe some of the psychodynamics involved in the incestuous relationship. We will deal mainly with the psychopathology in the father, and with his pathological relationship to his wife and daughters. We will touch briefly on the Freudian theory on incest as described in "Totem and Taboo", our own observations on this, and finally on the questions of prevention, recidivism and treatment.

PSYCHOPATHOLOGY

The psychopathology of the incestuous father can be traced as follows. The daughter replaces the wife. An incestuous father will sometimes give as excuse that he took the daughter in mistake for the wife; or, asked why he did not seek outside affairs as the solution, he will quite often explain that, "it is a sin to go with other women." The daughter is thus placed in the special role; she is not a woman outside the family with whom it is a sin to commit adultery, but someone who belongs to him, a permissible alternative to the wife.

When an incestuous father takes his daughter as a substitute for his wife, she is by no means the present aging wife, but the young girl he courted many years ago. This is often quite openly expressed, especially when the daughter resembles her mother. He will sometimes describe not only the beauty of his daughter but of his young wife, and two images merge. He thus recaptures in his daughter the image of his young wife.

As the incestuous father transforms his daughter into the young wife, he transforms himself in the same process. Though he may attempt to maintain and even to reinforce his role of an omnipotent father, he will at the same time behave towards his daughter as if he were a young man. He seems unaware of the incongruity of this situation, and there is here a great distortion of reality that permits him to forget his actual age and status and play the young lover.

He is now faced with the dilemma of reconciling the two figures, the daughter who has become the young wife, and his actual wife, whom he may have loved once, but who has disappointed him. Unconsciously his own wife now assumes for him another role, that of the mother. She is, however, a severe mother, a menacing figure who will punish him when she discovers what he is doing. This is actually a real danger, but what the incestuous father does not realize consciously is that in the wife he sees the punishing mother.

A further transformation takes place. The wife having been identified with the denying mother, he recaptures in this daughter not only the young giving and desirable wife he feels he has lost, but the early good image of the mother. In taking the daughter, he satisfies the unresolved incestuous craving for the mother of his childhood. This can be understood by the fact that the daughter represents more than a substitute for the young wife of his youth because when he originally courted his wife he was looking for a mother as much as for a wife. In taking the daughter, therefore, he is at last able to possess the mother he felt was denied to him in his childhood, and whom he can take because he is now powerful. In other words, he has found in his daughter the all giving maternal figures of his childhood dreams.

Incest, however, is self-defeating and disappointment is only perpetuated. Because he was frustrated in the oedipal situation, he was also disappointed and frustrated in the marriage; and in looking finally to his young daughter to find happiness, he suffers the keenest disappointment of all. In the end he is defeated and humiliated.

The process may be described in summary in five stages: (1) the daughter becomes the substitute for the wife; (2) the daughter is the substitute, not for the present wife, but for the girl he courted many years ago; (3) parallel to this, he, too, has the illusion that he is again the young man he was when he wooed his wife; (4) the real wife now symbolizes the forbidding mother; (5) the daughter herself has become transformed to the early giving mother.

FREUD'S INTERPRETATION OF THE INCEST TABOO

Freud's well-known explanation of the origins of the taboo on incest in "Totem and Taboo"[23] is that at one stage in the history of the race, the father had absolute right over all the members, and especially over the daughters whom he jealously guarded and initiated sexually. Freud postulates that the sons rose against the father and destroyed him because he did not allow them access to the young women. The origin of the incest taboo is seen as resulting from this revolt of the sons. After killing the father they were able to possess the women, but for their own protection, and because of guilt, they created a defence against the father/daughter incest.

How can we reconcile our material with Freud's hypothesis? There is one striking analogy, in the fact that the incestuous fathers we have observed are very possessive of the daughters, and rejecting of the sons; they also tend to be highly authoritarian husbands and fathers. This domination and possessiveness becomes even more marked once the incestuous relationship has been established. They almost literally make their daughters prisoners, both by coercion and by love. They also try to separate the sons from the daughters and the wife. In this kind of familial relationship, the sons undoubtedly become resentful and hostile to the father. In some of our cases the son was the one who disclosed incest, and occasionally a son has attempted incest himself, following the father's example. Here we discern the conflict between the son and father as described by Freud in his, perhaps allegorical, attempts to explain how the incest taboo originated.

However, we feel that Freud's emphasis on the revolt of the sons is only part of the picture. He did not perceive the effect of the father's total domination on the wife and daughters. The daughters in the end resist the father's exclusive possessiveness and revolt in their turn. This conflict becomes acute at the stage when the daughters realize that more suitable partners are available. They rebel against the father and achieve liberation. The omnipotent incestuous father thus loses his authority over all his children, daughters and sons alike.

One of the bases of the incest taboo is that in order to maintain his authority and respect, the father realizes that he must give up his right of exclusive possession over his children. In our society the feeling against incest is strong. The father, whether or not overtly incestuous, who exerts total domination over his family and prohibits the healthy social development of his children eventually is faced with revolt. When his possessiveness goes as far as incest he is defeated and humiliated, and he loses his role of father as protector and guide.

PREVENTION

Prevention appears not easily possible, unless one member of a family becomes aware that incest is likely to occur, and takes some action. This does not happen frequently to our knowledge. In some cases known to us, incest was prevented. In one instance, the wife came to see the psychiatrist because of her husband's behaviour to his 13-year-old daughter, which not only a-larmed her, but aroused her jealousy. She was further upset because he accused her of being needlessly jealous, and laughed at her fears. The wife reported that it seemed to her that her husband courted the daughter as he had courted her before their marriage. As she described his conduct towards the girl, his caresses and attentions, his preoccupation with her to the point of isolating himself and her from the rest of the family, it became evident that her jealousy was well founded. The relationships in the home were now very strained, as her husband was not interested in his son, and was abrupt and severe with the younger daughter, aged 8. In discussing her marriage, the wife stated that it had been on the whole satisfactory, but that in the past few years her sexual drive had diminished, and her husband had grown both less demanding and less interested.

The husband was seen and at first he denied everything, insisting that his behaviour was purely fatherly, and therefore permissible. He said that his wife's jealousy was highly unreasonable and that it was she who needed treatment. Questioned about his lack of interest in his younger children, he replied that as a father he would naturally not be as concerned over them, as they were still young and therefore the mother's responsibility. The more that he "explained" his behaviour, the more it was evident that he could not toler-ate being confronted with the clear-cut facts of his incestuous intention. When, however, he was asked how he would feel if he saw another man acting towards his eldest daughter in exactly the same way, touching and caressing her, taking her to movies alone, wanting to be exclusively with her and with-drawing her from others, he became aware of the real content of his feelings. He was able to discuss these, and from then the interviews went on to an-alyze his incestuous temptations. As a result, not only did his behaviour to his daughter change, but the marital relationship was more soundly establish-ed. In the course of relinquishing his daughter, he also became a better father to his son and younger daughter, both previously rejected.

In another case the wife reported that the relationship between her hus-band and daughter was abnormal, and that she was really afraid of the con-sequences unless something was done. The husband refused to see the psy-chiatrist, who therefore had to limit himself to discussing the problem with the wife, and give her help and relevant advice. She took the suggestion to remove her daughter from the home and sent her to a boarding school, thus avoiding the immediate possibility of incest. While this did not in itself clarify the relationships between wife, husband and daughter, she was thus at least able to protect the family.

In a third instance, the father was referred to us for a psychiatric pro-blem not manifestly related to incest. He was a very unstable personality, who displayed a compulsive sexuality, had rape fantasies, but was never pedophilic. Eventually he confessed his fantasies about his 12-year-old daughter and his incestuous desire for her, which frightened him. He had responded by being extremely severe to her, critical and punishing, in an effort, he said, to place distance between them, but also he wished to dominate her exclusively. He agreed that his daughter should be removed from the home, but before this plan could be carried out he left on his own account, because of the acute conflict, created by the fact that he had confessed to his wife.

RECIDIVISM

Recidivism in incest is rare. By this we do not mean the repetition of incestuous behaviour before disclosure, but afterwards. While it is not uncommon to see the incestuous father continue the relationship with one or more daughters, over a period of years, it is seldom that there is a recurrence after he has been discovered. Once incest has been disclosed, conflicts and relationships previously concealed are in the open. Every member of the family is sharply affected as the result.

The impact of disclosure is perhaps sharpest on the mother, who usually responds with shock, depression and with anger. Often the anger is partly directed against herself for having been so blind and permitted incest to occur. There may also be resentment against the daughter for not confiding in her, and some jealousy. After the discovery, if the marriage continues or is restored, incest will seldom recur. The mother having worked through her anger and depression will from then on be conscious of the problem, and be a better guardian of the children. Controls which should have existed in the first place are finally created, and new insights and attitudes are established. Should the family be disolved, the separation itself prevents recurrence.

The changes taking place in the father are equally decisive in the prevention of further incest. In studying the psychopathology of the incestuous father, we have noted that the daughter is a specific object relationship in whom the father attempted to recapture the mother of his childhood. After discovery, this specific relationship is no longer available. In the event that the wife is willing to resume a normal relationship, he will return to the marriage. Should this not be possible, or where there were extra-marital affairs prior to incest, it can be assumed that the father may return to these. We have discovered indications of this kind of solution in our study of some of our offenders in the penitentiary. The men recounted that during the first period of imprisonment, they continued to have fantasies and dreams about their daughters, but as time went on, they began to think of other women in their fantasies. The image of the daughter as a sexual object began to fade.

The most significant change is the father's new awareness of himself. True, he is no longer able to conceal his act, and he is under constant observation from family, social agency, court, etc. But added to this, he suddenly finds he is a man in middle-age who has mistaken his role and lost his status. He cannot retrace his steps.

All the children are more or less deeply affected by the disclosure of incest. The daughters who have not been victimized by the father, whether or not aware of what has happened, will be protected by the changes taking place in the parents, and the new attitudes that are established as the result. Disclosure erects a barrier between the father and the daughters. The position of the sons also changes, as the father is no longer able to exercise authoritarian power over all the members of the household.

The victimized daughter who has gained her liberation through direct disclosure or through having confided the fact of incest, is now in a situation where the father is at last no longer on the scene. This liberation is not achieved without emotional storm. The fact that in obtaining her freedom the father is humiliated, degraded and punished carries with it pain and guilt for her and some regret. It is rare for a victimized daughter to wish to inflict on the aggressor father punishment as harsh as that imposed by society. No matter how unwilling she may have been, an incestuous relationship is not possible without some love. Beyond the humiliation and devaluation of the father, one can venture that in the deep silence of the unconscious the image of the father returns, and remains forever the undefeated hero of a bygone childhood.

TREATMENT

Writers on incest agree that many cases occur that are never brought to light. Sometimes incest is disclosed only years after the event, in the course of clearing up another problem. To be noted is that these revelations are made by the victim, rarely by the initiator or aggressor. The daughter often informs that no-one in the family was aware at the time, not even the mother, or that the mother may have known but failed to intervene. We can only venture to speculate how incest ends when it is undiscovered. Our impression is that it does not continue indefinitely, but comes to a close in the normal course of family evolution, with the inevitable changes brought about by time, both in the father and daughter. The daughter rebels, seeks her independence, and leaves the home. In the face of his daughter's rejection, the father grasps that he is an aging man who cannot compete with younger boys. There is a greater or less degree of psychological damage to all concerned, but also a certain amount of self-healing.

In looking at the cases of discovered endogamic incest, we have noted that the psychopathology of the father prevents him from maintaining normal, healthy relationships within the family, or, failing this, finding satisfactions outside. Nevertheless, the framework of the family is maintained up to the time of discovery. There are undoubtedly mounting stresses of which various members grow aware, without necessarily knowing what is going on. The father realizes the cause of the growing tension, but, caught up in the incestuous relationship, he is both unwilling and unable to seek help, even if he feels guilt. He will, on the contrary, use every effort to maintain the situation. It is only after disclosure that some fathers will accept treatment, either to avoid prison, through an enhanced sense of guilt, through fear of losing their family; sometimes through a genuine need to understand the sources of their behaviour. To be noted, however, is that though most incestuous fathers cooperate in treatment, they will not seek it on their own account. This may be related to their passivity, to their fear of being humiliated, of being rejected by the therapist. None of our subjects came for treatment spontaneously because of the fact of incest. We approached some because we knew that they had committed incest, and others were seen by the psychiatrist primarily because of a depressive state, and from then on the incest problem was dealt with.

Treatment is often complicated and made difficult by legal procedures. Public knowledge, involving exposure, brings shame on the whole family and may be a great impediment to rehabilitation. An over-long sentence can also create hardship for all. When a case is conducted in camera, on the other hand, there are much better possibilities of arriving at a sound plan which takes into account the well-being of the whole family, not only the punishment of the offender.

Incestuous fathers usually have a great need to return to the family. In many cases, this may be the best solution, but the most important factor to be considered is the attitude of the wife. Treatment and rehabilitation are greatly affected by the wife's position on the subject, her wish for the return of her husband to the home, or her repudiation of him.

When the wife rejects her husband and is unwilling to resume the marriage, he usually passes through a depressive state with a feeling of almost overpowering loss. We have observed such cases in prison. An incestuous father will frequently ask for help because of severe symptoms of depression when his wife refuses to forgive him. He sees himself as losing everything, wife, family, the possibility of being at last a good father to his children. Sometimes, if the wife has accused the husband or turned against him, feelings of anger and bitterness supplant the depression. Depression, however, remains not deeply suppressed and whether the father is overtly angry and resentful or depressed, the feeling of great loss persists. His basic wish, despite the wife's rejection, is to return home.

In the therapeutic investigation the incest phase itself is usually short-lived. This is not so much because it is avoided, but it soon ceases to be the focus of treatment as the father grows more involved in his whole personal problem, of which incest is a part. The severity of the reactive depression is variable, depending greatly on the extent of punishment, whether there is a realistic prospect of reconciliation, or failing that, the degree of acceptance of reality of the loss, and ability to plan for a future without the wife and family.

Should the incestuous father remain in the home, the prospect of building a sound marriage depends largely on how much husband and wife both accept without too much recrimination their share of responsibility in the situation, though only one was legally guilty; and whether there is a possibility of a genuine change in the marital relationships, permitting husband and wife to assume normal roles and fulfill their proper function. They can then be of mutual help to one another in trying to establish a marriage on a healthier basis and in looking to the protection and eventual independence of their children.

In treating these husbands and wives, one becomes aware that incest is an extreme symptom of family maladjustment which existed from the beginning of the marriage, and that the incest was the last and most serious manifestation. The case becomes in effect one of family therapy, the outcome depending on the resources of husband and wife, their willingness to involve themselves, and to work together mutually towards a common aim.

SUMMARY

A study of father-daughter incest confined to men otherwise non-criminal or sexually deviant. Incest is here studied mainly in function of the psychopathology of the father. The father seeks to find in his daughter the young wife of his early years. Unconsciously, however, as a young man he was looking for a mother substitute in the girl he was courting. We face a paradox, that in taking the daughter the incestuous father is trying to return to the mother. Once incest is discovered, there is rarely repetition. Disclosure brings about a breakdown of preexisting family relations. This is followed either by separation of the participants, or a re-organization where conscious incest barriers now prevail.

NOTES AND REFERENCES

1. Weinberg, S. K.: *Incest Behaviour*. New York: Citadel Press, 1955.
2. Kennedy, Miriam: "Dynamics Involved in Family Offences Appearing Before the Court." *Can. J. Corrections* 1:50–55, No. 4, July, 1959.
3. Cormier, Bruno M. et al.: "Family Conflicts and Criminal Behaviour." *Can. J. Corrections* 3:18–37, No. 1, Jan., 1961.

4. Mannheim, Hermann: *Criminal Justice and Social Reconstruction.* New York: Oxford University Press, 1946, Chap. V, pp. 77–80.
5. Nurnberger, H.: "Inzestprobleme der Nachkriegszeit." *Deutsche Z. für gerichtliche Med.* 44:259–261, 1955.
6. Greenland, Cyril: "Incest." *Brit. J. Deling.* 9: 62–65, July, 1958.
7. Holder, Hans: "Zum Problem der Blutschande." *Schweizer Archiv für Psychiat. und Neurol.* 64:175–196, 1949.
8. Rennert, Helmut: "Zur Problematik des Inzest." *D.Z. für ger. Med.* 48:50–57, 1958.
9. Riemer, S,: "Research Notes on Incest." *Am. J. Sociol.* pp. 566–575, 1940.
   Riemer, S.: "The Background of Incestuous Relationship," in *Criminology* (Readings). New York: Dryden Press, 1955, pp. 301–307.
10. Szabo, Denis: "L'Inceste en Milieu Urbain." *L'Année Sociologique,* pp. 29–93, 1957–58.
11. Scherrer, P.: *La Sexualité criminelle en Milieu rural.* Paris: Masson & Cie., 1959.
12. Von Hentig and Viernstein: "Untersuchungen über den Inzest." Heidelberg.
13. Abraham, Karl: *Clinical Papers and Essays on Psychoanalysis.* New York: Basic Books, 1955, pp. 21–28.
14. Bender, L., and Blau, A.: "Reaction of Children to Sex Relations with Adults." *Am. J. Orthopsychiat.* 7: 500–518, 1937.
15. Barry, Maurice J., and Johnson, Adelaide: "The Incest Barrier." *Psychoan. Quart.* 27: 485–500, 1958.
16. Friedlander, Kate: *The Psycholanaytical Approach to Juvenile Delinquency.* London: Routledge & Kegan Paul, 1947, pp. 173–177.
17. Sloane, P., and Kapinski, E.: "Effects of Incest on the Participants." *Am. J. Orthopsychiat.* 12: 666–673, 1942.
18. Kinberg, Olaf et al.: "Incestproblemet i Sverige." *Natur och Kultur,* Stockholm, 1943.
19. Kaufman, Irving et al.: "The Family Constellation and Overt Incestuous Relations Between Father and Daughter." *Am. J. Orthopsychiatry* 24, No. 2, 1954.
20. Vestergaard, Emma: "Fader-datter Incest." *Nord. Tld. for Kriminalvid.* 48: 159–188, 1960.
21. Gordon, Lillian: "Incest as Revenge Against the Pre-Oedipal Mother." *The Psychoanalytic Review,* XLII, 1955.
22. Rascovsky, M. W., and Rascovsky, A.: "On Consummated Incest." *Int. J. Psychoanal.* 31: 42–47, 1950.
23. Freud, S.: *Totem et Tabou.* Paris: Payot, 1947.

Diary of an Alcoholic Wife

PAULINE K. AS TOLD TO JOAN GAGE

Women have been called "invisible alcoholics" because they can hide their drinking behind kitchen doors and drawn curtains. Yet an estimated two million American women suffer from this disease—and it is a disease. They are not immoral or undesirable women, but often busy, attractive housewives much like your own neighbors. One such woman is Pauline K., who was destroying her marriage, her children and her health with her drinking. She hopes that by telling her story she will encourage other alcoholics to take the two essential steps on the road to recovery.

Pauline K., 42, is the sort of slim, attractive suburban housewife whose photograph appears on the society page of the local paper. She looks equally elegant in a fur coat and sunglasses and in slacks and a sweater. Pauline lives with her husband and three children in a 175–year-old home surrounded by giant cedars, set back on a quiet road in suburban Connecticut. Inside, the house is immaculate, full of antiques, braided rugs, high, wood-beamed ceilings and sunlight.

Thanks to careful scheduling, Pauline manages to fit a multitude of activities into her day. She's the organizer of her college's fund-raising fair, eighth-grade class mother, avid gardener, expert tennis player, skier and bridge player. Pauline is all these and one thing more—she is an alcoholic.

The exact number of alcoholics in the United States is not known, but estimates range as high as nine million. Of these, almost two million are women, but the number may be much higher; women are often called the *"invisible alcoholics."*

Pauline hopes that her own experiences will encourage other alcoholics to take the two essentials steps of admitting they are alcoholics and asking for help. This is her story.

The first time I really got drunk was when I was 16. I was the maid of honor at my sister's wedding, and they had champagne. It tasted so good

I didn't stop drinking till I got loaded and had to be put up in my room. Everybody thought it was cute.

I did not come from a drinking background. My mother never drank and my father, a doctor, would have one Manhattan before dinner. If somebody came to visit, my parents didn't say, "Do you want a drink?" There was coffee and cake instead. On high school dates, if my date was a drinker, I would drink one-for-one with him. I liked people who drank. I went quickly from rum and cola (which most kids drank) to straight shots of bourbon with a beer chaser. I almost never got sick from drinking, I rarely had hangovers, and I could hold a lot of liquor. I know now that this is rather typical; an alcoholic tends to have a hollow leg in the beginning.

After high school, I went to a small girls' college in upstate New York. World War II was on my first two years there, so there weren't many dates and there wasn't much drinking. When the veterans came back, things changed. The fraternity parties I went to were wild. The boys had learned to drink in the Army. I drank a great deal of beer. Rarely hard liquor. We'd start a weekend party with milk punch in the morning and then drink beer from 11 A.M. straight through till four the next morning.

When I drank I was very up. I had to tell the funniest jokes and be the wildest, craziest person. Many people feel they have to drink to warm up; they are afraid of people. I wasn't. I just liked to drink, and when I drank I got wild. There's always one character in any group that people laugh with and at. That was me.

The morning after a big weekend I would think, "Oh the *stupid,* dumb things I did." I wasn't promiscuous in any way. These were just foolish things.

After college I went to work in New York. Sometimes at parties I would drink too much; other times, I wouldn't. After two years in New York, I went into the Foreign Service in Denmark—a drinker's heaven because you could buy duty-free liquor. Gin was 80 cents a bottle; the finest bourbon cost only $1.20. I drank Danish beer and aquavit a lot. One night I'd only have one cocktail at a party and another night, at the ambassador's party, I'd have six drinks, tell a dirty joke and *die* of embarrassment the next day.

After almost three years in Denmark, I came back to New York to work for a publishing house. When I came back from Europe I dated a terrific boy I had known in college. I really liked him. But he was a teetotaler. His father had been an alcoholic and he didn't drink. I wouldn't marry him because I couldn't spend the rest of my life with a guy who didn't drink! Alcohol had become vital to me.

Then I met my husband Jim. He drank; in fact, he was what you would call a heavy drinker. Sometimes he got more loaded than I did, but he could always turn it off. He could say, "I want one and no more."

We drank a lot before we were married. But for the first eight years of marriage my drinking wasn't a problem. I got pregnant right away and had two boys, sixteen months apart, and then I had a baby girl. I was a hard worker; I used to iron and scrub floors at night and maybe once or twice a year I would have too much to drink at a party.

In time I realized that my husband and I were not very compatible as far as drinking goes. After a certain number of drinks, he is a depressive. So he would be going *down* as I was going *up*. He'd give me dirty looks—and that would incite me to have another drink. We would fight after parties. He'd say, "It was a lovely party. Too bad you didn't let anyone else have anything to say all evening." Which was true.

Because of Jim's reaction to my drinking, I developed guilt feelings about it, which was a good thing. If I had been married to somebody who was the same way—the party-going, happy-man-type drunk—we'd probably both be roaring alcoholics right now.

Our whole social life was geared to drinking, and I think this is commonplace in America today. A football game? The most important thing was the Bloody Marys and the whiskey sours at the picnic beforehand. Skiing? The drinks *après ski* and at lunch. I can remember once when I was in a ski race. I emptied an aspirin jar and filled it with bourbon because I knew I was going to be nervous, and in the chairlift going up I drank it. I won a medal.

My drinking began to get out of control. I'd drink while the kids were eating or while I cooked their dinner, even if Jim was out of town. Once when he was on a trip, I had to go to the dentist. When I got home I couldn't open my mouth wide enough to eat, so I opened a bottle of bourbon. The next thing I knew it was four o'clock in the morning and I was lying, fully dressed, on the couch. I was scared. I went out to the kitchen and looked at the bourbon bottle; it was three-quarters empty.

In a month, maybe two, it happened again. This time I had another excuse: I was having a huge college alumni meeting in my home the next day. Absolutely stoned, I broke the whole set of good china trying to get it down from the cupboard. Again, terrible guilt. That same night I fell all the way down the cellar stairs and was covered with terrible bruises. Jim wasn't home.

There are people who become alcoholics because they *want* to get drunk, because life is so bad they can't stand it. But I didn't like getting drunk. I was happy. I liked being a housewife. I had worked for seven years and I really had no desire to go back to work. I didn't feel trapped or frustrated. I was always amazed that I would get drunk when I didn't intend to.

Around this time Jim decided to go into business for himself. It was a big step—making a change at 40. It could have been a total disaster for him, but I wasn't worried. He used to get mad at me because I didn't worry. But maybe I drank because I was worried and didn't realize it.

The new business kept Jim out of town a lot. I started drinking quite a lot after the kids were in bed. But before long I was drunk by the time they went to bed.

I had "telephonitis." I would call people. Once I even called the school principal. Mostly I called sympathetic friends, like a girl friend who was going through a divorce. I really don't remember what I said. It amazes people to hear that. I was coherent, but this was the start of the blackouts—the vital sign in alcoholism. You sound perfectly normal, you can talk and perform and drive a car, but you're in a total blackout. Often the next morning the phone would ring and some friend of mine would say. "Yes, I *can* do it today." And I didn't even remember having called her.

My husband was checking the liquor bottles by this time. I would still have my two drinks before dinner, but he wouldn't necessarily have a drink. He'd come home and find me with one. Many times it *would* be my first. But he'd say, "Oh, you're drinking." I'd resent the remark and I'd have another drink.

I'd have two drinks and eat dinner. Then I'd drink while I was doing the dishes. If we watched television in our bedroom, I'd think of some excuse to go downstairs to the kitchen. I'd have a little vodka. (I'd switched to vodka because it's cheaper than bourbon. Money was beginning to be a problem. I was drinking about a pint a day, which is $2.50, and I had to take that out of the grocery money. I was always delighted if my cleaning woman couldn't come because I could spend her money on liquor.)

When I was drinking in the kitchen, I'd close the door behind me. Suddenly, it would crash open and there would be my husband, saying, "What are you doing?" He went through different phases. He'd try to be sympathetic, and when that didn't work he'd say, "Do something about your drinking," and I'd cry. I cried and cried. I thought stopping was all a matter of willpower. I wouldn't *allow* this to happen to me! What am I doing? A mother, a housewife with a beautiful home. I clean the house, I take care of the garden, I'm president of my college club. How can I be an alcoholic?

But I kept on drinking.

I started having little tremors in the morning from drinking. The tremors made me so nervous I'd shake badly. I went bowling every Tuesday morning. I'd reach for the bowling ball and my hand would shake so. Thinking everybody was looking at me I'd say, "I have this neuritis in my arm and the heavy ball is making my hand shake." I couldn't write a check in the store because my hand shook so. Then I found that—and here's where the morning drinks start—I could cope with bowling if I had a little vodka in my orange juice.

Finally I quit bowling. I thought "It's the *bowling* that's making me nervous." I had so many excuses! "It's being president of my college club." Or

"I'm going through an early change of life and that's making me nervous." Or "It's the birth control pill. *That's* why I'm drinking."

I developed arthritis in my elbow and shoulders and then it started to go into my knees. I found out later that it's called "alcoholic arthritis." Drinking affects the joints. I'd go to bed with a heating pad. And of course I'd have to have some drinks for the pain.

My doctor didn't realize the truth. I was, to him, not the type of person to become an alcoholic. When I'd get drunk I'd say to my friends, "You know, Jim thinks I'm an alcoholic," and they'd say, "Oh, Pauline, you? Of *course* you're not!"

We went through stages where we would throw all the liquor out of the house. Drunk and crying hysterically, I'd say, "I'm not going to drink any more. Get rid of it." The first time Jim did this, he forgot the liqueurs in another cupboard—Benedictine, brandy, Cointreau. I drank it all.

I was buying my liquor at six different stores in the area. When you're an alcoholic you can never just go in and say, "I'd like a bottle of vodka." You have to go in and say, "Now. . . what was it my husband wanted? We're having guests tonight. Vodka! That's what it was!" The salesman stands there thinking, "Yeah, yeah." Every alcoholic does it. I'd be shaking trying to get the liquor into the house, as if someone were watching. And I wouldn't keep the bottles around. I'd empty the liquor into a pitcher or a mayonnaise jar in some back cupboard. And then I'd have to hide the bottles until the garbage man came. I'd hide one in the bottom of a garment bag in my closet or down in the basement in the hamper. One woman I met poured it into her steam iron, and she'd get up in the middle of the night and drink it out of the iron.

I was drunk most of the time now and I had two car accidents, one with all the children in the car. I'd been out to a friend's and had poured my own drinks, as usual, because nobody ever made them strong enough. I had two drinks, which were probably equivalent to six. I thought I was fine, drove home, rounded a corner and never straightened the car out. Eight hundred dollars' worth of damage to the car. A policeman came but I was not arrested for drunken driving because I was coherent.

There was *terrible* tension in the family. I was withdrawn, irritable. I never smiled. I just was so deep in my own concerns. You turn inward trying to figure out what's happening to you. "Am I going crazy?" you wonder. I had no time or interest for anything. My seven-year-old daughter would bring a little friend home and I'd be on the couch and she'd say, "Mommy's taking a nap because she's sick." The oldest boy knew what was going on. Often he'd pour my liquor down the sink. Not the whole bottle, but I think in his 12-year-old mind he figured, "If I can get rid of some of it. . . . "

Once when I was driving my oldest son to a friend's home, I drove the car out of the driveway and ended up in a ditch. He jumped out of the car and screamed, "You're drunk! You're drunk!" I was furious! I just drove off and left him. Imagine what my children were going through all the while.

The children saw the fights between me and Jim. One time I remember Jim took me by the arms and forced me upstairs. And I was screaming all the way up, "How dare you? Drunk? I've had one drink!"

My husband had begun to read Alcoholics Anonymous literature and he realized that alcoholism is a sickness. I would go through periods when I would stay off liquor for a couple of days, but I wasn't replacing it with any positive thinking. It was a matter of *will*. "I *will* not drink." Then I'd go right back on it.

When I first decided to call Alcoholics Anonymous, I was very drunk and I couldn't even look up the telephone number in the book. I dialed the operator and asked for AA. I got some woman on the phone. And for maybe a month I went to one meeting a week. At the meetings I didn't hear one word about alcoholism because I wasn't listening. I remember people talking about being arrested for drunken driving, being in hospitals, being in mental hospitals and being at an AA farm. I thought: "What am I doing here with all these crazy people!"

I went for about a month just to keep my husband happy, and I controlled my drinking. We went on two trips, one to California and one to the Caribbean. My husband was trying to do things to make me happy. He bought me a fur coat. I kept saying, "Look! I don't need AA. I went on two trips and I didn't get drunk so I am not an alcoholic." But the reason I didn't drink was because he was with me constantly.

Not long after the vacation I went to my doctor. He said, "Go without drinks for two weeks. That will prove you're not an alcoholic." He was wrong. So I went without a drink for 13 days. I figured, "Well, thirteen days, fourteen days, what difference does it make?" Most doctors don't want to get involved with alcoholics because of the trouble. Yet I can't understand *why* if they realize it's a sickness.

I started going to a psychiatrist, which was absolutely the worst thing for an alcoholic like me to do. You have to have sobriety before psychiatry. If you're drinking you are going to lie. You're going to cover up. And no psychiatrist can help you. What they should do is say, "Go get sober. And then come back."

I'd have to go get a bottle the minute I'd leave the psychiatrist. My husband would come home and find me drunk. I had failed him *again*. I couldn't stand that. Twice I ran away. The first time I left a note, and my oldest son read it. "I am drunk again and I am going to leave you . . ." I got in the car and drove away. I don't know where I went. But I came back in a couple of hours, took my bottle with me and went to bed.

I also talked about killing myself. "I'm going to end everybody's problems. It's the only way." But I didn't because I didn't want to die.

One morning, after the children had gone to school, Jim said, "This is it. I'm going to take the children and leave you." I could tell by his voice that he meant it. He said, "I'm sorry, but I cannot, for the safety of the children, allow this to happen any more. We're going down to see the psychiatrist right away."

We went to the psychiatrist's office. He called to find out about an AA rest farm, and he and Jim said, "All right, you're going away." I went into hysterics. Crying, wringing my hands. Not just ordinary crying. It was like the whole world had collapsed in on me. I begged, "Please, I'll do it myself!"

My husband later said that when he saw how upset I was he almost changed his mind. But he stuck to his guns. He took me home. I couldn't even pack my suitcase. I was totally drained of everything.

I know now what my reaction was. It was the surrender of my will. They have a saying in AA: "Let go and let God." I never was a religious person, but that is, in effect, what I was doing. I was saying, in effect: "I cannot fight it any more. I'm collapsed, finished, sunk. You take it."

I went to the rest farm for two weeks. I listened and believed everything they had to say. I felt like a child in school. My mind was completely washed of all the fight, all the excuses, all the self-deception, all the lying. They told me I had a disease that would lead to insanity or death, that I could never have a drink again, that I must live one day at a time. And I never *wanted* a drink again. It was giving up the fight that did it.

At the farm I learned that it takes five days for alcohol to leave your system. So when someone starts to drink, as I did after those 13 days of not drinking, it wasn't my body that wanted a drink; it was my mind. I *thought* I couldn't do without alcohol.

At the AA farm I saw people who were worse off than I was. Two have died since then. One is in a mental home. It was a powerful leveler. I realized that if I took a drink it would bring me despair, trouble, possibly death.

One woman there had seven years of sobriety in AA and then she stopped going to meetings and had one fall after another. She was on her way to Rome and ended up at this farm instead, with all her Rome clothes. She went into hallucinations and all we could do was sit around and listen to her hallucinate.

There was a man who'd been sober for about a week and he had delayed DT's. He thought people were coming after him. He tore the banister right off the staircase and crashed through the screen door beating at these imaginary people.

The farm can take 40 people. All the staff, including the cook, are alcoholics. There is a little farmhouse where the women stay and a couple of dormitories for the men. You have to promise that you will stay two weeks. It's $75 a week. Good meals; you help do the dishes and clean the rooms.

When you check in, you first go to sober up in a little dormitory with four beds. A woman helps you unpack. I thought, "Isn't this nice?" I was so naive. She opened up my bottle of astringent and sniffed it; half the people come in with liquor stashed in various things.

After breakfast you do the cleaning or what have you. They have croquet—no strenuous sports because a lot of people arrive in bad physical condition. Every morning the doctor comes for those who need him. You take lots of walks. You can take naps. The majority of the time is spent just talking. There is much camaraderie there, much laughter. I don't know of anybody who's been to the farm who doesn't feel, "This is like home."

There was a chapel service every day, plus an afternoon meeting you could go to and two evening meetings a week. At AA meetings somebody usually tells a story, his own story, and then people ask questions. At the farm, however, they gave us a pencil and paper to write down any questions if we didn't feel courageous enough to ask our own.

On Saturday nights there were open meetings—husbands or wives could come. Jim came to see me and said he had told the children that my mother was sick in Florida and that I was with her. I told him I thought he should tell the children the truth—and he did. They said, "We're so glad you told us because we thought she'd killed herself or run away and left us all forever."

Jim brought them up for a visit. They were looking around saying, "Is that one? Is that one? Gee, everybody's so terrific and attractive."

This idea of all alcoholics being Skid Row bums is crazy. A psychiatrist, a doctor, a priest and a lawyer were at the farm with me. The women were mostly housewives, including one mayor's wife. One woman, a grandmother, took her first drink at 52. After one drink she was an instant alcoholic, but that's not true of the majority of alcoholics.

After I got out of camp, Jim was a bit apprehensive. But, and this is very important, I did not stay sober for his sake. If you're going to try to keep sober for your husband or your children, it's not going to work. You've got to keep sober for yourself.

Another thing is that you can't worry about the past. If I worried about all the things I did when I was drinking and what I did to my children, I'd be in some mental institution, smothered with guilt. So I learned to live the Serenity Prayer, which all AA members know: "God grant me the serenity to accept things I cannot change, the courage to change the things I can, and the wisdom to know the difference." And when something bothers me I say, "Is this something I can change? No? All right, I won't worry about it." I learned, too, that self-pity and resentment are poison to an alcoholic. I'd get mad at my husband—and never tell him that I was mad or why. Now I do.

Jim stopped drinking for the first six months after I got out of the AA camp. I didn't like that because, when we were out at a party, people would notice if both of us didn't drink. So he went back to controlled drinking.

I didn't keep any liquor in the house for the first three months. Jim would keep it in the trunk of his car. If anybody came and wanted a drink, he'd pretend he had just bought the liquor and had forgotten it in the car. I felt safer that way. I knew I didn't want to drink, but my main concern was that I'd have a mental blackout—some crazy sort of thing—and I'd drink! If I had to go out to get liquor, I'd have time to think.

I went to the local AA meetings twice a week in the beginning. Some people go every day. Sometimes twice a day. I didn't feel this was necessary for me. However, any time that I felt tense or had a little problem I went to a meeting. There are two meetings every day in this area—one at lunch and one at night. Now I generally go once a week.

If you don't continue going to AA you can easily forget how bad it was. What AA does is constantly remind you, because you hear new people tell their stories—and you work with them and help them.

I haven't had a drink for over two years. After the first year, at the AA meeting, they had a birthday party for me, with a cake. That's the big step.

Since I've stopped drinking, my guilt is gone. I can take a nap now if I'm tired and not feel guilty about it. All the little things that I once would have lied about—like a dent in the fender—I can admit now. I feel so free.

How has this whole experience changed me? I think one of the big things is that all my life I always reacted *immediately*. I was on the defensive. But now I've learned to take that moment to think, "Is this really going to matter?"

I also know that until you hit some kind of bottom you can't really appreciate things as they are. I have such an appreciation of everything! Many people who drink have the feeling that life is not going to be any fun any more without alcohol. But the more I look back at the drinking times the more I realize they really weren't all that much fun. People didn't make sense at parties. Now I can really enjoy an evening because I'm sober.

I don't really know how to describe my change. But my husband and family and my life . . . it's just so peaceful. We scream and yell and get nervous sometimes because we're human. But I don't let it get out of control. If I get nervous I think, "So I'm nervous. I won't be nervous in another half hour. This, too, will pass."

If you seem to be drinking too much—to the point where it worries you—you may be interested in knowing more about Alcoholics Anonymous. Remember, only you can determine whether the AA program is for you (just as only your husband can decide if the program is for him). To help you make up your mind, here are 12 questions for you to answer Yes or No.

1. Have you ever tried to stop drinking for a week (or longer), only to fall short of your goal?
2. Do you resent the advice of others who try to get you to stop drinking?
3. Have you ever tried to control your drinking by switching from one alcoholic beverage to another?
4. Have you taken a morning drink during the past year?
5. Do you envy people who can drink without getting into trouble?
6. Has your drinking problem become progressively more serious during the past year?
7. Has your drinking created problems at home?
8. At social affairs where drinking is limited, do you try to obtain "extra" drinks?
9. Despite evidence to the contrary, have you continued to assert that you can stop drinking whenever you wish?
10. During the past year, have you been absent from work as a result of drinking?
11. Have you ever "blacked out" during your drinking?
12. Have you ever felt you could do more with your life if you did not drink?

What's your score? If you or your husband answered YES to four or more questions, Alcoholics Anonymous says chances are you have a serious drinking problem or may have one in your future.

Why does AA say this? Because their experience with tens of thousands of recovered alcoholics has taught them some basic truths about the symptoms of problem drinking and about people themselves.

If your score indicates that you have or may have a problem with drinking, you should realize that there is no disgrace in admitting that you have a health problem—*and alcoholism is a health problem.* The important thing is to do something about it.

If you think the AA program is for you, Alcoholics Anonymous will be glad to show you how to stop drinking. If you can't admit to the problem yet, that's all right, too. All AA asks is that you keep an open mind on the subject; when and if you need help, they will be glad to share their insights with you.

AA is a fellowship of men and women who share their experience, strength and hope with each other so that they may solve their common problem and help others to recover from alcoholism. There are more than 400,000 members and 14,000 groups in more than 90 countries. The only requirement for membership is a desire to stop drinking. There are no dues or fees. AA is self-supporting through contributions; it is not allied with any sect, denomination, political party, organization or institution. The primary purpose of AA is to help members stay sober (all are recovered alcoholics), and help other alcoholics achieve sobriety.

If you want additional helpful insights into the problem of alcoholism, you can send for two free booklets: *This is AA* and *AA for the Woman.* Write to: General Service Office, Alcoholics Anonymous, P.O. Box 459, Grand Central Post Office, New York, N.Y. 10017.

If you wish to contact AA in your community, consult your local telephone directory for the listing—or ask your doctor, clergyman or police officials.

A Junkie in the House

IRA MOTHNER

What can you do if there's one in your house? If you can't face up to it, you'll believe in him, protect him and try to find him an easy out—and that's how you'll hurt him and feed his habit. And one day you find out:

"We came home late and all the lights were on, and my daughter ran out and said the police were taking David in an ambulance."

Or you put it together:

"There were some things missing from around the house. She stole money from me. She sold my husband's camera. A watch, she sold. Little by little, things were missing."

You don't want to believe it:

"We all lied to ourselves. And he got busted on several occasions, but because dear old dad was a police officer, I could always go down and bring him home."

Even when your nose gets rubbed in it:

"This lady who lives around the corner told my wife's brother that if somebody didn't tell us Danny was using drugs, she would. Danny was then employed in the post office. He wasn't going to work, and this guy named Joe was calling up every day. Finally, Danny told us he owed this Joe, who is a loan shark, $154."

Even then:

"Even when Bobby got hepatitis, and even when the doctor and my wife told me he had needle marks on his arm, that he was a heroin addict, I still wouldn't accept it."

Bobby remembers how, before he left for the hospital, he confessed to his father: "I told him. And he said, 'Why didn't you tell me before? I would have given you money for clean spikes, so you wouldn't have to stick a dirty one in your arm.' And. . . he didn't understand."

From *Look Magazine* 35:38–39, Jan. 26, 1971. Copyright © Cowles Communications, Inc., 1971. Reprinted by permission of the publisher.

129

Bobby's father, Bob Carnival, understands now. But it's not easy for Bob or any parents in his encounter group to own up, to face what they did and didn't do. Getting straight with themselves so they can be straight with their kids is part of the program they bought when their children ended up at Phoenix House, New York City's residence program for drug-troubled young people.

Phoenix is no quick cure. It takes 30 months in one of the 15 houses run by former addicts and heavy on encounter therapy, rough discipline and work. "We're not just drying out dope fiends," says Dr. Mitchell Rosenthal, who directs Phoenix. "We're giving these kids a second crack at growing up," because somebody blew it the first time around.

That doesn't mean every youngster who goes to drugs is parented by ogres. The ten members of Bob's group may not have picked up fast on what was eating at their young, but they are all solid types who care about their kids. Their marriages seem rockier than most, but plenty are worse, and these have stuck together. What happened to their children could happen to almost anybody's. Acre zoning and a two-car garage are no insurance against it.

If you've got kids, you've got drugs. Maybe your youngsters haven't smoked, sniffed, snorted or shot anything yet (and you can't know for sure). Maybe they never will, but they'll have every chance because the drugs are there and very big on the adolescent horizon. Most young people, the lucky majority, will be in and out of pot or pills before their parents ever catch on. A good many others hang in longer, and some of them can't get out, can't get off whatever drug they've picked as their particular yellow-brick road, their way out of the real world. What it's all about, what should scare us, is not the kids who go out behind the gym once or twice to puff some pot. It's all those young people who are using drugs regularly to cop out on reality. They can use grass or hash or hallucinogens, and they can take the heroin route too, for heroin busted out of the ghetto sometime back. Now, anybody's child can get hooked. Not that it's a better deal to get heavily into amphetamines or LSD. Speed freaks and acid heads aren't "addicts," but their habits can be just as hard to shake, and they've chosen more efficient ways to mess up their heads.

Bobby Carnival started out when he was 13, "drinking beer and smoking pot." It wasn't much, but he didn't quit, and moved on to tougher hallucinogens. "I was about 15, and I used acid one summer, used it every day. In a period of two months, I dropped about 90 tabs. I was always like that. I went overboard with everything I ever used."

Bobby's habit is long gone, yet at least one druggy way persists—he exaggerates. But his basic tale is true.

By the end of that summer, he was off acid. "I finally took a bummer, a bad trip." By then, he was hallucinating even without the drug, "I always felt as if I was high on acid, even after I stayed straight for two-and-a-half months. I began to get desperate. And I got to a point where I didn't even like to come outside in daytime because the sun was too bright for me."

To switch off the kaleidoscope in his head, Bobby turned to depressants. "When I started eating barbiturates, it stopped. I was so messed up I didn't even notice the lights." But barbiturates only lasted two weeks before he found a deeper depressant—heroin. "Like I said, I go overboard with everything. And once I got introduced to heroin, it was like I fell in love with it. It was total Utopia. It was the only thing that really took my mind off everything that had me worried." He started, as most beginners do, inhaling the powder straight from its little glassine envelope. "I snorted half a bag of heroin that first day. The next nine days in a row, I snorted dope. The tenth day, I mainlined [shot into a vein]. From that first day, when I got turned on around the corner by the graveyard on Church Avenue, I stopped going to school."

For more than a year, Bobby got away with it. "When I started getting heavy into heroin, the only time I ever came home was at night. The only meal I ever ate was at night, when I used to come in and make sandwiches." He was busy. An addict has to keep at it, steal and shoot, deal and shoot, and Bobby dealt. He was no street-corner retailer, "I was selling weight, not bags, but ounces and half-ounces."

You don't need to know any 12 telltale signs of drug abuse to figure something is wrong with an adolescent living the way Bobby was. And his mother knew. She'd seen the spoons, needles, glassine bags, even the holes hi his arm. Bobby denied it, and her husband believed him. "She was the policeman," said Bob Carnival, "because I used to say, 'No, it didn't happen. Well, maybe he took a couple of pills.' She was looking for it. I didn't want to see it."

Bob and Edna Carnival were having a rough enough time without adding Bobby's grief. "There was never enough money," and there never had been. Edna had three older children from earlier marriages, and Bob had held down two jobs for years, driving a truck days, an ambulance nights. It was too much, and he switched to pushing a cab. That meant better money but never enough to move the family out of their downhill Brooklyn neighborhood. "What the kids needed or what they wanted, they got," says Bob. "That's the only thing we always agreed on. The rest of it . . . I mean, we couldn't get together. We couldn't sit down and talk for five minutes. It would end up in a big battle."

When Bob could no longer duck the truth about Bobby, he did as most parents in his group at Phoenix did—nearly everything wrong. The Phoenix gospel holds that shielding your kid, protecting him, believing his promises and lies doesn't help him: it helps his habit. There's a logic to this, for an addict must want to help himself, and he won't until the junkie's life becomes so difficult, so crummy and scary that he can no longer face it. It's not that old bugaboo, withdrawal, he's reluctant to go through; it's giving up his mental hiding hole.

Making it rough on their kids is hard for loving parents nagged by their own guilts. Bob Carnival wanted to trust his son. "He promised me when he was in the hospital, 'I'll be good,' and I believed him. I believed that thing, whatever it was, would go away. I thought he could be good."

But Bobby wasn't ready to quit. "I never really made an attempt. I started using again, and I started using heavy." He was hustling heavy too: dealing small stuff, rustling roast beefs from markets, lifting radios, snatching purses. Bobby now tells it like the adventures of some super cat burglar, but it was a grimy time, and he got caught.

The spring and summer when he turned 17, Bobby was arrested at least once a month: for possession, dealing, shoplifting and fighting with police. He was in jail and right out again. "I was Johnny-on-the-spot with the bail," says Bob. But he and Edna were desperate. They tried other programs before Phoenix, dragged Bobby to day centers. "I was leaving the house at eight, and I would go hustle, make some money, get high, go to the center, get out at three and get high again."

Even at the Phoenix Center, where youngsters are supposed to dump their habits before going into houses, Bobby was still faking it. But hustling was harder now; he was afraid to deal big. "I beat a lot of people out of money"—taking cash for drugs he didn't deliver. And he still conned money from his parents. Bob remembers: "After we thought he'd kicked his habit, he said, 'You know, Pop, the dope pushers are looking for me. I owe them money, and they want me to run a pound of something somewhere. If I get picked up, I'll get like four years.' So, I gave him the rent."

While Bobby wasn't making much progress at Phoenix, Bob and Edna were. So, after their son got picked up a fifth time, for purse-snatching, Bob didn't rush downtown with the bail. Even when the judge refused to turn the boy over to Phoenix, Bob held out and let Bobby go to jail.

He stayed there for seven months. "It seemed like seven years," says Bob. "I had to go up there every week and look at him through those bars." After a few months, he wanted Bobby out, "because it would make me feel better." But hardheaded former addicts at Phoenix warned him, "You'd be wasting your money. You'd be doing it for him again, and it wouldn't have any value for him."

Bob stuck it out, and Bobby stayed in jail until he was given five years' probation and sent to Phoenix House. "I figured I was going to stay for a couple of months," Bobby admits, "and then maybe my people would go for the fact that I was well." Only it didn't work that way. "After being honest in my groups and making friends and understanding what's going on here, I started to feel good inside. I started to really dig it."

Bobby has been at Phoenix for a year and a half now. Bob is chairman of a Friends of Phoenix group, laying it out for parents going through all the changes he did. "Get together," he tells couples, "and take a stand against your kid." Phoenix can help them. It did Bob and Edna.

For deep drug trouble, parents can't go it alone. They need a hand from someone who understands both kids and drugs. At Phoenix, Bob urges parents to get their youngsters into the program. "Tell him he can't live at home if he doesn't. Kick him out."

Plenty of Phoenix parents pass up encounter groups for themselves. The sessions can be painful, and some ugly realities pop up there. Most couples who make this scene have other children or hope someday to have their Phoenix youngster home.

It's hard to tell how much they learn or change. But when someone tells how his kid has split, quit Phoenix and gone back on the streets, the universal response is: "Have you changed the locks yet?"

PART 3

THE IMPACT OF INDIVIDUAL
DEVIANCY ON THE FAMILY

The introductory essay to this volume indicated the possibility, or more likely the probability, of an individual's deviant behavior having a profound and lasting impact upon the members of his family, his relationship to the other members, as well as upon the family as an integrated unit. The editorial commentary of Part 2 elaborated this eventuality. Deviant behavior raises the spectre of family crisis, at least in terms of its initial occurrence or discovery, or both. Whether or not this crisis precipitates a disruption or effects even stronger integration of the family unit depends upon the nature of both the deviant behavior and the effectiveness of the family's prior integration. However, no family confronted with deviancy ever emerges unscathed regardless of the disposition of the problem.

One variable reflecting the extent of impact on the family experiencing deviant behavior is the degree of permanent change attendant to the family structure as a result of the deviant act and its consequences. An alternate measure of trauma as a result of deviancy is the resiliency of the family or the extent to which it can restore or reassume its predeviancy or precrisis state of organization and integration. For example, if the deviant behavior results in the absence of one of the parents for a period of time, if not permanently, the possibility of a return to complete normalcy would likely be precluded. On the other hand, if the family response to the crisis of deviancy is sufficiently innovative or accommodative so as to return the family to a semblance of its precrisis state of organizational equilibrium, then the situation is likely to have a less damaging or disabling outcome for the family unit.

The variable of prior family integration is probably equally as significant as the nature of the deviancy in determining the degree and kind of impact on the family. With respect to this variable, however, two possibilities suggest themselves. The loosely integrated or partially disorganized family, characterized by a low degree of interdependence and with little psychological and emotional bonding, would seemingly have the more difficult time recovering from most crises. But, concomitantly, this type of family, precisely because of its loose structure, would perhaps also be prone to experience any impact to a lesser degree. The tightly integrated family, with its high degree of emotional and psychological interdependency and its higher level of interpersonal expectations, might be more vulnerable to a deviancy crisis, and thus more sensitive to its impact. However, this same solid structure which might be conducive to greater trauma could also provide the structural resilience which would facilitate recovery from crisis.

Accordingly, to adequately assess the social import of deviancy for a given family, it is necessary to have a clear understanding of both the nature of the deviancy involved and the cohesiveness of family integration. The former is easier to evaluate because most types of deviant behavior may be categorized according to the seriousness of the act and the severity of attendant stigma or punishment. Determining the level of family integration is difficult, but there are several variables, such as social class level, education, income, religiosity, and longevity of the marriage, which are indicative of integrative cohesion.

Another perspective on the impact of deviancy upon the family views divorce as a consequence of deviancy, based on the fact that many grounds or causes of divorce, both legal and actual, are in fact configurations of deviant behavior. For example, some of the most often cited grounds for divorce are desertion, cruelty, adultery, conviction of a felony, use of drugs, and drunkenness. These acts not only constitute deviancy from the standpoint of society, but most of them also represent violations of family norms and their commission is directed against the family and its members.

The disruptive effects of several types of deviant behavior are illustrated by the selections in this section. They are presented sequentially with respect to the seriousness of their impact upon the family. The initial articles emphasize the discovery and crisis brought on by deviancy, and the third and fourth articles describe disruption and displacement of the family. Although the primary emphasis here is upon the crisis which precipitated family disequilibrium, several of these readings also examine some coping patterns employed in response to the crisis exigencies.

DISCOVERY AND CRISIS

The first two selections address themselves to what might be termed "conventional" middle-class American families in which the deviant behavior of one of the children suddenly confronts the family and a crisis follows.

In the initial article, "Our Son Was Different," a mother quite unexpectedly finds evidence that a heretofore "model" son is involved in a homosexual relationship with a student friend. This case is similar to a number of others which have been reported in which the homosexual experimentations of the adolescent are accidently discovered by the parents. The discovery usually occurs when one of the parents finds a note or letter, or perhaps when the child is arrested under incriminating circumstances in the company of an adult.[1]

In the case described, the son had double-dated with a high school friend, and after arriving at the dance, he and the other boy became bored with their girls and returned to the car to engage in homosexual intimacies. The intimate episode in the car had been preceded by an exchange of affectionate notes which the boy's mother later found. The mother's initial response was to rush to the school psychologist, who assessed the contents of the note and advised her of the son's possible involvement in a homosexual relationship.

The parents convinced their son to undergo therapy and the psychiatrist also suggested therapy for the mother. Through this experience both mother and son gained insight into the failures of the relationship of the parents to each other and to their son during his early years. While such inadequate relationships appear to be common in the early lives of many homosexuals, great care must be taken before assuming any direct causal relationship. Evidence of causal factors of homosexuality is still quite scanty, especially in regard to whether or not the major cause is environmental or in some way physically inherent in the individual.

The subsequent article, "Not a Case History, Not a Statistic: Our Daughter," concerns an adolescent daughter and the effects of her unwanted pregnancy on herself and her family. The account is written from the mother's point-of-view and describes the daugher's development through childhood and adolescence, picturing her as having rebellious tendencies while being attractive and appealing at the same time. The boy with whom she becomes involved is a college freshman and only slightly older than the girl, who is still in high school. He is not atypical of the majority of unwed fathers reported in both case materials and survey research reports.[2]

As the couple's relationship develops, the boy gradually integrates himself into the life of the family, motivated to some extent by his immature dependency upon the girl. The mother grows apprehensive about the boy's constant presence, but is reluctant to interfere because it might provoke inappropriate acts of rebellious independence. As time goes on, the couple become increasingly deceptive about where they go and what they do, and the daughter becomes sullen and short-tempered. Subsequently, through a high school counselor who has become a confidante of the couple in their search for an abortionist, the mother learns of the pregnancy.

The article then relates the procedure undertaken by the family to obtain a legal abortion, and the processes of rehabilitation and reintegration experienced by the entire family as a result of the episode.

In both articles, it is the mother who first discovers her offspring's deviant activity. The literature suggests that this is a modal occurrence. The mother, with her household routine and her proximity to the child and his activities, is more likely to be aware of suspicious signs than the father. Also, she is more likely to enjoy a closer emotional and psychological relationship with the child, which may prompt the sharing of confidences or confessions.

These crises subject the family to great pressures and threaten to undermine the organization and integration of the family unit. The child as focal point of the difficulty is placed under great strain, but the other family members, and especially the parents, must endure considerable soul-searching and introspection. Concomitant with this reflection is an increase in the parents' feelings of guilt and inadequacy, and these feelings must be resolved along with the problem of the child's deviancy and its aftermath.

These accounts document a relatively satisfactory outcome inasmuch as these families are able to cope with the deviancy crises, due both to their high level of prior integration and their knowledge of and willingness to obtain professional help. However, these families can never be quite the same after having been confronted with such a situation.

DISRUPTION AND DISPLACEMENT

The second two selections in this section address themselves to some of the effects upon the family unit, and particularly upon the children, of the removal of one of the parents as a result of deviancy.

"Effects of Desertion on Family Life" concerns the impact of a deviant act which is committed directly against the family. Although desertion is usually considered a crime in the legal sense, it is infrequently brought to the attention of the authorities because the deserted members of the family may be reluctant to lodge a formal complaint. However, failure to complain about the deserter may presage even more suffering for the family because the absence of official certification may deprive it of aid and assistance to which it might be entitled.

Although desertion does occur with women, as evidenced in an article in Part 2, the overwhelming majority of offenders are men, and the article here is concerned mainly with the desertion of the husband and father. It explores the reactions of both the children and the mother. The child, like the mother, reacts initially to the loss of the father in the home, but also frequently has a secondary reaction caused by the mother's disturbance over the situation. Thus, the effects of the desertion may well reverberate throughout the entire family.

The most direct effect upon the child of the father's desertion is the feeling of insecurity brought about by the image of the father as the physical protector of the home and family. Furthermore, the father serves as the masculine role model which the son learns to imitate and from which the daughter learns the counter feminine role. Thus, loss of the father for a long, period of time or when the children are young would likely impair their role development.

The deserted spouse also feels a number of direct effects such as the immediate loss of financial support for the family, loss of sexual satisfaction, and certainly significant ego damage. The article examines both the psychological and practical aspects of the situation, and then documents a case history to illustrate the reaction of one family and the subsequent help it receives in the aid of a social caseworker.

"Inmate-Mothers and Their Children" reports partial findings of an extensive study of the female populations in two California penal institutions. That portion of the study reproduced here is a descriptive analysis of those women in the prisons who were mothers at the time of their incarceration. Also of significance in this article are the findings with respect to the disposition of the children after the mother is arrested. The problems created by the mother's deviant behavior and her subsequent imposed absence are compounded by the fact that in many cases the father is already missing from the home.

NOTES AND REFERENCES

1. Schreiber, Flora Rheta: "I was Raising a Homosexual Child." *Cosmopolitan* 154:60–65, No. 1, Jan, 1963.
2. Pannor, Reuben; Evans, Byron W.; and Massarik, Fred: *The Unmarried Father*. New York: National Council on Illegitimacy, 1965; also, Hansen, Barbara: "The Unwed Father." *Cosmopolitan* 154:68–73, No. 5, May, 1963.

Our Son was Different

LESTER DAVID

One dismal winter morning two years ago, Bess Alberton went to her son's closet to see whether any of his clothing needed cleaning or pressing. As she took his dark-blue suit from its hanger and swiftly ran through the pockets to remove the usual accumulation of odds and ends, a few scribbled words on a folded card caught her eye. As she read them, a cold fear took hold of her.

Bess couldn't bring herself to acknowledge, even to herself, what the words revealed. The school psychologist to whom she rushed that very morning said it for her.

He told her she had to face the possibility that her son Jed, nearly seventeen and a brilliant high school junior, might already be a homosexual.

Bess, who usually took pride in looking well-groomed at all times, had run from the house with an old driving coat flung over her housedress, her blonde hair barely combed. At 38, she still had a lovely figure and a soft, delicately rounded, pretty face. But now the face was filled with pain. At the psychologist's words, she winced as though struck a physical blow. Fighting a mounting dizziness, she pressed one hand against both eyes, and with the other gripped the chair arm until the knuckles perceptibly whitened.

The disclosure—which almost always comes suddenly—that a son or daughter has become a sexual deviate is a family calamity that can hardly be measured. It brings to most households the same desolate feeling of loss as a child's death.

After years of being swept under the rug, as venereal disease was two generations ago, the subject of homosexuality at last is being brought out into the open for full and frank discussion. Families, who are most intimately concerned with its catastrophic human effects, now can take a clear look at the extent of the problem, its consequences, causes, prevention and possible cure.

From *Good Housekeeping* 162:51, No. 1, Jan. 1966. Reprinted by permission of the author.

Of all the facts coming to light, two tower above the others:

First, the tragedy that struck the Alberton home cannot be viewed as a minor or isolated phenomenon. The deeply troubling truth is that male homosexuality is one of the most serious problems confronting our society at the present time and a direct menace to impressionable and emotionally unsure young boys.

Second, homosexuality is an illness that can be successfully treated. If caught in its early stages, it can be prevented entirely. So states the 40-member committee on public health of the New York Academy of Medicine, in a recent precedent-breaking report. The committee's findings, which followed an intensive investigation, shatter a widespread belief held by many persons, including many doctors, that homosexuality is incurable.

How widespread is the problem? Dr. Wardell B. Pomeroy, former director of field research for the famous Kinsey sex studies at the University of Indiana and a leading authority on the subject of homosexuality, reports that many thousands of American families learn each year—as the Albertons did—that a young son is veering toward or has already begun a life of sexual inversion.

While no accurate count is possible, medical and scientific experts variously estimate that from 1,250,000 to 6,000,000 adult American males— *or from two to ten percent*—are exclusively homosexual. Nobody can say for certain whether the number of homosexuals is actually growing. But the New York Academy of Medicine declares in its report that "there is an impression that at the present time the practice is increasing among the population at large."

The consequences of being homosexual in a world that does not accept your emotional and physical drives can be devastating. Dr. O. Spurgeon English, professor of psychiatry at Temple University Medical School, points out that only a minority of homosexuals lead constructive lives and contribute to society.

"When people are homosexual," he writes, "there is a tendency for them to be immature in their reactions, easily depressed and discouraged, frequently frustrated and with a tendency to involve themselves in love affairs with their own sex which often end in jealousy, disappointment, frustration, depression and quite frequently suicide."

The social and economic effects are spelled out as follows by Dr. Pomeroy, and by Dr. Robert D. Weitz, chairman of the subcommittee on youth guidance councils for the New Jersey Youth Commission:

The homosexual chooses a way of life that shuts out marriage and the creation of a family. He is forced to live a guilt-ridden double life, hiding his secret lest he be exposed and disgraced. He cannot get a U.S. civil service job. Every day of his life he faces the possibility of arrest (in all states but

Illinois, homosexuality is a crime). He exposes himself to blackmail. When he grows older and can no longer attract men, he lives a pitiful existence, scorned by younger males and forced to pay for the company he wishes.

Bess Alberton knew some of this and sensed the rest, and that is why she sat horror-struck in the school psychologist's office that Monday morning, hardly able to give him a coherent account of the events leading up to her finding of the note.

On the previous Friday, Jed had gone to the junior class dinner-dance, a 30-year tradition at Logan High that marks the end of the basketball season. He and a friend, Russ Thomass, had taken the Everett girls, sixteen-year-old cousins who lived on the next block. Jed rarely went to dances, Bess explained —"after all, he's not yet seventeen and very shy when it comes to girls. But everyone goes to this affair, so he went too."

"Jed got home—oh, maybe a little after midnight, and went right to sleep. I always stay up until I know he's home. This morning, after he went to school, I found this."

Bess handed over a folded dinner-menu, upon which three messages were scrawled in pencil. The first, in Jed's writing, read: "Russ dear—this is cruddy. Let's go to the car. 9 o'clock when the dancing starts." A suggestive sentence followed.

Beneath, in another handwriting, was Russ's acceptance and the question: "But what will we do with the girls?"

The third message: "Who cares? I'll tell them I'm sick."

The psychologist questioned Bess closely about Jed, then spoke gently. But his words were hammerblows.

"We cannot hide from the truth," he said. "We must suspect that your son and this boy are having a homosexual relationship. Please understand that we need to know a great deal more—what kind of relationship this is, how long it has been continuing, how intensely Jed is involved. Perhaps it may turn out to be experimentation, a phase that may soon end. But it is urgent that we find out."

Bess Alberton sat for a long time, one hand over her eyes, then abruptly rose and left the room. She doesn't remember how she reached home or whether she cried when she got there. She only recalls sitting alone in the house until midafternoon, when her husband telephoned. She told him to come home at once.

At the school psychologist's suggestion, the Albertons lost no time taking Jed to a psychotherapist, who confirmed their agonizing fears. Jed, in truth, was different. He was not merely experimenting but already preferred to obtain emotional and physical satisfaction from members of his own sex. The deviation, though in its early stages, was nonetheless clearly marked.

What went wrong? Was Jed "born that way"? Did his glands develop defectively? Did he fall under someone's evil influence? Was it something else?

A recent study, which took nine years to complete, by a special research committee of the Society of Medical Psychoanalysts is regarded as a milestone in research on the problem. It answers these and other questions. According to the ten scientists who conducted the study, there is no clear-cut evidence that heredity plays a part. Other studies have found that physical characteristics such as slightness of build and effeminate appearance, are not to blame either. Neither are "bad glands."

The psychoanalyst's investigation, which probed intensively into the lives of 106 homosexuals and 100 normal males, provides further evidence that *faulty parent-child relationships in the very early, very crucial years of a boy's life are the main causes of homosexuality.*

What, specifically, are these emotion-warping forces that can so twist a boy? They can differ widely with different sets of circumstances. To find the answers in Jed's case, let us look searchingly at the Albertons, man and wife, and the way they raised their son.

It is entirely possible that another boy, subjected to the same stresses as Jed Alberton, would have developed normally. Why this is so is a puzzle to experts in human behavior. For this reason, the Albertons' tragedy must be regarded primarily as one individual story of a family in crisis. At the same time, what happened in this household should not be ignored, because similar patterns of family behavior show up over and over again in case studies of male homosexuals.

The Alberton family consists of Bess and her husband Jack, a 43-year-old owner of a small wholesale electrical-fixture business, their son Jed and two younger daughters, Clarice and Jane, who are eleven and eight. Jed is a tall, slender boy with blond hair exactly like his mother's and a sprinkling of freckles around his nose. He has a shy, enormously appealing grin.

The family lives in a two-story attached brick house, one of a row of 18 identical homes built 15 years ago on the edge of a small city in a northeastern state. By this time, their owners have made enough additions and changes and planted enough shrubs and trees on the tiny plots to remove the once-uniform look.

It is a good home, run well and conscientiously by Bess Alberton. The children are well dressed and well fed. The small rooms are tastefully furnished and have an artistic flair about them. Bess points with pride to four needlepoint sofa cushions she made herself.

The Albertons are decent people who never knowingly broke the law and who wanted, in Bess's words, "only the best" for their children. Nonetheless, the seeds of catastrophe were sown in this pleasant little house, among all these good intentions, and they were planted by Bess Alberton and her husband Jack.

For Bess, unaware of what she was doing, feminized her son almost from the beginning. She discouraged him from becoming interested and involved in masculine things and at the same time bound him so closely to her that he was unable to become emotionally interested in other females.

And Jack was not father enough to prevent this sad twisting of his son. Weak and passive in his home, dominated by his wife, he set no strong masculine example for the boy to follow. And so Jed could build no respect for him, no wish to grow up to be like him and to do the things he did.

The causes of male homosexuality are many, deep and complex, and authorities do not always agree on the factors that may bring it about. However, this combination of excessively possessive, overprotective mother and detached, indifferent father is often to blame. Dr. Irving Bieber, the psychiatrist who directed the Society of Medical Psychoanalysts' investigation, reports that *these two factors were present in the lives of most of the homosexuals studied.*

What happened in the Alberton household?

Bess was an only child who had been left alone for long periods by her mother, a busy interior decorator. Actually, she was an unplanned, unwanted child, who came along at a time when her mother's career was at full height. Bess made a vow to herself that, when she became a mother, she would give her child all the attention and love she herself had yearned for.

And so, from infancy, Jed Alberton became the most important thing in his mother's life. Bess took over his care, feeding and management completely, never once permitting her husband to diaper or feed him. "Oh, what do you know about babies," she'd tell Jack as she bustled past him. "They need a mother's touch." Alberton, business on his mind, would shrug and turn away.

When he was fourteen months old, Jed developed a mild form of celiac disease, an inability to digest starchy foods, which calls for a strict diet. Terrified that he might be given cookies or other foods he should not have, Bess kept him with her constantly. She never allowed him to have playmates—she was his playmate. She invented games, talked to him by the hour and took him everywhere with her, long after the illness ended.

Bess watched carefully over Jed even after her second child, Clarice, was born. At six, the boy wasn't allowed to have roller skates ("Oh Lord, he'll split his head!") or a tricycle ("I'd be petrified every second").

She had read it was important to make an older child feel useful and wanted after the arrival of a new baby, so she gave Jed chores to perform. It is a sound idea, of course, moderately practiced. But at the age of six, when most boys are active in outdoor play, Jed Alberton spent nearly all his time happily helping his mother powder the baby, prepare her bath, fold and count the diapers and attach the jungle gym on the crib.

What was Bess actually doing by tying Jed so closely to her?

Most authorities agree that, fundamentally, homosexuality is a result of an inability to mature sexually. As a boy grows, he passes through various stages of physical and emotional development. One of these involves a strong attraction to other boys. The normal boy soon moves forward from this stage and winds up attracted in a healthy way to the opposite sex. By feminizing Jed, by crushing his natural impulses to act and feel like a boy, Bess was setting into motion forces that would thwart this normal flowering of his emotions.

Discouraged from normal childhood activities, Jed never could develop much interest or ability in sports and outdoor fun. Except when he was with his mother, he spent his growing-up years as a loner, occasionally taunted by other boys for being a "sissy," largely ignored by them.

Once, when he was in the seventh grade, his gym class was taught rope-climbing. Everyone but Jed climbed at least halfway. The teacher, young and inexperienced, had Jed try over and over, but the boy couldn't move upward. The teacher folded his arms and, as the class watched and giggled, grimly announced: "We're going to stand here and watch you all period long, if we must, until you learn to climb." Jed tried for 15 minutes, finally falling in exhaustion as the teacher turned away in disgust. "All the other boys can climb a rope but you can't," the incident taught Jed, "so you're not a real boy. Don't try to be like them. You aren't like them or as good as they are."

Afterward, Jed began to hate all forms of athletics and competition. He moved even closer to his mother, absorbing her interests in antique bric-a-brac and developing a fascination for fabrics and fabric design. Mother and son spent many weekend afternoons in antique shops, museums and drapery establishments. Jed looked forward to these trips as other boys would to fishing expeditions or Little League games.

Occasionally, Jack remonstrated with his wife. "For heaven's sake," he said, "stop making a sissy out of the kid." Bess would merely become furious and refuse to speak to her husband for days.

At his father's insistence, Jed joined a cub scout pack—but quit several months later on the day of a scheduled five-mile hike to a "haunted house." "Mother," he said indignantly, "would *you* walk five whole miles just to see a haunted house?" The question clearly showed that Jed was modeling his behavior on his mother's, not his father's. ("Mother wouldn't hike, so why should I?")

There were other aspects to Bess's deepening closeness with her son that played key parts in the boy's sexual maladjustment.

For one thing, Bess downgraded girls in Jed's mind, planting the conviction that they were silly, unreliable, conniving. Jed did make several dates with girls he met at the beach the summer he became sixteen, but Bess found fault with them all. One had "absolutely dreadful" taste in clothes, another was "too stupid for words" and a third, daughter of a handyman, was not in his social class. As a result, Jed was not given a chance to develop a normal interest in girls. Dr. English points out that in many homosexuals, "interest in the opposite sex has been shamed and discouraged."

Secondly, as Jed grew older, Bess Alberton's attachment to him began taking on seductive overtones. She would run her fingers through his hair, address him endearingly, ask his opinion on her clothes, even talk over some of her personal problems with him. The homosexual study reports that most mothers of inverts were "explicitly seductive, and even when they were not, the closeness of the bond with the son appeared to be in itself sexually provocative."

Needless to say, this attitude was entirely unconscious on Bess's part, but it had a damaging result. The shame and guilt Jed felt at emotions he could not understand caused the boy to be terrified of his sex reactions. Thus was created still another barrier that blocked his progress toward normal sexual development.

Doctors report that mothers of homosexuals sometimes act in a variety of other unhealthy ways that interfere with normal masculine development. Disappointed at having sons instead of daughters, they actually dress their boys like girls in childhood; they make confidantes of them, divulging highly personal matters, even "intimate details of marital sexual relationship"; they allow them into their beds, dress and undress in front of them, fondle them sensuously, bathe them long after they can bathe themselves. All these actions tend to feminize and sexually overstimulate boys.

Such, then, were the main influences that helped push Jed into a life of sexual maladjustment. But what about Jed's father? Jack Alberton, by himself, could have neutralized his wife's influence and stopped his son's drift toward homosexuality. Declares Dr. Bieber: *"Given a warm, positive, affectionate, constructive relationship of father to son, a homosexual will not develop in a family no matter how the mother acts or what she does."*

But Jack Alberton failed, too.

From the start, he never insisted upon his right to share in the rearing of his son. Rarely did he spend time with Jed to show the boy he liked him and enjoyed being with him. He never took a walk in the woods with him. He never kicked a football around with him. He never took him fishing, and only twice in his life went with him to an amusement area. He played checkers with him a few times but got bored and stopped. Once he asked if the boy would like to come down to his place of business on a Saturday, but Bess vetoed the idea—"it's too dirty there and he wouldn't be interested"—and he never again broached it.

Psychiatrists explain that a father needn't be a rugged, outdoors type or a star athlete in order to exert a strong, positive, masculine influence on his son. Far more important is his warm acceptance of the boy, coupled with firm discipline.

Writes Dr. Phillip Polatin, associate professor of clinical psychiatry at the College of Physicians and Surgeons, Columbia University: "A weak or passive father whose word counts for nothing in the home or an indifferent father who does not bother to make himself count is difficult if not impossible for a boy to respect and want to emulate."

Add up all these pressures—Jed's feminization, the fears that he was not like other boys, the contempt he was taught to hold for girls, the lack of a male example to follow. *They were powerful enough to prevent his sex desires from maturing normally. These remained fixed at the preadolescent level—the level at which boys are attracted to other boys.* This is the so-called latency period which starts about the age of five and extends to the time puberty begins.

And so Jed entered his sixteenth year desperately lonely, excessively shy and burdened heavily with the guilt of strange feelings that stirred within him. He recalls that time in his life without pain now, but what he says plainly reveals the agony he felt then:

"You know what it means to be lonely in this kind of a setup?" he asks. "If you're not in the crowd, you're just *nothing*. You say to yourself you couldn't care less, but you care. The other kids go around calling you a fink and you see they're having a ball, you care all right."

"Like I say, you're lonely and you feel like an oddball. You're all tensed up inside, most of the time. Then you get this feeling in your mind that you're a different kind of kid and this gets you more tensed up, especially since you're not sure what it is. So one day you meet up with a kid and you know right away he feels like you do."

The feeling can be summed up this way: Jed, and doubtless Russ too, were riddled by fears. They feared they were failures among boys their age, who held them in contempt. They feared girls could not possibly like them. They feared they were incapable of coping with the increasing problems of adolescence. Dr. Bieber points out that these fears, present in boys like Jed and Russ, "pave the way for the prehomosexual's initiation into the less threatening atmosphere of homosexual society, its values and way of life."

Jed had known Russ Thomass for several years, but the boys did not become friendly until just before Thanksgiving, in their junior year. Russ had a completely equipped ham-radio outfit, and the two boys spent hours together, sending and receiving messages. The incident at the dinner-dance, when the fateful notes were written, was the third time the boys had engaged in homosexual acts.

The days following the discovery of the notes are a blur in Bess's memory. "I was in a state of shock, I suppose," she says. "Then, when the numbness went away, I started to get wild thoughts. I wanted to pack a bag and run away, anywhere, just to hide. But thank God my husband calmed me down. He was the sensible one, and all along I thought I was."

It was true. Once Jack Alberton realized that his family was in crisis, he found the strength to take control. He called a doctor, who gave Bess a sedative and, next day, he spoke quietly to her about their responsibilities to their other children and to Jed. "He needs help," he told Bess, "and we'll see that he gets it. It will be expensive, but we'll find the money some way. We would if it meant saving his life, wouldn't we?"

Jed was young and wanted to be helped, and this counted a great deal. The New York Academy of Medicine report states that although treatment is difficult, it can be successful and effective, depending upon how deeply the perversion is entrenched and the strength of the patient's desire to modify it.

For two years, Jed was under a psychotherapist's care. Those years must be telescoped in this account, but they were not easy ones for Jed. He had to discover many things about himself and his parents that were hard to face. Had he not been so desperately anxious to find a way out of his unhappiness, he might not have found the strength to continue. But he did, and gradually he came to understand the forces that had acted slowly and subtly upon him. He began to see himself, his mother, girls and the entire world of men and women in a new and totally different way. He discovered that he was not a weak, worthless "finky kid" at all, but a person with qualities of his own that were admirable and of which he could be proud.

Jed never knew when the change came about, but it did. He kept growing in inner strength, and as he began to look upon himself as a boy growing into manhood, the sickness started to lose its grip.

The Albertons played key roles in their son's emotional changeover. For the boy's mother, the ordeal involved was especially severe because she was forced to face a number of harsh truths about herself. After two years, her face shows signs of the terrible strain she underwent. It is sharp-featured, and there are dark circles under her green eyes; she has also developed a mild but noticeable twitch in her left eye, a nervous tic the doctor says will disappear in time. Under professional guidance, Bess came to understand what had happened and most importantly *why* it happened, and now she can say: "I can't believe I was once so blind. I wouldn't blame Jed if he hated me the rest of his life."

At first, Bess found it impossible to realize that her love for her child could have helped create the damage it did. Once, early in her own consultations, she cried out to her doctor: "But this is stupid, what you're trying to have me believe! How can you love your own baby too much?" She sobbed hysterically for ten minutes and was unable to continue that day. But Bess was to discover that the wrong kind of love can indeed hurt; that possessive love, arising from unhealthy causes, can be destructive.

Sipping coffee in her sun-splashed kitchen, Bess recalls: "When I understood at last, I had to fight to cure myself. You know, I felt like an addict of some kind, struggling to free himself from something—and when I explained this to my doctor he said that was exactly the kind of experience I was going through. You know, withdrawing. I had to fight with myself to stop smothering and coddling my son.

"I can't count the times I wanted to run to him and comfort him when I knew he was having a hard time. Once I heard him crying in his room. I couldn't stop myself; I burst in and tried to hug him and say everything would be all right. But he pushed me away and screamed at me to get out. I never did that again."

Although there were times when Bess failed, she succeeded more often. As the months went on, she was able to master her own emotions and to convey to her son the thing he most wanted to know—that she had confidence in his own ability to help himself.

Jack Alberton, too, helped his son. As Bess moved away from Jed, the natural thing happened—she moved closer to her husband. Thus Jack began to assume his rightful place in the family, as a real father to his son and his two daughters.

Jack was not an athlete nor was he adept at any hobby. But he didn't need to be in order to establish true father-son and father-daughter relationships. He was a man and had much to give Jed in the form of experience and advice. He began spending much more time with his son, talking to him, telling him stories about his early life, asking about the boy's own interests. Father and son discovered after a while that they were both nice people, interesting people. Jed found, somewhat to his surprise, that he had a good new friend to whom he could talk on a man-to-man basis.

Jed had shown no interest in cars, but suddenly, shortly after he reached his seventeenth birthday, he wanted to learn to drive. Jack, an expert at the wheel, took his son out on weekends and showed him how. "He was wonderfully patient," Jed says. "Other boys say their dads either refuse to teach them to drive or growl and even swear at them. We used to go out to some country road and keep at it. Later, we'd have lunch in some quiet place and talk. We'd gab about my future—you know, college and what I'd like to study and all. I got to like my dad."

The last sentence was a tremendous statement. It meant that Jack Alberton had arrived as a father and was helping his son become a man.

Today, two years after the shock of Bess Alberton's discovery, Jed is away at the state university, holder of a full four-year scholarship. He has a small circle of friends, as brilliant and artistic as he. He has been discharged from treatment but still sees his therapist once in a while for talks. There is the possibility that, under unusual stress, Jed may yet move backward, but the doctor does not believe it will happen.

The Alberton house now buzzes with the chatter of two growing girls and their friends. A happier and emotionally healthier family lives there now. It has a real father at its head and it has a mother who has learned a great lesson: That mothers can love their sons deeply and show affection in countless ways, but at the same time they must avoid doing the things that can destroy their masculinity.

Sadly, the shadow that has moved away from the Albertons can descend on other homes. The causes may be quite different from those operating in Jed's case. Psychiatrists emphasize that a variety of neurotic conflicts, rooted deeply in a boy's background, can prevent him from walking across the emotional bridge into manhood. As one authority has stated, "There are many routes to homosexuality."

A boy, for example, may develop manly traits such as great proficiency in athletics and yet be so paralyzed by fears that he is unable to make a normal sexual adjustment. It is a mistake to believe that all homosexuals are effeminate in action or appearance. Many normal men have some feminine ways about them, while some virile-looking and acting males are practicing homosexuals.

Experts stress that there are many gradations of homosexuality. The New York Academy of Medicine report states that some men are bisexual, engaging in both kinds of sexual activity, while in the exclusively homosexual there are dominant and latent types. Moreover, homosexuality occurs with varying degrees of intensity "from the confirmed inveterate to the more lightly affected."

Authorities point out that if the problem does arise, parents should seek professional help quickly: The earlier treatment is started, the more successful it will be. Advice should be sought from a physician, clergyman or qualified psychologist. The school guidance counselor or psychologist can suggest places to go, which may include a local mental health clinic or family service agency.

And Jed Alberton? Recently he wrote a letter home from college that read in part: "I hope you won't mind, but Janice, the girl I'm going with, has asked Ed, Bill and me to her house for Easter. It's O.K.—her folks will be there and a few of the girls from her sorority. It means I won't be home, but I love you all anyway. . . ."

Bess handed the letter to Jack. They both laughed until the happy tears came.

Not a Case History, Not a Statistic: Our Daughter

JUDITH MARCH

As Maria lay in the hospital bed, in the far sleep of anesthesia, barely stirring, safely rescued from a pregnancy nobody could tolerate, she was someone I hardly knew—all warmth, all animal spirits drained beneath a white, white skin. She stirred with a small moan, the first sign that misery was filling the vacuum of postoperative non-being.

Dan, my husband, sat with his chin on his fist, more anxious than contemplative—because he is an easy prey to anxiety and because this child was the quicksilver in the graying areas of his subsurface, middle-aged emotions. She was a child who sang as part of her breathing, who tossed her impulses about as carelessly, yet as artfully, as her great length of chestnut silk hair.

I sat quietly, aware of the ergotrate dropping slowly through the intravenous equipment, down through Maria's arm, which was held rigid on a board, her palm open and vulnerable.

I was still wondering, futilely, if I could have held her back from her physical relationship with Jeff. From becoming pregnant. Even as a young child, Maria had never been willing to learn through precept, only through experience—no matter what the danger, no matter what anger or punishment could follow. How did she feel now? How could I know—unless she confided in me? Would I ever see it as she did, for all my mother antennae and woman's memory of my own youth?

Maria at seventeen gives a strong impression of beauty. Her looks are a compound of vitality, radiance, humor, appetite, sexuality—in short, of life and youth. She can be soft and beguiling, all five-feet-eight of her; or hoydenish and ungainly, like an animal in too small a space. She is nature's child: attuned to the morning sun and the full moon, to insects, fish and all things living. She shares her room with a Dalmatian, a Siamese cat, goldfish

From *McCalls* 94:76, No. 11, Aug. 1967. Reprinted by permission of Curtis Brown Ltd. Copyright © 1967 by the McCall Publishing Company.

and two white mice in a cage. She'd keep a horse if she could. She did not develop into a student. But we consoled ourselves: one can't have everything. We were delighted—sometimes snowed—by her charm, her pleasing looks; much less enthralled with her disposition, which ranged from infectious high humor to infuriating ill-temper. I must smile wryly as I recall that a few months before Dan and I were complimenting ourselves that we still had the upper hand.

When Maria reached high school, we were stricter than other families about hours, cars and boys, because of our knowledge that she was headstrong, not willing to accept the simplest "no" without countering; not easily constrained from acting out her wishes—and being "sorry" afterward.

It is understandable, I think, if a parent sees a child as special rather than typical. To both Dan and me, Maria was especially fascinating. By sixteen, she had grown into her final coat of personality, always on the edge of a strong emotion, whether it was compassion for the retarded child down the street, anger at a social injustice that had momentarily caught her attention or an explosive pleasure in being alive, which she would express by hugging the person or animal nearest her. Dan and I were only too conscious that this feelingful child would not be held back, would not hold herself back from sexual experience for long—not in today's setting of provocation and non-prohibition.

We were not the only ones who saw the problem. Our family doctor—no staid, fatherly prototype, but a handsome man in his early fifties with a nice appreciation for women—told me one day: "Maria's grown into a charming young woman. If she were mine, I'd have a talk and give her contraceptives."

As the mother in this matter, I played Hamlet. I could not resolve the question. I was hung up between the totally rational view, which says: "For the new mores, give the new pill," and the deep wells of constraint, within which I had guarded my own impulses and now sought to guard Maria's. I could not look on sex as a casual, mechanistic act. I hoped only to set up fences Maria might break down—at the right time. Contraception, finally, was a go-ahead I could not, did not give her. My deep instincts won out, for once. But not so much in a clear-cut victory as a long, dull draw.

As I look back, it was not *this* decision that brought us to the morning in Maria's hospital room; it was the many decisions made long before and the non-decisions in the critical time after Jeff arrived.

It all began like the usual teen-age romance, and it was some time before I realized that Jeff was no longer just "a" boy. When he first arrived, I was fully occupied in battling the sick onset of hepatitis, the bleak February snowstorms and the arrival of a new Siamese kitten (Maria's, naturally). Only later did I notice that Jeff, whose family lived in our neighborhood, was coming home from college weekend after weekend—to our house.

Maria and Jeff were shiningly new with each other—she entranced with the attention of an "older" man, and he intrigued with the fun and volcanic life-force he had suddenly encountered.

Our privacy at home was much curtailed. Jeff was on the phone, at the door, honking in the driveway. I could be caught in my own kitchen at unexpected hours of the morning or night, my hair up and my guard down. He was underfoot with the persistence and appeal of an eager young puppy. Maria was never ready when he arrived, so while he waited, he would join me in the kitchen or in the den. He talked about sports, weather and small things, but more about life at the fraternity, which seemed to center on drinking.

We sometimes invited him for Sunday supper. But when he was back in school, we still had him at the table by proxy—"Jeff says . . . ," "Jeff thinks . . . ," "Jeff went . . ." became the replacement for Maria's former conversation. At times, she seemed indifferent to my opinion of Jeff; at others, anxious for my approval: "He's nice, isn't he?" "You do like him, don't you?"

My attitude, only half formed, was one of surprise, not objection. Maria, who could be equally fired by civil rights, folk music, Beethoven and the entire race of boys, who preferred blue jeans to any dress, had chosen a boy who wore shoes and jackets, who cut his hair regularly and who didn't know SNCC from a snack. To me, Jeff was one more humbling lesson in what every mother does not know about her own child. Dan was glad; he thought Jeff was "safer" than boys with the new look.

Soon after meeting Maria, Jeff dropped out of college. He was within blocks of our house; he had a car, a job and parents who exercised no demands, exacted no disciplines. We held the line on "weekends only" for dating and on Maria's keeping sensible hours.

Jeff didn't change our life so much as join it. In the process of going out together, he and Maria did an amazing amount of staying home. I began to take it as a matter of course that I'd find them lounging in the den on a Sunday afternoon along with Dan. Jeff was at home with us. He'd walk the dog at night or drive the Sunday-school car pool with great willingness. But he would not wash a plate, even for Maria, or think of clearing away the apple cores and ashtrays he accumulated around himself. As time went on, I found myself scolding him as though he were our child. In truth, he was our a priori son-in-law.

He and Maria settled down as a steady thing, without any announcement, but with a clear understanding between themselves. Maria would wear Jeff's sweaters, his jackets, his signet ring. She would not go out with other boys—"There's no one else I like." There was an openness in their relationship that many of us do not achieve after years of marriage. No small pretenses and defenses. No locked-up feelings. No holding back of opinions—or demands.

"They're sweet," said the waitress in the coffee shop where they often went for hamburgers and Cokes. "They're adorable together," said Jeff's mother on the telephone. And as I watched them walk down the front path together, take each other's hands, I had to admit the appeal of their youngness, their self-discovery. But there were elements that troubled me: They were not only confiding in and learning about each other, they were leaning and building on each other, putting into the relationship all the weight and ceremony of a first year of marriage. Wasn't this too early? Too serious? A shadow play without foundations?

On Sundays, Maria would often cook a steak supper. She would serve Jeff the choicest, largest portion; he, in turn, would compliment her on the cooking. They're playing house, I thought. While it looked sentimentally appealing, I knew it was dynamite. It was child's play in which neither one expected, or was prepared, to take on the more boring, burdensome aspects of responsibility—be it familial, economic or sexual.

In this setting, sex could simply become one more aspect of playing house. Where could such closeness go—except to bed? Yet I could not make myself project forward to a physical relationship and possibly pregnancy, let alone to abortion and that eventual room in the hospital. The life style of the young, I reminded myself, had changed since my day.

I could not, did not meet head on with Maria about sex with Jeff. I would have been embarrassed and confused. I was not the mother of a child but of half a child, half a woman; and mother-in-law, before the fact, to a boy-man, sometimes nineteen going on nine. I relied on *understood* standards. I was not permissive, but somehow I permitted what I feared by default.

We felt secure in saying to Maria, at seventeen, that she *must* do her homework, *must* be in at twelve-thirty on a weekend, *must* do her share in the house. But we could not, with sense or sensitivity, order her to end an ostensibly harmless relationship. We had to allow for choice—even when it did not dovetail with our own. We could only hope that she would outgrow it or grow up in it without the heartbreak and scars of a too-early marriage.

During our annual family holiday at the shore, I could hardly look on Jeff as a passing phase. We had no sooner unpacked the bedclothes and the groceries than Jeff arrived—by arrangement with Maria. He took a room nearby only because I said no, he could *not* bring his sleeping bag and use the floor of our living room. But at nine in the morning, he'd arrive, and Maria would serve him fresh orange juice, bacon and eggs, toast and coffee. At midnight, he was still on hand. He integrated into the family scene: helped with the shopping and the driving, took part in Maria's tangles with her sister, Toby, and was polite to Grandma. Before I could catch myself, we were One Happy Family.

What I saw of Jeff and Maria at close range in that two-week period did not put me at ease. The dependency no longer struck me as appealing. Jeff could not let Maria out of his sight. Maria, who always had a deep need for private time, was never alone. I suspect that the many small frictions between *us* at the shore were her escape valve: reaction to loss of privacy. Maria began showing traits we had fought doggedly against for years: she would become short-tempered, unreasonable, downright nasty with Jeff. But in quick compensation, she would turn to him with love, bacon and eggs or an enthusiastic plan for the day.

Jeff was undoubtedly better-natured than Maria, yet at times I wanted to shake him, to make him stand up for his rights. But he'd tell me, "You don't understand, Mrs. March. I know she doesn't *mean* it," and Maria would say, "You don't understand, Mom. We're not like this when we're alone."

The "alone" was preying on me in unavoidable, insinuating fashion. Jeff and Maria would go down to the beach and spread a blanket far from the rest of us—but not far enough to blot out the sight of their physical closeness, their bodily ease with each other. I had to look the other way.

Then something snapped. Suddenly I found the situation had become totally untenable. I did not know where to turn in my frenzied worry. Dan had been called back to town on business. But even at home he could display a maddeningly detached attitude toward the problem. There were times when his masculine approach leavened my more emotional responses; but at other times, I *knew* he was not facing the possibilities of the situation.

I vacillated, characteristically, between taking Maria and Jeff's visible conduct as a sign that this was the full extent of their physical relationship and the conclusion that they had consummated their togetherness.

The sex aspect was disturbing, but secondary. My overriding fear was that they might run off and get married. Within only a few months, both would have the legal right to sign their names in a marriage registry. Soon Jeff would come into a small legacy from his grandfather, which must have looked to him like security.

I had one oblique talk with Maria while we were still at the seashore. I asked her to walk with me along the hard-packed sand at the water's edge. With my eyes more on my feet than on her face, I told her I thought their public display of affection was tasteless. I had never tried to create an aura of intimacy between us in sexual matters. She never came to me with questions. I assumed that any child who knew so much about animals, who read Indian love poetry, Harold Robbins and Henry Miller with equal interest must know the sexual facts.

I skipped Biology One. I did not ask her if she was having sexual relations with Jeff. I did not expect her to tell me. But I felt no confusion or constraint in telling her that the association with Jeff was not good for her; that Jeff was immature and that, in a marriage, she would very soon chafe at his dependency; his boyish charm would not wear well. Only at this point did Maria speak up: "Don't you think I know all that?" But she must have repeated every word to Jeff. The term "public affection" became a light joke. The humor insulated us, kept us safe with one another. But it did not stave off the outcome.

I was glad to have school start again and the rule of weekends only invoked once more. Even back in the autumn schedule, however, the more they went together the more freedom they assumed. It grew impossible to know where they were at all times, and it was niggling and uncomfortable for me to ask their whereabouts. They'd go off on a Sunday afternoon—"downtown," "over to the duck pond," "to Jeff's house." Jeff's parents made a fuss over Maria. They'd invite her to informal Sunday-evening suppers. "Too bad they're not five years older," commented Jeff's mother. I kept my opinion to myself.

I was equally guarded with my friends and would smile when they asked, "Is Maria still going with Jeff?" I even managed an unperturbed exterior when a busybody on Jeff's street asked, "Isn't that your daughter I see so much at Jeff Kohler's house? I saw her there just yesterday."

Yesterday, they'd said they'd been bowling. It had to mean what I suspected: that Jeff and Maria were often at the Kohler house when his parents were not home—in outright violation of one of our strictest, oft-stated rules. I could not be a policeman if I wanted to. How could I accuse? How could I handle what was not out in the open?

But as I look back, the signals were clear. Maria was in foul humor; she would snap at any of us, would sit morosely at the dinner table, would hardly respond when spoken to. I would find her in front of the television set after school, although it was agreed-upon homework time. She seemed to be talking more than ever on the telephone. Then I began to find her asleep after school. She'd always been such a hypochondriac that I did not pay attention to her "tiredness" until it became impossible to ignore. I set up, almost as a routine, an appointment with the family doctor for a checkup. Maria protested with a vehemence that aroused my fears.

The next afternoon, Bessie—who's been "doing" our house on Wednesday for years—said, "Something wrong with Maria, Mrs. March. I think it's serious trouble. I'd talk to her if I were you."

My stomach turned over. I was sick with dread. I realized that Bessie was trying to be helpful without violating the confidence Maria had placed in her. I did not press Bessie further.

When Dan came home, I called him aside.

"I'll ask Maria," he said, with masculine directness.

"Absolutely not," Maria told him. "I'm not pregnant."

The reassurance lasted ten minutes. It might have lasted a few days, even a week, if our younger daughter had not come into my room. She'd heard the quarreling over going to the doctor—as Toby always seemed to hear everything. "I don't know whether I should tell you," she began hesitantly, "but I think I know what's wrong with Maria. I heard her talking to Mrs. Dunnock. Maria's pregnant."

Mrs. Dunnock! A woman I hardly knew, but whose name will always be inseparable from that night and from the aura of uneasiness and uncertainty that still remains. Mrs. Dunnock was a school counselor in our community, avowedly prejudiced in favor of children—a friend to every sensitive, rebellious child with a problem. She had known Jeff and his family for many years. She had recently met and taken a fancy to Maria. It was not the important matter at that moment, but I felt a twinge. Mrs. Dunnock knew. We did not.

"Call Mrs. Dunnock," said Dan, "and ask her."

Ask if *our daughter* was pregnant! I was aware of my pride, even while I knew it was inappropriate to have pride in these circumstances. I felt and heard the pulses pounding in my body.

Mrs. Dunnock had something of Bessie's loyalty to Maria and to Jeff, as well. "Maria has a problem" was all she would say at first. She knew little of me as a parent. She was testing: "What would you do—if it *were* so?" I was being challenged to come up with the right answers, so that I might deserve to know the truth. I must have said what was expected of me. Frankly, I cannot remember. Mrs. Dunnock decided: "I'll call Maria and call you back."

It was insane. I could not go directly to my own child, talk to her—even accost her, if necessary. In the midst of these delicate negotiations, I had to put away my hurt that someone else was closer to my child than I was.

Maria came into my room. "I have to see Mrs. Dunnock for five minutes. May I take the car?" It was, under normal conditions, a wild time for visiting: ten o'clock on a Wednesday night. But nothing was normal. The house had the dread expectancy that comes with crisis or deathly illness. While we waited, Dan and I played a mindless game of backgammon. We had to focus, had to make small, nervous moves.

At eleven-thirty, Mrs. Dunnock telephoned. "Maria wants you to come over." She was speaking to me, not to Dan. "The kids want to tell you themselves."

Why me? Why not both of us? If I had been in possession of myself, I should never have agreed to go alone. It was frightening. And odd. We were both her parents, and we would act together, no matter what differing emotional signals we might give off in the process. But in the turmoil of that moment, I think I was so relieved to be included that I did not stop to take a stand.

I threw a coat over my pajamas and drove the few blocks to Mrs. Dunnock's with my hands rigid on the wheel. What was I to say? What was I to do? My own attitudes, training, reading were in a jumble.

Jeff opened the door for me, and as I started up the stairs to Mrs. Dunnock's study, he said to my back, "We have somthing to tell you. Maria is pregnant."

There it was.

I walked into the room, and there was Maria, beaten down, sitting slumped over her knees on a small couch, old and new tears mingling on her face. I found tears in my own eyes—the first—with relief at knowing what we had to know. I held her, more numbed and drained than warm and motherly.

"Oh, Mommy, I'm sorry. I'm sorry," said Maria, over and over.

I said repeatedly, equally compulsively, "We love you. You belong to us. We love you."

In truth, I had not a single small impulse to scold, moralize or say, "I told you so." We sat on the couch together, and Maria leaned on my shoulder. I held her hand tightly in one of mine; with the other, patted her on the back—she might have been a tearful two-year-old.

Jeff sat, stunned, in a chair across the room. Mrs. Dunnock hopped around like a solicitous bird. She offered me coffee, which I accepted, although a tranquilizer would have been more to the point. I wanted to be alone with Maria, to take her home, where she belonged. But they were talking. It was a review for my benefit—and their own. Jeff and Maria had apparently been going from one "doctor" to another, trying to make certain that Maria *was* pregnant, trying to arrange for an abortion. I thanked God that they had located neither the "doctor" nor the money for a back-room abortion. There was not, never had been, any question of having the baby— only of finding a way out.

No one mentioned marriage except Mrs. Dunnock: "They're very much in love, you know. They plan to get married one day." Maria, tucked into my arms, still said nothing but "I'm so sorry, Mommy." Mrs. Dunnock reassured her: "There are lots of kids like you and Jeff. We can't say it's wrong. We can't say that *any* communication between two people is wrong."

How could I, at that moment, if I had found my own thoughts and words, have taken a less generous attitude? No, it did not behoove me to debate the ethics or philosophy of the situation with Mrs. Dunnock that evening. It was to be months before I could know even part of the meaning for myself.

We now had the problem of what to do: Let the child be born—disrupt Maria's life for a life that was not wanted? Force them to marry? The implications of the first troubled me deeply. But as for the second, I would far rather that Maria have an abortion than enter into a marriage which, under more favorable auguries, would still be a bad bet. Dan and I were the grown-ups, with resources, but we did not know the way out any more than the children had.

The need for action called forth all Dan's adrenalin and reflexes. He thought systematically of the doctors among our acquaintances who might give us some guidance and came up with Dr. Bailey, an obstetrician who often lectured on sex education to young adults. Dan planned to see Dr. Bailey the following morning.

Meanwhile, Maria came up with an important fact learned from a girl friend: A *legal* abortion could be performed if one had a psychiatrist's letter advising it.

I called Dr. Asch, a woman psychiatrist who had seen Maria a few times during grade school when she'd been giving us a rough time. Yes, Dr. Asch told us, it was true; most hospitals require one or two consent letters from psychiatrists before permitting an abortion. Dr. Asch was instantly alerted to our problem and was willing to write such a letter once she talked to Maria.

Dan called to report that Dr. Bailey would perform the abortion if we had Dr. Asch's letter, but Maria would also have to see a psychiatrist on the hospital staff, whose approval—or disapproval—would be the final hurdle.

The following day, by appointment, Maria and I went to Dr. Bailey's office, which was filled with young women patients at every stage of pregnancy. There were a few middle-aged mother-types, to make me feel less conspicuous.

I was more nervous, more self-conscious than Maria. I turned the pages of a high-fashion magazine, seeing little. Maria sat quietly, her hands in repose, until Dr. Bailey called us in.

He addressed himself chiefly to Maria. "We are not here to make a moral judgment, but to help you, Maria. We are concerned with your well-being, your peace of mind." He turned to matters of fact: When did she have her last period? When did she think she might have conceived?

Maria did not blush, she did not hesitate for words. If she was embarrassed, she gave not one inkling.

"But first, let's be sure you *are* pregnant," Dr. Bailey said.

When he'd examined her, he was almost positive she was pregnant, but took the usual tests, to verify his judgment. With Christmas holidays coming in ten days, we thought it best for Maria to continue at school, to enter the hospital—if approval was forthcoming—on the last day of school and return after New Year's Day. "In the meanwhile, we want to make you as comfortable as possible," Dr. Bailey told Maria, as I would guess he tells every newly pregnant woman who goes to him.

In the intervening week, we did everything to support Maria. We did not avoid the subject at the dinner table. We talked about the plans with Maria. I handled the matter more casually, more offhandedly than I would have thought possible. I was still under the influence of Mrs. Dunnock and of Dan, who said, "Remember, we were young once. I think."

Maria, who can be astonishingly open as well as devious, said, "I never realized how much I wanted to stay in school until this happened. Maybe something good will come of it, after all!" Another time, she told me, "Well, at least I know I can have babies."

I allowed myself one pronouncement, out of deep feeling: "It's sad, darling, that your first pregnancy should have to end like this. It should be one of the thrilling moments of your life."

Maria listened. She said nothing. But sometimes as she was putting bread into the toaster or backing the car out of the driveway, she would turn to me. "You're wonderful, Mom! I love you so much!" I recognized relief. I recognized gratitude. Yet the cynic within me whispered that both are among our most ephemeral emotions.

We waited a long week for word from the hospital. During that time, Maria confessed, "I was beginning to think about having it!"

Finally, approval came. We could now pass the problem on to professional hands, much as Maria and Jeff had passed it on to us. For the time being, I said only, "We are doing everything we can to help you. There is one thing *you* must do. You must see Doctor Asch, the psychiatrist, when you come home from the hospital." Although I would not force her, for the moment, to come to honest terms with us, I could not let her escape coming to terms with herself. Whether it had been rebellion, hostility, impulse—or some of all three—*she* had to know it, even though we might never be clear. I took Maria's silence for agreement. . . .

I was calmer before than after the surgery (known on the records as an "interrupted pregnancy")—a classic case of reaction. In the hospital room, I felt a frightening separateness from Maria and the medical details of the abortion. I was as anesthetized, in my own way, as Maria.

Alerted to her slightest pain, she was a demanding patient, quick to ring for a nurse, frank about all the anatomical details. For Dan, who is squeamish, it was punishing.

As she was fighting her way back from anesthesia, I could hardly believe it was Christmas Eve. The hospital was even more remote from life than usual; the floor was emptied of all but the most acute cases, the nurses did not bustle about.

Our house had something of the same dull emptiness. I missed Maria and her delight in the small habits and surprises of our usual Christmas. After opening our presents on Christmas morning, we had our special breakfast of steak, blueberry pancakes and fresh strawberries. But we could not pretend to even the most spurious cheer. Maria's chair was overbearingly present in her absence.

Grim as the day was, we were lucky that the holidays had always been a close, private affair among the four of us. In a widespread family celebration, we would have had the task of covering up for Maria—for we took an uncompromisingly traditional stand: to keep the whole episode as quiet as possible.

In spite of us, the news undoubtedly spread. I told one close friend because, as I explained to Maria, "*I have to* tell someone." Jeff's parents knew because he had told them. (This is a point on which I cannot dwell comfortably: They knew when we did not know, yet they neither told us nor made any effort to resolve the situation. The responsibility in this situation has not been modernized, but remains squarely with the girl and/or her parents.) Maria, in her early panic and indiscretion, had confided in two girl friends; one of them, she later learned, had told *her* girl friend. Maria reported this angrily; but here was the hard pragmatism of the young: she was resentful of their thinking her "the fool who got caught."

Before I could carry up Maria's first lunch tray when she came home, Jeff arrived. Throughout, he had been simpler than Maria: visibly shaken, openly guilty and abashed, eager as a child to make amends. "I'll pay the bills. Let me pay the bills"—his way of salving his dignity once we had taken over the reins. We had not permitted him to visit Maria in the hospital; this would have been more casualness than I could tolerate, although I had seemingly tolerated so much else.

Jeff was back on our doorstep: faithful, thoughtful and attentive. "I prayed while Maria was in the hospital," he told me. Even while I was preparing dinner in the kitchen, he would drive out for hamburgers and pizza, because "that's what Maria wants."

Why didn't we forbid him to come to the house afterward? Because we remained the enlightened parents Dan and I agreed that outright opposition now, as earlier, would only bind them closer. We later learned from Mrs. Dunnock—who, like Toby, always seemed to know what we should have known—that they were both amazed and grateful when we did not play the heavies. Actually, we were hoping that this "incident" might cause the relationship to fall of its own weight. To the contrary, it seemed stronger than ever, and we had to face Jeff's comings and goings once more.

How does one feel, how does one act toward a boy who has been having sexual relations with your unmarried daughter and who has made her pregnant? I had no guidelines for how to behave. It would have been impossible for Jeff to win. If he'd neglected Maria, I'd have said angrily, "See?" But his reappearance in our house, with an assumption of old privileges, enraged me equally.

I realized that Dan, whose innermost feelings were perhaps even more complex than mine, was putting off the task of talking to Jeff. Something *had* to be said. But Dan was unexpectedly called to California on business, and it became my task.

I sat facing Jeff in the den. I told him that he must know I was angry, that I could not accept or welcome him in our house in the same way, that I felt duped by his pleasant manners, his seeming acquiescence to our ground rules. I felt pompous, doling out judgment. I could not escape from myself, from a lifetime habit of trying to be objective, to be fair to young people, to adjust to the cold war between the generations. Suddenly I was *counseling* him: "You know Maria must talk with the psychiatrist when she's recovered. But it wouldn't hurt you to go, too—to find out how you could let this happen if, as you say, you love Maria."

He's young and vulnerable, I thought, remembering that it was he who said to Maria, "You should be grateful," took her to task when she fussed over her boredom, her slow recovery. But when he said, "I know I've caused a great upset, but I cannot feel there's anything dirty or wrong about loving each other," I shrugged angrily at the cliché, at the naiveté, the ego of youth— totally unmindful of any*one,* any*thing* other than their own momentary emotions. Yet I do think he behaved more admirably under pressure than at any time in the year we'd known him. He was right when he said, "I've grown up a lot."

It was Maria who troubled me. Following that first night at Mrs. Dunnock's house, she had given no sign of remorse, of awareness that there had been anything wrong on her part. She continued to concentrate at home, as in the hospital, on her bodily well-being, her own comfort and amusement.

We did come, finally, to one moment of angry, distorted truth telling. It began casually. Maria came into my room for some small thing—an aspirin, I believe. I dismissed her brusquely: "When I finish on the phone!" I was out of patience with the Camille role. Maria stormed out, and I hung up quickly, regretting my lack of control.

I found Maria on her bed, sobbing and screaming, "*You* hate me! *Daddy* hates me! You *all* hate me!" I was terrorized by the outburst of such passion after so much control.

Jeff walked onto the scene with the usual bag of hamburgers. I stood by, paralyzed, while he sat on the bed and tried to stop Maria's wild sobs. Within I was as uncontrolled as Maria. I was racked with guilt. Suddenly I was the villain. How had that happened?

I sent Dan up. I recognized that it was our place, not Jeff's, even though I was numb. Dan talked with Maria for an hour. He didn't say much when he came out, just "Maria wants to see you."

"I'm sorry, Mom," she said. A comically polite ending for that storm of naked anger and emotion. When I stopped shaking, I was relieved. For a moment, the playacting had stopped.

"Maria, I don't know your feelings about this," I said. "You never told me." Her response, immediate, without pretense or defense, was: "I don't know." We talked, then, about Jeff and sex; about her feeling that Mrs. Dunnock was right, that sex was a "communication between two human beings." Maria did not feel it was wrong. She said, contemplatively, "I've never had a close relationship with a boy before."

I was nonplused when she told me that "Dr. Bailey says if I have to continue in this relationship, I should come to him for contraceptive pills." What could I say? "You can't," "You shouldn't," which I wanted to say, but was constrained by inadequacy, ineptitude? The new morality was being spelled out for me in my living room. Maria said openly: "I won't say I won't do it again." Weakly, I moved from sexual relations to the dangers of promiscuity. (I did not even *think* of the possibility of another unwanted pregnancy until later.)

"I'm not going to get into bed with every boy!" she protested, as though I were unknowledgeably young and she the woman of the world. I felt a mixture of embarrassment and admiration at her candor. But even more, I felt deep regret that it could not be otherwise.

The episode is past now. Maria has been going to Dr. Asch once a week, refers to her as "Edna-baby" and discusses everything freely with us except the pregnancy. Even as I write, the relationship with Jeff has deteriorated to quarreling, bickering and short, nonlasting reconciliations. "You're smothering me" is Jeff's complaint; and Maria cries in her bed at night because "I don't understand. I've been so honest with him!" Sad echoes of any marriage on its way out. But for Maria, being Maria, there are sounds of new boys in the air—Rusty, Dave, Richard—on the telephone, at the door.

Our family doctor, when I saw him last, said, "You handled it well." I wonder. We did not drive Maria into a rash, unpromising marriage; we did not compel her to accept the life of an unwanted child; on the surface, we did not estrange her from home and family.

The story, in its telling, must arouse different reactions in different parents. Some enmeshed in a situation like ours, may think we did "the best we could"; others, that we were fools at a dozen different points: for letting Jeff make himself at home; for letting Maria take advantage of, while we gave her the benefit of, our open-ended doubt; for being the parents that we are—indecisive, anxious to understand, afraid to trust reputedly outdated instincts and impulses.

Still others, I hope, will recognize that love makes fools of us all.

Throughout this account, I sense that I have been struggling to tell myself what I have learned, what I really believe and feel. It may be a long while before I see fully who and what we were during this critical time, how it will affect our future lives. We behaved in the spirit of the children's generation, practicalists meeting immediate dictates without thought of deeper sanctions or morality.

But have we, in the process, created a philosophic Frankenstein's monster—a generation with the non-need to face responsibility, with a super, self-centered arrogance that precludes any *obligation* on their part, any *rights* on ours? Can we, in truth, give them the privileges and the freedoms of adults? Can we say, "Go ahead and express your sex freely," providing them with contraceptives as both caution and precept?

In this era of multiple meanings and interior analysis, it would be foolhardy to cling, for security's sake, to the once-simple, clearly understood directives we were taught. How can we, as one writer has wryly asked, put the genie back in the bottle? We have learned, through our intellect, that our animality is natural, our impulses and drives costly if contradicted. Can we then ask our children to do what is unnatural and inhibitory? Because we are not clear in our minds, we are not convincing when we say or imply "no." We have built fences and left the gates wide open.

I ask myself: Where would I draw the line? I may not be able to prevent a premature sexual acting out of the young (although I frankly admit I wish I could!)—but I can cease to sponsor it. It strikes me that in allowing our children to make their sexual practices so public, we are not resigning ourselves to their independence but fostering dependency. When our daughters and sons behave so openly, it is more than the characteristic self-centeredness of the young. It is anger. They are chafing, showing us, *because* our hold is so strong, so hard to break. If they were truly independent, they would go about their business, not involving us, not forcing us to react to their hostility, to their defiance.

I no longer wish to denigrate my own "square" belief that there are values that outweigh momentary desire. I no longer believe that responsibility will be the spontaneous result of a child-oriented home, as we once romantically hoped. I believe that responsibility has to be taught, painstakingly, like the habit of brushing one's teeth. I wish I had given houseroom to the antique notion of "what our children owe us"—if only to give them practice in living with others. I wish I had reminded myself of what I knew all along: that freedom is the most difficult human privilege to use and enjoy.

But above all, I wish I had allowed myself an honest moment of anger and bitterness as ugly, open and honest as Maria's moment of truth. I love Maria enough to be angry with her and to withstand the anger I might have stirred in her. We might have avoided the small, nasty resentments that crop up now in the wrong place, with wrong emphasis. The past will not release the present from tentacles of memory and guilt.

Sadly, I feel that Maria and I are not closer, but one step more removed from each other than before—perhaps because each of us has abandoned a part of her traditional role.

Maria is a woman in her sensuality; in her relations to us, she is still the child. How do we resolve the dilemma—by ignoring the child or ignoring the woman? Everything within our culture abets her (as we did) in playing a woman's role with a child's responsibility, while it seduces us into parental confusion and inaction.

When I was the mother of young children, I worried about my ability to love a child with a perfect love. But now it is equally hard; it is imperative that I find my way through attitudes old and new toward the widsom to be a mother to a young girl, barefoot, in blue jeans—who, in turn, must find the wisdom to be wife, mother and her own woman.

Effects of Desertion on Family Life

SAMUEL H. LERNER, M. D.

Most social workers have had some experience with cases involving desertion of one of the parents. Desertion is relatively frequent in our society and causes untold misery to all family members. I shall not discuss the problems of marital conflict which lead to desertion, but shall confine my comments to the problems that occur after a parent has left the home.

If we look up the meaning of desertion in the dictionary, we find that to desert meants to abandon, to forsake, to relinquish. Desertion is the act of abandonment, especially in violation of duty or obligation; in the eyes of the law, it is a wilful abandonment, especially of one's wife or husband, in violation of legal or moral obligation. Desertion, therefore, has two distinct meanings: a broad one relating to abandonment in a general sense, and a narrower one relating to wilful abandonment, especially of one's wife or husband in violation of legal or moral obligation.

Feelings of being deserted or abandoned are found early in life. The baby, at birth, is one of the most helpless of all mammals. It is completely dependent upon the outside world, usually the mother, for its very existence. Without her care, her nourishment, her protection from the natural elements, and her tenderness—or that of her surrogate—the newly born infant would perish. It can be preserved from destruction only by the kindness of the adults in the world around it. Most animals are dependent upon their mothers for only a few short weeks and then become independent and able to take care of themselves. By contrast, the baby is completely dependent upon the mother for the first year of life; were it to be abandoned, it would die.[1]

But even after its period of infancy, the child is not independent: it does not know how to obtain its necessary food and shelter or how to defend itself from various forms of attack. The human animal needs fourteen or fifteen years before he can get along without adults and take care of himself. It is important, therefore, for the child to have his mother near at hand to satisfy his needs—a function that lies within her power. The child, using the instinct

From *Social Casework* 35:3–8, No. 2, June, 1954. Reprinted by permission of the publisher.

of self-preservation with which he is endowed, attempts to preserve this maternal care as long as he needs it. As long as his mother is close, within sight or hearing, he feels safe. When she is gone, however, his anguished crying reveals generalized feelings of discontent and dissatisfaction. Here is the expression of the first feelings of desertion experienced by the human being. Without his mother, the child is helpless.

Soon the relationship between child and mother goes far beyond the mere striving for life. The child wants to be near his mother; he longs for her even when his hunger is satisfied and there are no dangers from the outside world. We then say that the child loves his mother. Because of this intimate relationship, the child would be completely content if his mother devoted all her time to taking care of him, feeding him, loving him. Almost from the beginning of life, however, there are disruptive factors affecting this universal desire. Usually the mother has household duties to perform and there are other members of the family to whom she devotes time and energy—the father and siblings. The child feels resentment and jealousy toward those who deprive him of what he considers rightfully his. This feeling of being deserted, abandoned, is an inevitable feeling of childhood, especially if the child is left for any prolonged period of time. A person may express it later in life by saying, "I felt lost, bewildered, and afraid."

Since this type of trauma, however, is universal to a greater or less degree, one may ask why it is not an overwhelming blow in the child's emotional development. Certainly the daily shopping tours or the vacations taken by the parents—unless these are too extended when the child is very young—do not appear to have catastrophic consequences. If we observe the child carefully, we see that he finds a solution to the loss of a loved object—in this instance, the mother. The child learns that with the passage of time his mother returns. He shows joy and pleasure upon her reappearance. Gradually, as he grasps the concept of time, he is able to allow her to stay away for longer periods, certain that she will return as she has in the past. We can all remember the great pleasure we experienced in playing childhood games whose main theme is the finding of what has been hidden or lost—hide-and-seek, buried treasure, and similar games. Adults too, in an unconscious way, play this game with children when they cover their eyes with their hands and then release them, causing the child to burst into gales of laughter.

REACTIONS OF CHILDREN TO DESERTION

What happens when the child is faced, not with a temporary desertion, but with a much more permanent one, when weeks and months go by without the sight of the person familiar to him? In all cases where persons feel themselves deserted as a result of death, war, divorce, or other similar phenomena, the situation is characterized by the loss of a loved object for a long period of time or even forever. Social workers and others experienced in dealing with the problem of desertion know that statistics on desertion are difficult to obtain, since it takes many forms and can be relatively permanent or intermittent. For instance, an unmarried mother is not considered technically to have been deserted, and yet realistically her child has been deserted by the father before birth.

It is far more common for a man than a woman to desert a family. Women, in general, show less tendency to avoid responsibility, especially where children are concerned, than do men. There are a number of social, economic, cultural, and psychological reasons for this. Economically her earning capacity is almost always less than a man's, which tends to keep her at home. The woman is usually more dependent and less aggressive in an overt way. She bears the children, and not only does society expect her to accept the major share of responsibility for rearing the children, but usually she herself also accepts this role. Since she is in closer contact with her children, caring for them physically, her feelings about leaving them are likely to be much stronger than those of her husband, whose role in the child's early development is less active. When a 4-year-old was asked who his daddy was, he replied, "Oh, he's the man who comes home evenings, sits in his chair, and reads the paper." For the very young child, desertion by the mother is a much more severe blow than desertion by the father, as evidenced by the importance of the early relationship between child and mother. However, even the father who sits and reads his newspaper is an important person to the child. Since it is more frequently the father who deserts the family, I shall discuss the effects of the loss of the father on the child; first, the direct effects, and, second, the effect through the influence of the mother who reacts with disturbance to the desertion of her husband.

DIRECT EFFECTS ON CHILD

To the child, the father represents the natural protector, a person who gives him a feeling of security. The child needs a father not only as someone to love, but as someone to serve as a pattern for his own life. This is especially true for the boy, but the father also sets a pattern of masculinity for the girl as a model for her future love object. In many ways, the father is the controlling force in the life of both the girl and the boy. The attainment of normal femininity or masculinity is more difficult for the child who grows up without a father. We often hear it said that if desertion occurs very early in the child's life, the trauma will not be great because the child does not understand. On the contrary, there is evidence that the younger the child when this loss occurs, the more serious will be its influence. Even before he is a year old the effects of such a loss are evident. The child may be too young to understand the meaning of what has happened, but this only makes his suffering more acute.[2]

If we examine the normal psychological development of a child with reference to the influence of the father, we see that the father plays almost as important a role as the mother in introducing the child to the world. As already stated, the constant reappearance of the mother is the foundation of the child's feeling of security. However, the infant is unstable emotionally and has to pass through stages of jealousy, relinquishment, and renunciation, for in reality the infant cannot possess the mother as completely as he desires. He thus experiences feelings of rage, sorrow, and conflict. Ideally, the parents should respond to these inevitable emotions with a steady affection and remain adult in their reactions. Gradually the child learns that the father is more grown-up than he is, that the father has an importance for his mother which he cannot have, and that the father can do things that he cannot do. Thus he comes to recognize his own value and becomes acclimatized to being a child, which he is.

Without the child's emotional tie to the father, the mother is likely to indulge excessively the child's infantile wish to possess her completely. This can be catastrophic to the child's development. Normally, too, the father usually gives the child a respect for danger. This is quite different from a fear of danger or a defiance of danger. The mother, without the support of the father, is much more likely to betray her anxiety in a dangerous situation. Since children imitate their parents, this factor is important in the child's development. The child, with his feelings of jealousy, rage, and conflict, can best solve his problems by identifying himself with his father; in this way he will have no need to defy him.

The meaning of the father to the child, obviously, varies with different periods in the child's development. To the infant, the father is the big figure who stands for security. To the small child, the father is the man who can "beat up" all the other children's fathers; who is not afraid of burglars, policemen, or thunderstorms; who gives fair reprimands for naughtiness and yet is not forbidding enough to make all mischief impossible; who is the defender and the model. To the boy, the father is the model to copy. To the girl, he is the means of attaining a normal attitude toward femininity; he is someone who shows respect and love for a woman—the mother.

This, then, is the picture of the normal or ideal relationship between the father and his children. In desertion this relationship is disturbed. Even in the first year of the child's life, the disappearance of the father arouses a feeling of loss and great anxiety. Children at the age of two can verbalize their feelings. "Why doesn't Daddy come home?" they ask. To the young child the father's not coming home means that the father does not love him, that he does not want to come home. The boy especially has strong feelings of guilt because of his love for the mother and rivalry with the father. The child is placed in the position of being the father before he is ready chronologically to assume this role. Sometimes, in desertion, a mother fosters this attitude in her son by telling him that he is now the man in the family. This creates strong anxiety in the child because what has formerly been a fantasy approaches the proportions of reality. We see evidence of this clinically in the child's attempt to ward off his anxiety and guilt through fantasies of reuniting the mother with the deserting father.

The loss of the father also means to the child the loss of his protector and all that this entails in the way of a comfortable home, food, and clothing. The child develops a strong feeling of insecurity and dread of the future. We may expect to see a number of symptoms in such children. Many times the child clings to the mother in an overpossessive way; he fears losing her and feels guilty because of his aggressive wishes. This kind of clinging is always a sign of guilt. Sometimes the child becomes rebellious and defiant toward other children or toward persons in authority. There may be outbursts of delinquency. In such cases the child is imitating his father or trying to incur punishment for his guilt feelings. Or the child may respond by becoming withdrawn, listless in school, and generally apathetic. Some children cannot stand any expression of sympathy, as though this implies an accusation of their guilt.

CHILD'S REACTIONS TO MOTHER'S DISTURBANCE

Children may be further disturbed by the fact that the father's desertion usually causes the mother to become upset. The woman who loses her husband becomes unconsciously a child, and many childish traits, such as dependency, frustration, and rebellion, may become active. She may respond with strong aggressive feelings toward the husband, and these feelings may be displaced onto the children. Frequently she feels guilty, as though her husband had left because of some fault of her own—lack of love or lack of care. This guilty feeling may undermine her capacity to deal with the problems of her children.

The loss of a woman's husband, especially if it occurs unexpectedly, can affect her in many ways. Usually she loses her financial security and is confronted by many practical problems in earning a living and caring for the children. Also, she loses sexual satisfaction, and her thoughts may be concentrated on how long she can endure this lack. In addition, she loses the person who once gave her a feeling of value. The desertion may mean to her that she is worthless, since otherwise her husband would not have left her. It also arouses her hate and bitterness. Many times this feeling is projected onto the world in general, and she feels that everyone is against her. She is envious of women who still have their husbands. She feels increased responsibility to the children, in order to make up to them for the loss of the father. This anxiety may be transmitted to the children, so that in addition to losing a father—even though he may be a poor one—they feel the extra burden of the mother's anxiety.

Whether the children will be a stimulus and a solace to the mother or an intolerable reminder of future burdens varies with the individual mother. Often she requires help in caring for her children. Sometimes she may look for a person of authority, a mother figure, and react with extreme dependence. Such a reaction will be unfortunate for the children, since it will arouse their contempt when they need to feel respect. Sometimes, following desertion, the mother becomes restless; she rushes around doing one thing after another, finding a job, breaking up her home, and so on. Or she may plunge into wild pleasures, with an overly gay and cheerful attitude. Such behavior deprives the children of her stabilizing influence. They feel the loss of the father and need time to express their bitterness, sadness, and love, but the mother's attitude encourages them to affect a meaningless mask of gaiety. If the mother remarries immediately, the children may become jealous of the new partner and regard the mother's marriage as a desertion of themselves.

HELPING THE MOTHER AND CHILDREN

In cases of desertion, what help can be given by caseworkers, especially to the children? Definitely the mother needs support—often in a practical way and certainly in a psychological way. If she can be encouraged to express her strong feelings in her talks with the caseworker, there will be less chance of her acting impulsively and she will be better able to have a stabilizing influence upon her children. We must recognize that no matter how bad a character structure the father has, his loss will be a major event in the child's life and cannot fail to affect his future development. Even if it can be said that in the long run the child may be better off without such a father, we must still expect the child to have strong emotions over such a loss. The loss of the father cannot wholly be made good; there is no substitute or external help that can make up for this.

In most cases the child will have to find his own solution to this trauma. We can, however, offer help and understanding. The mother's reaction is more immediate and noticeable than the child's. Often many months may go by before any reaction can be observed in the child. He relives his infantile fantasy that the father will return, and many times it is only when this fantasy becomes incompatible with reality that the child shows disturbance.

In giving support to the mother, one can point out to her the needs of her children. Often a mother makes a demand on her children that they show no feelings, especially if these feelings do not correspond to her own. She should learn to tell her children the truth—not in a harsh, brutal manner but in a kindly, understanding way. Her problems cannot be kept from the children, for they will hear of them through their playmates, neighbors, and relatives. It is an obvious fact that the father is gone, and the children should receive their information about this traumatic event from their mother, if possible. On the other hand, the mother should not demand of her children that they express aggression, nor should she talk constantly about the desertion. She should tell the children the truth and then speak about the subject in a frank way whenever they bring it up.

Another way in which the mother can help is to bring the children in contact with men who can be substitutes for the father—friends, relatives, or grandfathers. She can also encourage her children to form friendships with other children. The children can be taught to work through their feelings in any type of expression that is suitable, such as art, music, hobbies, or athletics. Teachers can sometimes help in these activities. Normal competitiveness often becomes inhibited in the boy whose father has deserted the family, and he can be helped to work out some of his rivalry and aggression through approved ways, particularly in athletics.

One can advise the mother against expressing her loneliness by sleeping with her child. Following desertion, children often desire to sleep with their mother in order to comfort both themselves and the mother. Anxiety and guilt then arise. The more guilty the child feels in his belief that he is the cause of his father's leaving, the more he will seek intimate bodily contact with the mother. A vicious circle can result, with the child permanently tied to the mother's needs, and the mother turning to the child—particularly the boy— to satisfy her longings for affection. The boy cannot fill his father's shoes. The mother may demand that the boy hate his father and join with her against him. The child may try to take his father's place, but his inevitable failure causes him to accumulate resentment toward the mother and secretly to idealize the father. His resentment toward his mother may prevent him later from turning to other women as objects of love.

I shall conclude this discussion with a case illustration of a boy, John A. His father, after earlier temporary absences, deserted and was subsequently imprisoned for embezzlement when John was 14 1/2. John was referred for casework help because of complaints from the school that his work had deteriorated and that he had become noisy, boisterous, and talkative, creating a constant disturbance. He seemed to have gotten along fairly well in school until the time of Mr. A's imprisonment. One day in class the teacher asked each student to rise and tell his father's occupation. John stood up and said that his father was in the army. Another boy rose and declared this to be a lie, thereupon telling the entire story.

Following this episode, Mrs. A gave John money one day to buy lunch. Another boy complained that his lunch money was missing. The teacher then searched John, found the money that his mother had given him, and accused him of having stolen it. John became very upset and ran to his grandmother's, since his mother was away from home working.

John's mother was an anxious, indecisive woman, but she showed warm feeling for John and his two sisters. She stated that her husband had always been restless, never staying in one place very long. (Mrs. A had first met her husband while he was roaming the streets one night. She was looking for a certain street, he attempted to help her, and they both got lost. He felt himself attracted to her and suggested that they get married, which they did the next day.) When the children were small, she traveled with her husband since he was so restless, but this became too difficult as they grew older.

The mother's chief complaint about John was that he lied constantly and had a terrible temper. It soon became clear that this behavior was an imitation of her own. She had encouraged the children to lie about the father's whereabouts, for he was frequently in conflict with the law. With regard to John's temper, it was very similar to her own when she came home in the evening, after her day's work, and found things in a mess. She had no control over John, and if she remonstrated with him, as she did when he stole the money she had saved to pay for dental work for one of her daughters, he would say in a gentle, seductive way, "Now you know, Mother." She commented that John was "a good lad but the same as his father—nervous, jumpy, and impetuous"; that he "couldn't stay in one spot very long"; that he "had seen a lot of that from his father and was turning out the same way." She declared that John came in late every night, lied constantly, and stole money from the house.

Clearly, in this case, John was identifying himself with his father and with the mother's unconscious approval of the father's antisocial acts. John could not decide whether his father was a hero or a devil, especially since his own delinquencies coincided with his father's embezzlement. He identified himself with his father's the-world's-against-me attitude, especially since his mother seemed to approve of this attitude in the father. Society, however, as represented by the children and teachers, condemned his father.

John was seen by a caseworker who treated him with understanding but also with firmness and authority. John began to express his anger at his father and his guilt over his wish that the father would leave. At the same time the worker's personality provided John with a more healthy identification. The worker did not condemn the father but permitted John to condemn him. During this period the mother attempted to form a relationship with a man but dropped him when he turned out to be very much like Mr. A. She then found another man to like, who fortunately took an interest in John.

John's symptoms disappeared, and his school work improved along with his behavior.

This case presentation illustrates some of the points emphasized in this paper. The mother's comment that John behaved like his father made John try to be like his father. John recognized that his mother loved his father and wanted him back. He was aware of his mother's yearning and relief whenever the father returned. What John meant by "Now you know, Mother," was essentially that she loved his father, who possessed these undesirable traits himself. His mother did not help him to distinguish between his father's undesirable traits and the worth-while characteristics that she loved. John tried to substitute for his father, whom he knew his mother missed. Complete success in this unhealthy identification would have been costly.

NOTES AND REFERENCES

1. Freud, Anna: *Psychoanalysis for Parents and Teachers.* New York: Emerson Books, 1935.
2. Isaacs, Susan; Riviere, Joan; and Sharpe, Ella Freeman: *Fatherless Children.* London: Pouskin Press, 1945.

Inmate-Mothers and Their Children

SERAPIO R. ZALBA

Understanding of the social welfare needs and problems of imprisoned mothers of minor children must be predicated upon a base of knowledge about the social and demographic factors that may influence the attitudes and actions of these women, and that may be the same or different from those characterizing imprisoned women who either are not mothers or have children who have reached adulthood. Consequently, an early task of this study was not only to identify which of the inmates of the California Institution for Women were mothers of minor children, but also to provide data that would permit a comparison of the characteristics of these mothers and the remaining group of inmates. These data were gathered in two stages, and the findings are presented here.

The data were obtained from institutional records—the Warden's Cards and the case files—and from questionnaires completed by the inmates. Cognizance should be taken of two points with regard to these sources. One is that the information provided by the inmates about themselves did not always coincide with the information contained in the records; these disparities are noted in the text that follows. The other is the matter of the samples used and the administration of the questionnaire to the inmates.

Although the population of the institution was 885 inmates when the first stage of the study had been completed, the number had increased when the second stage was begun. The questionnaire was administered to all of the inmates in order to avoid identifying to the rest of the population those thought to have minor children; in addition, this gave researchers the opportunity to try to identify other inmate-mothers with minor children who had not previously indicated that they had children.

During two consecutive evenings, while the women were in their rooms

From *Women Prisoners and Their Families,* in collaboration with Lois M. Tandy and Cynthia E. Nesbit. Sacramento: California Department of Social Welfare, 1964. Reprinted by permission of the Department.

and before "lights out," the project staff distributed the fourteen-item questionnaire to a 100 percent sample of the California Institution for Women population. To underscore the assurance of confidentiality that had been given the women in the preliminary group meetings, the project staff remained available to answer the questions of the women regarding the forms, then collected them. Eighty percent of the women returned completed questionnaires at this time. There was one follow-up effort—including group meetings conducted by the project staff to interpret once again the project's goals and activities—to obtain completed questionnaires from the 190 inmates who had not submitted usable documents. More than half (52%) of this group responded by completing usable forms. In all, 840 were completed and returned.

CHARACTERISTICS OF THE TOTAL POPULATION

Offense

The 885 inmates comprising the Institution's population in the first stage of this study had been convicted of crimes ranging from bad checks to murder. The largest percentage of women (45%) were imprisoned in the California Institution for Women for such crimes against property as bad checks, forgery, embezzlement, receiving stolen property, etc. Only 35 percent of the men in California prisons were convicted for similar crimes. The men more often were convicted of crimes of physical harm or threat, such as strongarm or armed robbery, assault, rape and homicide. But homicide as the specific crime of conviction accounted for a higher proportion of the women's population (14%) than for the men in California prisons (8%). It should be noted that in actual numbers, however, as of December 31, 1962, there were 97 women prisoners convicted of homicide as compared with 1,439 men. Nevertheless, a prisoner at the California Institution for Women was more likely to have committed homicide than would a prisoner in a California prison for men—a fact that has special import for family relationships and outlook. Such crimes carry extremely pathogenic potential for the children in the female inmate's family: Pollack has indicated that homicides by women tend to have members of the immediate family (husband, children) as their victims. Also, homicide offenders serve longer sentences in the institution, hence are separated from their minor children for longer periods of time. Mrs. A. M., for example, shot and killed her husband under conditions of extreme provocation, which involved a threat to the mental health of her children. The five children she left behind her have been split up into three different household units. There is considerable evidence that Mrs. M. was a good mother, but by the time she is paroled, she probably will have been away from her children for from three to five crucial years of their lives.

Social Class, Ethnicity and Marital Status

Social Class. The use of the Hollingshead two-factor index of social position based on formal education and occupation revealed that the majority of California Institution for Women inmates were from the lowest of Hollingshead's three social classes: 69 percent of the inmates had not completed high school, and 82 percent had worked on unskilled or semi-skilled jobs. These data support the findings of others that the bulk of prison populations come from the lowest socioeconomic classes.

Ethnicity. Social class membership, or identification, affects the individual's perception of crises or needs for social welfare services, as well as his perception as to which of the community's resources are actually available to him. This has a special significance for Negroes who are disproportionately represented in the California Institution for Women population: they account for 27 percent of the Institution's inmate population, and only 6 percent of California's general population. The picture was not clear with regard to Mexican-Americans, whose problems might be expected to be somewhat similar to those of Negroes. Technically, Mexican-Americans could have been included in the Caucasian category. However, a distinction was made in this study because membership in this sub-cultural group exposes its members to de facto discrimination, and it has implications of barriers, either real or imagined, in utilizing the social welfare institutions of the dominant culture. The data differed with the sources supplying them. Thus, from the records, the figure was found to be three percent. Yet eleven percent of the inmates identified themselves as Mexican-American in answering the inmate questionnaires. It would seem more likely that members of such groups would identify themselves with the majority advantaged groups in society, than vice versa.

Marital Status. A high percentage of inmates (82%) reported having been married at some time in their lives, according to the Warden's Cards, which also indicated that currently 24 percent were divorced, 21 percent separated, 6 percent were widowed; only 34 percent had intact marriages. Joan Henry, in her study of a British prison, noted a propensity among women offenders to represent themselves as married when they were not. This was found to be true in this study also, for the inmate questionnaries identified 11 percent of the relationships as "common-law" rather than the one percent noted in the Institution's records.

Probably, they preferred to have the official records show them as married instead of divorced or maintaining relationships not legally or socially acceptable. Furthermore, there may have been some expectations that revelations of common-law arrangements, especially to persons in the dominant culture, might have led to embarrassment or ostracism.

Age

Age is of special significance in a study focused on inmate-mothers and their families. The majority of inmates (68%) were 35 years of age or less, so many had a number of child-bearing years ahead of them; social welfare services that might help them become more adequate persons and mothers could affect an as yet unborn group of children.

Religion

Almost all (98%) of the inmates claimed some religious affiliation. The high degree of reported church affiliation is probably not a true reflection of the institutional population's religious constancy or commitment. There seemed to be recognition among many inmates of value in apparent religious conformity. In addition, in prison, church services are perceived by some as diversionary activities as well as religious observances.

Perhaps of more significance than a claim to a religious affiliation is the high percentage of inmates (42%) who specifically identified themselves as Catholics. Nine percent of those who identified themselves as Catholics were Negroes born in South Central states, notably Louisiana and Texas.

CHARACTERISTICS OF THE INMATE-MOTHER POPULATION

From the inmate questionnaires it was determined that 59 percent of the total California Institution for Women population had minor children. An additional six percent indicated that they had adult children only. The total incidence of motherhood revealed by the questionnaires was 65 percent, although the Warden's Cards indicated 68 percent. The project staff speculated that the discrepancy may have derived from either or both of two possibilities: some residual misunderstandings, stemming from literacy problems, as to whether adult children were to be noted on the questionnaire; and some fear that the identification of minor children might result in their being taken away.

Family Size

The 460 inmates with minor children accounted for 1123 children, 41 percent of them belonging to inmates convicted in Los Angeles County. Inmates from the urban centers of Los Angeles County and the San Francisco Bay Area tended toward slightly smaller families. Although the families of the inmate-mothers ranged in size from one to nine children, the median family size was two children, with 38 percent of the mothers having only one child. The average family size was 2.4 children. Mexican-American familes were slightly larger than either Negro or Caucasian families.

Offense and Length of Stay

The average length of stay at the institution was twenty-two months, but inmate-mothers tended to be sentenced to slightly shorter terms than did non-mothers. Fewer of the mothers were convicted of crimes of violence and more of them convicted of crimes against property, and the consequence that mothers tended to have shorter sentences is therefore not surprising.

Birthplace

Considerable attention has been focused on the influx of population into California and its possible effect upon the rates of crime and financial dependency. While no data were obtained about the inmate's length of stay in the state, it was found that in contrast with the 22 percent of the general California population twenty years of age and over born in the state, 31 percent of the inmates were born in California. According to the Institution's records a slightly higher proportion of the inmates born in California had children (70%) than did women born elsewhere (67%).

Family Background

Data on the mother's childhood, which might be related to her current circumstances, fell in the two categories of economic deprivation and family emotional problems. The inmate-mother was considered by the project staff to have had an economically deprived childhood if it were so indicated explicitly in the case file of the Institution—usually in the probation officer's pre-sentence report or the California Institution for Women correctional counselor's social summary. This category was used to reflect a lack of those necessities of life generally termed survival needs: food, clothing and shelter. In accordance with this conservative criterion, fourteen percent of the inmate-mothers were classified as having been economically deprived as children.

The existence of a history of family emotional problems was determined on the basis of the inclusion in the case records of any of the following: severe marital discord between parental figures; death, alcoholism, drug addiction, criminality or mental illness of parental figures; or the existence of such special living arrangements as formal or informal foster homes and institutions. Miss B. N.'s record contained an example of family emotional problems:

Her parents argued incessantly. Finally her father beat her mother severely enough to require hospitalization. He then moved out of town, leaving his wife and children to care for themselves as best they could.

As children, almost two-thirds (65%) of the inmates had experienced one or more of the situations listed above. Even though a high proportion of the inmate-mothers had some emotionally disruptive experiences as children, 81 percent of all the mothers were maintaining some contact through letters and/or visits, with their familes of orientation—father, mother and siblings.

Inmate-Mother's Crime History

A longitudinal look at the inmate-mothers' records of arrest along with their youthful marriages and subsequent divorces offers some indication of the chronic nature of the personal instability characterizing these women.

More than half (54%) of the mothers had been arrested by the age of twenty-one, and 40 percent had juvenile records. Although this was the first *felony* conviction for 80 percent of the mothers, three fourths of them had already been identified as individuals with problems.

Other Deviant Behavior

Another indication of problems in the social adjustment of the inmate-mothers was the extent to which histories of deviant behavior other than crimes, pre se, existed among the cases in the sample whose case files were analyzed: 77 percent of all the inmate-mothers had histories of other deviant behavior, often in more than one category. For instance, 42 percent of the mothers had used opiates, 31 percent had drinking problems, 32 percent had been convicted for prostitution, 9 percent had been involved in overt homosexuality, 6 percent had been committed to a mental hopital, and 5 percent had attempted suicide. There was little overlap in the last two categories; 10 percent of all mothers had either attempted suicide or had been committed to mental hospitals.

Marital History

The marital histories of the inmate-mothers also presented a picture of instability and discord. Ninety percent of the mothers had been married; however, only 34 percent considered their marriages to be currently intact. Of the women who had been married, 46 percent had been married two or more times. Some clue as to the instability of the marriages may be found in the ages of the mothers when they were first married.

Eighty percent were twenty-one years old or less, and 54 percent were under 18. In addition to these legal alliances, 56 percent of the inmate-mothers had been involved in one or more common-law relationships, 34 percent of these women having had their first such relationship when they were 21 years of age or younger.

The difficulties the inmate-mothers may have encountered in providing stable homes for their children were possibly aggravated by their tendency to marry men who also had histories of anti-social behavior. . . .

Of the mothers who had married legally, 44 percent had been married to men with criminal records. In 11 percent of the cases, the husband had at some time been convicted as his wife's crime-partner. One out of four of the legal spouses was incarcerated at the time of this study, and an additional 3 percent were currently on parole.

Performance as a Mother

When the mothers still were living in the community, 62 percent had at some time left their children in the care of relatives, friends, or agencies.

Mrs. C. O. used heroin; in order to get the money this required, she resorted to prostitution. As an addict she spent much of her time around other users and sources of supply. When she realized that she was becoming re-addicted, she left her child with friends. Her motivation for placing the child was partly a matter of concern for the child's welfare; primarily, however, it was a matter of convenience in pursuing her own activities.

Despite their extensive use of substitute child care arrangements, only 13 percent of the inmate-mothers had relinquished children for adoption. Eleven percent of the inmate-mothers had histories of verified child neglect or abuse; these were actual arrests and convictions, or compelling evidence of gross child maltreatment.

The children of Mrs. D. P. were picked up by the juvenile authorities in response to a complaint by neighbors. The children, ages three and five, were often left locked in the home alone during the day and many of the nights, without provisions being made for care, supervision or, at times, even food. The children were undernourished, dirty, and bewildered.

In five percent of the cases, the inmate-mothers had involved their children in the crimes, with the children as crime partners in three percent and as the victims of the mother's crime in two percent of the cases.

WHEREABOUTS OF THE INMATE-MOTHERS' CHILDREN

Despite the generally assumed high degree of disorganization and disintegration present among the families of offenders, 74 percent of the questionnaires completed by the inmate-mothers revealed that relatives—especially the children's maternal or paternal grandparents—constituted the main resource for the care of the inmates' children.

There appeared to be an association between the size of the inmate's family and the use of foster homes for care of the children. There were such placements in 22 percent of the families, and these tended to be the larger families. It is probably easier to find relatives willing to take a smaller number of children into their homes. The data available in this stage of the study did not indicate clearly whether the children in larger families who were placed in foster homes generally were placed in a single home.

The extent to which fathers assumed responsibility for their children during the mother's incarceration is reflected in the fact that some of the minor children in 29 percent of the families were living with their fathers. While some of the children were with fathers currently married to their mothers—10 percent of all families—in seven percent of all families children were living with fathers from common-law, and even casual relationships.

The minimal usage of foster home placement, and the reality problems of any father trying to care for children without the help of their mother, probably account for the placement of fully half of the children with relatives other than the father. With an increase in the age of the inmate, a greater proportion of the children were found to be living with fathers, and fewer were living with other relatives.

In each ethnic category it was found that at least half of the families had children living with relatives other than the father. This was true in the familes of 74 percent of the Negro inmate-mothers as compared with 50 percent of the Caucasians and 58 percent of the Mexican-Americans. This fact poses questions for consideration. Is it that the internal sub-cultural values of Negroes militate against placing children outside of the family? Or is the status quo more closely related to the differential availability of social services, including foster care facilities, depending on the client's ethnic characteristics? Whatever the reason, foster homes were used to place children from only 10 percent of the Negro families, as compared with 25 percent of the Caucasian, and 29 percent of the Mexican-American families.

The other demographic factors found to be particularly related to the differential use of foster home placement were family size and county of inmate's residence. As noted previously, there was an almost steady progression of increased foster home use as family size increased. This did not necessarily mean that other kinds of placements were used less; rather, where large families existed, a number of resources were tapped in accommodating the many children in the family. When data regarding foster home placement were cross-tabulated with county of residence data, it was found that inmate families in the most urbanized areas had the lowest rate of foster home use. For instance, only 15 percent of the families in the San Francisco Bay Area, and 18 percent of the families in Los Angeles County used foster homes, as compared with 33 percent for the other counties in the state. It should be noted that the Negro population in California is concentrated primarily in Los Angeles County and the San Francisco Bay Area; this may account for the differential rate of foster home use. Another possibility is that in rural areas there tend to be stronger community reactions to the deviant behavior of the mother, culminating in the placement of the children away from the family, in foster homes.

PART 4

INDIVIDUAL FAMILY MEMBERS AS VICTIMS OF DEVIANCY

Just as an individual's deviant behavior may have a profound effect upon the family as a unit, such deviancy may also have a serious impact upon particular members within the family. The focus of this section is on the types of individual reactions to the deviancy of other family members. Here again deviancy may be divided into two broad categories, one concerning violations of specific family norms and statutes and which in a sense are directed against the family, and the other concerning extra-familial deviant behavior. Invariably, given the nature of the family in our society, a deviant act or pattern of behavior by any member of the family unit will have some effect upon not only the unit itself, but also upon each individual member.

In our society, both familial and nonfamilial deviant behavior committed by adults is considered more serious than deviant acts of children. Furthermore, deviancy on the part of adult family members as opposed to deviant acts of the children tends to have a far greater impact upon the family and thus renders reconciliation and adjustment more difficult. Evidence of this was provided by several cases in the previous section, for example, the instance in which the daughter became pregnant and the one in which the son was becoming a homosexual. Both of these families managed to effect a satisfactory readjustment under the circumstances. The families of the deserter and the hit-and-run driver, however, suffered more lasting trauma. In our society, in spite of the emphasis on youth and children, the parents remain the pivotal members of the family and it is upon their behavior that the fortunes of the family rest.

While this section concentrates on deviancy of adult family members and its consequences for young children, one article also demonstrates the impact of one spouse's suicide upon the other mate. Among the possible consequences of deviancy for family members are emotional insecurity, physical injury or impaired academic performance among children, and the social stigmatization which may accrue to any members of a family containing a deviant.

EMOTIONAL INSECURITY

Although our society greatly deprecates any violation of norms or laws that presages harm to the family, perhaps no behavior is more disparaged than that which does or threatens to do harm to children. Our normative structure reflects the ingrained societal belief that any unusual or abnormal occurrences involving children may well have profound and lasting effects on both the current and future emotional and psychological life of the child. Thus society makes great attempts to buffer or shelter the child. Such concern for the protection of children may reach unreasonable proportions, and often manifests itself in irrational if not hysterical reactions to incidents such as sexual molestation or homosexual abuse of children. Many individuals are vehement in their objection to the exposure of children to pornography or television violence because they are socially defined as damaging to the child's emotional development. Realizing the emotional support engendered by these norms concerning the protection of children, some political and social propagandists have manipulated public sentiment by portraying certain proposed social programs as potentially harmful or particularly beneficial to children. For example, both opponents and proponents of sex education in schools have played on the emotional responses of the public to gain support for their cause. Without regard to the logic or rationality of norms relating to the security and protection of children, it goes without saying that they are very much an integral part of the American value system.

Although the evidence suggests that the violation of some of these protective norms for children seems to have little or no effect upon the child's later life, there are several forms of child-directed deviant acts which appear to have serious and lasting consequences for the child who is victim to the act. The results of physical abuse and emotional and psychological neglect on children have been thoroughly researched by experts in the areas of child welfare and therapy and their findings are well documented.

One enigmatic aspect of such deviant acts involving children is the fact that they persist in the face of strong public support for the norms and severe social censure as well as legal sanctions for violations. Because the perpetrator of neglect, child abuse, or abandonment is most often a parent of the child, many persons have difficulty reconciling this fact with the socially prescribed affective and protective role of the parent in our society.

The first article in this section, "The Abandoned Child," offers some insights into the causes or motivations leading to the abandonment of children, as well as a discussion of some of the possible effects on the children. Of particular interest is the description of some modal characteristics of parents who abandon their children. Most children, for example, are abandoned by their mothers rather than by their fathers. This is attributable to the fact that such mothers frequently have been abandoned or deserted themselves by the husband/father. This desertion may well have contributed to the dilemma in which the woman finds herself—that of being unable to properly care for the child or children without the help and support of her spouse. Thus, her behavior may be a final development in a long chain reaction of social and economic circumstances, and it represents the most efficacious albeit deviant option open to her.

Another common characteristic of this situation is that the abandoned child, contrary to popular belief, is almost never a retarded or handicapped child. Apparently the burden of guilt which would accrue to the mother as a result of abandoning this type of child would be beyond her ability to bear. Another interesting point is that the abandoned child is invariably clean and dressed very neatly, usually in new clothes. This probably represents the mother's attempt to have the child more readily accepted by whoever finds him.

The loss of material comfort and support is not the major negative consequence of child abandonment, for usually the child is found and his material needs are immediately served by one of several appropriate public agencies. The most serious consequence is the possibility of psychological or emotional injury. Extensive investigation of the immediate and long-term effects of abandonment indicates that these children tend to lack the ability to respond emotionally to others, and in being unloved, they also lack the ability to love others or themselves. This situation also disrupts the normal development of the child's self-image; his normal identity does not progress to the point where he has a socially adequate conceptualization of himself.

The selection also describes the procedures employed in placing the child in a temporary home while attempts are made to locate his parents. If these efforts fail, the child is faced with spending the remainder of his youth in one or more foster homes. The article suggests that laws relating to this matter are not particularly useful as a remedy inasmuch as "neglect" statutes are not designed to restrain the deviant parent, but rather to keep the family together. Furthermore, desertion statutes, designed to apply to males, have little application when a mother abandons her child.

PHYSICAL INJURY

The basic similarities between abandonment and childbeating are that in both instances the child is the victim of the parents' deviancy and that both acts constitute lamentable violations of both social norms and legal statutes. For the most part, the similarity ends here because the motivations for and the consequences of each act are quite different.

Craig Taylor's article, "The 'Battered Child': Individual Victim of Family Brutality," offers a comprehensive survey of the case literature and research findings concerning willful child abuse. Statistics on the frequency of childbeatings are very scanty, and those available are thought to be grossly underrepresentative of the true frequency of this type of deviancy. The reason for the lack of accurate data concerning child abuse is that the individual cases rarely reach public attention, unless the child dies, and even then the cause is laid to an "accident," rather than to abuse by the parents.

Furthermore, those who are in the best position to detect child abuse, medical doctors, are also the most reluctant to inform authorities. Since evidence for proof in prosecution is very difficult to obtain, the doctor may be left in a rather precarious legal position, facing charges of false accusation by the parents. Also, the innocent parent frequently tries to protect his deviant spouse, and both will deny that the child was injured by either of them. The parents of a "battered" child often go to a different doctor each time the child is injured by their violence, so that the doctor has little or no reason to suspect that the child has not simply fallen or suffered some other accident.

The reasons or motivations for childbeating may be seen as both simple and complex, as indicated by the article. Simply put, the child has become the scapegoat on which the parents take out whatever day-to-day frustrations they encounter. Presumably, the personality problems of these adults weakens their ability to cope with their environment, and the child serves as a convenient object of their aggressions and hostilities.

There are also several more complex sociological reasons underlying child abuse, however. The disappearance of the extended family, for example, means that the young mother has no one to whom she may turn at short notice to care for the child when she is feeling ill or indisposed. There is, in effect, no respite from the constant responsibility of parenthood and little if any assistance from kinsmen in discharging this responsibility. Additionally, there is some evidence to indicate that a large portion of "battered" children were either illegitimate or of doubtful paternity. Such children, being both unexpected and unwanted as well as being the source of stigma to the mother (and her husband if married), would undoubtedly generate considerable resentment in the parents, who would direct their violent frustrations toward the children.

Of particular interest in recent years is the formation of a number of organizations which might be referred to as "Childbeaters Anonymous" because they operate according to principles similar to those of Alcoholics Anonymous. Parents who are aware of their tendency to beat their children excessively or violently meet with other parents to discuss their mutual problems and attempt to gain insights into their motivations. Also, the members try to be available to help each other when crisis situations arise. For example, if a mother feels herself developing a mood of depression and realizes that she might aubse her child while in this mood, she can call one of the other members, either for moral support or perhaps to have her come to care for the children while she tries to compose herself—for example, by going to the beauty parlor. Early reports indicate that these organizations are having considerable success not only in preventing further child abuse, but also in improving the total outlook and attitudes of the parents.

IMPAIRED ACADEMIC PERFORMANCE

Previous articles have demonstrated some of the myriad ways in which parents' deviant behavior tends to affect their children. In "The Adjustment of Children of Jail Inmates," Friedman and Esselstyn report some results of their study of the children of men who have been sent to prison. The study focused on their school adjustment and relied upon teacher ratings of the children on a number of attitudinal and performance factors.

The children of the inmates were located through the prison records and through interviews with the inmates themselves. This group represented the experimental group, and two other randomly selected groups were employed as control groups with which to compare the children of the inmates. The teachers rated the students of each of the three groups without knowing to which group the children had been assigned or what membership in the group represented.

On most of the rating factors, the children of jail inmates scored significantly lower than did the children in the control groups. Of particular interest is the fact that female children of inmates were rated even lower in performance than were the male children of inmates. Apparently the stigma of one's father having been sent to prison presents greater adjustment problems for daughters than for sons, which is perhaps an ultimate reflection of the normative structure in our society which defines crime as being more acceptable to males than to females.

SOCIAL STIGMA, GUILT, AND SHAME

Perhaps one of the least understood forms of deviant behavior is suicide, especially in those instances where the individual has a family for whose care he or she is responsible. However, the article presented in this section is not so much concerned with the causes or correlates of suicide, but rather with some of the residual effects of suicide upon the surviving spouse. "The Legacy of Suicide," by Albert Cain and Irene Fast, is one of several research reports by the same authors based upon an intensive investigation into a number of cases of families after a suicide had taken place.[1] This research was unique in the fact that it did focus upon the aftermath of the event rather than upon the event itself.

A suicide sets into motion a number of particularly unpleasant events which taken either individually or as a group tend to have a traumatic impact upon the remaining family, especially the spouse. The remaining spouse is usually the wife, since a significantly higher proportion of men than women commit suicide. Shortly after the event takes place, the police are called to confirm that the death was in fact a suicide and not homicide. Subsequently, there may also be a coroner's investigation, as well as additional investigations by insurance companies. The entire investigative process tends to reinforce existing suspicions in the community concerning the cause of death. Even in the absence of all official doubts as to the fact of suicide, a residue of community suspicion tends to remain.

Further problems are engendered in some instances by the fact that several religious denominations will not allow the normal type of funeral service, since suicide is considered an unforgivable sin. Thus, many of the religious rituals and practices that normally serve to comfort bereaved persons upon the death of a loved one are denied in the case of suicide. There tends also to be a pattern of avoidance on the part of friends and relatives, apparently due to the shame and stigma attached to suicide. The bereaved spouse finds little support in the community and not infrequently encounters an atmosphere of accusation among relatives, especially inlaws. The prevailing sentiment is that the remaining spouse must have driven the other to take his own life.

The ultimate outcome of these unpleasant processes, and the community stigma and avoidance, is that the remaining spouse frequently tends to internalize all of these reactions to the point of extreme shame and guilt about the death of the mate. Not infrequently, the situation of the spouse deteriorates to the point where she may have to leave the community and seek anonymity in some new place.

The article delineates five distinctive patterns of adjustment, although these patterns might be described as being somewhat pathogenic, as opposed to adjustment in the positive sense of the term. Several of these patterns involve a new marriage through which a number of neurotic needs, brought on by the suicide of the spouse, might hopefully be met.

NOTES AND REFERENCES

1. Cain, Albert C.; and Fast, Irene: "Children's Disturbed Reactions to Parent Suicide." *American Journal of Orthopsychiatry* 36: 873-880, 1966.

The Abandoned Child

ARTHUR HENLEY

A small, bewildered face looks out of the newspaper; the picture also shows a kind-looking policeman offering milk and cookies or ice cream; the brief story below tells how the child was found wandering alone last night in the city railroad terminal. The headline asks: "Do you know this little boy?" He is an abandoned child.

At the height of a recent Christmas season, a boy and girl, age five and four, handsome and healthy and dressed in spanking-new clothes, were found huddled in the darkened toy department of a large department store, long after shopping hours. The children, clutching each other's hands, had been told to "wait here for Mommy." Pinned to the pocket of the boy's coat was a note reading: "I am the mother of these children. I love them dearly but have no money for food and no place to go. Please help them." They were abandoned children.

In a crowded bus station in Indianapolis, on a hot summer night, a four-year-old girl with big, sad blue eyes and a tangle of long blonde hair sat alone on a bench for many hours, until a policeman noticed that no one came for her. Too frightened to move or answer questions, she could not be identified and was finally taken to the county home for waifs, where a doctor examined her to determine whether she was mute. He found her perfectly healthy, but apparently shocked into silence by fear. She was an abandoned child.

And in a lawyer's office on Long Island, a seven-year-old boy with bright-red hair and a tooth-shy smile patiently held the hand of his smaller sister while they waited for their mother to come back. The two were dressed in a collection of incredibly shabby hand-me-downs, but they knew their names and their full address, and were safely returned home. When they arrived, the mother burst into tears and cried, "*Why* can't I get rid of you?" The police learned that she had made several previous attempts to abandon her children and had even said to the boy, "Why don't you run away?" He had answered, "You know I can't cross the street by myself, Mommy."

From *McCalls* 91:126, No. 8, May, 1964. Reprinted by permission of Curtis Brown, Ltd. Copyright © 1964 by the McCall Publishing Company.

Who are the abandoned children? Sometimes called "orphans of the living," they are the hundreds of thousands of youngsters who have one or both parents living but, for any one of countless reasons, have suddenly been left to fend for themselves. Rejected, deserted, neglected, mistreated, given up—such terms all describe the loveless act of abandonment, and authorities use them interchangeably with the stark but legally hazy term "abandoned."

Accurate statistics concerning abandoned children are difficult to find; but it is known that there are now over a quarter of a million *homeless* children in the United States. Some are newborn babies left at hospitals and never claimed; some, deprived of love and care, turn up lost, stranded, or as runaways, and they are not legally considered "abandoned." Thousands of others are abandoned in their own homes, locked in or chained to beds, left with neighbors or strangers and then never called for, deposited on church steps, in barrooms, stores, train stations—even tossed into curbside ash cans. Sometimes a tag is found attached to the child's wrist or clothing, with a scrawled message from his mother or father, pleading for kindness or listing minute, painstaking details about the proper feeding formula to give "my baby."

On November 18, 1962, a man strolling down East Sixty-First Street in New York City thought he heard a cat meowing. Then he spotted a small blue bundle on a stoop—no cat, but a two-month-old baby boy, wrapped in a blanket. A note pinned to the bundle read: "Please understand that I had no choice but to leave him somewhere. . . . I do not want to give him away; I will come for him when I can care for him properly. We will name him John Smith for the time being. His father was from Malaya. He probably is part Negro. I am from New York, white. Perhaps this small bit of information will help in placing him." She also left the baby's formula and a bottle. The case record reads: "Abandoned male No. 2631." The mother never came back.

In almost all cases where a child has been deliberately abandoned, he or she is found scrubbed and shining, immaculately dressed in bright *new* clothing—not just a freshly laundered worn suit. This is usually the final act, child-welfare authorities explain, of a mother's desperation. Says Robert Mackreth, of the Federation of Protestant Welfare Agencies: "After her impulsive decision to abandon her child, the mother performs her last act of love for him by making him as appealing and presentable as she can. She says, in effect, to whoever finds him: 'I was, after all, a pretty good mother—just see how nice my child looks.' "

Yet beneath the crisp new jacket or dress, the abandoned child often shows the marks of severe mistreatment; social workers call these youngsters "battered children"—they have been abused physically, not just emotionally. Most often, the battered child is a boy under three.

The abandoned child is rarely a defective or handicapped youngster. Authorities say that this is because the parent of such a child would be burdened with too heavy a sense of guilt—heavy enough to outweigh her motives for wanting to give him up.

What kind of unbearable pressure could drive a parent to abandon a child? The authorities tick off emotional immaturity, alcoholism, drug addiction, poverty, broken home, mental or physical illness, aloneness, ruthlessness, despair—as the "common contributing reasons." In almost all cases, it is the mother who does the abandoning, for most abandoned children are first the victims of broken homes, and in a broken home, it is usually the mother who has been left with the children.

Many such mothers sometimes become so frightened and unbalanced that they try to sell or trade their children before actually deserting them. In Chicago, a mother tried to sell her daughters, age two and three, to raise rent money; in Salt Lake City, Utah, a young couple attempted to trade their six-month-old baby for a new car. At the Children's Aid Society in New York City, Mrs. Nora Johnson, director of Foster Care Services, recalls a woman who tried to sell a baby and when asked, "Are you sure he's yours?" replied, "Sure I'm sure. I paid twenty-eight dollars for him."

Often, a mother on her own and sometimes a couple abandon several children at once. In such cases, say the authorities, the reason is that the responsibility of parenthood has weighed more and more heavily until, by the time the third or fourth child is born, the burden has become too great to bear at all.

Why don't such troubled parents surrender their unwanted child for adoption instead of abandoning him? Mrs. Mildred K. Wagle, director of Child Adoption Services, State Charities Aid Association, says, "It takes a lot of courage to face someone and say 'I want to give up my child.'" For this is a woman in crisis, a mother whose emotional state cannot countenance the endless questions and innumerable delays imposed by most agencies that accept such children. Abandonment seems by far the less painful way out.

When an abandoned child is found, what happens to him or her varies widely from state to state and even from city to city. In New York, if he is under two years of age, he is placed at once in the Foundling Hospital; if he is over two but under sixteen, he is turned over to the Bureau of Child Welfare. If he is found at night, police take him to a temporary shelter (the Children's Shelter, for boys age two to fifteen and girls age two to six; Callagy Hall, for girls age six to fifteen). If the child cannot be identified through questioning, clothing, or papers, a footprint check is made, a report filed with the Missing Persons' Bureau, and the newspapers, television and radio stations called on to help by printing and broadcasting descriptions and photographs. If no one responds after several months, the child is assigned a name, a religion, a birthday (decided on after a physical examination), and a serial number. Then he is placed in foster care, through an agency, or, if possible, in an adoptive home.

Once in a while, the parent who deserts her child has a change of heart or is found and brought in; when this happens, she almost always has an excuse for her actions ("I thought she was with her grandma," or "I was sick and couldn't come for her"). Her child almost never blames her; social workers say it is characteristic of the abandoned child to *protect* his mother, even when all evidence proves she has willfully forsaken him. In the children's shelters, most arguments among small lost inmates start when one child says something mean about another child's mother and the other youngster snaps back in angry defense. The more abused the child, the more fiercely he defends his parents, whether from fear or the need to be loved.

Children from forty states turn up at New York's welfare agencies with heartbreaking regularity. When parents are tracked down, few charges are pressed. Sometimes even a parent from a distant state turns up voluntarily, explaining, "I just got fed up with everything and went out to get drunk. Now I feel better and want my baby back."

One such repentant mother, a young Indianapolis woman who left her four-year-old daughter, Cindy, in a bus terminal one summer, showed up two weeks later at the police station and claimed her. "She was lost," the mother explained. "It was a mix-up." When brought face to face with Cindy, she hesitated and did not hug the child, while Cindy stared blankly at her, not saying a word. "Don't you remember me?" the mother asked finally. The reunion was so unsuccessful that the police made the child pick out her mother from a "lineup" of four women. This time, Cindy did better. "Take your real mommy's hand," a policewoman directed. After an endless moment, Cindy did.

The law is handicapped in dealing with such parents because, in many cases, courts have little or no jurisdiction over them; in some states, it is not even possible to compel them to come into court. Neglect statutes are not designed to punish them, but merely to help keep families together. And so the abandoning mother rarely is charged with having committed a criminal act—and even when she faces the courts on a minor misdemeanor charge, she usually wins a suspended sentence or outright dismissal.

The child whose mother is not found and does not return most often is boarded with a foster family for approximately $100 a month in some states, far less in others, and up to twice that sum if handicapped, paid for by the welfare agency.

Albert J. Neely, director of the Children's Division, Cook County Department of Public Aid, Illinois, reports: "Between September 1, 1962, and March 1, 1963, we looked after 46 abandoned children and 183 deserted children (the difference being one of intent). We looked after an additional 377 children during that period, who were categorized as physically abused, deprived, and otherwise neglected. I have a case here where a mother abandoned all her eight children, on and off, for several days at a time. It costs about $1,200 a year to place each one in foster care. That means it would cost us nearly $10,000 for these eight children. And chances are they'd have to be so cared for for about ten years, which brings the total cost to about $100,000. But we'll have to spend it if these kids are to have a chance."

The luckiest abandoned child is the one who is classified "readily adoptable": He is under five, white, of at least average intelligence, and has no serious physical disabilities or severe emotional problems. The good-looking youngster usually fares better than the one not so well-favored. And while three out of four white children available for adoption do find an adoptive family eventually, only one in twenty Negro babies is so fortunate. In our great cities where the Negro is the most deprived citizen, there is a preponderance of homeless Negro children.

When no adoptive family can be found, the abandoned child becomes a ward of the state for an indefinite time. In New York, a foundling abandoned in infancy automatically becomes available for adoption at the end of one year; in other states, the waiting period may be two years or more. But the rejected child whose parents are known to the authorities may wear out many years in a succession of temporary shelters, waiting for someone to love him.

There is such a tangle of laws and technical language concerning the problem of abandonment and the treatment of it that there is no clear picture of how wide and deep a social illness it has become. The United States Children's Bureau reported in 1961, on the basis of statistics submitted by 42 states, that 388,506 children were receiving care from adults other than their parents. This figure included children in homes for the neglected and dependent, foster-family homes, group homes, homes of relatives, temporary shelters, treatment centers, and adoptive homes. The states of New York, Pennsylvania, Illinois, Ohio, California, Tennessee, Kentucky, and Georgia led in volume of cases.

And it is acknowledged by all authorities that abandonment is steadily increasing. As the birth rate continues to rise, so does the abandonment rate. Since emotional strain is in great part responsible for child desertion, the dramatic increase in mental disturbance also has its effect on the rising rate of abandonment. Another factor is the steady changing of the American social pattern—with what many authorities feel are alarming declines in the responsibility of the family unit and the once strong influences of religion and a high moral code.

Still another key to the puzzle is the fact that by far the largest number of abandoned children are found in urban areas. A small town or a rural community undoubtedly provides parents with more resources for hanging on—or else the closeness of a friendly neighborhood bolsters pride and discourages desertion. It is not so easy to "lose" a child when nearly everyone in town knows everyone else. Authorities have found that fewer children are abandoned in stormy weather or times of intense cold than in bright, sunny weather. Some lingering sense of responsibility urges a mother to protect her children from the elements.

Or she may join that even more callous breed of "psychological abandoners." These are the parents who keep their children with them at home, but mistreat them so cruelly that a horrified neighbor or relative finally reports the situation to the police. The victims of psychological abandonment may be locked up, chained, beaten, kicked, starved, or molested, not only by their parents, but by other members of the family—brothers, sisters, uncles, cousins—with the parents' consent and approval. Often, a mother is unable to love one of her children, as a result of a difficult pregnancy or because the child is unmanageable or shows personality conflicts. A woman whose husband has deserted her may transfer her affection to an older son, but abandon or mistreat a younger daughter. And still another deserted mother may vent her hostilities on a son because he reminds her of the husband who left her.

A mother in Flushing, Long Island, Mrs. Ellen Davis, confessed bitterly to welfare aides that she "took a lot of things out" on her six-year-old son, Bob, "because he's the spittin' image of his father." The father had walked out on them when she was pregnant with her second child, a little girl now four years old.

When the problems of raising her youngsters alone grew too great for Mrs. Davis, she began to abandon her children "temporarily." "I'd put them out in the hall and tell them to get lost when they became impossible," she explained. "And when I got real mad, I walked out on them—figuring a neighbor would look after them. Sometimes I did it just long enough to go have a cup of coffee and cool off. I kept wanting to get rid of them somewhere, anywhere."

Occasionally, it is a father who abandons—first his wife, then his children. In Chicago, there was the case of Dan Roberts, a towering hulk of a man who liked to be on the go, dragging his family with him as he moved restlessly from job to job (day laborer, railroad worker, carnival hand) or casually leaving them behind. His wife, Dorothy, was just as irresponsible. Throughout their marriage, they frequently drifted away from each other—until, finally, they separated for good, and Dan filed for divorce. He called his wife a "floater" and was awarded custody of their four children—two boys, four and seven; two girls, six and ten.

For the most part, Dan lived in Michigan, never staying long at any one address. Dorothy went to Arkansas, married again, and never bothered to keep in touch with her children.

About a year ago, Dan, his four children, and his current lady friend packed into an old car and drove out of Michigan. When they reached the outskirts of Chicago in late afternoon, Dan pulled up and parked off the turnpike. He took a grimy piece of torn carpeting out of the car trunk, laid it on the grass away from the main road, and told the children to get out of the car and sit together on the rug. "I'l be back. Just stay here," he said. The children didn't question him; they had been taught to obey. Then Dan climbed back into his car and drove away with his lady friend. An hour went by; then another hour. It began to grow dark and quite cold; the wind had come up and whipped about the children huddling together on their scrap of rug. Finally, the cold and darkness became too much. The older girl, Edna, told her sister and brothers to stay where they were while she went for help. She walked to a nearby house and knocked timidly at the front door. A woman answered, and Edna said, "We are waiting for our daddy, but he's late, Can we please come in where it's warm?"

The startled woman sent her husband to fetch the children, then telephoned the police. She sensed at once that the children had been abandoned. Police managed to track down the father by circulating a description of the car and the children's photographs. A car dealer in a Michigan city recognized them and later identified the father, who was picked up in Illinois. When reunited with his children, he showed little emotion, and they displayed no tears or feeling for him. He said he had not meant to abandon them, but was so busy looking for work that he had not been able to return for them.

His excuses failed to convince the police. He was tried, found guilty, and sentenced on charges of child abandonment. The children were placed in a foster home and are still under court custody. It isn't likely they will rejoin either parent. If they are lucky, loving foster parents may help heal their emotional scars.

But even when care and tenderness are finally given to the child who has been abandoned, the tragic effects of earlier mistreatment are often very hard to overcome. The authorities who try to help such children know the first signs of psychic damage extremely well: disturbed eating habits, nightmares, bed-wetting, extreme passivity, infantile behavior, loss of speech. Miss Elizabeth K. Radinsky, associate director of the Jewish Child Care Association of New York, drew this brief portrait: "Most abandoned children are so frozen that they've even lost their right to cry." The far-reaching effects are harder to predict. The way an abandoned child develops, the kind of adult he grows up to be depend on his native strength and resilience, his intelligence and personality. The neglected youngster who cannot laugh or cry when he is found often works with all his might to attach himself to someone he thinks might love him: it is not at all unusual for such a child to cling to the first social worker who questions him kindly when he is brought into a shelter. Pathetic as this may seem, the youngster who responds this way stands the best chance of growing into healthy, emotionally sound adulthood. The abandoned child who is able to cling to any kind of family image—no matter how remote—or who wants to arouse the interest of any one person is likeliest to find again the great healing gift of love, regardless of what he has suffered.

Jack Scott, born on Skid Row in Chicago twenty-five years ago and abandoned by his mentally ill parents, is a spectacular example of this remarkable recovery pattern. He was the son of an immigrant couple who had fled intolerable living conditions in their native country, only to find they could not surmount language and social barriers and grinding poverty in America. Both parents had been committed to mental insitutions by the time Jack was two years old. The child became a ward of Family Court and was placed in a foster home by the Illinois Children's Home and Aid Society. At first, he could neither laugh nor cry and seemed incapable of reacting in any way to the attention of caseworkers or his new parents.

Fortunate enough to be assigned to a dedicated caseworker and to be placed with a warm and loving foster family, he gradually emerged from his hard little shell and began to return their affection. Once he had established excellent relationships with his family, and later with schoolteachers and classmates, Jack turned into a happy, outgoing child. When he was eleven years old, his foster parents became ineligible for further public aid, and the boy was returned to the agency. He was soon placed with a second foster family, and again he adjusted well. When he reached his late teens, the second foster father died, and the mother remarried. Then Jack decided to strike out on his own. He graduated from high school, worked at two jobs, and earned enough money to finance his first year at college.

Throughout the rest of his college career, he worked part time to support himself and kept up a faithful correspondence with his old caseworker, though he was no longer a ward of the agency. The agency had, in effect, become his family, for it had been the most constant and stable influence in his young life. He invited the caseworker to visit him at college and treated her as if she were a parent, entertaining her where his classmates took their mothers to dinner and proudly showing her off to his friends. Only after he had established in her the parental "image" he so desperately needed could he face without pain or bitterness the fact that his real parents were alive, and feel compassion for them.

Scott is now an engineering draftsman and has chosen to live in a small town in Minnesota. He married another college graduate, and they have a son, whom they love devotedly. The young father is a good-looking, good-natured, intelligent, popular man, who seems to have no insurmountable problems in life. He even contributes to the support of the parents he never knew. Yet "even today," he admits, "I think of the Illinois Children's Home and Aid Society as my real family."

Jack Scott may have been exceptionally lucky, remarkably strong, or simply endowed with a crisis-proof spirit. But for every Jack Scott, there are, of course, hundreds of abandoned children growing up alone in society, unable to reach out to anyone or anything that has touched their crippled lives. These are the hopeless ones who will repeat the tragic pattern their parents set for them when they deserted them. Their sense of abandonment stays with them, and they reach maturity racked with fear, timidity, self-distrust, and deep depression. Often the pain of such total aloneness leads to insanity or suicide. Material success or fame may have little effect. Marilyn Monroe, who seemed to have pulled herself up out of despair to a dazzlingly desirable life, never escaped the haunting past of her abandoned childhood and the many unhappy years she spent in the foster homes where she had never really belonged.

If psychological scarring could haunt a Marilyn Monroe and force her to end her life, uncounted thousands of others, lacking her energy and talent, drift through their days in the drab emptiness of a lonely, unmarked existence, and end in tragedies not even noticed by the world in which they never find a place.

Jeff Shaw, age fourteen, was one of five children abandoned in 1957 by their unstable, hard-drinking, desperately unhappy parents. Jeff was eight when his parents left him and his brothers and sisters for the last of many times. Jeff was placed in an orphanage for three years and then transferred to a boarding home. But the boarding home was shut down when authorities discovered it was not being run properly, and when Jeff was not quite twelve, he was placed in the Montanari Clinical School and Treatment Center in Hialeah, Florida, where severely disturbed children are sent for treatment. His brothers and sisters had all been adopted, and Jeff deeply resents the fact that he, alone of the five, has been unable to find someone to love him.

Jeff, born in Los Angeles, has lived in many places. Psychologists say that at fourteen, he still wets his bed, has frequent violent temper tantrums, and is often aggressive toward other children. And he is very much concerned about someday having a home—a gift he feels he can earn only by being "a good boy."

When asked to draw a picture in class, Jeff drew a frightening skull and crossbones. As he is considered virtually "unadoptable" because of his age and background, his future lies only in the direction of institutional care or another foster home. The teachers and doctors who know him say that without continued love and care, he is unlikely ever to become a useful member of society; chances are greater he will grow up into a rebel, a delinquent—or worse.

The problem of the homeless child has far outstripped the sentimental image that appeals readily to all persons of good will. It is too overwhelming to be handled by the benevolent relative, the well-meaning neighbor, or even the charitable philanthropist. It swamps the family courts and the welfare services, most of which are understaffed and overworked. It takes an extraordinary bite of every tax dollar. But most disturbing of all is the extent of its present toll in human suffering.

As the number of abandoned children increases, the number of potential adoptive families dwindles. The disheartening tangle of laws and red tape surrounding adoption have driven away many couples who long to adopt a child. The wide differences and lack of teeth in laws concerned with abandonment—and the incredible difficulty of devising *any* law to deal justly and wisely with what, after all, is not so much a crime as a deep symptom of moral and emotional disturbance—indicate that there are no easy answers and that there can be no instant cure.

All experts involved with the problem of abandonment agree that such solutions as there are must begin with the parents; thus, the great need is for society as a whole to learn how to listen to the cries of human beings who are alone, in pain, desperation, and fear. The need is for help and understanding for the sufferings of parents who cannot face the responsibility of parenthood. The need is not only to relieve the suffering of their children now, but to keep those children from growing up unable to give love to their own young, and so perpetuating the vicious circle. The abandoned child touches every individual with the lessons that it is easier to love when you are loved and that the sense of being cared for—or cared about—in some critical split second of distress may make all the difference in generations of lives.

The only cure for abandonment lies in prevention of the hopelessness that makes it happen.

The "Battered Child":
Individual Victim of Family Brutality

CRAIG TAYLOR

Four-year-old Jenny was admitted to a hospital with a broken leg and signs of old bruises. Her mother reported that the child had fallen. Routine X-ray examination revealed that in her young life Jenny had had both arms and a collar bone broken and her skull mildly fractured.

Five weeks after he left the hospital with his parents a healthy, new-born infant, Steven was back in the hospital, this time with a skull fracture, intercranial bleeding and a broken arm, the victim of a savage beating by his parents.

Year-old Jimmy would not stop crying. His mother shook him, then in frustration threw him against a wall. His body when autopsied showed signs of previous physical abuse and raw, open sores from persistent diaper rash.

These cases represent tens of thousands of similar occurrences in the United States every year. The extent of child abuse as a social problem only came to public attention in the 1960's when hospitals and clinics began to make routine X-ray examinations of the bodies of infants who were brought in with serious injuries. These examinations revealed that many of the children had been the victims of repeated injuries inflicted by their parents. This phenomenon is so common that it has been given a name, the "battered child syndrome," and doctors are becoming increasingly aware that a problem of serious proportions exists. They must look for signs of a history of abuse when confronted with an injured child, the circumstances of whose injuries are questionable. Medical associations, welfare agencies, and public health services, the police and the mass media have all become involved in the treatment of this problem, and public awareness has grown, largely through the publication of the gruesome details of the more sensational cases. The tragic irony of this situation is that these children are being vic-

From Bryant, Clifton D. (ed.): *Social Problems Today*. Philadelphia: J. B. Lippincott Co., 1971, pp. 210–216. Reprinted by permission of the publisher.

timized in their own homes by those persons who are supposed to be responsible for their welfare.

A pioneer study by the American Humane Association of cases of abuse reported in newspapers in the U.S. in 1962 found that of 662 cases 55.7% of the victims were under the age of 4 and 27% of the children (178) died. The most vulnerable are the younger children. Of the 178 who died, 53.98% were under 2 years of age. Fathers alone abused 38.25% of the children, mothers alone abused 28.86%, and both parents joined in abusing 5.4% of the children. Mothers accounted for 48.54% of the fatalities while fathers were responsible for only 22.22% of the fatalities. Parents accounted for 72.57% of all abuse and 75.85% of all fatalities.[1]

An attempt to estimate the possible size of the child abuse problem was made by Brandeis University and the National Opinion Research Center of the University of Chicago in 1965. They asked a national sample of 1,520 adults if they personally knew any of the families involved during the preceeding year in incidents in which children were physically injured or killed by their parents or other persons caring for them such as teachers or baby sitters. The abuse in question had to be in anger or deliberate; it could not be accidental. Three percent of the respondents (45 persons) reported 48 separate incidents. Extending this to the U.S. population of 190 million persons, with statistical error taken into consideration, the researchers estimated the upper limit of child abuse to be from 2.53 million to 4.07 million cases, or from 13.3 to 21.4 incidents per 1,000 population.[3]

Statistics dealing with child abuse are apt to be misleading and to present a distorted view of the problem. Accurate social data is difficult to collect for normal behavior and the problem is much more difficult when the activity being studied is of a criminal nature. The medical profession has found, for example, that parents who repeatedly injure a child may take the child to a different doctor for the treatment of each injury so that the doctors will not be able to identify a pattern of abusive behavior. Second, lower-income and non-white parents are more apt to be suspected of child abuse by doctors and their child's injuries reported to authorities than are middle-class and white parents. Third, the private or "family" doctor who depends on the good will of an established clientele will be less apt to report suspected abuse than will clinic and public health doctors, the type most patronized by the lower-income families. Forth, abuse resulting in death is more apt to be reported than those injuries which are not fatal and the fatal injuries are most apt to be inflicted on infants under three years of age. Therefore non-fatal abuse, abuse to older children and middle class abuse are underrepresented in official statistics. Fifth, when confronted with the possibility of criminal prosecution parents are apt to present a united front against officials and insist that the child had an accident. Evidence in child abuse cases is difficult for the prosecution to acquire.

These problems sometimes lead to the general impression that child abuse is primarily a phenomenon of the lower classes, particularly when they are dealt with in conjunction with such behavior as drinking and sexual promiscuity. The public is prompted to feel that such behavior is all that can be expected of those people and that they must not be "right." However, this obscures the fact that child abuse is also an increasing problem in the middle class.

Historically, the situation of American children is probably more secure than that of children at practically any other period in history. Fathers do not have the right of life or death over their offspring, nor can they sell them into slavery or offer them as human sacrifices to God. It is indicative of the change in public attitudes toward the general status of children that reports of their physcial abuse by parents do result in moral outrage, intervention by welfare agencies and criminal prosecution. Attitudes are not always perfectly consistent with one another and while many Americans would agree that a man's home is his castle and that to spare the rod is to spoil the child, they would still have some limit on the physical harm which a parent might inflict on his or her children.

There is, of course, a difference between judgements of what constitutes punishment and other aggressive behavior. Burning a child with cigarettes, placing caustic materials in body orifices, beating it with a lamp cord, or scalding it under a hot water faucet, all practices which have been encountered by doctors and by police departments' forensic pathologists, clearly exceed the general norms governing punishment. These forms of behavior are so excessive that they suggest a serious pathological situation.

Americans expect children to be protected by their parents within the shelter of the home. However, the isolation of contemporary nuclear families places the child at the mercy of the parents to a greater degree than is true of an extended-family situation. The pressures of contemporary society are brought increasingly to bear on the quality of family life and the victim of these pressures is too often the child in the home. Here we focus on two aspects of the complex situation of child abuse. One aspect is those characteristics of children which make them likely victims of abusive behavior. The other is the change in the family structures and roles resulting from urbanization and industrialization.

There are characteristics of some classes of children which make them prone to be targets of abuse. Among the most abuse-prone are those children who have digestive disorders which render them constant!y irritable. A frequent response of an abusive parent when questioned after a child had been thrown, beaten or scalded is that the child wouldn't stop crying. Children are rendered ill-tempered by diaper rash and hunger. Forensic pathologists reporting on the condition of the remains of babies killed by parents indicate that a frequent condition is severe diaper rash, generally serious enought to result in scars. Children in tropical climates such as India who do not wear diapers or pants are free from diaper rash because there is no cloth present next to the skin to trap and hold the acid in the urine and to culture bacteria in excretions.

In India a common practice has been to still crying babies by applying opium to their fingers. When the fingers are sucked the opium makes the baby sleepy. This use of opium does not result in addiction because it is discontinued when the child is a few years old. American pediatricians sometimes prescribe mild sedatives for infants who have colic and are not getting sleep because of crying. The relief which this provides for the infant's mother should not be underestimated because the presence of a crying infant may aggravate the familiar post-partum depression and produce nervous strains which in turn may result in abuse of the child.

Education and financial considerations work to the disadvantage of the infant in lower income families. The lower income mothers are those least apt to have the knowledge and resources to keep an infant well fed, clean and healthy. The new disposable diapers, the rash and colic medications and the pediatrician with his prescription medications and advice are prohibitively expensive for the low income mothers. These women in urban slums are also miles and generations removed from wild-growing herbs and other folk remedies with which their ancestors dealt with the common complaints of childhood. Migration to urban areas has left behind the wise old women who were the repositories and teachers of such information and the disorganized urban poor are left to their own resources with such help as they can get from public agencies.

Other characteristics also increase the chance that the child might be victimized. One of these is its status as legitimate or illegitimate. The illegitimate child may be resented by the mother, particularly if it infringes on her freedom, reminds her of a dissertion by a lover or of rape, or makes her subsequent marriage an unlikely prospect. Illegitimate children are also apt to be resented by the child's grandparents and by subsequent boyfriends of the mother whom the child serves to remind of the woman's previous attachments.

Formal legitimacy is not proof against such attitudes toward a child. The U.S. government has recently estimated that 1/3 of all first births to women in the U.S. are conceived out of wedlock. Of these, 6/7 of the women marry and the child is born in wedlock. Only 1/21 of the first conceptions are born out of wedlock. This leaves 2/7 of all first births *within marriage* having been conceived out of wedlock. Many of these marriages are variations of the "shotgun" variety, actually having been precipitated by the occasion of the pregnancy. Such children are frequently among those referred to as "unwanted" or, at least, "unplanned." The marriage they cause may be ill-advised, between partners who would not have married each other had not biology and social pressure intervened. Either or both parents may feel trapped in the situation and the infant may be the scapegoat. If the marriage provides financial burdens which the father is unprepared to assume, prematurely cuts short his adolescence or interferes with his educational or career plans, he is apt to resent the child. It should be noted that within this last category are the bulk of the abused middle class children. Young middle class males are apt to experience more disturbance in their educational and career plans than are the lower-class youths. The plans of the middle class male require more time and money than those of the lower class male. This is not to suggest that the middle class male is more apt to marry a pregnant girlfriend than is the lower class male, but rather that the "pregnancy-precipitated" marriage contains more sources of potential resentment for the middle class male than for the lower class male.

Another class of legitimate child which has high potential as a target of aggression is the child whose paternity is in doubt. If the young father feels he has reason to doubt that he is in fact the biological father of the child, whether he is or not, it is highly possible that he will be physically aggressive toward the child. Similarly, if a woman's pregnancy is the occasion chosen by her husband for an extramarital affair while she is not in shape to compete, the mother may resent the offspring.

One of the casualties of the urbanization and industrialization of contemporary society has been the extended family system. Families are more mobile as youths go to college and then are transferred from position to position within companies with the young husband and father quickly becoming the head of his own household. Patterns of housing construction reflect this trend as most homes are built with the nuclear family in mind, not making allowance for the presence of the aged within the home. In the typical extended household situation child care involves a number of female relatives, many with extensive experience. The young mother is not left to her own resources to deal with the full range of activities of child care and consolation. Further, in such a situation a young mother will have observed, in most realistic situations, siblings and cousins in their infancy. The modern young mother, particularly those from middle class homes, will not have had such experiences. Orientation toward motherhood is more apt to be an extension of the sex-role orientation of playing with dolls. Parenthood, rather than having been learned gradually through lifelong exposure, is a cram course of magazine articles, advice from pediatricians, warnings from mothers and gossip with peers, mostly encountered with the onset of pregnancy. When the cooing, wetting dolls of girlhood are replaced with reality of colicy, messy, smelly, demanding, crying babies the young mother, though better educated and with more labor-saving devices than her ancestors, may justifiably feel ill-equipped to cope.

The impact of this situation is compounded if the girl feels that she has chosen motherhood as a career as opposed to other career possibilities she might have been considering. If she has placed most of her emotional eggs in the basket of fulfillment through motherhood the crying child or the child who refuses to eat poses a serious threat to her identity. The child is, to her, telling her that she is not a good mother. In the absence of a close group of related females who can assure her that such infant behavior is normal and who can take over while she gets away from the house, the woman can only deepen her sense of failure. Whereas Green pointed out that the 24-hour attention given to the middle class child tended to absorb the child's personality, it may be noted that for many young mothers motherhood is also a 24-hour trap which may absorb *her* personality. The constant and unrelieved contention with an uneasy infant may produce a serious strain on the nerves of the young mother and if she resents the child for any reason she is apt to respond violently to the child in moments of anger.[2]

Young fathers frequently bring home the tensions and frustrations which are encountered in their occupation and convert these to aggressive behavior in the home. Age at marriage has been declining in recent decades and so has the age of parents at the birth of the first child. Parenthood has been assumed by persons less and less prepared for it, emotionally and financially, and with the resulting frustrations that the child has become an increasingly likely target of aggression. Since nearly 1/3 of the couples married are expecting a child at the time of marriage there is little time for them to establish sound personal relationships before they are faced with the burdens of parenthood. It would seem reasonable to assume that most of these pregnancies are unplanned, although some will point out that the pregnancy may have been planned by the woman to trap a husband. Whether the pregnancy was an intentional trap or not, the "trapped" feeling resulting from hasty marriages under such circumstances are widely discussed and the male's resentment toward their wives and babies an ever-present possibility. A hasty marriage frequently results in drastic changes in the young man's plans. His freedoms and personal expenditures are curtailed as, in many instances, are his career plans. For the lower class male marriage may be viewed as a chance to demonstrate to the community that he is a man. However, as Leibow suggests in *Tally's Corner,* for the Negro male in the low income neighborhood marriage and parenthood are a major source of proving manhood, but they place him in a situation in which the effects of failures are maximized.[4]

It is possible to identify important qualitative changes in physical abuse of children by parents. Historically, much child abuse has been criminal but much has been within the acceptable normative context of the society. Corporal punishment has been approved for defying authority, as a remedy to drive out demons or other spiritual purification, to teach stoic acceptance of pain, and as punishment for dishonoring the family name or breaking taboos which would anger the gods and result in the suffering of the collectivity of which the child was member. Children have been sacrificed to gods and maimed to inflict caste marks, to conform to standards of beauty as in the instance of Chinese foot-binding of females, and to render them pitiable and hence effective beggars as is done today in India. These acts are, within the norms of the groups in question, rational acts of conformity which increase the solidarity of the society and add to the integration of the family into a larger collectivity.

By contrast, perhaps the most disturbing aspect of child abuse in contemporary society is that it tends to be irrational or nonrational, is in and of itself a deviant act, and performs no integrative function relating the family to the larger society unless it is to call the family and its problems to the attention of legal and welfare authorities. Child abuse today in America is sometimes interpreted as a covert plea for help by troubled parents who cannot cope with the extra-familial pressures of contemporary life.

The family is one of the basic persistent social groupings of society which has traditionally been the focus of such activities as education, religion, procreation and social placement. When asked to explain the universality and persistence of the family, students of social institutions point to prolonged physical dependence of the human infant and the time required for social maturation in the absence of instincts. With the departure of such functions as education and religious observance from the family to extra-familial institutions the major functions retained by the family are procreation, the nurture and protection of children and social placement. The irony of child abuse, therefore, lies in the failure of the institution which is vested with the responsibility of protection and the nurture of children. In our culture, which is frequently described as "child-centered," having children remains major justification for continuing, sanctioned sexual relations between adults. The child-centeredness of thousands of homes today consist of the child being the target of parental hostility and brutality.

NOTES AND REFERENCES

1. DeFrancis, Vincent: *Child Abuse: Preview of a Nationwide Survey.* Denver: American Humane Association, Children's Division, 1963.
2. Green, Arnold W.: "The Middle Class Male Child and Neurosis." *American Sociological Review,* Feb., 1946, pp. 31–41.
3. Helfer, Ray E., and Kempe, Henry C. (eds.): *The Battered Child.* Chicago: The University of Chicago Press, 1968.
4. Leibow, Elliot: *Tally's Corner.* Boston: Little Brown & Co., 1967.

The Adjustment of Children
of Jail Inmates

SIDNEY FRIEDMAN AND D. CONWAY ESSELSTYN

How are children affected by the jail confinement of their fathers? Does the fact that their father is in jail have any meaning for them? If so, is it associated with good adjustment or bad adjustment? Or are they not affected at all? These are the questions which the present authors sought to explore.[1] So far as is known, the subject has not been investigated.[2]

Humanitarian considerations, educational and psychiatric consequences, influences upon future potential as a productive worker and effective consumer—all combine to suggest that steps be taken to determine what effect the jail confinement of the father has upon the child.

The same arguments, as well as additional ones, concern the effect that jail confinement of the mother has upon the child. However, that subject was not included in the present study because of administrative problems and the small number of mothers confined in jail and available as a point for initiating an inquiry.[3] When one asks how children are affected by the jail confinement of their fathers, many serious methodological problems arise. Most of these have to do with forging a tight causal link between the fact of the father's jail confinement and any adjustment problems which might be observed in his child. It was felt that these problems could not be resolved profitably at this time. Therefore, the decision was made to state the problem in an alternative way: Do children whose fathers are jail inmates differ from children whose fathers are not jail inmates? The problem, then, is one of discovering differences and measuring, or otherwise indicating, the scope and direction of these differences, if any exist. The causal connection would then have to be postponed, and would have to remain at present as an inference.[4]

METHOD OF STUDY

The method by which the problem was investigated involved the identi-

From *Federal Probation* 29:55–59, No. 4, Dec., 1965. Reprinted by permission of the publisher.

217

fication and selection of jail inmates who were the fathers of children whom they acknowledged, the location of those children, and the application of a measuring devise to them and to their controls.

The jail inmates were those who were confined in the Elmwood Rehabilitation Center of Santa Clara County for periods longer than 6 months during the year 1963.[5] It was felt this was the minimum length of time which would be necessary for the father's absence from the home to be reflected in the behavior of his children. Inmates were identified as fathers by consulting available records and by interviews during the orientation period. They were advised of the scope and purpose of the study. Cooperation was solicited with no representation of influence upon sentence or jail regimen. Confidentiality was assured. With his consent, the inmate was selected as a father for purposes of this study and this process was continued until a sample of over 100 children was obtained.

The children were located in the school system through the cooperation of the Santa Clara County Office of Education.[6] The total number of children involved in the entire study was 328. This population was derived from three groups.

Group III was the experimental group—children of jail inmates. These children were distributed throughout all the elementary grades from kindergarten through the seventh grade.

Groups I and II were controls selected for purposes of comparison. These children were selected by employing a table of random numbers, using two numbers out of 35. The pupil above the name of a child on the Group III list was assigned to Group I, the pupil below was assigned to Group II. The children in Groups I and II thus had the same grade distribution as those in Group III since they were chosen by random lot from the same class lists.

Principals and administrators were consulted as to whether the fathers of any of the controls had a history of jail confinement. None was discovered. Some thought was given to devising a method of verifying replies on this point but none could be constructed readily. If one may judge from the great amount of intimate knowledge which school officials showed they had about their pupils, it is doubtful whether any system of verification would have turned up a substantial degree of error regarding the absence of jail histories among the fathers of the controls.

The same age range was observed among all three groups. While the groups were not compared socioeconomically, it is anticipated that if such comparisons were made, the differences, if any, would be minimal since the children in all three groups came from similar localities.

Ethnically, there is a different problem. Group III was composed of children, 60 percent of whose fathers had surnames indicating Mexican ancestry. This is about 20 percentage points higher than appeared to be the case for children in control groups I and II. This overrepresentation of the Mexican-American enclave in the jail population is part of a larger constellation of social problems in Santa Clara County and is beyond the scope of this study. There is no way to determine how ethnicity influenced teacher ratings, but general community folkways suggest that the distortion was minor. Beyond ethnicity as a variable, the three groups were comparable racially.

The distribution by sex for all three groups is that shown in Table 1.

The sex distribution in all three groups was similar. The excess of boys over girls was deliberate. Originally, an all-boy sample was planned. Girls were added later to provide tentative comparisons.

The measuring device applied to the three groups of children was the University of Pennsylvania Pupil Adjustment Inventory, Short Form. This provides for ratings of the following traits or characteristics:[7]

Age	Health
Achievement	Participation
Attitude	View toward school
Sociability	Attendance
Acceptability	School's influence
Companions	Economic status
Temperament	Family interest
Self-concept	

Each of these characteristics is arranged on a five-step continuum so that a teacher may rate a pupil from below-average to above-average on each item or trait. The wording of the five steps on each continuum varies with each trait but follows the general theme:

Conspicuously below expectations
Below expectations
Equal to expectations for this age and grade
Above expectations
Far above expectations

In the present study, all ratings were "blind," that is, in order to eliminate rating bias, teachers were not informed which pupil was in the experi-

TABLE 1. DISTRIBUTION BY SEX

	Total	Boys	Girls
All Groups	328	244	84
Group I	104	74	30
Group II	107	80	27
Group III (Experimentals)	117	90	27

mental group (Group III) and which pupils were in the controls (Groups I and II).

These teacher ratings were later totaled separately for each characteristic and the totals were converted to percents of each group by sex. In this process all ratings to the left of the midpoint position on the Short Form were compressed as below-average accomplishments, abilities, or adjustments, and all to the right were compressed as above-average. This procedure is consistent with the way the Pupil Adjustment Inventory is designed.[8]

These steps may be illustrated by examining the distribution of ratings on one of the traits. The trait "Attitudes Toward School Work" is selected arbitrarily for this purpose. The five steps on the continuum for this item are:

Almost never attempts any school work
Below estimated aptitude
Equal to estimated aptitude
Above estimated aptitude
Far above estimated aptitude

The third step—"Equal to estimated aptitude"—denotes the average position. All to the left are below average, and all to the right are above average. The ratings which the teachers gave for this trait are shown in Table 2.

TABLE 2. ATTITUDE OF BOYS TOWARD SCHOOL WORK AS RATED BY TEACHERS

	Percent Below Average	Percent in Average Category	Percent Above Average
Group I	23	45	32
Group II	30	48	22
Group III (Experimentals)	42	52	6

Table 2 shows that 42 percent of the experimentals, and 23 and 30 percent of the two controls, were rated below-average on attitude toward school work. On the right of the midpoint, 6 percent of the experimentals, and 32 and 22 percent of the two controls, were rated above average on this characteristic. Thus, relative to comparable controls in the same school grades, a higher proportion of the sons of jail inmates was rated as displaying average attitudes toward school work. By the same test, a significantly higher proportion of these pupils displayed below-average attitudes and a conspicuously lower proportion displayed attitudes which teachers rated as above-average. Since the teachers did not know which pupils were in which groups, the likelihood of a halo, or its reverse, around any one group was reduced, even eliminated.

Hence, it appears safe to regard these ratings as operationally objective and not reflective of bias or unconscious wish.

FINDINGS OF THE STUDY

Limitations of space prevent our presenting here a detailed report on the volume and the percentage distribution of teacher ratings on all three groups for all 15 traits.[9] However, the data support the following three principal findings of this study:

1. The sons of jail inmates are rated below-average in the school world on important social and psychological characteristics more frequently than are comparable controls.

2. Some boys are rated above-average, but they are far outranked by comparable controls.

3. The same statements apply to daughters, but there appear to be even greater differences between them and other girls with whom they may be compared.

Considered in detail, the data in Table 3 show comparisons for boys within the three ranges.

TABLE 3.

	Group III (Experimentals)	Groups I and II (Controls)
Below-Average	Higher proportions generally. Not much difference on sociability and attendance. Great differences everywhere else.	Represented in the below-average range, but except for 2 traits, they are here in far lower proportions.
Average	Outrank the controls on 9 traits: achievement, attitude, sociability, companions, self-concept, participation, view toward school, attendance, school's influence. In 4 of these (sociability, participation, view toward school, and school's influence), the difference is 8 percentage points or better. In the other 5, the difference does not appear significant.	Outrank the experimentals on 6 traits: age, acceptability, temperament, health, economic status, family interest. All of the differences are significant except for health.
Above-Average	Represented in the above-average range on 13 traits; i.e., all except age and home economic status, but in comparatively low proportions.	Represented in vastly higher proportions on 12 traits. On 2 traits, temperament and attendance, the differences are not so vast. On 1 trait, economic status, the differences are present but are not significant.

Considering the girls, their numbers were so low in all groups as to require caution on all statements. Tentatively, however, and subject to the limitations of small groups, two observations may be offered. First, the direction of the difference for Group III girls, compared with Control Group girls is the same as for Group III boys compared with their controls. Second, the magnitude of the difference is greater—a greater proportion is below-average, a lesser proportion is above-average, than is true of Group III boys.

The suggestion is, therefore, that girls whose fathers are jail inmates pose more extensive adjustment problems than boys.

With further regard to the Group III boys on this level of comparison, the ways in which they outrank the controls on the average range—especially the traits of attitude toward schoolwork, acceptance of school as a normal activity, and school's influence upon him—all this may be contrary to what one might logically expect. Insofar as Group III boys are products of a deprived background, one would anticipate that they would have negative feelings about school, and much in our current literature supports this expectation. However, the favorable ratings here tend to undermine that position and lend some degree of support to the ideas of Roebuck and Richardson. Although they dealt with delinquents, one should be prepared for a connection between their views and the discovery that Group III boys have surprisingly good feelings abut school.[10]

The foregoing compared Groups I and II with Group III on ratings, shown as percents, within each entire range. The following discussion compares the proportion of ratings evident on each trait between all three ranges.

Thus, for the characteristic, "attitude toward schoolwork," shown above 58 percent of the Group III experimentals are rated average and above, and 42 percent are rated below. However, from 70 to 77 percent of the controls are rated average and above, while 23 to 30 percent are rated below.

On sociability, 76 percent of the Group III boys are rated average and above. Seventy to 85 percent of the controls are so rated. Fifty-five percent of the Group III boys are shown as having average or above-average concepts of the self, 71 to 86 percent of the controls are rated in this direction.

And so the pattern unfolds for comparisons on each trait between the three ranges. The proportion of Group III boys in the average or better category is lower, the proportion in the least favorable category is higher. The same trends hold for girls, except that the proportion of unfavorable comparisons for the Group III girls is everywhere more striking.

SUMMARY

The implications of this study may be summarized briefly. There is more than suggestive evidence here that committing a father to jail is soon accompanied by a depression in the school performance of his children—not alone academically, but in all other particulars as well. The link between the jail commitment of the father as family breadwinner and the financial problems of his wife has long been known. It is now time to explore the link between jail confinement and the education of their young.

It is also striking, although the numbers involved are small, that girls seem to be influenced more adversely than boys. The causal connection, as noted in the opening paragraphs, cannot be articulated precisely at present and it may turn out to have nothing at all to do with the father's jail confinement. But there is clear evidence of greater damage in the girl when the father is committed, and thus one might well assume that if a father is committed to jail, his daughter needs expert guidance immediately.

Finally, a suggestion can hardly be resisted even though it goes beyond the specific data. Vital and continuous cooperation and coordination is required between correctional, welfare, and educational agencies. Provision for special attention to children at the time of their fathers' confinement should be part of general social service practice everywhere. It should be well-planned, effective, and part of standard operating procedures. It should not be left to chance or the unusual incident.

NOTES AND REFERENCES

1. This study was part of the County Project in Correctional Methods, Norman Fenton, Ph.D., Director. The Project was supported by a grant from the Rosenburg Foundation of San Francisco, and was cosponsored by the Institute for the Study of Crime and Delinquency, Sacramento. Sidney Friedman was the principal investigator for the present study. Data were analysed and the report was prepared by Mr. Friedman and Dr. Esselstyn jointly. General direction was provided by Dr. Fenton.

2. Recent literature abounds with references to jail conditions and routines, and to the jail confinement of juveniles. However, except for Zalba (see footnote 3), no study has been discovered on how the jail confinement of a parent affects offspring.

3. For a discussion of the relation between mothers undergoing incarceration and their children, see Serapio P. Zalba, *Women Prisoners and Their Families*, Los Angeles: Delmar Publishing Company, 1964. The problem under review there was different in important particulars from the one considered here. However, the two reports do agree that children of incarcerated parents merit special attention.

4. Since the literature is silent on how the jail confinement of fathers affects their children, the question arises as to whether the removal of the father from the home by means other than arrest and incarceration provide any

model in the present concern. Examples might be, his absence or removal because of illness, military service, job change, extended vacations, and the like. It was felt that none of these removals are comparable to removal because of breaking the law. The only feature they have in common is that the father is away. The crucial difference is that types of removals such as those listed, however devastating are socially approved. Removal for the purpose of serving a jail sentence never is in any culture, however tolerated in some subcultural levels. The only type of removal that might be comparable to removal for jail confinement would be desertion. But even here there is a question. Nominally and legally, the deserting father absents himself with intent not to return. In the present study, a high proportion of the fathers intended to re-unite with their wives and children. Thus, the literature on the adjustment of children from all of these types of disrupted homes appears irrelevant on a theoretical level and is not reviewed here.

5. Grateful acknowledgment is herewith expressed for the invaluable assistance rendered by the following officials of the Santa Clara County Sheriff's Department: Sheriff John Gibbons; Rehabilitation Officer George K. Williams; Former Assistant Rehabilitation Officer Erl R. Kirk; Captain James M. Geary; and Lieutenant Melvin E. Riley.

6. This step could not have been accomplished without the help of the following listed persons and grateful acknowledgment is made to the Santa Clara County Office of Education, Dr. C. R. Timpany, County Superintendent of Schools; D. Carl Gelatt, director of attendance and juvenile services; R. E. Arnold, former director of attendance and juvenile services; the Alum Rock Union Elementary School District, Richard E. Conniff, district superintendent; San Jose Unified School District, Dr. Earle P. Crandall, superintendent; Roy Bursch, director of guidance and pupil personnel; all of the school district, administrators, and teachers who participated, and especially to R. E. Nino, chief juvenile probation officer, Santa Clara County, who allowed the principal investigator the use of physical facilities without which the study could not have been conducted.

7. Educational Service Bureau, School of Education, University of Pennsylvania, *Pupil Adjustment Inventory Rater's Manual,* Boston: Houghton Mifflin Company, 1957. Reproduced as shown by permission of the publisher, which permission is hereby gratefully acknowledged.

8. *Rater's Manual, op. cit.,* p. 1.

9. Completed tabulations may be obtained by writing the authors directly.

10. Julian Roebuck, and Harold Richardson, "Attitudes of Delinquents Toward School," *California Youth Authority Quarterly,* Winter 1963, pp. 40–43. For further evidence on the generally favorable attitude of

disadvantaged youths toward school and the generally favorable influence of schools upon them, contrary to many current beliefs, see Harrison Salisbury, *The Shook-Up Generation*. New York: Harper, 1958, p. 164.

AFFILIATIONS AND ACKNOWLEDGMENTS

1. Mr. Friedman is Training Officer, Santa Clara County Juvenile Probation Department, California. Dr. Esselstyn is Professor of Sociology, San Jose State College, San Jose, California.

The Legacy of Suicide:
Observations on the Pathogenic Impact
of Suicide Upon Marital Partners

ALBERT C. CAIN AND IRENE FAST

Early pioneer work in the scientific study of suicide, long fallow, has in the last decade been followed by a revival of interest, culminating in new empirical studies and conceptual work, heightened preventive activity, and, perhaps most significantly, a breaching of the taboos in the psychological sciences on the investigation and open discussion of suicide. In this paper we attempt to extend the psychological study of suicide into a relatively unexplored sphere—the effects, the "legacy" of suicide. Recently we have been engaged in a clinical study of a large number of children, one of whose parents had committed suicide.[1] But these children's reactions could not be studied in isolation. Our previous work in bereavement[2] strongly suggested that one can rarely meaningfully investigate, much less therapeutically deal with, object-loss reactions in the bereaved child alone, so complexly interdependent are the reactions of the surviving parent and the children. While exploring such interrelationships, we were struck by quite incidental findings of pathological patterns of behavior in the surviving parent—the marital partner of the suicide. It is these initial findings, rather striking though still fragmentary, that are reported here.[3]

The original study, whose case material came primarily from the University of Michigan's Children's Psychiatric Hospital and secondarily from nearby child-guidance settings, focused on forty-five disturbed children, one of whose parents had committed suicide. The case materials included, in most instances, a developmental history of the child, psychiatric interviews with the child and surviving parent, diagnostic testing of the child, and re-

From *Psychiatry* 29:406-411, No. 4, Nov., 1966. Reprinted by permission of the authors and by special permission of The William Alanson White Psychiatric Foundation, Inc., copyright 1966 the Foundation. This paper stems from a larger investigation, "The Mourning and Familial Loss Project," supported in part by The Grant Foundation, Inc.

ferral materials, plus theraɒy notes from outpatient or inpatient treatment if initiated. The present reɒort is based principally on an intensive review of all relevant recorded materials from the interviews with surviving parents, the extended casework notes —which were available in approximately half the cases—plus additional discussions with the caseworker or family therapist when available. The total number of surviving spouses had included sixteen husbands and twenty-nine wives, but six of them had died or deserted before our contact with the child. In all other cases the surviving spouse was available for clinical contact. The mean period between the suicide and the psychiatric referral was slightly over four years.

The nature of the data on the surviving spouse permits little meaningful statistical analysis. The period that elapsed between the suicide and the clinical contact ranged from a few days to more than ten years; the parents were seen at clinics with different recording practices and by different staff members; the major focus was upon the child rather than the surviving parent; and the clinical material (from previous, closed cases as well as current patients) varied in nature and completeness. While all of these circumstances suggest caution about generalizations from our data, one particular caution should be underlined. The sample is drawn from an exclusively clinical population: These were parents of markedly disturbed children who were referred for psychiatric evaluation and treatment.[4] Thus there is every likelihood that these families were located toward the most disturbed end of the spectrum of all families who have experienced a suicide, allowing us relatively little opportunity for studying the more adaptive, integrative modes of coping with a suicide.[5]

Sociological and psychological studies have long concentrated on a host of variables regarding *the suicide himself,* such as his age, residence (urban or rural, or particular type of urban), race, sex, socioeconomic status, religion and psychiatric status or diagnosis; and more clinical investigations have dealt with the nature of his intrapsychic structure and conflicts. Recently, paralleling general developments in personality theory and dynamic psychiatry, there has been a strong emphasis upon the interpersonal aspects of suicide. Yet, oddly enough, given the heightened emphasis upon the interpersonal, object-related nature of the suicidal act, there has been minimal interest in the fate of the suicide's real human objects following the suicide. By contrast, our data suggest that the implicit interpersonal tugs and pulls of the suicidal person's general presuicidal behavior and ultimate suicidal act have profound effects upon his actual external objects—effects lasting long after the suicidal act—which virtually cry out for study and intervention. In this area, the older medical-psychiatric literature supplies little more than intriguing tales of identical suicides within families, and generations of suicides within families (leading some early writers to a hereditary concept of suicide), and the more recent literature adds only some studies indicating a high indicance of past suicide in the families of psychiatric patients who themselves commit suicide.[6]

Careful analysis of the inherent nature, context, and almost inevitable consequences of suicide gives strong indication of why the impact of a suicide upon a spouse may have pathogenic potential distinct from and well beyond disruptive factors generally surrounding and following a death. Frequently there were involvements of a quite unpleasant, if brief, nature with the police, who overtly or implicitly considered the alternative possibility of murder rather than suicide; and sometimes, following close behind, there was a similar encounter with the coroner's office. Often added to these were no less unpleasant contacts with insurance representatives. In a number of instances ministers would not conduct typical burial services, and in a few instances burial was refused in church grounds.

But perhaps the most crucial of the malignant external agents was the blame frequently heaped on the suicide's surviving spouse by his community, his neighbors, and his family—especially his in-laws. This phenomenon, repeatedly visible in our clinical data, involved two somewhat distinct damaging factors. Often almost no support was provided the bereaved spouse. This is in marked contrast to the typical reaction to a bereaved spouse; ordinarily friends, relatives, and neighbors offer emotional support by providing opportunity for catharsis, by reassurance, by the sharing of grief, by efforts to reduce guilt, and the like, at the same time offering specific, concrete assistance with the practical management of day-to-day details. Frequently the spouse of the suicide was offered no such support, but rather felt that he was obviously being avoided by many of those from whom he would ordinarily expect and receive sustenance. But the reaction generally did not stop at this, for there was in many cases active finger-pointing at the surviving spouse. The phrase "drove him to it" tends to reverberate through the thoughts and conversations of the community following a suicide, as it engages in flurries of gossip and careful scrutiny of the couple's recent life for signs of marital strife. Such community reactions—and expectation of them—heighten the shame engendered by suicide, shame that leads to widespread underreporting of suicide, frantic family efforts to conceal suicide, and potentially lethal masking or minimizing of the significance of unsuccessful suicide attempts.

In at least five of our cases, the remaining spouse was hounded out of his community by gossip, accusations, and ostracism. Under the spotlight of suicide, the survivor hastily moved in order to avoid the relatives, neighbors, and business associates "who knew"—in the process adding important new strains. Concerns regarding a residual family stigma from the suicide were often manifest. Well-meant efforts by others to reduce such concerns and related guilts, efforts which usually took the form of explaining the suicide as the product of mental illness, often produced not the intended reassurance but a further burden, with associated concerns about heredity.

Far more destructive, though, was the fact that the shame and guilt typically brought about a massive avoidance of communication regarding the suicide, which in turn virtually prevented the working through of mourning. Denial, concealment, and refusal or inability to talk about the suicide tend to freeze or halt the mourning process in its earliest stages and allow minimal opportunity for it to take its normal though disruptive course.[7] The conspiracy of silence which tends quickly to surround a suicide sharply limits the bereaved spouse's opportunities for catharsis, for actively checking distorted fantasies against the realities of the suicidal act, for clearing up a variety of gross misconceptions, or for fully dealing with and eventually resolving the irrational guilts and particularly the angry reproaches felt toward the person who committed suicide.

The role of irrational guilt following bereavement has been amply recognized, but the ferocity of guilt in the survivors of a suicide is particularly striking. In part this stems from one qualitatively distinct element in suicide: the intentional, volitional quality of the act.[8] The deliberateness, the overtness of the rejection of the world and its immediate human relationships and objects are rarely mistakable to the suicide's survivors, whatever the suicide note may say.

In addition, typically there are other particularly intense elements fostering guilt and shame, even disregarding such special guilt-engendering instances as those labeled "psychic homicide" by Meerloo,[9] and those in which the surviving spouse had at least preconscious awareness of the forthcoming suicide and made no effort to stop it.[10] There is the almost inevitable reverberation to the suicide's active rejection of his world and those closest to him. Suicide regularly implies that the suicide's spouse could not or did not help him toward happiness, or at least out of despair. And indeed there was not infrequently, within the context of the suicide, an easily visible plea directed toward the spouse, or a complaint or grievance lodged against him. Thus, the entire history of the marital relationship often seemed put on trial for its "responsibility" for the suicide: Here the subtly guilt-inducing qualities of many depressive suicidal persons exacted their ultimate toll. Quite aside from guilt over presumed long-term responsibility for the suicide's anguish, the surviving spouse was regularly tortured by guilt phrased in terms of not having understood, much less helped his suicidal mate; having been blind to his torment and eventual suicidal intent; and having failed somehow to prevent the suicide—by not forcing him to get help, by concealing his previous suicidal attempts, by signing for his release from a mental hospital, and the like.

These factors perhaps make comprehensible the marked degree of disturbance we found in individuals whose spouses had committed suicide. As indicated earlier, the nature of our sample and our clinical data permit only minimal meaningful statistical analysis. We shall attempt no further generalizations, noting only the marked incidence of severe disturbance, and the significant etiologic role that the marital partner's suicide appears to have played.

It is apparent that many of these people had had serious personality problems long before their spouse's suicide, and in some instances, their disturbances appear to have been crucial in their selection of an eventually suicidal marital partner, as discussed under Pattern 5 below. But the manifest content of their disturbances, the material emerging during diagnostic or casework interviews, and the timing of the appearance of their symptomatology suggest that important elements of their present difficulties were contributed by the spouse's suicide. To illustrate concretely these suicide-engendered forces, we shall briefly present some recurrent patterns in our clinical data.

Pattern 1

This pattern appeared to involve reparation via a damaged object. Approximately half of the spouses remarried, and in seven cases, the new marriage was obviously neurotically determined and ill-fated in various ways that had a common theme. The new spouses were either chronically ill, were grossly physically handicapped, or were grossly handicapped in some other way—being, for example, in advanced stages of alcoholism. In five of these cases the suicide's spouse plunged into the marriage within less than a year after the suicide, against the entreaties and advice of friends and relatives. It was clear, when one probed into these new relationships, that whatever their adaptive features, their primary nature for the bereaved spouse had a pathological cast; the choice of the new spouse was almost totally dominated by a defensive effort to give, nurture, repair, and undo, and the bereaved spouse was attempting to define himself, in the face of postsuicide guilt and accusations, as good, as loving, and, most of all, as *not* destructive.

Pattern 2

Closely related to this pattern was that of reparation by means of "world-rescue" plans and activities, found mostly among scientists and other professional people, of whom there was a disproportionate number, since the sample was drawn in part from a university town. These interests included grand economic designs, cancer cures, ultimate paths to religious experience, inoculations against mental disease, food production from special substances to feed the world's population, and the like. Such efforts, although they were at best on the very fringes of the conceivable, were always extensively legitimized and rationalized. These pursuits—their unrealistic aspects becoming ever more obvious—increasingly expanded, eventually becoming a total preoccupation, a near fanaticism, to the detriment of the person's other interests, activities, responsibilities, and professional reputation. Although this pattern was obviously reparative in nature, it was, of course, like the first of these postsuicide paths, in the larger sense inevitably self-destructive.

Pattern 3

More direct, openly self-destructive impulses and behavior were also encountered among these spouses. Three of the surviving spouses themselves later committed suicide, their children having been subsequently brought to us by relatives. Four others had made suicide attempts; and many spoke of having struggled with suicidal thoughts and impulses during the period following the spouse's suicide. For some the suicidal fantasies seemed alien or related only to their despondency; but others experienced them quite consciously as self-punitive, identificatory, or even in a distorted way vengefully retaliatory.

Pattern 4

A quite different mode of managing the suicide-bred guilts through a new marital relationship was seen in at least five cases. These cases seemed to involve externalization and mastery of superego accusations. Here, rather than attempting reparation and undoing, the suicide's spouse apparently selected or used the new marital partner to assuage his savage superego pressures by playing out in the relationship with this partner the complaints, grievances, and accusations—real or fantasied, justified or inappropriate, implicit or overt—of his previous partner against him. The fierce repetitiveness of these accusations, condemnations, and criticisms, matched only by their irrationality, made a virtual nightmare of the new marriage.

Pattern 5

A small but remarkable subgroup of the spouses appeared to have an unconscious attraction to suicidal persons. After the suicide of the spouse they proceeded to become involved with other suicidal persons, eventually marrying people who either had previously attempted suicide or were obsessed with ideas of suicide. By far the most striking instance of this pattern was a woman in her late forties. She had three times married suicidal men, two of whom did commit suicide; during these marriages and between them she had affairs with other suicidal men. When she was not involved in such a relationship, she became depressed and preoccupied with suicidal fantasies herself. It appeared that these persons used marital partners or other relationships to vicariously act out their own suicidal fantasies.

The patterns described of course do not encompass the full range of disturbed reactions to a marital partner's suicide. Much less do they do justice to the more successfully adaptive modes of coping with a suicide. Furthermore, we have not here dwelt on the adaptive strengths manifested amid the disturbed reactions we have described. But these patterns do reveal a number of basic constituents of the bereaved's postsuicide reactions, some of the repetitive, driven efforts at mastering the psychologic impact of the suicide.

The major origins of these enduring disturbed reactions appear to be the especially intense sources of guilt evoked by a suicide; the manner in which the shame, denial, and concealment often associated with suicide inhibit or distort the normal mourning process; and the community's tendency to respond with blame and implicit accusation rather than emotional support for the surviving spouse. Clinical data and an analysis of pathogenic factors inherent in the sequelae of suicide strongly suggest the need for postsuicide preventive interventions with the bereaved.

NOTES AND REFERENCES

1. Cain, Albert C.; and Fast, Irene: "Children's Disturbed Reactions to Parent Suicide." *Amer. J. Orthopsychiatry* (in press).
2. Cain, Albert C.; Fast, Irene; and Erickson, Mary E.: "Children's Disturbed Reactions to the Death of a Sibling." *Amer. J. Orthopsychiatry* 34:741–752, 1964. Fast, Irene; and Cain, Albert C.: "Disturbances in Parent-Child Relationships Following Bereavement." Unpublished paper presented at the 1963 Annual Meeting of the American Psychological Assn.
3. We omit from any extensive consideration here the impact of repeated suicide threats and unsuccessful suicide attempts. However, we would like to note that clinical data indicate that suicide threats often appear to be successful in achieving their external purposes with a spouse. The data also indicate that the visible effects of such threats upon the children include marked separation anxieties, pervasive fright, even latent panic—while at school, when the phone rang at night, when the house seemed especially quiet—that "he [the suicidal parent] might have done it," and heightened guilt and related smothering of behavior which was or might be construed as upsetting to the threatening parent. Linked with such reactions were the children's increasingly exasperated, vengeful wishes that "he'd go ahead and *do* it," growing unspoken contempt and derogation toward the parent who made repeated threats and unsuccessful

attempts, and identification with the manipulative, exploitative aspects of the threats and attempts.

4. See note 1.
5. Recently we have begun to see families on a preventive basis immediately following the suicide, permitting more study of such responses. However, virtually all the case material referred to in this report comes from families seen in the course of standard child psychiatric referrals.
6. Jameison, G. R.: "Suicide and Mental Disease: A Clinical Analysis of One Hundred Cases." *Arch. Neurology and Psychiatry* 36:1–12, 1936. Moss, Leonard M., and Hamilton, Donald M.: "The Psychotherapy of the Suicide Patient." *Amer. J. Psychiatry* 112:814–820, 1956. Wall, J. H.: "The Psychiatric Problem of Suicide." *Amer J. Psychiatry* 101:404–408, 1944.
7. Bowlby, John: "Processes of Mourning." *Internat. J. Psychoanalysis* 42:317–340, 1961.
8. Hence its description as an "insult to mankind."
9. Meerloo, Joost A. M.: "Suicide, Menticide, and Psychic Homicide." *A.M.A. Arch. Neurology and Psychiatry* 81:360–362, 1959.
10. These are somewhat more frequent features of suicide than is generally assumed, if our clinical data are at all representative.

AFFILIATIONS AND ACKNOWLEDGMENTS

1. Albert C. Cain, B.A. 54, Ph.D. 62, Univ. of Mich. Ford Foundation Fellowship 55; Psychology Intern, VA Mental Hygiene Clinic, Detroit 56–57; Asst. Psychol. 57–59, Staff Psychol. 60–63, Chief Psychol. 64-, Univ. of Mich. Children's Psychiatric Hosp.; Rsc. Asst., USPHS Psychotherapy Rsc. Project 59–60. Candidate, Chicago Inst. for Psychoanalysis, Rsc. Training Program 61-. Asst. Prof. 62–65, Assoc. Prof. 65-, Depts. of Psychology and Psychiatry, Univ. of Mich. Member, Amer. Psychol. Assn., Amer. Orthopsychiatric Assn., Soc. for Rsc. in Child Development.
2. Irene Fast, Ph.D. Univ. of Mich. 58. Psychol., Psychol. Clinic, Univ. of Mich. 58–59; Psychol., Counseling Division, Univ. of Mich. 59–63; Lect., Univ. of Mich. 58–63; Chief, Psychol. Services, San Fernando Valley Child Guidance Clinic 63–65; Lect., Dept. of Psychology, Univ. of Mich 65-; Rsc. Assoc., Dept. of Psychiatry, Univ. of Mich. 66-.

PART 5

THE MEANING AND MOTIVATION OF DEVIANCY IN THE FAMILY

Previous chapters have examined various configurations of internal family behavior inappropriate in light of traditional customs and norms. Subsequent parts have addressed themselves to the impact of deviancy on either an individual member of the family or the family as a whole, viewing either impact as a dependent variable in the deviancy process. Family may not only constitute an independent or dependent variable in the analysis of deviance but may also be considered as a context within which deviancy occurs, as well as a constellation of pressures and motives which may precipitate deviant behavior. Inasmuch as the family may also mediate, negate, or channelize various social forces and exigencies which come to bear on individuals within the family, even those of a positive nature, it can also constitute an intervening variable in the social processes which may lead ultimately to deviancy. This section attempts to articulate some of the motivations manifestly attributable to deviant family members as well as to focus on the manner in which they redefine violation of various norms and values, and ascribe social meaning to such deviancy.

THE EXTERNALIZATION OF FRUSTRATION AND HOSTILITY

The family has been termed the "matrix of personality"; it might better have been labeled the "cauldron" of personality. The family grouping demands a deeper involvement, offers more intense interaction, provides a greater degree of intimacy, and thus self-revealment, and produces a higher level of emotional interaction and individual response than perhaps any other social configuration. The family affords a cathartic and occasionally therapeutic foil against which the individual members may act out their frustrations and aggressions in reaction to the social stresses and conflicts which they experience both within and without the family. Not infrequently this acting out of frustrations and hostility manifests itself as externalized hostility and violence.

Traditionally, the family has served as a mechanism of social control and as such has had the legitimated capability of administering sanctions. The so-called sharp-tongued wife might verbally "lash" the errant husband, and the authoritarian husband might effectively admonish the wife deficient in fulfilling her domestic responsibilities or guilty of some other social indiscretion. The family also is authorized to effect control of the behavior of minor children through the administration of sanctions including physical restraint and corporal punishment. In some instances even today the husband

237

might retain the legal right to utilize corporal punishment on his disobedient or delinquent wife provided the physical punishment is not excessive. Many wives do apparently accept such sanctions as appropriate. Furthermore, many husbands and wives indulge in ongoing conjugal battling which may involve some display of physical force such as throwing objects at each other and mild physical blows or slaps in addition to verbal abuse. Such behavior appears to be endemic to many marriages, especially among some socioeconomic and ethnic groups. Behavior of this type may be both ritualized and functional in that it permits a measured release of tension and marital frustrations and facilitates a return to a former state of conjugal equilibrium after a marital dispute.[1]

Generally, family behavior involving physical violence, such as that described, represents a kind of normative occurrence and does not include some of the pathological manifestations of family violence. Child abuse or the occurrence of the so-called battered child in our society has become increasingly prevalent in recent years.[2] Some researchers have estimated that perhaps as many as four million children a year are killed or physically injured by parents or other persons caring for them. Because the battered child does not always come to the attention of the medical or legal authorities, the actual incidence may be somewhat higher. Such injuries include skull and bone fractures, burns, scaldings, cuts, bruises, and internal as well as external bleeding. These injuries are deliberately inflicted and not accidental.

The findings of research studies on child-inflicted violence suggest that it often grows out of parental tensions, strains, and frustrations generated by situations external to the family. Such situations include occupational stresses or status strivings, and financial problems as well as marital discord, disaffection, and dilemmas arising, for example, from having given birth to an illegitimate child, forced marriage, the restrictive demands of parenthood, and resentment toward marriage or spouse. Often the child abuse resulting from the parental externalization of rage and hostility is triggered by an infant's irritability or illness, especially if the child is prone to crying or fretfulness.

Even the so-called normative corporal punishment administered ostensibly for disciplinary reasons may be a thinly disguised display of latent frustration. As Dr. David Gil of Brandeis University, in referring to corporal punishment, has put it, "Usually it is the attacking adult who is seeking relief from his own uncontrollable anger, frustration and stress."[3] The depth of despair of parents who abuse their children has been echoed by Dr. Vincent Fontana, chairman of New York City's Task Force on Child Abuse and Neglect, when he stated that, "Many women who abuse their children are actually crying out to society, 'Please take this baby away from me!' "[4] The family as a personality arena is a social configuration of volatile potential for the infant and child members. Leo Ryan, California State Assemblyman, has said, for example, "We all have within us the potentiality to beat our kids to death."[5]

In a situation where frustration is intolerable, and few, if any, alternatives or escapes are available, the impotent rage simply externalizes itself in the form of violent behavior directed at the nearest victims—all too often other members of the family. However, externalized violence is not restricted to the victimization of children in the family. "Mate beating," as one report terms it, "is one of America's most hushed-up crimes."[6] The President's Crime Commission found that 31 percent of all aggravated assaults involved family altercations, often involving spouses. It is sufficiently serious to have prompted some police departments to have set up special mechanisms for dealing with it. Although more characteristic of lower socioeconomic groups, it is by no means infrequent among middle-level and upper-level income groups, or among any ethnic, racial, or socioeconomic group. August Gribbin in an article on the subject pointed out that "one fifth of all police deaths have been attributed to family dispute calls."[7] On the basis of national polls on the subject, one sociologist found that 25 percent of America's adults "actually approve of husband-wife slapping around."[8] Often attributed to alcohol, drug addiction, and economic problems, among other factors, spouse-directed violence appears to be the result of more deeply seated problems with such factors constituting more a symptomatic syndrome than a cause. Some writers speak of couples who are unable to externally articulate their hostility and frustrations and instead channelize these stresses into overt spouse-directed violence. As the Rev. Kenneth Mitchell, a Menninger Foundation marriage counselor, phrased it: "The man who explosively gives his spouse a clout in the chops has usually been desparately frustrated in trying to get his partner to truly listen. The episode can be a 'scream,' entreating, 'Hey, we need help!' "[9] It has also been suggested by John E. O'Brien that the superordinate-subordinate husband-wife role relationship found in the American family may strain toward violence, in that violent behavior seems to be "most common in families where the husband was not achieving well in the work/earner role and where the husband demonstrated certain status characteristics lower than those of his wife." The husbands' violence then is seen as an attempt to reassert his superior ascribed sex status in the face of status inconsistency.[10]

The first selection in this part, Leroy G. Schultz's "The Wife Assaulter," takes an intensive look at four cases (out of a caseload of fourteen spouse assaulters) where an individual was convicted of assaulting his wife with intent to kill, where a common characteristic pattern was found. In this instance all of the offenders were Negro adult lower socioeconomic males with at least an eighth grade education and a history of employment stability.

There was no history of alcohol or narcotic habituation and none was involved at the time of the assaults. In three of the four cases, the victims had been previously married, and three of the assaulters had previous wives. All of the offenders had a history of assaulting their present or former wives. All of the assaults were preceded by a "perceived threat of breaking off the marriage."

It appeared that the assaulters had domineering and rejecting mothers who tolerated little hostility or aggression from their children. Similarly the assaulters had married "very masculine, outspoken, domineering women" who had much in common with their mothers. The husbands tended to play a generally submissive role toward their wives as they had toward their mothers. These wives, aware of their husbands' passiveness and dependency tended to exploit these weaknesses by withholding affection, sex, or threatening divorce or affairs with other men, all with profit gains in mind. The husbands, as with their mothers, would hold their hostility toward their wives in check, as long as their needs were satisfactorily met by their wives. When the husbands felt that this dependency gratification was being threatened or cut off, they could no longer hold their hostility under control and reacted with aggressive outbursts, often in the form of physical assaults. In this particular study then, spouse-directed violence grew out of an inadequate or inappropriate husband-wife relationship and its attendant interaction, and the inability to properly channelize hostility and frustration growing out of the situation.

Spouse directed violence in the family is not limited to assaults and beatings. Not infrequently such violence results in homicide. Contrary to popular opinion, murder is not a crime usually inflicted upon a stranger, rather it is most often a crime among intimates and acquaintances. As Wolfgang has put it:

Criminal homicide is probably the most personalized crime in our society. Because motives do not exist in a vacuum, the subject-object, doer-sufferer relationship is of prime importance in this particular crime. Homicide is a dynamic relationship between two or more persons caught up in a life drama where they operate in a direct, interactional relationship.[11]

As a primary group harboring intense and emotional interaction, it is also a significant loci of homicidal violence. As perhaps the relationship of greatest emotional potential, the husband-wife relationship is also a frequent dyadic pattern in murder. Family and marital disputes may grow into physical altercations and lead subsequently to the death of one or more of those involved. The angered spouse, regardless of past control, on discovering their mate's infidelity or disloyalty may in their uncontrollable rage become a sudden murderer.[12] The husband or wife trapped in an intolerable marriage situation may resort to murder as a means of resolving the dilemma with absolute finality. A variety of pressures and strains on the family may prove to be contributory or precipitant factors in family violence and homicide. Nor are these strains only concomitant to periods of societal economic declines. Bowdouris points out:

As economic conditions improve, inflationary pressures, socioeconomic competitiveness, and family budgetary problems are greater sources of family maladjustment than when the society as a whole is experiencing crises, as in the economic depression of the 1930's.[13]

He also suggests that "the largest category of family homicides may represent a problem in family relations and maladjustment . . . ."[14]

The second reading in this section is Marvin E. Wolfgang's "Husband-Wife Homicides." Based on a study of 588 consecutive criminal homicides committed in Philadelphia during the late 1940s and 1950s, Wolfgang concluded that among the homicides studied which involved husband-wife murders, the husband was slightly more prone to kill the wife than the wife to kill the husband. The more severe forms of violence resulting in murder were more likely to be committed at home. "Thus, husband-wife homicides were violent to a greater degree than homicides in general." The overwhelming majority of husband-wife murders occurred in the home and the largest percentage of these took place in the bedroom. This was particularly the case with husbands. Wives on the other hand were more prone to murder their mates in the kitchen. Of this entire number of cases more than one-fourth were victim-precipitated with the victim being the spouse to first resort to violence or show and use a deadly weapon. Husbands appeared more often to provoke their wives to violence leading to their own homicide than did wives. Finally, husbands who had murdered their spouses were more often than wives found guilty of more serious degrees of homicide.

In the final analysis, the family often serves as an arena of personality conflict and clash, and also not infrequently fails to adequately insulate its members against external pressures and problems while subjecting them to unique stresses and frustrations. In addition as Goode points out, the family, like all social systems, is a power system, and its members are often moved to serve the ends of the family by force or threat of force.[15] At times the application of force on one member by another may be inappropriate or excessive. Given these exigencies, it is not surprising perhaps that frustration and hostility may often be externalized in the form of violence within the family group leading at times even to murder.

ECONOMIC MOTIVES

Among its other duties, the family fulfills an economic function. Traditionally, the family has served as an economic production unit collectively producing many of the goods required by members of the family as a whole. In recent years, however, the family has come to fulfill its economic function primarily as a consumption unit with certain members of the family going outside the family, working in the marketplace, and bringing back the wages received to the family in order that it may consume as a unit, especially in terms of the basic family needs such as food, housing, utilities, and so forth.

With the shift more from ascribed to achieved status and with the contemporary emphasis on economic style of life and material possessions as a means of legitimating claims for social deference, the family has experienced increasing pressure for economic striving and a high level of consumership. Regardless of how broad a base of distribution modern industry has achieved and in spite of the advances of modern technology in producing relatively low priced goods through the use of improved manufacturing techniques and synthetic materials, the great American dream of an extravagant economic life style and an almost unlimited economic capacity for acquiring consumer luxury goods has not been universally or completely realized. As a result of the socioeconomic competitive pressure on the members of a family as well as the family as a whole, it is perhaps not surprising that family members and whole families have resorted to a variety of devices, both illegitimate as well as legitimate, as a means of subsidizing family income or the economic resources of individual members.

In spite of the reduced length of the work week and the concomitant increase in hourly wages and weekly salaries, many Americans have not tended to take full advantage of this new opportunity for leisure and rest. Rather, many, goaded by economic desires and pressures, return to the marketplace during their time off from their first job to seek second and sometimes third jobs. These moonlighters, as several million such Americans are known, are not so much seeking the economic necessities as the economic luxuries. They probably hope to be able to afford a second color television set, or third automobile, or even a motor boat rather than simply being able to put food on the family table and a roof over the family's head. For some, however, the second job has become more of a necessity in recent years as inflationary pressures erode family income levels and thus attendant economic styles of life.

Where the second job will not suffice to generate economic resources perceived as adequate for conspicuous consumption, an alternative or additional device for maximizing family income is the employment of the wife. (In fact, this may have been a necessity prior to the second moonlighting job.) Where some years back the working wife was relatively rare and most often associated with the lower socioeconomic level family, today the working wife is fast becoming more the rule than the exception, and in the middle and lower middle income levels as well as the lower. By the 1960s almost one third of all married women living with their husbands were employed and among widowed, divorced, and separated women, the figure rose to above 40 percent. Unfortunately, not all married women who wish to work, or need to work, can do so. Many have responsibilities associated with child-rearing that hinder their obtaining or maintaining employment. In some instances they have no training or skills readily salable in the marketplace. In other instances the social position (or perceived position) of the family may seem to preclude the wife's employment as an efficacious economic alternative to bolstering the family's financial resources. The husband, for reasons of male pride as a breadwinner, may be particularly vehement in opposing his spouse's employment. In any event, the economic pressures remain and not infrequently increase and if the family is to survive socially, if not in terms of sustenance, some supplemental economic resources must be found. As one solution, some family members, like teenagers, steal as a means of supplementing their own individual resources. While some teenagers steal for thrills, others steal as a means of stretching their allowance. Shoplifting is a preferred and convenient means of larceny. Many colleges today are faced with an increasing number of students who shoplift minor items from grocery and department stores as a means of supplying their food, cosmetics, and apparel needs in the face of a seemingly inadequate parental stipend. Such students are not necessarily the product of an economically deprived household, however, in that the physician's daughter or the accountant's son may feel the pangs of relative deprivation along with the offspring of the sanitation worker. In one large Southern city, the manager of a small grocery adjacent to a home for aged women was faced with the dilemma of some of these women securing their daily needs of cigarettes, candy, snuff, and notions by shoplifting them from his store. He was usually aware of the guilty parties but could hardly move to prosecute the offenders for fear of the adverse publicity and possible public reaction. Other members of a family may steal out of partially altruistic motives in an attempt to better "manage" the family budget. In this connection, shoplifting has been recently labeled by some writers as the "housewife's crime" in reference to the increasing frequency with which housewives, and even middle and upper-middle income housewives are apprehended in the commission of store thefts. As one such writer put it:

According to one recent study, the woman who stretches her household money by 'clipping' a pound of coffee or a new sweater is generally married to *a white-collar worker or a professional man. She belongs to a bridge club, to a churchwoman's group, and to the PTA. She lives in a comfortable home, drives a car, and has approximately $60 a week for household expenses. She most emphatically does not think of herself as a criminal, or even as a thief. (She speaks of 'taking,' not 'stealing.') In fact, she is inclined to view her actions self-righteously as her way of 'helping out at home.'*[16]

For some wives, other avenues of family income supplement seem more feasible. The next article by the Editors of *Newsweek* documents the efforts of "The Call Wives." In this case some fifteen housewives from a Long Island, New York, suburban community were arrested as prostitutes. Ranging from 20 to 45 in age, they were frequenting local bars and restaurants seeking customers and extra income. According to the article, "Nearly all of them by their own account, were merely trying to cope with a classic suburban problem: keeping up with the Joneses despite a limited budget." A similar saga occurred in a medium-sized Southern town several years ago, only in this instance the women involved were all wives of local physicians. It seems they were both bored because of their husbands' medical routines as well as feeling deprived with what they felt were inadequate household allowances and were attempting to amuse themselves while they acquired some extra "pin" money.

For some individuals extra pin money is not enough and they live vicarious lives of desperate desire and aspiration. For such persons one of the few sustaining, if not rewarding, activities is gambling. Gambling holds out the hope of the big win and instant wealth. Psychiatrists speak of compulsive gambling as a disease akin to alcoholism or narcotic addiction and some have suggested that the compulsive gambler may unconsciously even want to lose.[17] His gambling, so they say, is a plea for approval with winning as a symbolic affirmative response. In spite of such deeper attempts at analysis, the gambler consciously articulates a desire to win, usually for economic gain. Gambling has always enjoyed considerable popularity in our country although in times past it was limited to certain segments of the population and some forms of gambling were essentially the province of either the wealthy or the shadier elements of our population. Today, however, gambling in various forms is enjoying something of a popularity boom, and with practically all segments of the population.[18] For many, gambling is part of the new pattern of affluence and the upper middle class couple may enjoy an exciting weekend of gambling at Reno or Las Vegas with the same aplomb that the executive or professional man may casually drop $100 with his bookie betting on a Big-10 football game. For many Americans, however, gambling still remains a means for making dreams, even if modest, come true and getting the economic monkey off the family's back. The ghetto family in

Spanish Harlem may pool their pennies to play the numbers and the harried blue-collar worker may overindulge in poker in the hopes of the windfall. The recent boom in gambling may be as much the result of inflationary economic pressures and overly aggressive status drives as a mark of an affluent society. For fun or profit, it is interesting to note that housewives, typically the major bearers of the family financial burden, are showing up in increasing numbers at horse tracks to wager.[19] Bingo may continue to do yeoman duty in quenching the gambling thirst of many women but the larger action these days is at the track and the casino, and many women require increasingly larger action.[20] Gambling often, unfortunately, moves beyond harmless amusement and vicarious fulfillment of economic drives and becomes more a form of family deviancy, even if seemingly for a good cause.

The next selection in this part takes up such a situation. In Dorothy Disney's description of "Gambling Fever: Winner Lose All," she chronicles a compulsive gambler husband who had experienced economic pressures since childhood and sought "a feeling of independence and freedom" that only gambling afforded. Beset by marital conflict and personality difficulties the husband compounded these with his gambling activities until they led to economic disaster and near family disintegration.

The family is an economic unit, whether productive or consumptive, and it is often within the family that we rise or fall financially with its attendant implications for status and life style fulfillment. It is therefore not surprising that deviant behavior committed by family members often has economic roots regardless of whether the motivation is for individual gain or the collective good.

RECREATIONAL OUTLETS

The traditional proverb had it that, "the family that prays together stays together." However, with the increasing dilution of sacred and religious values and the growth of secular values, it may well be more appropriate today to postulate that "the family that plays together, stays together." For some time the automobile and mass public transportation have permitted the individual members of the family to scatter and pursue emotional and recreational gratification among peer groups or within the context of commercialized public entertainment or both, but the family, sensing danger to its integrity, has more recently moved to rectify this erosion of family solidarity and has often done so to the rallying cry of "togetherness."

The family today seeks togetherness in many guises. The recent boom in boating activities, particularly the houseboat popularity, suggests such an attempt to lure the wandering members back to the bosom of kith and kin. Excursion traveling, with attractive family rates, has also been immensely popular. For those families of lustier (and perhaps earthier) mien, outdoor hiking and camping provide togetherness on mountain tops and in forests, not to mention along the highways and byways of America where the convenient campgrounds which dot the countryside beckon the family to shelter, complete with communal showers and often an organized program of group recreation. Attendance at all sorts of sports and entertainment events are at record highs and the emergence of the plush "theme" amusement parks springing up around the country serves as additional evidence of collective family participation in fun, inasmuch as parks like Disneyworld and the Six Flags group clearly and flagrantly are designed and advertised as "family" amusement parks.

The home itself has become more geared to family fun and frolic. The multiple television (often color television) home is becoming more the rule than the exception today and even the homes of more modest income levels of the broad upper middle class may boast of game rooms with pool tables, stereo hi-fi's, bars, and even swimming pools, often with adjoining sauna baths. Husbands and wives (and sometimes offspring) enthusiastically embrace golf, bowling, and skeet shooting, not to mention rebuilding antique automobiles and raising poodles.

Today's home with its recreational schedule and facilities may be a far cry from the Sunday afternoon ice cream picnics and Saturday night sing-alongs around the parlor piano, but for many families it is tame fare indeed and hardly likely to titilate the jaded appetite for fun. For such couples recreational activities with more zest are often sought and sometimes encountered in the form of communal chemical "trips." Marihuana, as some reports suggest, is even becoming endemic to suburbia and allegedly is replacing scrabble, bridge, and charades as the weekend "thing." For a smaller minority more sophisticated drug enterprises are the order of the day.

Bruce Jackson's account of a "White-Collar Pill Party" details the social events at a veritable multi-course chemical feast. No wild bacchanalian debauch, simply a middle class social gathering of genteel comportment and exemplary proprietous behavior. Like any other party of well behaved people, except that the smorgasbord featured is illegal drugs rather than buffet fare. As Jackson described the affair:

. . . there had been nothing wild about the party at all, nothing. There had been women there . . . but there had been none of the playing around and sexual hustling . . . . : no meaningful looks, no wisecracks, no 'accidental' rubbing. No one had spoken loudly, no one had become giggly or silly, no one had lost control or seemed anywhere near it. Viewed with some perspective, the evening seemed nothing more than comfortable.

For the new mod family dabbling in drugs may be little more than another evening's attempt to enliven the drab social circuit without regard to the seriousness of the deviant recreation, or the possible import to family and self.

For some Americans, however, hedonism is a way of life, and the more traditional pursuits of the flesh hold more zest and thus recreational appeal. Although maintaining something of a facade of social propriety, if not puritanical morality, in the area of sexual comportment many couples have been actively indulging their sexual fantasies in something less than a vicarious fashion and in flagrant violation of religious, social, and legal norms.

The extramarital affair has long been more American fact than fiction even if often discreetly hidden from public scrutiny. As Alfred Kinsey and other sex researchers of recent decades have pointed out, a significant number of American married couples admit to having had sexual affairs with partners other than their spouses. While perhaps not entirely new to the American conjugal scene, the rapid erosion of marital sexual fidelity and the increased public acceptance of extramarital affairs, particularly since the beginning of World War II, suggests a new era of sexual permissiveness and the pursuit of individual gratification.[21] Rapid geographical and social mobility, the new "fun" morality, the sexual awakening of women, and an urgency in finding or attaining perceived self realization or self actualization, were all contributory in sending married individuals in search of sexual excitement and response outside the marital bond.

In relatively recent years, however, a new variety of extramarital sexual deviancy has appeared, with increasing and widespread frequency. This new form of sexual misadventure is group sex, wife swapping, or "swinging," as it is more popularly known.[22]

Swinging has apparently grown into a recreational pastime of significant proportions. A number of films such as *All the Loving Couples* and the better known *Bob and Carol and Ted and Alice* have served to familiarize, if not popularize, the "sport" with the public. Some swingers have even effected a stance of indifference, defiance, or militancy in the face of public repulsion. One group of swingers, so it was reported, held a national convention a year or so ago. Cosmopolitan in orientation, swingers often look outside their circle of regular intimates for participants in their sexual soirées. To this end, several swinger magazines are published with news of signal swinging gatherings and events, not to mention personal ads and notices featuring pictures, postures, and particulars for the rest of the faithful to pursue in window-shopping fashion. Curiously, it is also reported that many swingers have an inordinate fear of emotional entanglements arising from their sexual encounters and often swing only a few times with any other couple.[23] This, in a sense, tends to depersonalize the sexual encounters and, hopefully, avoids marriage-threatening involvement. This would appear to be a form of sexual activity oriented toward fun or recreation and an opportunity for personal sexual gratification in what is perceived to be more stimulating but socially sanctioned situations. Some couples apparently have succeeded in establishing more lasting and meaningful friendship relations with participating couples but in other instances swinging, rather than sustaining a marriage, may have been a precipitating factor in its breakup. In any event, swinging apparently provides for some an opportunity to fulfill sexual fantasies with social facility and the swingers of more sophisticated taste and fuller experience have turned to sexual experimentation of a broad spectrum of idiosyncratic taste involving costuming, unusual combinations of sexes (and animals), and a whole repetoire of sexual "cultures" including French (oral) and Greek (anal). Swinging as a recreational pattern often assumes routinized and ritualized configurations and perhaps offers diversion (albeit of a deviant, and sometimes pathological, nature) to as many as several million married Americans, by some estimates.[24] Swinging in essence is consensual adultery and permits a structured form of family deviancy for ostensibly recreational purposes, but which allows the couples involved to violate traditional sexual norms while monitoring each other's behavior. Thus, while the deviancy occurs within a permissive context there are, in fact, sanctioned limits.

In the next reading, "Before We Began to Swing," Sara Harris tells of one woman's account of her own and her husband's gradual involvement in swinging as a recreational (and therapeutic) activity. Although the couple had their recreational horizons widened so to speak, as their group sex took on more bizarre forms and as their own values of propriety and morality began to erode, they slipped away from the conventional norms of conformity and tradition and even began to proselytize to their married children.

Given the impact of rapid technological and social change, the growth of the mass media with its urgent and insidious comparisons of life styles and modes of behavior, and the gradual decline of extended families and other primary social groupings, it is perhaps not surprising that families are driven to the extreme edge of deviancy in their quest for stimulation, recreation, and diversion from the monotony of life in the mass society.

INEFFECTIVE PARENT-CHILD RELATIONSHIPS

As previously pointed out by Goode, the family as a social system is a power system. As such, it involves various superordinate-subordinate power relationships based on age, sex, and kinship. (Such relationships may, however, be ephemeral due to the changing composition of the family, the aging process of members, and even the employment state of various members at any given time.) Both the equilibrium of the family as well as the emotional security and well being of the individual members may well depend on the appropriateness with which such reciprocal role relationships are maintained and the degree to which such role playing is mutually rewarding and personally satisfying and meaningful. Such role relationships should ideally be viable, reflecting changes in family situations, social exigencies, and the personality of the individuals involved.

Inappropriate imposition of normative restrictions on various members of the family, inadequate recognition and response, or deficiency or ineffectiveness in playing parent or spouse roles may lead to a disturbed marital relationship, fail to provide emulative parental role models, create reference group conflicts for individual family members, and generally create a family situation deemed intolerable by some family members if not pathological by community standards.

Our society, like others, makes provision for various socially sanctioned patterns of evasion from overly restrictive norms. Thus the young person confronted by family resistance to an intended marriage may, if over age (and in some instances even if not), elope even at the expense of parental blessing. The wife or husband unable to tolerate the idiosyncratic whims and demands of an overly-rigid spouse may under some circumstances be able to effect a legal separation or divorce. By violating existing legal and social norms the harassed spouse may also undertake to escape or evade the role pressures and conflicts through desertion, or effect a temporary relief through extramarital affairs, or in some instances through a resort to extreme physical violence.

The child in a family generally has open to him no socially sanctioned means of evasion in the face of intolerable family role conflicts and pressures. In such a situation, the child or young person may similarly resort to deviant evasions and compensatory behavior such as promiscuity or other behavioral excesses away from the family, or in some cases he may escape the situation by running away.

Such a modal deviant evasion is described in "The Runaway Girl: Reaction to Family Stress." Here the authors examine a number of cases involving adolescents brought before a court clinic for running away from home. Running away, while often treated lightly by authorities and even parents, is a form of legal delinquency. The authors saw in these teenagers "a consistent pattern of family interaction . . . basic to the etiology of running away." This pattern included an attitude of rebellion against their offspring role and its discomforts which arose out of insufficient warmth and affection from the mother and an attempt on the part of the mother to subtly force the child into increased responsibility and assumption of the maternal role. The father is often ineffective in demonstrating parental control over the girl's impulses and behavior and the mothers are often the dominant figures in the household. The father reacts to his ineffectiveness with temper outbursts and may become overly restrictive with the girls, creating additional tensions in the home and adding to the already disturbed marital relationship. In effect the social pressures for early dating and sexual maturity, and the mother's efforts to assign excessive responsibilities to the daughter, coupled with the father's overreactive restrictiveness and hostility, act to produce role conflicts and blockages which are intolerable to the girl. In desperation and defiance she runs away and thus attempts to alleviate her conflict through deviancy.

Other avenues of evasion and escape from unsatisfactory role configurations exist in the form of illicit drug use. Like their adult counterparts who cannot adjust to rejection or excessive strain and conflict and turn to alcohol and drugs as a chemical escape, even if temporary, young people may also seek similar release. In an article focusing on teenage family satisfaction and drug usage, Nechama Tec examines the relationship between "Family and Differential Involvement with Marihuana." Based on a survey of more than 1,700 high school teenagers in an affluent Eastern suburban community, Tec found a negative relationship between the degree of marihuana involvement and general satisfaction with the family situation. Teenagers, it appears, are less likely to use marihuana if parents provide adequate models of behavior conformity. In effect, the teenagers from broken homes or with separated parents, or with parents who use hard liquor, tranquilizers, or sleeping pills, are more prone to marihuana use than those whose parents provide conformity models for behavior. Similarly, if associations with the family unit are rewarding in terms of recognition, respect, and personal satisfaction, the teenagers are also less apt to be involved with marihuana. Finally, if parental controls and family demands are perceived as excessive and unfair, and not accompanied by warmth, the likelihood of marihuana usage increases. In short, if the teenager experiences a family situation which is repressive, lacking in response and social meaning, and deficient in providing adequate parental role models, he is apt to seek evasion, escape, or relief through marihuana.

The family with its intimate and restrictive power control and its elaborate normative structure may often prove to be a sufficiently unsatisfying, disaffective, and conflict-laden mode of conformity as to generate rebellion and deviant violations on the part of its members.

FAMILY STRESSES AND DISORGANIZATION

The family as a social system (and as a power system) is also a system in equilibrium. As such, it enjoys a symbiotic balance of structured interpersonal relationship with the attendant interaction among members. The intimate interrelationships of the family together with the emotional intensity of the interaction and deep ego involvement of its members make the family particularly vulnerable to disruption and disequilibrium, especially in the presence of deviant behavior. Earlier chapters have examind the impact of family deviancy on individual members as well as the impact of individual deviancy on the family as a whole. Here the basic relationship of family disorganization and deviant behavior is examined. Deviant behavior often grows out of family disorganization as a confused or inappropriate response to anomic conditions, or as overreaction to stress, hostile interaction within the family, and oppressive family requirements for conformity. Deviant behavior as a pathological behavior pattern of a member, in a sense, feeds on other pathological patterns within the family. Individual deviant behavior, then, is but an external extension of internal family disequilibrium.

In the next article the authors focus on "The Interrelatedness of Alcoholism and Marital Conflict." Various sociopsychological and sociopsychiatric perspectives of alcoholism have pointed to personality defects and character disorders, as well as unconscious conflicts, difficult life situations, social anxieties, and interpersonal frustrations as possible factors in the genesis and etiology of alcoholism. In this study the "marital interaction and the interpersonal relationship in marriages in which the husbands were alcoholic and their wives were nonalcoholic" are examined. Based on a study of counselor interviews of such couples, the authors conclude that in the couples studied both partners tended to have difficult family backgrounds and emotional problems. The personality problems of the partners were important factors in their marriage selection and their marital conflict was often of long standing, even in some instances extending back to the premarital relationship. Marriage had apparently not fulfilled the personality needs of the partners and further emotional disturbance in each partner and greater marital conflict were often the result. In some instances, the wife was the dominating family figure while in other cases the wives demonstrated "strong dependency needs and feelings of inadequacy." These latter wives sought strong emotional support from their husbands. In both the former and latter instances, the alcoholic husbands were inadequate in their male family role and given to anxieties, jealousies, and frustrations. The alcoholism compounded the marital conflict in that the wives often displayed resentment, hostility, and withdrawal reactions to their husbands' drinking, such reactions "sometimes stemming from disturbed relationships with their [own] fathers." Overall, it would appear that, in this study, alcoholism was as much the effect as the cause of family stresses. Often growing up in disorganized families themselves, the spouses sought support and emotional security in marriage, only to discover that their personality configurations were incongruous and incompatible and thus the marital relationship with its attendant interaction was stressful.

These stresses contributed to the husbands' drinking which in turn precipitated negative reactions to the drinking and an increase in family disorganization and general marital unhappiness for both partners.

Deviant behavior concomitant to family stress and disorganization may take forms other than that of alcoholism or narcotic addiction as an escape mechanism. The genesis of various antisocial behaviors may also be attributable to certain anomic conditions characteristic of the family experiencing excessive stress and disorganization. Cormier and associates address themselves to this problem in "Family Conflicts and Criminal Behavior."[25] Studying a group of 176 latecomers to crime, they examine men who committed their first offense after marriage. They conclude that in many cases the criminality "resulted from a conflict of relationship between husband and wife and children. A conflict which was acted out in a variety of offenses within or outside the family." The article articulates four types of offenses based on the offenders studied which may result from some type of unfavorable or disorganized family constellation: offenses committed entirely within the family such as incest, assault, and nonsupport; combination offenses occurring both within and without the family like nonsupport and public drunkenness; offenses where criminal breakdown occurs outside the family but where it is often directly related to a crisis in the family; and finally, offenses occurring outside the family where there may be no direct connection with family crisis, but where the husband has a severe personality problem and family stresses compounding the problem may precipitate a criminal act. A fifth residual group of offenses demonstrated no meaningful connection between crime and marital or family stress. In all of the first four instances the deviant or criminal patterns are directly or indirectly related to marital problems and family stress.

The authors further conclude that harsh or excessive punishments may encourage an antisocial attitude in the offenders where none existed previously. These men were not habitual criminals but ". . . people who break under the continuing stress of a highly conflicting and damaging family relationship." The separation of husband and family imposed by a correctional sentence often only further disorganizes and dislocates the family, punishing all members of the family. The treatment of such offenders should not be just the helping of an individual with inadequacies and personality problems, rather it should be the treatment of the family itself, in an attempt to help resolve the neurotic marital relationship with the frustrations, stresses, and conflicts which plague it.

Disruption and family conflict place a heavy burden on the conformity of members of a family. Expectations of behavior and attitude are difficult to fulfill in the face of stress, oppressive restriction, and lack of response and recognition as reward. The individual not therapeutically supported by the family milieu, or permitted to obtain intellectual and emotional gratification from parents or spouse may well elect to violate social norms, both internal and external to the family, and thus externalize his frustration in deviant behavior.

DEFENSIVE AGGRESSION

The family may rally to aid and defend the deviant family member, shielding him from a critical community, tolerating the stresses which he precipitates, or providing emotional and social support. The errant member, however, is upsetting to family routine and equilibrium, erosive of family and community status, and potentially divisive to family cohesion. Not infrequently in the face of deviant behavior committed by a member, the family may move to assume a defensive posture even to the extent of acting aggressively toward the offending member in its own defense. The family faced with the alcoholic member, for example, may initially attempt to deny or eliminate the problem, rallying collectively to resolve the threat to family well-being. Failing in this and faced with possible disorganization and disintegration, the family may move to eject the errant member or to modify his family status and thus dilute his functional significance to the family, thereby buffering the impact of his deviancy. The family may reorganize itself around the failure of the alcoholic father to discharge his responsibilities and redistribute his family roles. As Jackson described this situation in families with alcoholic husbands, "The alcoholic husband is ignored or is assigned the status of a recalcitrant child by the wife and children."[26]

In other instances the family, in aggressively defending itself, may find it difficult or inappropriate to expel, ignore, or modify the status of the deviant members. In such instances the offending individual may come to be used as the object of aggression internal to the family, particularly where the other members of the family attribute the family's difficulties and stresses to the member's deviancy.

The last article in this section examines such a pattern of defensive aggression. Roslyn Ganger and George Shugart look at "Complementary Pathology in Families of Male Heroin Addicts" and focus on "familial forces affecting male heroin addicts and the obvious and subtle ways in which family members in their defensive systems use the addict as a scapegoat." Based on a study of various members of the families of more than 100 male heroin addicts, the authors attempt to analyze the aggressive reactions of family members to the deviant addicts. The mothers of the addicts were characteristically "domineering, compulsive, anxious, and self-pitying." The mothers had apparently experienced emotional deprivation at an early age themselves and also had not been permitted to express anger toward their parents. Faced with their sons' heroin addiction, these mothers attempted to maintain their sons in a dependency position, becoming overly preoccupied with both their sons' narcotic addiction and day-to-day life activities. They interfered with their sons' heterosexual activities, and assumed "a clinging seductive" manner with them. By maintaining a sense of inadequacy and guilt on the part of the addict sons, the mothers were able to prevent them from asserting themselves and were, in effect, keeping the sons bound to their own neurotic needs and anxieties.

The fathers were often absent from the home or if they remained in the home, played only an indifferent role. In a few families the fathers were overly aggressive, possibly as an "overreaction to the mothers' subtle, though real, control," but on the whole the fathers were unassertive and subordinate to the wives' wishes. They were often adequate providers but did not take full advantage of their work opportunities. The fathers were essentially weak, apathetic, and unable to establish meaningful relationships with the sons.

The brothers and sisters of the addicts were often jealous of the addict sibling. These brothers and sisters were envious of the "addict's monopoly of parental attention and concern," as well as "the hold he exerted on the parents through the problems he created and the parents' involvement in the minutiae of his daily life." This jealousy and envy often expressed itself in the form of excessive sibling rivalry and in some instances as aggression, physical violence, and even cruelty. Initially, in the addict's narcotic history the other siblings may have rejected him or become involved in family efforts to rehabilitate him, while later, however, even concern often changed to punitive or moralistic aggression. The siblings, generally speaking, were successful but were still envious of the addict because of the mother's over-involvement with him.

It would appear that the narcotic addict in his deviant behavior disturbs the equilibrium of the family and its conventional patterns of interpersonal relationships. It arouses pathological responses on the part of other family members who find that they are not able to adequately play their family roles or receive appropriate responses from yet other family members. The family members' behavior toward the addict occurs in a manner often best calculated to serve their own neurotic needs and to chastise him for his disruptive deviancy.

NOTES AND REFERENCES

1. As a former army military police officer, one of the editors has vivid recollections of a number of couples on an army base where he was stationed who engaged in such battles with disturbing regularity. In almost all instances if the M.P.s intervened, the couple would either

present a cohesive front in dealing with the M.P.s or if one was a complainant, they invariably changed their mind by the next morning, dropped the charges, and often derided the M.P.s for interferring.

2. For an elaborate discussion of this phenomenon, see, Taylor, Craig: "The 'Battered Child': Individual Victim of Family Brutality," (Reprinted in Part 4 of this book); see also, Gil, David H.: "Violence Against Children." *Journal of Marriage and the Family* 33: 637–648, No. 4, Nov., 1971; and Giovannoni, Jeanne M.: "Parental Mistreatment: Perpetrators and Victims." *Journal of Marriage and the Family* 33:649–657, No. 4, Nov., 1971.

3. See Harvey, Paul: "Suffer Little Children." syndicated in the *Park City-Bowling Green Daily News,* Friday, May 19, 1972.

4. *Ibid.*

5. *Ibid.*

6. Gribbin, August: "The War of the Spouses: America's Most Hushed-up Crime." *The National Observer,* March 11, 1972.

7. *Ibid.*

8. *Ibid.*

9. *Ibid.*

10. O'Brien, John E.: "Violence in Divorce Prone Families." *Journal of Marriage and the Family* 33: 697, No. 4, Nov., 1971.

11. Wolfgang, Marvin: *Patterns in Criminal Homicide.* Philadelphia: University of Pennsylvania Press, 1958, p. 203.

12. For an examination of emotionally precipitated homicide, see Lamberti, Joseph W.; Blackman, Nathan; and Weiss, James M. A.: "The Sudden Murders: A Preliminary Report." *Journal of Social Therapy* 4: 2–15, 1958.

13. Bowdouris, James: "Homicide and the Family." *Journal of Marriage and the Family* 33:673, No. 4, Nov., 1971.

14. *Ibid.,* p. 675.

15. See Goode, William J.: "Force and Violence in the Family." *Journal of Marriage and the Family* 33: 624–636, No. 4, Nov., 1971.

16. Maynard, Fredelle: "The Housewives' Crime—and What Makes Them Do It?" *Good Housekeeping* 165: 99, Oct., 1967. For a general account of middle class shoplifting, see, Wharton, Don: "Shoplifting: Our White-Collar Scandal." *Reader's Digest* 82: 73–77, April, 1963.

17. See, Berry, James R.: "What Makes a Gambling Addict?" *Today's Health* 46: 20–23, Oct., 1968.

18. See, Axthelm, Pete: "Everybody Wants a Piece of the Action." *Newsweek* 79: 46–52, No. 15, April 10, 1972.

19. Willig, John: "Housewives at the $2 Window." *The New York Times Magazine,* April 1, 1962, pp. 48.

20. One of the editors of this volume has worked as a bingo counterman in a carnival and can testify to the urgent, if not possessed, manner in which many women gamble. In the process of playing bingo some women, even grandmotherly types, seem to completely change personalities and appear to almost lose their grip on reality.

21. For an elaborate examination of changing American sex values and behavior, see, Packard, Vance: *The Sexual Wilderness*. New York: David McKay Company, Inc., 1968. For other accounts of adultery in our society, see, Hunt, Morton: *The Affair: A Portrait of Extra-Marital Love in Contemporary America*. New York: The World Publishing Company, 1969; and, Boylan, Brian Richard: *Infidelity*. Englewood Cliffs, N. J.: Prentice-Hall, Inc., 1971. For treatments of the sexual revolution, see the articles in "Sex and the Contemporary American Scene." *The Annals of the American Academy of Political and Social Science* Vol. 376, March, 1968; and the articles in "The Sexual Renaissance in America." *The Journal of Social Issues* Vol. 22, No. 2, April, 1966; also, Lipton, Lawrence: *The Erotic Revolution*. Los Angeles: Sherbourne Press, Inc., 1965.

22. See, Denfeld, Duane; and Gordon, Michael: "The Sociology of Mate Swapping: Or the Family that Swings Together Clings Together." *Journal of Sex Research* 7:85–99, No. 2, May, 1970; see also, Breedlove, William and Jerrye: *Swap Clubs: A Study in Contemporary Sexual Mores*. Los Angeles: Sherbourne Press, 1964.

23. For a detailed discussion, see, Palson, Charles and Rebecca: "Swinging in Wedlock." *Transaction: Social Science and Modern Society* 9:28–34, No. 4, Feb., 1972.

24. Denfeld and Gordon, *op. cit.*

25. For other studies of the relationship of family disorganization and delinquency, see, Simcox, Beatrice R., and Kaufman, Irving: "Treatment of Character Disorders in Parents of Delinquents." *Social Casework* 37:388–395, No. 8, Oct., 1956; Jaffe, Lester D.: "Delinquency Proneness and Family Anomie." *Journal of Criminal Law, Criminology, and Police Science* 54:146–154, No. 1, June, 1963; Simcox, Beatrice R.; and Kaufman, Irving: "Handling of Early Contacts with Parents of Delinquents." *Social Casework* 37:443–450, No. 8, Oct., 1956.

26. See, Jackson, Joan K.: "The Adjustment of the Family to Alcoholism." (Reprinted in Part 6 of this book).

The Wife Assaulter

LEROY G. SCHULTZ

This is a report on a series of cases in each of which a husband was convicted of assaulting his wife with intent to kill. Four cases were selected from the writer's caseload of fourteen spouse assaulters when it was noted that a common pattern was characteristic of all. The purpose of this paper is to present a picture of the common dynamic core underlying these selected cases and what was done with them through the probationary treatment process.

There is little literature on wife assaults, although some exists where the assault resulted in the spouse's death.[1,2,3] Actually many of these studies are highly applicable to these four assaulters as it was their intention to kill the spouse and only a quick dispatch to a hospital prevented it. The spouse-to-spouse relationship (victim to offender), if understood, usually throws considerable light on the offense dynamics and motivation. The victims in spouse assaults can always be assumed to have played a crucial role in the offense, and may have directly or indirectly brought about or precipitated their own victimization.

GENERAL GROUP CHARACTERISTICS

All four assaulters were Negro males ranging in age from 34 to 47 years and were of the lower socio-economic class. (Criteria used were occupation, education and residence.) All had migrated from farm areas of the South as adults. All had employment stability, the shortest continuous employment period being seven years and the longest fifteen. Educationally, all offenders had reached at least the eighth grade. In two of the four assaults the victim was the second wife, in one the third, and in the last the first. The marriages ranged from six weeks to fourteen years' duration at the time of the final assault. In three of the cases the wives were motivated to prosecute and in

From *Corrective Psychiatry and Journal of Social Therapy* 6:103–111, 1960. Reprinted by permission of the publisher.

one the wife died of her wounds before she could be interviewed. The assault, in every case, was preceded by a perceived threat of breaking off the marriage. In two of the four cases a gun was used and in the two others a knife. In one case one shot was fired, entering the victim's stomach; in one case two shots were fired; only one of which entered the neck of the victim. In the stabbings one husband stabbed eight times, the other four times. Hospitalization for the victims ranged from four to eight weeks and only one died of her wounds. Two of the husbands turned themselves over to the police and two were arrested within twelve hours near their homes. All offenders were cooperative with police officers, pleaded guilty without a trial and were able to afford defense counsel and make bond. None had a criminal record other than previous assaults on their wives. In one case the husband had assaulted each of his three previous wives once each; in two cases the husband had assaulted his second wife three times and in the last case four assaults preceded the final one.

All three surviving victims opposed probation for their husbands and felt a longer sentence than the court recommended was in order.

There was no history of alcoholism, narcotics or venereal disease and no husband had been drinking or had taken narcotics at the time of the assaults. There was no history of mental illness in three cases and in the fourth the husband had a two-week hospitalization following a suicidal attempt, which he admitted was designed to bring his deserted wife back to him, three years before the final assault. This was the only case of the four in which aggressivity was turned toward himself, unless one considers injury to one's love object as self-injury.

THE TYPICAL CASE

The case of Jim (pseudonym), as in many, was typical of the pattern found in the lives and offenses of all the assaulters.

Jim, 47, is a lower-class Negro who was born on a large plantation-type farm in the deep South. He is the oldest of seven children born to illiterate parents. Living conditions were substandard during his youth and adolescence, with chronic shortages of money and clothing. The parents were sharecroppers, worked long hours in the fields and usually came home exhausted, with little time, energy or patience for Jim's supervision and emotional needs. The parents showed concern only when he did something wrong or forbidden or deviated from parental dictates. Such deviation brought quick, harsh punishment. Punishment included being knocked unconscious with a frying pan, withholding of meals and being suspended from a beam in the smoke house in a potato sack. Jim's primary function in the home was for household chores. As new children were added he became a baby-sitter, meeting the needs of others when his own needs were not met, a problem never expressed or discussed. Such self-minimizing was characteristic of Jim's whole life. His greatest joy was to attend school, but he was permitted to attend only on days when the weather did not allow farm work. Failure to do assigned work brought punishment out of proportion to the incident. Jim learned that submission to maternal authority and demands could guarantee some form of affection and protection and that any display of hostility only brought further rejection and harsher punishment. He learned to control and inhibit at all costs hostile feelings felt toward his mother.

Jim described his mother as a good, strict woman whom he loved dearly. Asked about the harsh punishment, he replied that he was an "evil child" and deserved anything he got. He remembered little of his father, who was away from the home most of the time working on a railroad track-laying gang.

When Jim reached the age of 15 his mother asked him to quit school so he could help support his large number of siblings. He felt that his mother used him for her own gains and that he missed out on many normal adolescent privileges. There was little in his account of his youth to indicate that it was happy or that his mother was a warm loving figure.

At 15 Jim went to work for a white physician, doing general porter work in the doctor's office, and turned over his small earnings to his mother. He began dating farm girls, but soon devoted full time to Sue. After five years of courting, Jim's mother gave him permission to marry. Sue and Jim rented a small farm and both worked hard the first two years to make it a success. Then Jim came home by surprise one day and discovered his wife in bed with a neighboring farmer. He said he did not know what to do and merely closed the door and returned to the fields and cried. He added that he could have done "something" as there was a loaded rifle in the room adjoining the bedroom. Jim never brought up his wife's infidelity and she, seeing so little objection, became more bold in her affair. The paramour began staying for meals and on several occasions stayed overnight. Jim voiced no objection and even lent the paramour money, seed and farm equipment, as well as labor. Finally, after this arrangement had gone on for three years, the paramour took a truck to Jim's farm while the latter was away, loaded up the household goods and livestock, as well as Jim's wife and four children, and took them away. Jim, though surprised at his wife's and children's absence, did nothing to find out where she was or to attempt to bring her back, nor did he ever approach his wife's lover. Instead he returned to live with his mother. Asked about losing his four children, Jim replied that he was not sure that any of them were his. Four years after the wife's desertion, he obtained a divorce.

During the war years Jim heard of the high wages in northern was plants and left home. He got a job at once and worked at it some fifteen years.

Eight years after Jim's first marriage, he married Gloria after a six-month courtship. She had already failed in two marriages. Jim admitted he knew Gloria was "hot-tempered" and that she had killed her second husband, but he married her anyway. During the first three years most disputes were kept at a verbal level. Then Gloria asked Jim if she could go down south to visit friends and relatives He had heard her speak of her adolescent sweetheart there and he refused permission, buttressing his refusal with a blow to her face. Gloria responded by stabbing her husband over the eye with a fork. Both were arrested but neither would prosecute the other. Thereafter, at approximately two-year intervals up to the final assault, minor assaults occurred, resulting in both spouses' arrest. However, these assaults differed from the first in that Gloria always prosecuted Jim. The result was a series of heavy fines, which the family could ill afford.

A severe assault preceded the final one. Jim and Gloria were having their usual argument over Gloria's alleged interest in another man when Jim began to draw his knife. Gloria anticipated his move and drew a large knife, slashing Jim's arm from wrist to elbow. Gloria was charged with assault with intent to kill, but Jim again refused to prosecute, ignoring the times his wife had prosecuted him.

The final assault occurred one morning after Jim returned home from work. He asked his wife for his usual kiss. Instead she berated him for not picking her up at the beauty shop the night before. Jim apologized to no avail for the family's unoperative automobile. Gloria then informed him that he need never pick her up as she had found a paramour with a car who would be glad to furnish transportation. Jim thrust his knife into her chest four times. He then turned himself in to the police.

PATTERN-DYNAMICS

In general, the youth of the sample of assaulters was characterized by a domineering, rejecting mother relationship, where the child experienced primarily aggression. The mother, on the other hand, at no time tolerated any action or expressed thoughts of a counter-hostile nature from her child. The child's reaction to the situation was passive submission to maternal authority and learning that rebellion was futile and resulted in further rejection and punishment. The child identified with his mother (the aggressor), internalized her dictates and responded to his own superego with compliance, rationalization and rigid control over aggressive impulses. As the child grew up he became more perceptive of parental aggression and more intense efforts were made to prevent anger from reaching conscious levels. Should this defense break down, the child knew that retaliation from the parent would follow. The result was a submissive, passive individual who avoided conflict at all costs. The child did not appear to integrate normal patterns of aggression.

Such a uniformly poor child-mother relationship makes for a frustrated dependency in which the child's emotional needs are never truly met. This dependency influences choice of mate and subsequently is transferred from the mother to the wife, where the child-mother relationship is duplicated. Children who cannot permit aggressive impulses to break through during their youth have difficulty as adults in entering interpersonal relationships that do not duplicate the original dependency of the child to the parent. In short, the attitude of the husband to his wife may reflect a reaction originally adaptive to the child-mother relationship.[5,6] The husbands tended to parentify their wives[7] and appeared foredoomed to take a submissive role toward them, as they did toward their mothers.

It is when these dependency needs are frustrated or where frustration appears, or is perceived as imminent, that aggression breaks through. In short, it is where the husband senses that his dependency gratification is being cut off that he overtly attacked the frustrating object, his wife. The conflict is one between hostility toward the wife and dependency on her. The first was held in rigid control as long as the second was satisfactorily met. The aggressive outbursts came when the husbands felt that dependency gratification was being permanently cut off, as in the wife's admission of having a lover or her stating she was going to get a divorce or separation. Such a threat of both physical and psychic withdrawal of love was intolerable to the husbands, whose ordinarily rigid hostility-control system broke down. Any interest in another person by the wife was viewed by the husband as a failure in satisfying his permanent hunger, conjuring up the dangers of desertion and loss of gratification.

A series of interviews was held with the three surviving wives. They were found to be very masculine, outspoken, domineering women who had much in common with their husbands' mothers. The wives, in general, tended to exploit and profit from their husbands' passiveness and dependency. In one case, a condition obtained by the wife as a promise not to leave her husband was that he send her to beautician school and then set her up in her own shop. In another case the wife forced her husband to buy a large home as a condition of continued marriage despite their limited income. Denial of sex relations also was frequently used by the wives to obtain their own ends. In one case the husband tolerated threats of sadistic acts from his wife, who demanded money or gifts not to go through with the acts.

TREATMENT

One of the functions of probation is to provide the controlled psychosocial medium through which correctional changes may be brought about in the offender's environment and personality while he remains in his own community, rather than in prison, the goal being the prevention of recidivism. It is hoped that the correctional changes brought about in treatment will carry over into the offender's post-probation life.

Two specific probation conditions were ordered by the court at the direction of the probation officer. These were (1) that the husband-wife (victim-offender) relationship be severed, and that all visits or contacts of the spouse occur only with the probation officer's approval, and (2) that the probationer not remarry or form a paramour relationship without the probation officer's consent.

The rationale for these conditions was to give the court and community some assurance that the spouses would not again be victimized and that no newly acquired spouses or paramours suffer the same fate. It was felt that the type of marital situation described, if allowed to continue, could have resulted in murder of the spouse.[8],[9] Marital disharmony accounts for a large number of spouse murders[10] and many murderers have been found to have had a record of previous assaultive behavior involving personal violence of a felonious nature.[11],[12] Three of the four probationers had a previous history of offenses involving violence toward their spouses that fell short of murder. In addition, the probationers needed a nonthreatening environment (separation) where old anxieties could not easily develop.

The probation conditions, in general, also acted as an aid, support or crutch to the probationer's superego, tended to stabilize and clarify his life situation and indicated a real interest in the probationer's problems by the probation officer.

The problem of giving help when class and race differ between the treater and the treated has been receiving increasing attention.[13],[14],[15],[16] It was not felt that a total removal of social distance was possible or necessary. Whyte found in his relationships with lower-class gang members that they did not expect the outsider to be just like them, but rather that he take a personal interest in them.[17] The idea of strict appointments does not seem to fit into the lower-class concept of time. Appointments were made very general (within three day period) with no specific hour of the day. In addition, learning to communicate[18] with the lower-class probationer in argot peculiar to the lower-class and Negro race of this area was considered an aid. Role-taking and empathy were facilitated by familiarity with lower-class Negro cultural values, social norms and marital behavior, as well as day-to-day problems. Another asset in fostering communication was for officer and probationer to share something, such as food, drink, a common problem or experience. In general, the officer differed as much as possible from the Negro's negative stereotyped concept of the white.[19],[20]

As anxiety mounted, the probationers reacted by over-eating, a flight into religious activity or long hours of solitary brooding, and coming into the office without an appointment. Efforts were made to encourage and teach the probationer to ventilate hostility through verbalization with the accepting officer.

The secondary treatment phases were characterized by going over the actual assaults; their dynamics and meaning, with emphasis on the self-damaging and negative aspects. The probationers were shown how their marital behavior had not achieved its purpose, how they had brought pain on themselves and how compulsive modes of marital adjustment had resulted in failure and lack of happiness. Although they voiced self-devaluation and minimizing, this slowly waned as positive strengths were stressed and built on.

Complete separation and ultimate divorce were felt to be decidedly within the family's as well as the community's best interest. In view of the violence pattern and the danger between spouses, marital reconciliation was contraindicated, although where the patterns of violence are exceedingly less this may be the goal.[21] No great personality reorganization was attempted.

By the final treatment phase the probationers were beginning to express some insights into themselves as husbands, their problems and new methods of handling similar situations in the future. Their feeling about women as wives had been favorably altered, as well as their own self-esteem. At the termination of probation, the four assaulters were encouraged to return when they felt a need. All four probationers made excellent adjustments to their probation status and appeared to have profited by it.

Some readers may feel that the officer's goals for his lower-class Negro probationer were in direct violation of their class norms. The Negro lower class has been described as having "unrestrained aggressive conduct,"[22] a "strong propensity to physical violence,"[23] or an "idealization of personal violence."[24] More important are the findings of Drake and Cayton in their extensive study of the urban Negro lower class.[25] They found that the lower-class Negro has an accepted standard of what constitutes a good spouse and this is one who may "slap and curse" at her but will never put his spouse's life in danger whether drunk or sober. To this extent the four probationers violated their own class norms and this problem was individual to them, as they engaged in an excessive amount of violence not sanctioned by their group. In this context their offenses cannot be considered primarily derived from their cultural background but resulted from individual emotional pathology related to a Southern rural matricentric influence during their developmental years.

CONCLUSION

In general, two conclusions can be stated regarding some wife assaulters: (1) they engage in behavior that foretells of serious hostile acts towards their spouses, which has implication for courts handling their minor offenses, and (2) some spouse assaulters can be treated within an authoritative setting to the individual and community's well-being.

NOTES AND REFERENCES

1. Berg, I., and Fox, V.: "Factors in Homicides Committed by 200 Males." *Jour. of Soc. Psych.* 26:108–119.
2. Kurland, A.; Morganstern, J.; and Sheets, C. A.: "Comparative Study of Wife Murderers Admitted to a State Psychiatric Hospital." *Jour. of Social Therapy* 1:7–15, 1955.
3. Wolfgang, M.: "Husband-Wife Homicide." *Journal of Social Therapy* 2:263–271, 1956.
4. Dollard, John et al.: *Frustration & Aggression.* New Haven: Yale Univ. Press, 1939, p. 34.
5. Powdermaker, H.: "The Channeling of Negro Aggression by the Cultural Process," in Kluckholn, C., and Murry, H. (eds.): *Personality in Nature, Society & Culture.* New York: Alfred A. Knopf, 1950, p. 476.
6. Mittelmann, B.: "Analysis of Reciprocal Neurotic Patterns in Family Relationships," in Eisenstein, V. (ed.): *Neurotic Interaction in Marriage.* New York: Basic Books, Inc., 1956, pp. 84–85.
7. Ackerman, N.: "The Diagnosis of Neurotic Marital Interaction." *Social Case Work* 35:142, No. 4.
8. Kurland, *op. cit.,* pp. 7–15.
9. Meyer, A.; Apfelberg, B.; and Sugar, C.: "Men Who Kill Women." *J. of Clinical Psychopathology* Vol. 7 and 8, 1946–47, Parts 1 and 2.
10. Gillin, J.: "Murder As A Sociological Phenomenon," in *Murder and the Penality of Death.* Am. Acad. Pol. Soc. Sc. 284: 22, 1952.
11. Berg, I., *op. cit.,* p. 111.
12. Cruvant, B. Waldrop: "The Murderer in the Mental Institution," in *Murder and the Penalty of Death.* Am. Acad. Pol. Soc. Sc. 284:38, 1952.
13. Martin, Jr.: "Social Cultural Differences: Barriers in Casework with Delinquents." *J. of Soc. Work.* 2:22–26, 1957.
14. Ginsburg, S.: "The Impact of the Social Workers Cultural Structure on Social Therapy." *Soc. Casework* 32:319–325, 1951.
15. Fantl, B.: "Integrating Psychological Social and Cultural Factors in Assertive Casework." *J. of Soc. Work* 3:30–38, 1958.
16. Leighton, A. et al.: *Explorations in Social Psychiatry.* New York: Basic Books Inc., 1957, p. 304.
17. Whyte, W.: *Street Corner Society.* Chicago: U. of Chicago Press, 1959, p. 304.

18. Schatzman, L. Straus: "Social Class and Modes of Communication." *Am. J. of Soc.* 60:329–338, 1955.
19. Cothran, T.: Negro Conceptions of White People." *Am. J. of Soc.* 56: 458–467, 1951.
20. Lewis, H.: *Blackways of Kent.* Chapel Hill: Univ. of North Carolina Press, 1955, p. 179.
21. Reynolds, R. Siegle: "A Study of Sado-Masochistic Marriage Partners." *Social Casework* Dec. 1959, pp. 545–551.
22. Dai, B.: "Some Problems of Personality Development Among Negro Children" in Kluckholn, C., and Murray, H. (eds.): *Personality, Nature, Society and Culture.* New York: Alfred A. Knopf, Inc., 1950, p. 444.
23. Hollingshead, A., and Redlich, F.: *Social Class and Mental Illness.* New York: John Wiley & Sons, Inc., 1958, p. 364.
24. Dollard, J.: *Caste and Class in a Southern Town.* New York: Doubleday & Co., Inc., 1957, p. 274.
25. Drake, S., and Cayton, H.: *Black Metropolis.* New York: Harcourt, Brace & Co., 1945, pp. 586–587.

Husband-Wife Homicides

MARVIN E. WOLFGANG

Most homicide literature does not analyze the relationship between victim and offender, but instead concentrates attention on either the victim or the offender. As a result, a static structural analysis of homicide is usually presented that fails to take cognizance of the dynamic elements in the social situation. The relationship between victim and offender is of special importance in this crime. Homicide is a dynamic phenomenon between two or more persons caught up in a life drama where they operate in a direct, interactional relationship. More so than in any other violation of conduct norms, the relationship the victim bears to the offender plays a role in explaining the reasons for such flagrant violation. All offenses against the person involve direct contact between victim and offender, but homicide usually means a greater degree of intensity or longer duration of this contact than is true for any other offense. Those slayings in which a husband kills his wife, or vice versa, represent the most personalized nature of the crime of homicide.[1]

There is, unfortunately, a paucity of studies and of data that describe and analyze husband-wife homicides. In his review of 100 males committed to the Massachusetts State Prison on conviction of homicide, Stearns[2] noted that eight had killed their wives. In *The Illinois Crime Survey*,[3] Lashly reported that, of 760 killings during 1926 and 1927, the Chicago police recorded 55 husband-wife slayings. Arthur MacDonald[4] pointed out that in England and Wales between 1886 and 1905, of 487 murders committed by men, 26% of the victims were wives of the slayers. More recent statistics from England and Wales may be found in the Report of the Royal Commission on Capital Punishment,[5] which reveals that, between 1900 and 1949, 20% of the 1,080 males convicted of murder had killed their wives. In contrast, only

From *Corrective Psychiatry and Journal of Social Therapy* 2: 263–271, 1956. Reprinted by permission of the publisher.

10% of the 130 females convicted of murder had murdered their husbands. German statistics for 1931 cited by von Hentig[6] supply some brief information regarding husband-wife slayings. Of all male relatives who were victims of murder, 14% were husbands killed by their wives; and of all female relatives who were victims of murder, 62% were wives killed by their husbands. Finally, in a recent study by Albert Kurland and his associates[7] at Spring Grove Hospital in Maryland, it was reported that, of 52 psychotic murderers, 12 were men who had killed their wives and two were women who had slain their husbands. Beyond these few studies, there is very little information reported by students of criminology.

THE PHILADELPHIA STORY: METHODOLOGY

The present study is part of a larger work which includes analysis of 588 consecutive criminal homicides recorded by the Homicide Squad of the Philadelphia Police Department between January 1, 1948 and December 31, 1952. All told, there were 621 offenders and 588 victims; the number of offenders being larger than that of victims because in several cases more than one person was responsible for one homicide. In husband-wife slayings the relationship always involved one civtim and one offender.

To safeguard against loose generalizations, the chi-square test of significance has been used wherever cell-size of the variables being tested permitted such treatment. The conventional use of a P value of less than .05, or the 5% level of significance, has been employed as the limit of statistically significant association. Therefore, whenever the term *significant* is used in italics, the reader may assume that a test of association has been made and that a chi-square with P less than .05 has been found.

RACE AND SEX

Of the 136 victims who had a familial relationship to their slayers, there were exactly 100 husbands or wives, 9 sons, 8 daughters, 3 mothers, 3 brothers, 2 fathers, 1 sister and 10 other types of more distant relations. The primary focus of attention in the present study is with the 100 mate slayings. Of these, 53 wives were slain by their husbands, and 47 husbands by their wives. *Significantly,* the number of wives homicidally assaulted by their husbands constituted 41% of all women who were killed, whereas husbands homicidally assaulted by their wives made up only 11% of all men who were killed. Among those killed by a spouse, Negro husbands numbered 40, Negro wives 40, white husbands 7, and white wives 13.

When a man was killed by a woman, he was most likely to be killed by his wife. Of 75 Negro males slain by Negro females, 40, or 53%, were husbands slain by their mates; and of 9 white males killed by white females, 7 were slain by their mates.

When a woman committed homicide, she was more likely than a man to kill her mate. Of 89 Negro female offenders (for whom a victim-offender relationship has been identified), 40, or 45%, killed their husbands; and of 15 white female offenders, 7 killed their husbands. On the other hand, of 321 Negro male offenders, only 40, or 12%, killed their wives; and of 118 white male offenders, only 13, or 11%, killed their wives.

Combining the races, we may note that when the 104 identified female offenders committed homicide, they killed their husbands in 45% of the cases; but when the 439 identified male offenders committed homicide, they killed their wives in only 12% of the cases.

VIOLENCE

All criminal homicide implies that some kind of violence has been employed and that the death was not a natural one. But some slayers kill their victims with one shot, one stab or one blow; while other offenders brutally and much more violently kill. It may be a purely arbitrary and statistical artifact to attempt to draw quantitatively a line between violent and nonviolent homicide, but the study by Berg and Fox[8] provides some useful insight into this problem. These authors, like the present one, consider two or more acts of stabbing, cutting or shooting, involved in the process of slaying a victim, as violent homicide. If a severe beating is the method by which the victim met death, it too may be classified among violent homicides, although determination of a severe beating is probably a more subjective evaluation by the researcher. If more than five acts were involved in the death, the slaying may properly be labeled "excessive violence." Although previous analysis in the larger work, which is concerned with all 588 cases, showed no positive association between the intimacy of interpersonal relationship and violence of the homicide in general, there is a *significant* association between violence and spouse slayings. Husbands killed their wives violently in a *significantly* greater proportion than did wives who killed their husbands. Among the 53 husbands who killed their wives, 44 did so violently, but among the 47 wives who killed their husbands, only 18 did so violently.

The excessive or severe degrees of violence in which more than five acts were involved were most likely to have a home for the scene, and of all violent homicides, 18% involved more than five acts of a stabbing or shooting. However, among husband-wife homicides, the category of "more than five acts" constitutes 24% of all violent mate slayings. Thus, husband-wife homicides were violent to a greater degree than homicides in general. To this extent, violence and intimacy of personal relationship are associated.

PLACE AND METHOD

With respect to place of occurrence, 85% of husband-wife slayings occurred in the home and only 15% outside the home. The single place where most of these slayings occurred was in the bedroom. Arguments, emotional conflicts, tensions that arise before a couple enters the bedroom, are ordinarily resolved to enjoy the primary purposes of the room, which are sleep and sexual intimacies. The primary purposes appear to become secondary, however, for most persons involved in husband-wife homicide. In those cases where the interpersonal conflicts are carried into the bedroom, or that arise there in the first place, the sleep or sex drive that conducted the couple there becomes subordinated to the tension issues between them. Thus the physical proximity of husband and wife, required largely by institutional expectation in the case of sleep, and of biological necessity in the case of sex, provides a setting in the bedroom for unresolved conflicts. Most women who kill, as we have seen, kill their mates, and since they are not generally in direct contact with their husbands during the working hours of the day, it is not unlikely that when domestic quarrels, pangs of jealousy or desire for revenge arise, they should occur during the evening hours and, if unresolved, are taken into the bedroom. Sex differentials are important to this generalization about the frequency of bedroom homicides. Whereas 24 (45%) of the 53 wives were killed in a bedroom, only 11 (23%) of the 47 husbands were killed there. Thus, proportionately and *significantly*, the bedroom is a more lethal place for wives than for husbands.

With respect to the kitchen, a reverse situation appears to be true, for only 10 wives were slain there compared with 19 husbands. Wives usually stabbed their mates, as indicated by the fact that 30 wives used this method to kill their husbands and only 15 shot them. Husbands were less discriminatory, and killed their wives in almost equal proportions of the leading methods. In 19 cases they shot their mates, in 16 they stabbed them, and in 15 beat them to death. Of the 45 wives killed in the home, 17 were shot and 15 were beaten; of the 40 husbands killed in the home, 23 were stabbed. When a husband was killed in the kitchen, his wife usually used a kitchen instrument (a butcher knife or paring knife most commonly) which was easily accessible. This fact indicates that most kitchen slayings were committed in the heat of passion, during a quarrel and on the spur of the moment. Mealtime is one of those family rituals[9] often used for discussion of problems affecting the individual members of the familial group. As a frequent family meeting place; as a place for family discussion during which tempers may rise and frustrations accumulated during the day may find vent among primary group members; as a place where wives raise questions about the family budget and suggest that their husbands are spending too much money on liquor and perhaps other women, and as a place where butcher knives and other deadly weapons are handy, the kitchen more often than any other room in the home provides a setting for women who kill their husbands.

Of the husbands killed in a kitchen, 17 were stabbed with a kitchen knife and only 2 were shot. Of the wives killed in a kitchen, 5 were stabbed with a kitchen knife, 3 were shot, 1 was beaten to death with a broomstick and 1 was severely cut with a hatchet. Of 11 husbands killed in a bedroom, 4 were stabbed with a kitchen knife, 4 were shot with a pistol, 1 with a shotgun, 1 was cut with a jagged drinking glass and 1 was soaked with kerosene and burned to death. Of 24 wives killed in a bedroom, 9 were beaten or strangled, 6 were stabbed with a kitchen knife, 4 were shot and 1 each was slain by a mop handle, an electric iron, an iron pipe, an overdose of barbiturates and a push from a third-floor apartment. Among these wives killed in a bedroom there were 12 beatings, 6 stabbings, 4 shootings and 2 by miscellaneous methods. When a husband was killed in any place in the home other than the kitchen or bedroom, his wife used a pistol in 4 cases, a shotgun in 1, a penknife in 3, a kitchen knife in 2. When a wife was slain in any place in the home other than the kitchen or bedroom, her husband used a pistol in 9 cases, a shotgun in 1 and a penknife in 1.

VICTIM-PRECIPITATED CASES

In the analysis of criminal homicide in Philadelphia, the term *victim-precipitated* homicide applies to those homicides in which the victim is a direct, positive precipitator in the crime.[10] The role of the victim is here characterized by his having been the first in the homicide drama to use physical force directed against his subsequent slayer. The victim-precipitated cases are those on which the victim was the first to show and use a deadly weapon, to strike a blow in an altercation—in short, the first to commence the interplay of resort to physical violence. In seeking to identify the victim-precipitated cases recorded in police files, it has not been possible always to determine whether the homicides strictly parallel legal interpretations of sufficient provocation to reduce a murder charge to one of manslaughter. In general, there appears to be much similarity. Mutual quarrels and wordy altercations do not constitute sufficient provocation under law, nor are they included in the meaning herein applied to victim-precipitated homicide. The victim, in these cases, must be the first to resort to physically assaultive methods of attack.

Of the 550 identifiable relationships between victims and offenders among total homicides in the larger study, 150, or 26%, have been designated as victim-precipitated homicides. An impression derived from analysis of husband-wife slayings inferred that a higher proportion of husbands than of wives provoked their mates into killing them; that is, first struck their mates and changed the level of social interaction from that of verbalizing to assaulting. Of 38 family slayings among victim-precipitated cases, 33 are husband-wife killings, while of 98 family slayings among non-victim-precipitated cases, only 67 are husband-wife killings. This proportional difference results in a *significant* association between mate slayings and victim-precipitated homicide.

Of these victim-precipitated mate slayings, 28 victims are husbands and only 5 are wives; but of non-victim-precipitated mate slayings, only 19 victims are husbands while 48 are wives. Thus, there is a *significant* association between husbands who are victims in mate slayings and victim-precipitated homicide. This fact—namely, that *significantly* more husbands than wives precipitate their own demise in spouse slayings—means that (1) husbands actually may provoke their wives more often than wives provoke their husbands to assault; or (2) assuming that provocation by wives is as intense and equally as frequent, or even more frequent than provocation by husbands, then husbands do not receive and define provocation stimuli with as great or as violent a reaction as do wives; or (3) husbands may have a greater felt sense of guilt for one reason or another, and receive verbal insults and overt physical assaults in a marital conflict without retaliation as a form of compensatory punishment; or (4) husbands may withdraw more often than wives from the scene of martial conflict, and thus eliminate temporarily a violent overt reaction to their wives' provocation. This is only a suggestive, not an exhaustive list of probable explanation. In any case, we are left with the undeniable fact that husbands more often than wives are major precipitating factors in their own homicidal deaths.

DISPOSITION OF OFFENDERS

The following breakdown shows the disposition according to marital status of offender:

	Husband	Wife	Total
Guilty	34	26	60
Not Guilty	2	16	18
Nolle Prosequi	2	2	4
Pending	3	2	5
Suicide	10	1	11
Died Before Trial	1	—	1
Fugitive	1	—	1
Total	53	47	100

Below is the court designation of the homicide according to marital status of the defendant:

	Husband	Wife	Total
First Degree Murder	10	—	10
Second Degree Murder	10	4	14
Voluntary Manslaughter	10	15	25
Involuntary Manslaughter	4	7	11
Total	34	26	60

These data reveal that:

(1) a higher proportion of husbands (64%) than of wives (55%) were found guilty;

(2) a higher proportion of wives (34%) than of husbands (4%) were acquitted;

(3) more husbands (19%) than wives (2%) commited suicide after having killed their mates;

(4) husbands were convicted of more serious degrees of homicide than were wives. The majority of husbands were convicted of murder while five-sixths of the wives were convicted of manslaughter. None of the wives, but about a third of the husbands, were convicted of first-degree murder. Less than a sixth of the wives, contrasted with three-fifths of the husbands, were convicted of either of the degrees of murder.

An immediate and common conclusion from these data suggests that the courts treat wives with greater leniency than they do husbands. Such an interpretation of differential treatment assumes that all other things are equal—i.e., there is no major difference in the actual types of homicides committed by wives and husbands. Examination of these mate slayings reveals, however, that it is not necessarily true that the courts treated wives with unjustifiably greater leniency than they did husbands, for in 28 cases of female defendants, the husband had strongly provoked his wife to attack; and, although she was not exonerated on grounds of self-defense, there had been sufficient provocation by the husband (as the victim) to reduce the seriousness of her offense. In contrast, such provocation recognized by the courts occurred in only 5 cases in which husbands killed their wives.

Finally, it is interesting to note that in only one of the 47 cases in which a wife killed her husband did she later commit suicide; but that in 10 of the 53 cases in which a husband killed his wife did he commit suicide.[11] Close examination of mate slayings ending in suicide implies that this differential is due to greater feelings of guilt and remorse on the part of husbands. We know from previous analysis of victim-precipitated mate slayings that 28 husbands and only 5 wives were victims who contributed to their own death by making the first assault. The wife who killed her husband after he had slapped or beaten her is less likely to feel remorse or guilt than if she had not been so provoked. Husbands killed their wives *significantly* more often without provocation. These facts suggest that husbands had greater guilt and remorse feelings and hence more frequently committed suicide after slaying their mates.

HUSBAND-WIFE CRIMINAL HOMICIDE, BY RACE, METHOD, PLACE AND VIOLENCE, PHILADELPHIA, 1948–1952

	Husband Killed by Wife	Wife Killed by Husband	Total
Both Races	47	53	100
Negro	40	40	80
White	7	13	20
Method			
Stabbing	30	16	46
Shooting	15	19	34
Beating	—	15	15
Other	2	3	5
	47	53	100
Place			
Bedroom	11	24	35
Kitchen	19	10	29
Living Room	4	7	11
Stairway	6	3	9
Highway (public street, alley, field)	4	4	8
Taproom	2	1	3
Other commercial place	1	3	4
Other	—	1	1
	47	53	100
Violence	18	44	62
Non-Violence	29	9	38
	47	53	100

NOTES AND REFERENCES

1. This study is part of a larger work on patterns in criminal homicide to be published by the University of Pennsylvania Press.
2. Stearns, Albert W.: "Homicide in Massachusetts." *American Journal of Psychiatry* 4:740, July 1924-April 1925.
3. *Illinois Crime Survey.* Chicago: Illinois Association for Criminal Justice and the Chicago Crime Commission, 1929, p. 610.
4. MacDonald, Arthur: "Death Penalty and Homicide." *American Journal of Sociology* 16: 96–97, 1911.
5. Royal Commission on Capital Punishment: *1949–1952 Report.* London: H. M. Stationery Office, 1953, p. 330.

6. Von Hentig, Hans: *The Criminal and His Victim*. New Haven: Yale University Press, 1948, p. 392.

7. Kurland, Albert A.; Morgenstern, Jacob; and Sheets, Carolyn: "A Comparative Study of Wife Murderers Admitted to a State Psychiatric Hospital." *Journal of Social Therapy* 1:7–15, Jan. 1955.

8. Berg, I. A., and Fox, Vernon: "Factors in Homicides Committed by 200 Males." *Journal of Social Psychology* 26:109–119, Aug. 1947.

9. Bossard, James H. S., and Boll, Eleanor: *Family Ritual*. Philadelphia: University of Pennsylvania Press, 1950, p. 99.

10. For some theoretical suggestions on the role of the victim as a determinant in crime, see von Hentig, *op. cit.,* pp. 383–450. For excellent legal discussions of the rule of provocation, see Perkins, Rollin M.: "The Law of Homicide." *Journal of Criminal Law and Criminology* 36:412–427, March-April 1946; and Weschler, Herbert, and Michael, Jerome: "A Rationale of the Law of Homicide." *Columbia Law Review* 37:1280–1282, May and Dec. 1937.

11. If the 10 husbands who killed their wives and then committed suicide had killed themselves in the same proportion as wives, the number of husbands convicted of first degree murder would have been much higher. Judgment of these 10 homicide-suicides of husbands, by competent observers, places them in the first-degree murder category. Should the cases have gone to trial, likelihood of conviction for murder would have been great.

Suburbia: The Call Wives

Throughout the sandy reach of Long Island, where New Yorkers in the postwar hundreds of thousands have settled down to learn outdoor cookery and cultivate mortgages, the towns thickly clustered along the tendrils of the Long Island Rail Road are scornfully labeled by the sociologists as big-city bedroom communities. The sociologists christened better than they knew.

It came to light last week that housewives there have been doubling as call girls. Fifteen of them ranging from 20 to 45 years old were rounded up in after-dark raids on split-level ranch houses and roadside restaurants, accused of selling their favors for $25 to $100. One woman, a Nassau County grand jury was told, earned $30,000 in pin money in one year.

Nearly all of them, by their own account, were merely trying to cope with a classic suburban problem: keeping up with the Joneses despite a limited budget. The new friends were mostly men who came to watch the trotters at Roosevelt Raceway and picked up just the right telephone numbers in the neon-spangled nightclubs and cocktail lounges nearby.

In some cases, the women were loosing the kirtle of virtue while their husbands, all unknowing, were wearing the tight white collar of middle-class desperation in the city. "In at least one instance," District Attorney William Cahn said, however, "the husband knew what his wife was doing and even babysat for her. His income was insufficient and she did it to help."

How did the authorities get onto it all? An old story, Cahn sighed; the housewives helped to draw attention to themselves by squabbling with resentful professional prostitutes in public places. Keeping up with the Joneses, in short, is no game for amateurs.

From *Newsweek* 63:18, No. 18, Feb. 17, 1964. Copyright Newsweek, Inc., 1964. Reprinted by permission of the publisher.

Gambling Fever:
Winner Lose All

DOROTHY CAMERON DISNEY

Gambling, legal and illegal, is one of the biggest industries in the United States. Recently the commissioner of Internal Revenue, who should be qualified to judge, told a U. S. Senate committee that illegal bookmakers did at least a 50-billion-dollar business annually in off-track betting, and this is only one form of organized gambling.

Marriage counselors of my acquaintance, all over the country, are disturbed by the increasing number of youthful husbands and fathers who impoverish their families and wreck their homes by gambling. They squander wages earmarked for rent and grocery bills in poker parlors, on floating dice games, by placing bets on baseball, football, basketball, hockey and prize-fights. Inevitably, wives and children suffer. No good marriage can be built under the handicap of heavy gambling.

With the possible exception of alcoholism, a husband's gambling confronts a wife with her most complex and rugged challenge. I mean *excessive* gambling. Nowadays, only the most rigid moralists see evil in an occasional small flier at fortune.

Gambling is as old as history. Most of us, when we take a chance, have the normal desire to win. Without undue difficulty we are usually able to hold our losses to a sensible limit, set a reasonable bedtime hour. The compulsive gambler is different. He seems literally unable to tear himself away from the game so long as he has a dollar in his pocket, a blank check in his checkbook. In these conditions, profit becomes a virtual impossibility. As a professional bookie once told my husband: "This fellow wins five dollars, he wants ten; he wins ten dollars, he wants twenty; he wins twenty, he wants forty dollars . . . so why won't he go home and quit a winner? What is it this fellow wants? Win still more? He wants to *lose!*"

From *Ladies Home Journal* 80:18, No. 18, March, 1963. ©1963 Downe Publishing, Inc. Reprinted by special permission of the *Ladies' Home Journal*.

Most researchers agree that men gamble to excess for the same sub-conscious reasons that other men drink to excess. They seek escape from pressures of which they are unaware on a conscious level but cannot tolerate.

In many cases there appears to be a definite link between gambling and sexuality. There are unquestionably gamblers who substitute the thrill of the pari-mutuel machine or roulette wheel for the satisfactions of sexual love. Some husbands gamble because they feel their wives are cold and unresponsive; others gamble because they subconsciously doubt their own masculinity.

Other gamblers seem bent upon self-destruction. They are weighed down by feelings of shame and guilt and seek to lighten the load by punishing themselves. They are happy only when they are miserable.

More common in my experience are gamblers driven by rebellion. Rebellion against responsibility, against boredom and monotony, against childhood disaffections, rebellion against their wives. Their situation is by no means hopeless. They *can* quit, and frequently do. Oddly enough, in many instances their regeneration seems to depend more on co-operation and changed attitudes on the part of their wives than on their own sworn pledges to reform.

There are reasons. Gamblers often attract, and are attracted by, women whose personality difficulties are as acute as their own. These problem wives unerringly, if unwittingly, apply the very pressures their husbands cannot tolerate.

"Wives," Professor Donald M. Maynard of Boston University told me recently, "cannot isolate a husband's gambling from the difficulties of their marriage as a whole. She knows what he is doing wrong. But what is she doing wrong? This is a problem that almost always has two sides."

I first heard of Ina and Fred Warner through caseworker friends at the Family Service in New Haven, Connecticut. When 30-year-old Ina, a tall, intensely shy woman, appealed to that admirable organization for counseling, she was desperate. Thirty-two-year-old Fred had just gone on the most calamitous gambling spree of the couple's chaotic, up-and-down marriage. Fred's prosperous auto-supply business had been taken over by creditors. His $25,000 home had been foreclosed by the mortgage holders. He was $8,000 in debt.

Said Ina: "Fred insists he loves me and our three youngsters. He depends on me, I know. Yet his gambling has made our lives a misery. Our sons are camping out with my mother right now. She doesn't want them, and she is a bully and a nag besides. For twelve years I've tried to keep a careful watch on Fred, but it's done no good. Bill collectors knock constantly at our door; process servers haunt us; we've been sued time after time. I'm ashamed to hold up my head in public.

"Even when Fred and I met as high-school students and were church-mouse-poor, he ignored my protests and used to risk part of his pitiful wages on football games. But he also helped support his younger brothers, whereas my two brothers have never supported anybody and have grown up to be as worthless as my father. Not only did my father gamble but he also threw away his money on other women until mother divorced him. She warned me not to marry Fred. But he was the only boy friend I ever had—I was too tall, too shabbily dressed, too shy to be popular—and I was so sick of her bossiness I wouldn't listen.

"I just don't understand Fred. The morning we were evicted, he broke down and cried. He looked so pathetic that I hated myself for my mean thoughts. He seemed like one of the children. I put my arms around him, and I cried too. I have never loved him more than I did at that moment.

"I've sacrificed everything for Fred—fun and recreation, the companionship of other women, peace of mind, the welfare of our sons. I've devoted myself exclusively to Fred. On Fred's account, I have lived like a hermit. Yet my best efforts to help him have failed . . . . "

By Ina's own admission, she felt her love for Fred most deeply when he was beaten and distraught. Why? Subconsciously she feared that if he acquired the gumption to mend his ways, his dependence on her would be lessened. Ina put no faith in her abilities either to hold a husband or to attract a feminine friend. From girlhood she had been ashamed of her background and her appearance. It wasn't Fred's fault she lacked friends, had few resources of her own, lived like a hermit.

Fred's gambling was the result of years of frustration—frustration as a boy and as an adult. His father early deserted the family. In boyhood Fred was overburdened by the financial and emotional demands of his mother, a woman who wept on his shoulder, expected him to act as a father to a pack of younger brothers, hand over his earnings to her. His only relief was to hold back a few dollars to make small wagers on high-school sports events. Win or lose, he experienced a feeling of independence and freedom and learned to equate gambling with the rare and pleasant emotion.

Ina leaned on Fred as heavily as his mother had, and created the same emotional atmosphere. His mother was changeable and moody and played favorites among her children, so that Fred never knew where he stood in her affections. Ina was as changeable as her mother-in-law. She alternately treated Fred like a cherished infant or a prospective embezzler.

Moreover, although Ina was unaware of it, she was as domineering in a soft-spoken way as *her* mother. Early in the marriage she cut Fred off from masculine friends on the theory that an evening out might lead to gambling. Actually she was jealous. She had frequently embarrassed him before fellow workers by calling in person at his place of employment to collect his salary check. He countered by borrowing the money for a gambling stake.

Fred gambled to find release from the tensions and strain of a marriage that was a repetition of his tension-ridden boyhood. In gambling he found a way to take revenge on Ina, his omnipresent if benevolent jailer.

Ina was intelligent enough, after counseling, to recognize and correct her mistakes. It wasn't easy, but she conquered her excessive shyness, joined the PTA, developed other outside interests. She stopped pressuring, maneuvering and checking on Fred, eventually mastered her worries, suspicions and excessive fearfulness.

When she learned to trust Fred to behave like a man of strength and standards, the whole emotional climate of the marriage changed. And Fred changed too. He became more dependable, more relaxed, a stronger personality. The Warners are still in debt, but Fred now has a well-paid job and is whittling the debt load down to size. Both Ina and Fred are convinced that his gambling days are behind him.

Before We Began to Swing

SARAH HARRIS

An amiable, young, well-bred face, a mouth smiling with a gamin wistfulness, and a very low drawl. Certainly there's nothing sinister about this Adele McLean, who had been chosen, out of the eight members of a Westchester wife-swappers' club, to give structure and sequence to what was to me, on the day I met her, a jumble of facts and impressions stored in my mind. Surely swappers couldn't participate in such weird rites; they couldn't openly confess their doings, making such statements as: "My wife's an angel in her fashion—and I'm not being ironic when I say 'fashion'—but" or: "It's meant so much to me being married to my husband. Being his wife's been the loveliest thing in my life. I love him, I really do, he's my favorite person in the world. But, you see, our marriage—"

I had been steered to Adele's swap club by Jean (swappers are some of her best customers) and by the Midwest vice lieutenant. I had met Adele in a midtown restaurant. She had said at the beginning of our meeting, "Really, I'm not very knowledgeable about swinging. Paul and I are fairly new members of the swingers." She sounded as if she envied the older clubbers' full life before she and her husband had also become swingers or "modern marrieds," as the wife-swappers throughout the country, from Los Angeles to Boston and Denver to Miami, identify themselves to each other.

As Adele bent very low to talk to me, I felt like a predator as I fingered my long list of pious, disrespectful questions—a list headed by that fatuous question: "Tell me about it. Why do you do it?"

This, of course, is what four out of every five interviewers have always asked the female—especially fastidious female—swap-club members. What a futile question! It is the same question that is thrown at prostitutes, and it deserves the same answer they provide whenever their customers put the query—the first thing that comes to mind in hopes of politely blocking more presumptuous queries. Why shouldn't they be on the defensive before the

Reprinted by permission of G. P. Putnam's Sons from *The Puritan Jungle: America's Sexual Underground* by Sarah Harris. Copyright © 1969 by Sarah Harris.

lynxlike curiosity of men, who, though they use them in private, have been educated to "spit" on them in public?

Similarly, why should a wife-swapper surrender her caution and wariness to people who not only may identify her but cause her to be condemned by the upright, respected citizens who accept her because they know nothing of her swapping activities?

Some women wife-swappers, of course, are not defensive at all; indeed, they blatantly let you know that their life adjustment is better than yours. They tell you, because they believe it, that unlike you, who out of cowardice are saddled with mental and physical frustrations, they have found the way, the only way (for to them sex is the only way) of facing life honestly.

Fully convinced that, although you may not altogether grasp their meaning, you nevertheless must covet their liberation, they do not hesitate to lay bare the most intimate secrets of their lives with their husbands and swap-partners. For the true believers in "modern-marriedism," no detail of their sexuality is too personal; not, at least, once they have come to know you and to trust your promise to protect their anonymity. And the higher up they are in their social circles, the more pride they take in their activities.

Anita Lewis is a mini-skirted ingenue wife of a Chicago lawyer, who, although she is a psychiatric social worker, looks like a musical-comedy star. She blows the most impeccable smoke rings, flicking ashes from her constantly lit cigarette with excessive daintiness as she throws out confidences that would startle debonair women twice her age: "I haven't got sufficient words to describe the satisfaction, the stimulation, the delight in our own marriage as well as in our 'co-marital partnerships' my husband and I have experienced since we came to our understanding and began swinging."

Anita is like all consecrated "modern marrieds" I met individually or with their spouses or in groups as large as twenty, or with whom I corresponded by mail. She sharply distinguishes "co-marital" exchanges of two or more husbands and their wives from "extramarital" affairs, which she considers "disreputable."

Marlena Anderson, a forty-three-year-old grandmother living in Washington, D.C., and married to a man of more than middling importance in governmental circles, echoes young Anita. Marlena, who practically pushes on friends and acquaintances pictures of her two young grandchildren, invariably wears brave, large hats and black dresses specially cut to attract men's stares to her bare, white shoulders and voluptuous breasts. One dress and tricorne hat in particular makes her look like nothing so much as the cover illustration for the book *In Praise of Older Women by a Young Man.*

Once she let herself go with me—it took a long time—Marlena talked far more recklessly and freely than Anita about her marriage in relation to her "co-marital" sensations and emotions, experiments and experiences.

"My feelings about my husband," she said, "used to be, especially as we both grew older, equally divided between love and hate. I loved him for his brilliant intellect, his genuineness, his kindliness, his love and passion for me which continued through twenty-five years of marriage. But I hated him because his aging body reminded me that I was aging too, although he kept flattering me whenever we made love, and it was often, because George is still today, at fifty-three, a very passionate man—disgustingly passionate, I thought before we became swingers; he literally nauseated me in bed in spite of my respect for him as a person. You see, he'd had an illness two years before we started to swing that turned him scrawny, made his complexion bad, caused his skin to turn slack and sag so I couldn't stand any sort of bodily contact with him.

"Of course, he was too perceptive not to realize how he revolted me physically, although I did my best to hide it from him, out of compassion, to say nothing of my love for him.

"Strange as it may seem, it was George who first suggested we become swingers. And, you know, though I was fully aware, naturally, that he was considering my needs rather than his own, I was deeply hurt. I felt snubbed, rejected. And I couldn't understand how such an idea could have occurred to a man of his intellect and status. I mean, all I knew about swinging then came from titles I'd only glimpsed on covers of cheap magazines I'd never dream of buying. It certainly didn't seem an answer for people like us.

"At first, I laughed, sure that George must be joking. Then, when I discovered how deadly serious he was, I flew into a fury and began raving and ranting at him. What did he think I was, anyhow—some dime-store clerk, some whore? Or maybe he thought I was oversexed. Well, *he* was the oversexed one. As far as I was concerned, I didn't care if I never went to bed with a man again. And I didn't mean George alone, either; I meant any man.

"The grandchildren weren't born then, but both my daughters were grown—Jean was nineteen and Lisa was twenty-two and engaged to be married. So you can see how ridiculous the whole notion seemed to me. But George had done a lot of soul searching himself before he broached the idea to me, and he just kept at it and at me, selling the merits of the whole swinging situation.

"And then, a couple of months after he and I had first begun talking about swinging we spent a long weekend at Rehoboth Beach with two very dear friends. Lou's a doctor and Anne's what I guess you'd call a perennial student. She's got her master's degree in psychology, her Ph. D. in sociology and she still goes to school. Also, she paints and is a wonderful pianist though she's never performed publicly, out of fear, I think, rather than because she isn't good enough.

"Lou's thirty-six and Anne's thirty-one. But the difference in our ages made no difference in our friendship. Washington is like that, different from every other place in the United States I've ever known in that age isn't half as important in your relationship with people as mutual interests. Our friends, I mean, good, close friends, range from couples in their twenties to some in their late sixties and early seventies.

"I guess I'm going about it the long way, but, what I mean to say is that the four of us swung that weekend at Rehoboth and are still swinging now (we get away together twice a month or thereabouts) without any thought of age difference."

Marlena admitted to being somewhat horrified at her first swapping experience. Too many of those recollections seemed—despite the delight she says she will treasure for the rest of her life—a "shattering tragedy." There was scarcely a minute during the three nights she spent with Lou and Anne with George, "except, of course, when we made love and I forgot everything but Lou"—with his firm resilient body—that flashes of her daughters were not evoked. During the times Lou slept, Marlena lay tossing and sleepless beside him, thinking of Joan and Lisa. She could not help imagining how, with their conventional upbringing, much like her own, her daughters would have loathed the thought of their mother in the arms of a man other than their father. She fought those thoughts with every defense she had—to no avail. No matter how she tried to block her thoughts, she could visualize the inevitable scene—the girls furious, and herself attempting to appease them with lies and promises she knew she might or might not be able to keep.

She could think of only one way to end the nightmare dominating her: wake Lou and make love again. But how could she do such a thing? Although Marlena may appear a woman of sophistication, actually she is—or was—extremely reticent and modest as befits the daughter of resolute Baptist parents who taught her that the only kind of lovemaking any woman would engage in—even with the man she married—was what both Marlena and her husband now refer to as "conventional."

I spoke with George later on and he reiterated all Marlena had told me. He said that although he loved her now as he had from the day they were married, he had always been frustrated by her refusal to engage in any sort of foreplay to intercourse. Through twenty-five years she clung to her feminine modesty, stubbornly refusing to yield to any of his needs for stimuli.

"I would have done anything to stimulate her," George said. "Out of selfish as well as unselfish reasons, because I myself become far more exicted and aroused when I'm able to rouse her. But she insisted—before we began to swing, I mean—that these 'unnatural games'—that's what she called all sexual foreplay—had no place in love between a woman and a man.

"She still has a beautiful body," he said. "But she'd never allow me to see her nude in all the many years before we began swinging. Can you imagine? To have been married to a woman for years and never to have been allowed to see her?

"I don't know, to this day, how or why I stood for it, except that I loved her so much and kept on hoping something would happen to change her."

Marlena laughed when I told her, with his permission, all George had told me. "It was a long wait, wasn't it? And if not for the swinging it would have been longer still. Poor George. But the swinging's changed me, not only with Lou and Jim, who is part of the one other wonderful couple we swing with occasionally, but also George when he and I are making love. And George is so delighted in the change in me." She told me that before she had begun swinging, she felt herself forced to cling to her "mother's and grandmother's customs. I wanted to perform the act quietly buried beneath a blanket in a dark, secluded bedroom." She laughed.

"But getting back to my first night with Lou—because, really, in its way, that's what changed all our lives—I wakened him after I found myself so miserable over the kids. Being who I was then, you can't imagine what it cost me to do that."

She talked passionately as she described how, despite her firm belief that a woman ought never to be the aggressor, she kissed Lou awake with her searching mouth.

"I could not believe it was me behaving so wantonly."

What happened next, Marlena said, she will never forget.

" 'I didn't want to waken you,' I told Lou, 'but I need you, now.'

" 'I'm glad,' he said, and immediately removed my nightgown and his pajamas and turned on the bed lamp, something I'd never let George do in all the years of our marriage. He literally pored over my body for half an hour, and, though I was embarrassed, I wouldn't have had him stop for anything in the world. And then he caressed me all over."

When George had caressed her through her nightclothes, she said, "even at the beginning of our marriage, I'd occasionally—but only occasionally—permit him to turn on the light. But, far from being stimulated, my whole mood for lovemaking would be spoiled. And I don't believe it was because of George. I just felt his embraces and especially his tongue kisses to be more than I could take—especially in the light. I think that before swinging freed me, I'd have felt the same no matter whom I'd been with."

Her first night with Lou, though, she was aroused as she knew he was also to a state of intense excitement by the most thorough, unhampered preliminaries. And instead of keeping her eyes closed as she had all her life during the sexual act, she opened them wide and looked directly at Lou. Soon something that had never happened before and that she never could have envisaged happening occurred. She began exploring Lou's chest, arms, cheeks, neck, legs.

"Neither of us slept all night except on and off," she said, "and we both had several orgasms."

In the morning, the two couples met for breakfast in the hotel dining room. Covering her embarrassment with an attempt at acting bold, Marlena preceded Lou to the table where George and Anne were sitting, looking like two people who throughly knew and accepted each other. Coming upon them like that, Marlena was surprised at her shiver of jealousy; could George's night with Anne, young Anne, have been as heady and intoxicating as hers with Lou? She admits she was horrified at the prospect.

Seeing George so obviously delighted and betraying none of the inadequacy he did after she and he made love, she felt her own exhilaration give way to guilt again. She found herself shaking with rage at her husband, eating breakfast so calmly while all she felt like was crying over her daughters deceived by their faithless parents.

She waited for the tears to come, but they didn't. Instead, she turned to Lou and the heady, intoxicating feeling she had when she was in his arms returned. George smiled at her lovingly, his face full of devotion; and then Anne softly complimented her on George's technique as a lover, his tact and finesse. "He goes to such elaborate lengths to please a woman," she told Marlena.

Marlena didn't know what Anne meant "although, as I've said, I certainly know now," but she wouldn't admit it to Anne or any other living soul. Having seen another woman in relation to George, she suddenly realized that though Lou enraptured *her* (as George, of all people, seemed to have delighted Anne), her basic attachment was to her husband just as Anne's was to Lou.

"After breakfast," Marlena said, "the four of us went swimming and later we looked for a new restaurant—we're all gourmets and one of our real kicks is exploring new restaurants."

At lunch, over too many drinks, Lou and Anne told Marlena that they had engaged in swapping activities for over three years—beginning some four years after their marriage. They told dozens of stories, not only of their co-marital relationships but also of their different activities as members of swapping groups of six, eight and even ten people.

"I seem to have blocked out much of what then was, to me, their 'vulgarity,' " Marlena said. "They talked about the 'little erotic games they and the larger groups they'd swung with played, so they could become animated, incited, call it what you will, to the swinging mood.

"I do remember, though, that George didn't seem embarrassed at Anne's and Lou's conversation." Marlena remembers sitting there, her hands flat on either side of her chair "to prevent myself from getting up and running away, I guess, and smiling down at my shoes and hoping nobody could read my thoughts. Then, suddenly, Anne asked, 'Are you listening, Marlena?'

" 'Yes,' I said, feeling goose bumps on my arms because I had really been thinking that it was one thing to go to bed in private with a man who attracted you, though even that was bad enough, God knows . . . but this . . . to consciously swap your husband for your friend's; seemed fighting against everything human. We seemed animals instead of ordinary, maybe somewhat extraordinary people.

"I came up for air just in time to hear Anne explaining about games people played when they attended swap-parties. She talked of the 'underground movies' they'd show to make people hot. That was Anne's word, 'hot,' and you'd have to see her to imagine how really incongruous it sounded coming out of her mouth. She's so—well, delicate and refined. I was really shocked at her description of the 'movies to put you in the mood.' But I was most revolted by her explanation of the swap-party games. I was horrified at them.

"If you'd ask me now why that was, I don't believe I could tell you. Now that I swap myself, I mean." She glanced down at her long, tapered hands resting in her lap. "Oh, the games Anne explained weren't different from ordinary card games people play except that, when you lost, you gradually stripped off items of clothing. They were both single—like poker and blackjack—and double-handed, which I've since learned most swingers, especially accustomed ones, choose over singles. These included hearts, pinochle, canasta. In them, you see, husbands and wives are allied against other husbands and wives. The winners undress the losers; the winning husband undressing the losing wife and vice-versa until everybody's in the nude. Naturally, a great deal of touching, kissing and caressing goes on till everybody's sort of excited or, anyhow, stimulated.

"Then there are the kinds of games with variations. Children's party games with variations. Remember Musical Chairs you played when you were a kid? Well, some swingers play Musical Laps. When the music begins, the women standing on the inside of the circle move in one direction and the men standing on the outside move in the other. Then, when the music stops, the men and women nearest each other dash to the closest chair. The man sits first and the woman sits on his lap. The couple remaining without a chair must, of course, pay the penalty." Penalties are diverse and largely subject to the inclination of the group's leaders and the inhibitedness or lack thereof of the membership. Penalties range all the way from the removal of one garment to stripping one another nude or having public intercourse in one of many positions.

"There is one game," Marlena said, "that has become practically standard in swapping circles, especially the larger ones. It's called Sheets, and

since it is a piece of buffoonery and depends upon trickery, which, once perceived, will never fool anyone again, it is tried, as are fraternity absurdities,
only with new pledges. The new member is sent out of the room and informed
that Sheets is a strip game which calls for him or her to exercise intuition and
imagination. Then 'it' returns to the room completely dressed, and fully
covered by a sheet, and is told that the group has decided on an item of clothing 'it' must discard. The new member must keep discarding clothes until
he or she hits on the mystery item—which happens rarely, leaving him or her
nearly completely nude, since the item the group has chosen is the sheet in
which they have wrapped him.''

Marlena looked into her coffee cup, seeming for all the world like the
respectable, infinitely desirable, upperclass matron she is, and smiled,
momentarily.

"Lord, Lord, honey," she mimicked her Negro maid, "here I sit, listening to Miss Anne and Mr. Lou, talking about underground movies and card
games and such, and not welcoming the talk nohow. And next thing,"
she looked up and shook her head slowly from side to side, "here I am, involved in an orgy, a saturnalia—anyway, a bit of high living if you know what
I mean. And, well, not altogether disliking it.''

The "orgy," the "saturnalia," took place at Anne and Lou's home where
Dick, a fifty-year-old prominent San Francisco lawyer and his third wife,
Dorothea, twenty-two, bright-eyed, cherry-cheeked, looking dainty as a
doll, but in reality more worldly-wise "sexually speaking" than either
Marlena or Anne, came to spend three days in the spring.

Marlena and George were also invited. They arrived the night before the
morning Dick and Dorothea were due, and slept together instead of swap-
ping. They rose early, but to their surprise, Lou and Anne were also up.
After preparing breakfast, the men went off to stock up on supplies, leaving
Marlena and Anne, who had given her maid a vacation "for good reason."
Anne, regarding Marlena, asked if she was uncomfortable about any of this.

Marlena could not return her gaze. "I suppose so. What makes you ask?"

"Look, with the six of us here, some may get too carried away, become
too impossible. So if the going gets rough, a little scary"—it was as though
Anne were thinking back to her own first such experience—"look, Marlena,
the rest of us won't lose our respect for you, if you find you can't—on your
first time with the six of us . . . ''

"I know, but I'm looking forward to it; really I am." And in a way she
was, despite her fear of the new experience.

Dorothea and Dick arrived and the afternoon was a pleasant one.
After an excellent lunch, the three couples sat around the living room, listening to records, particularly an album of Arthur Rubinstein playing Chopin
preludes. Later, they took a drive through Washington and Rock Creek Park.

Just before dinner a full-fledged thunderstorm broke out and the couples sat before the picture window, sipping martinis and watching the great flashes of lightning come across the sky. Dick said he hoped the storm lasted through dinner and the whole night for that matter. He had always liked making love to thunder and lightning.

Suddenly, Marlena, quite drunk on martinis by now, felt that she was going to cry. No one but Dick noticed, though. "You all right?" he asked.

"I'm all right."

"You better have a drink. Hey, Lou, give the lady another martini."

He eased her into an easy chair and sat close beside her. "He fed me that silly martini as though I were a baby." "You're gorgeous," he said, while she sipped at her drink. "I didn't know that you were a queen, Marlena."

Comfortable in Dick's arms, as through a haze Marlena noticed Dorothea completely nude ("It's hot in here," she said), sitting with Lou, ruffling his hair and "touching him all over till you could hear him panting because be wanted her so badly. Drunk as I was, I could see she was completely uninhibited (she was younger than my elder daughter), and so was Lou with her. George and Anne were nowhere around, and I surmised they'd gone to a bedroom together.

"But I couldn't have cared less. Somehow, I couldn't keep my eyes off Lou and Dorothea. She undressed him and then let herself down on the floor, and pulled him till he lay there on her. I watched them: I just couldn't keep my eyes off them as she kept moaning and moving beneath him.

" 'They're having a long, hard great time, aren't they, honey?' Dick asked me. And he took the martini glass out of my hand so there'd be nothing between my body and his. Almost beside myself, hardly knowing what I was doing, I let my hands come up and touch his face. And I put my arms around his neck and clung to him.

"Even through my high, I was unable to believe I was me. I felt Dick's lips touch my lips and neck and ears and heard him say, 'Honey, you're the greatest.' He lifted me up and carried me upstairs.

"In bed, he turned me over on my back and moved against me. I knew what he would do—and, you see, I'd never done that before. I was so afraid, and, still speaking through my drunken haze, I said, 'Oh Dick, don't hurt me, please.'

"He said, 'Hurt you? Why should I want to hurt you?' And then he said, 'Oh, I see you've never had it the Roman way before. I won't do it if you don't want me to.' And he didn't—that night.

"Well, we never got up to have our dinner or anything else, and we stayed in bed till noon. And in the morning, we did have anal intercourse. I'd always thought it disgusting when I'd thought about it at all which, I can assure you, was not often. But with Dick, the new sensation was wonderful.

He, like Lou, helped rid me of the sexual millstone you might say I'd worn all my life. I guess I sound like I'm on a soapbox, now, but no one can imagine how beyond belief it is to discover the joy in sex—not love and sex— *just plain sex*—at my age. And George's. In one way, that was the greatest couple of days any of us had ever had. Everyone said that. I spent two nights with Dick and one with Lou. Dorothea and George slept together two nights, and she and Lou had their last night together. Anne was with George and Dick. We were all delighted, really.

"Then, on Sunday, a few hours before Dorothea and Dick had to leave, we had the wildest party of George's and my swapping career. We had several threesomes, you see, and neither George nor I had ever had a threesome before. First, Dorothea and I worked out with Dick. At times, Dick was the link between Dorothea and me. And at times I was the link between the two of them. At other times, of course, Dorothea was the one who lay between Dick and me.

"Then George, my George, of all people, hit upon a magnificent idea. He suggested that each man hold his own wife while someone else made love to her. You know, it was like a pipe dream come true. I found myself passionate toward the men who made love to me and thrilled with my own husband, the way he held me.

"You know, so much has happened since those days when I first felt guilty about swinging, and ashamed if my children knew. They know now." Seeing my look of sudden disbelief, she repeated it. "I told them because it's meant so much to me. I've tried particularly hard to explain it all to my daughters and their husbands. The boys are hostile, of course, but even the girls look at me like a stranger when I tell them what I do and try to show them what they're missing by not becoming swingers while they're still so young. 'All these wonderful, wonderful years ahead of you,' I say, 'if only you'd take advantage of them before waiting till you're as old as I to discover the truth.' Their retort is always the same. 'I love my husband. I love my husband.' They refuse to see. Besides, they're rather ashamed of George and me. I know they'd be humiliated if any of their friends were to discover our swinging beliefs. Not that we'd tell them, of course. To begin with, our lives, especially our sex lives, are our own business. But, like too many other people in this world, they aren't sufficiently broad-minded to think straight on this subject of sex.

"It's my fault, and George's too, that Joan and Lisa can't live unfettered as we do. But we learned, too late, to repudiate the proprieties and dictates of the Mrs. Grundys of this country. The happiness I've achieved is right within their grasp if only they'll open their minds and hearts to it. George, who's not religious in any sense of the word, can only hope for our girls' conversion. But I—I pray for it."

Highly respected citizens like Marlena, George and their swinging companions are no longer unique in the swinging movement. During the past several years, the way-out cliques of bohemian swingers, found only in the more sophisticated cities, have been far outnumbered by people one would never suspect—couples, not only of the upper class but more significantly, of the proper middle class.

According to the Institute for Sex Research at Indiana University, there are approximately five million married couples in the United States who have exchanged partners with other married couples on some occasion, if not frequently, not only for purposes of sexual intercourse or engaging in group orgies, but also for the voyeuristic satisfaction of watching their own wives and husbands making love to others. Other authorities have estimated the number of regular swingers (excluding far-out bohemians and admitted debauchees, dissolutes and prodigals, traditional hedonists) at one to three million.

Actually the stories that have been written about swapping present only half the picture. They tell only of the satisfied swappers, seldom of the unwilling, reluctant, sad ones. The reason, of course, is understandable since those writing from the outside are generally biased and do their stories from the viewpoint of the hedonists they believe all swappers to be. And the satisfied swappers, like Marlena, consider themselves sexual revolutionaries and either don't want outsiders to know or just aren't aware of the unwilling swappers in their ranks.

But there are many, usually wives, who find the swapping life sordid and sickening but nevertheless remain for various reasons. You seldom hear about swapping wives whose lives drive them to various types of violence, ranging from suicide to assault and battery. Neither do you often hear about those wives who live their lives in fear of the day when husbands may arrange new swapping activities for them.

Only a few psychiatrists approve of swapping and some of these are swappers themselves. The majority damn the swapping philosophy more for their patients' sake than from outraged morality. Dr. Arthur A. Rhodes, the distinguished California psychiatrist, states: "You know, when a man and woman are on the verge of divorce and blame the difficulty entirely on sexual maladjustment, which, of course, it hardly ever is, I discuss with them the patterns of their marriage through the years. Usually, they've been rigid—coitus performed at, literally, planned-out times rather than spontaneously. And, of course, they've observed the *rules* of *proper* intercourse. You've no idea how many times, in my practice, I hear those two words, *rules* and *proper*.

"Naturally, then, I urge such people to give expression to their real sexual instincts, and, in fact, to explore those instincts. I try to make them see that nothing is perverse when performed with mutual pleasure. But, really, I mean this sexual liberation to be limited to the marital bedroom.

"I don't know for a fact, except through my own colleagues, but I feel I have every reason to surmise that most reputable psychiatrists and marriage counselors take a dim view of swinging as being extremely dangerous to marriage, despite all the protestations that 'it saved our marriage!' "

Reporting on cases of swingers he has known, Dr. Walter R. Stokes, a distinguished psychiatrist and Fellow of the American Association of Marriage Counselors, declares: "In each instance unhappy and tragic complications have ultimately arisen and the marriage has broken up. . . .

"[There is] the heavy risk that one of the spouses may become seriously attached to an extramarital partner, after which interest in the spouse rapidly wanes and the marriage goes on the rocks. I have known this to occur repeatedly. For these reasons, I am emphatic in discouraging this type of behavior."

These psychiatrists and others like them say that swingers are bored, jaded, sick people who need either psychotherapy or marriage counseling, not an orgy of condoned adultery. In a truly sound marriage, this view holds, a husband should be able to continue to find sexual excitement and satisfaction with his wife, and she with him. If it takes swapping to accomplish this, something is seriously wrong—either with one partner, both, or the marriage.

White-Collar Pill Party

BRUCE JACKSON

> There was a thing called Heaven; but all the same they used to drink enormous quantities of alcohol. . . . There was a thing called the soul and a thing called immortality. . . . But they used to take morphia and cocaine. . . . . Two thousand pharmacologists and bio-chemists were subsidized in A.F. 178. . . . Six years later it was being produced commercially. The perfect drug. . . . Euphoric, narcotic, pleasantly hallucinant. . . . All the advantages of Christianity and alcohol; none of their defects. . . . Take a holiday from reality whenever you like, and come back without so much as a headache or a mythology.
>
> Aldous Huxley, *Brave New World,* 1932

Drugs, like chewing gum, TV, oversize cars, and crime, are part of the American way of life. No one receives an exemption.

This was made particularly clear to me recently by my four-year-old son, Michael, who came into the kitchen one evening and asked me to go out and buy a certain brand of vitamin pills for him. Since he is quite healthy and not observably hypochondriac, I asked why he wanted them. "So I can be as strong as Jimmy down the block."

"There isn't any Jimmy down the block," I said, whereupon he patiently explained that the clown on the 5 P.M. TV program he watches every day had *told* him the pills would make him stronger than Jimmy, and his tone gave me to understand that the existence of a corporeal Jimmy was irrelevant: the truehearted clown, the child's friend, had advised the pills, and any four-year-old knows a clown wouldn't steer you wrong.

For adults the process is modified slightly. An afternoon TV commercial urges women to purchase a new drug for their "everyday headache" (without warning them that anyone who has a headache every day should

From *The Atlantic Monthly* 218:35–40, No. 2, Aug., 1966. Copyright ©1966, by the Atlantic Monthly Company, Boston, Mass. Reprinted with permission of publisher and author.

certainly be consulting a GP or a psychiatrist); a Former Personality with suggestive regularity tells you to keep your bloodstream pure by consuming buffered aspirin for the headache you are supposed to have, and another recommends regular doses of iron for your "tired blood." (It won't be long before another screen has-been mounts the TV commercial podium with a pill that doesn't do anything at all; it just keeps your corpuscles company on the days you ate liver and forgot to have a headache.)

One result of all the drug propaganda and the appalling faith in the efficacy of drugs is that a lot of people take a lot more pills than they have any reason to. They think in terms of pills. And so do their physicians: you fix a fat man by giving him a diet pill, you fix a chronic insomniac by giving him a sleeping pill. But these conditions are frequently merely symptoms of far more complicated disorders. The convenient prescription blank solves the problem of finding out what the trouble really is—it makes the symptom seem to go away.

Think for a moment: how many people do you know who cannot stop stuffing themselves without an amphetamine and who cannot go to sleep without a barbiturate (over *nine billion* of those produced last year) or make it through a workday without a sequence of tranquilizers? And what about those six million alcoholics, who daily ingest quantities of what is, by sheer force of numbers, the most addicting drug in America?

The publicity goes to the junkies, lately to the college kids, but these account for only a small portion of the American drug problem. Far more worrisome are the millions of people who have become dependent on commercial drugs. The junkie *knows* he is hooked; the housewife on amphetamine and the businessman on meprobamate hardly ever realize what has gone wrong.

Sometimes the pill-takers meet other pill-takers, and an odd thing happens: instead of using the drug to cope with the world, they begin to use their time to take drugs. Taking drugs becomes *something to do*. When this stage is reached, the drug-taking pattern broadens: the user takes a wider variety of drugs with increasing frequency. For want of a better term, one might call it the white-collar drug scene.

I first learned about it during a party in Chicago last winter, and the best way to introduce you will be to tell you something about that evening, the people I met, what I think was happening.

There were about a dozen people in the room, and over the noise from the record player scraps of conversation came through:

"Now the Desbutal, if you take it with this stuff, has a peculiar effect, contraindication, at least it did for me. You let me know if you . . ."

"I don't have one legitimate prescription, Harry, not *one!* Can you imagine that?" "I'll get you some tomorrow, dear."

" . . . and this pharmacist on Fifth will sell you all the leapers [amphetamines] you can carry—just like that. Right off the street. I don't think he'd know a prescription if it bit him." "As long as he can read the labels, what the hell."

"You know, a funny thing happened to me. I got this green and yellow capsule, and I looked it up in the Book, and it wasn't anything I'd been using, and I thought, great! It's not something I've built a tolerance to. And I took it. A couple of them. And you know what happened? *Nothing!* That's what happened, not a goddamned thing."

The Book—the *Physicians' Desk Reference,* which lists the composition and effects of almost all commercial pharmaceuticals produced in this country—passes back and forth, and two or three people at a time look up the contents and possible values of a drug one of them has just discovered or heard about or acquired or taken. The Book is the pillhead's *Yellow Pages:* you look up the effect you want ("Sympathomimetics" or "Cerebral Stimulants," for examples,) and it tells you the magic columns. The pillheads swap stories of kicks and sound like professional chemists discussing recent developments; others listen, then examine the *PDR* to see if the drug discussed really could do that.

Eddie, the host, a painter who has received some recognition, has been awake three or four days, he was not exactly sure. He consumes between 150 and 200 milligrams of amphetamine a day, needs a large part of that to stay awake, even when he has slipped a night's sleep in somewhere. The dose would cause most people some difficulty; the familiar diet pill, a capsule of Dexamyl or Eskatrol, which makes the new user edgy and over-energetic and slightly insomniac the first few days, contains only 10 or 15 milligrams of amphetamine. But amphetamine is one of the few central nervous system stimulants to which one can develop a tolerance, and over the months and years Ed and his friends have built up massive tolerances and dependencies. "Leapers aren't so hard to give up," he told me. "I mean, I sleep almost constantly when I'm off, but you get over that. But everything is so damned boring without the pills."

I asked him if he knew many amphetamine users who have given up the pills.

"For good?"

I nodded.

"I haven't known anybody that's given it up for good." He reached out and took a few pills from the candy dish in the middle of the coffee table, then washed them down with some Coke.

The last couple to arrive—a journalist and his wife—settled into positions. The wife was next to me on the oversize sofa, and she skimmed through the "Product Identification Section" of the *PDR,* dozens of pages of pretty color photos of tablets and capsules. "Hey!" she said to no one in particular. Then, to her husband, "Look at the pretty hexagonal. George, get the Source to get some of them for me." George, across the table, near the fire, nodded.

I had been advised to watch him as he turned on. As the pills took effect something happened to the muscles of his face, and the whole assembly seemed to go rubbery. His features settled lower and more loosely on the bones of his head. He began to talk with considerably more verve.

A distractingly pretty girl with dark brown eyes sat at the edge of our group and ignored both the joint making its rounds and the record player belching away just behind her. Between the thumb and middle finger of her left hand she held a pill that was blue on one side and yellow on the other; steadily, with the double-edged razor blade she held in her right hand, she sawed on the seam between the two halves of the pill. Every once in a while she rotated it a few degrees with her left index finger. Her skin was smooth, and the light from the fireplace played tricks with it, all of them charming. The right hand sawed on.

I got the Book from the coffee table and looked for the pill in the pages of color pictures, but before I found it, Ed leaned over and said, "They're Desbutal Gradumets. Abbott Labs."

I turned to the "Professional Products Information" section and learned that Desbutal is a combination of Desoxyn (methamphetamine hydrochloride, also marketed as Methedrine) and Nembutal, that the pill the girl sawed contained 15 milligrams of the Desoxyn, that the combination of drugs served "to both stimulate and calm the patient so that feelings of depression are overcome and a sense of well-being and increased energy is produced. Inner tension and anxiety are relieved so that a sense of serenity and ease of mind prevails." Gradumets, the Book explained, "are indicated in the management of obesity, the management of depressed states, certain behavioral syndromes, and a number of typical geriatric conditions," as well as "helpful in managing psychosomatic complaints and neuroses," Parkinson's disease, and a hangover.

The girl, obviously, was not interested in all of the pill's splendid therapeutic promises; were she, she would not have been so diligently sawing along that seam. She was after the methamphetamine, which like other amphetamines "depresses appetite, elevates the mood, increases the urge to work, imparts a sense of increased efficiency, and counteracts sleepiness and the feeling of fatigue in most persons."

After what seemed a long while the pill split into two round sections. A few scraps of the yellow Nembutal adhered to the Desoxyn side, and she carefully scraped them away. "Wilkinson's the best blade for this sort of thing," she said. I asked if she didn't cut herself on occasion, and she showed me a few nicks in her left thumb. "But a single edge isn't thin enough to do it neatly."

She put the blue disk in one small container, the yellow in another, then from a third took a fresh Desbutal and began sawing. I asked why she kept the Nembutal, since it was the Desoxyn she was after.

"Sometimes I might want to sleep, you know. I might *have* to sleep because something is coming up the next day. It's not easy for us to sleep, and sometimes we just don't for a couple or three days. But if we have to, we can just take a few of these." She smiled at me tolerantly, then returned to her blade and tablet.

When I saw Ed in New York several weeks later, I asked about her. "Some are like that," he said; "they like to carve on their pills. She'll sit and carve for thirty or forty minutes."

"Is that sort of ritual an important part of it all?"

"I think it is. She seems to have gotten hung up on it. I told her that she shouldn't take that Nembutal, that I have been cutting the Nembutal off my pills. It only takes about thirty seconds. And she can spend a good half hour at it if she has a mind to. I told her once about the effect of taking a Spansule; you know, one of those big things with sustained release [like Dexamyl, a mixture of dextroamphetamine sulfate and amobarbital designed to be effective over a twelve-hour period]. What you do is open the capsule and put it in a little bowl and grind up the little pellets until it's powder, then stuff all the powder back in the pill and take it, and it all goes off at once. I'll be damned if I haven't seen her grinding away like she was making matzo meal. That's a sign of a fairly confirmed head when they reach that ritualstage."

Next to the candy dish filled with Dexedrine, Dexamyl, Eskatrol, Desbutal, and a few other products I hadn't yet learned to identify, near the five-pound box of Dexedrine tablets someone had brought, were two bottles. One was filled with Dexedrine Elixir, the other with Dexamyl Elixir, Someone took a long swallow from the latter, and I thought him to be an extremely heavy user, but when the man left the room, a lawyer told me he'd bet the man was new at it. "He has to be. A mouthful is like two pills, and if he was a real head, he'd have a far greater tolerance to the Dexedrine than the amobarbital, and the stuff would make him sleepy. Anyhow, I don't like to mess with barbiturates much anymore. Dorothy Kilgallen died from that." He took a drink from the Dexedrine bottle and said, "And this tastes better. Very tasty stuff, like cherry syrup. Make a nice cherry Coke with it. The Dexamyl Elixir is bitter."

Someone emptied the tobacco from a Salem and filled the tube with grass; he tamped it down with a Tinkertoy stick, crimped the tip, then lighted it and inhaled noisily. He immediately passed the joint to the person on his left. Since one must hold the smoke in one's lungs for several seconds to get the full effect, it is more economical for several people to turn on at once. The grass was very good and seemed to produce a quiet but substantial high. One doesn't notice it coming on, but there is a realization that for a while now the room has been a decidedly pleasant one, and some noises are particularly interesting for their own sake.

I leaned back and closed my eyes for a moment. It was almost 5 A.M., and in three hours I had to catch a plane at O' Hare, "You're not going to *sleep* are you?" The tone implied that this group considered few human frailties truly gauche, but going to sleep was surely one of them. I shook my head no and looked to see who had spoken. It was Ed's wife; she looked concerned. "Do you want a pill?" I shook my head no again.

Then, just then, I realized that Ed—who knew I was not a pill-user— had not once in the evening offered me one of the many samples that had been passed around, nor had anyone else. Just the grass, but not the pills. His wife suggested a pill not so that I might get high, but merely so that I could stay awake without difficulty.

"I m not tired," I said, "just relaxing." I assured her I wouldn't doze off. She was still concerned, however, and got me a cup of coffee from the kitchen and offered some Murine from her purse.

The front door opened, and there was a vicious blast of winter off Lake Michigan. Ed kicked the door closed behind him and dumped an armful of logs by the fireplace, then went back into the kitchen. A moment later he returned and passed around a small dish of capsules. And this time it was handed to me. They looked familiar. "One a Days," he said. I had learned enough from the Book to see the need for them: the amphetamine user often does not eat for long periods of time (some days his only nourishment is the sugar in the bottles of soda which he drinks to wash down the pills and counter their side effect of dehydration of the mouth), and he not only tends to lose weight but also risks vitamin deficiencies. After a while, the heavy user learns to force-feed himself or go off pills every once in a while in order to eat without difficulty and to keep his tolerance level down.

Later, getting settled in the plane, I thought, What a wild party that was. I'd never been to anything quite like it, and I began making notes about what had gone on. Not long before we came into Logan, it suddenly struck me that there had been nothing wild about the party at all, nothing. There had been women there, some of them unaccompanied and some with husbands or dates, but there had been none of the playing around and sexual hustling that several years of academic and business world parties had led me to consider a correlative of almost any evening gathering of more than ten men and women: no meaningful looks, no wisecracks, no "accidental" rubbing. No one had spoken loudly, no one had become giggly or silly, no one had lost control or seemed anywhere near it. Viewed with some perspective, the evening seemed nothing more than comfortable.

There are various ways to acquire the pills, but the most common is also the most legal: prescriptions. Even though there is now a federal law requiring physicians and pharmacists to maintain careful records regarding prescriptions for drugs like Dexamyl, many physicians are careless about prescribing them, and few seem to realize that the kind of personality that needs them is often the kind of personality that can easily acquire an overwhelming dependency on them. Often a patient will be issued a refillable prescription; if the patient is a heavy user, all he needs to do is visit several physicians and get refillable prescriptions from each. If he is worried that a cross-check of druggists' lists might turn up his name, he can easily give some of his doctors false names.

There are dealers, generically called the Source, who specialize in selling these drugs; some give them away. They do not seem to be underworld types but professional people in various capacities who, for one reason or another, have access to large quantites of them. If one is completely without connections, the drugs can be made at home. One young man I know made mescaline, amphetamine, methamphetamine, LSD, and DET and DMT (diethyl- and dimethyl-tryptamine, hallucinogens of shorter duration and greater punch than LSD) in his kitchen. In small lots, dextroamphetamine sulfate costs him about 50 cents a gram; a pound costs him about $30 (the same amounts of Dexedrine at your friendly corner druggist's would cost, respectively, about $10 and $4200).

In some areas, primarily those fairly distant from major centers of drug distribution, the new law has begun to have some significant effect. In one medium-sized city, for example, the price of black-market Dexamyl and Eskatrol Spansules has risen from 15 cents to 50 cents a capsule, when one can connect for them at all.

In the major cities one can still connect, but it is becoming more difficult. The new law will inhibit, but there may be complications. It would be unfortunate if the price should be driven up so high that it would become profitable for criminal organizations to involve themselves with the traffic, as was the case with opiates in the 1940s and 1950s and alcohol in the 1920s.

There was talk in Manhattan last winter, just before the new law took effect, that some LSD factories were closing down, and I know that some Sources stopped supplying. For a short time the price of LSD went up; then things stabilized, competition increased, a new packaging method developed popularity (instead of the familiar sugar cubes, one now takes one's dose on a tiny slip of paper; like a spitball, only you don't spit it out), and now the price for a dose of LSD is about 20 percent *less* than it was a year ago.

Since most of the pillheads I'm talking about are middle-class and either professional or semiprofessional, they will still be able to obtain their drugs. Their drugs of choice have a legitimate use, and it is unlikely that the government's attempt to prevent diversion will be more than partially successful. If our narcotics agents have been unable to keep off the open market drugs which have no legitimate use at all—heroin and marijuana—it hardly seems likely that they will be able to control chemicals legitimately in the possession of millions of citizens. I asked one amphetamine head in the Southwest how local supplies had been affected by the new law. "I heard about that law," he said, "but I haven't seen anybody getting panicked." Another user tells me prices have risen slightly, but not enough yet to present difficulties.

There are marked differences between these drug-users and the ones who make the newspapers. They're well educated (largely college graduates), are older (25 to 40), and middle-class (with a range of occupations: writers, artists, lawyers, TV executives, journalists, political aides, housewives). They're not like the high school kids who are after a kick in any form (some of them rather illusory, as one psychosomatic gem reported to me by a New Jersey teen-ager: "What some of the kids do is take a cigarette and saturate it with perfume or hairspray. When this is completely soaked in and dry, they cup the cigarettes and inhale every drag. Somehow this gives them a good high"), or college students experimenting with drugs as part of a romantic program of self-location. The kids take drugs "because it's cool" and to get high, but when you talk to them you find that most ascribe the same general high to a wide range of drugs having quite diverse effects; they're promiscuous and insensitive. There is considerable evidence to suggest that almost none of the college drug-users take anything illegal after graduation, for most of them lose their connections and their curiosity.

It is not likely that many of the thousands of solitary amphetamine abusers would join these groups. They take drugs to *avoid* deviance—so they can be fashionably slim, or bright and alert and functional, or so they can muster the *quoi que* with which to face the tedium of housework or some other dull job—and the last thing they want is membership in a group defined solely by one clear form of rule-breaking behavior. Several of the group members were first turned on by physicians, but a larger number were turned on by friends. Most were after a particular therapeutic effect, but after a while interest developed in the drug for its own sake and the effect became a cause, and after that the pattern of drug-taking overcame the pattern of taking a specific drug.

Some of the socialized amphetamine-users specialize. One takes Dexedrine and Dexamyl almost exclusively; he takes other combinations only when he is trying to reduce his tolerance to Dexamyl. Though he is partly addicted to the barbiturates, they do not seem to trouble him very much, and on the few occasions when he has had to go off drugs (as when he was in California for a few months and found getting legal prescriptions too difficult and for some reason didn't connect with a local Source), he has had no physiological trouble giving them up. He did, of course, suffer from the overwhelming depression and enervation that characterize amphetamine withdrawal. Most heads will use other drugs along with amphetamine—especially marijuana—in order to appreciate the heightened alertness they've acquired; some alternate with hallucinogens.

To the heroin addict, the square is anyone who does not use heroin. For the dedicated pillhead there is a slightly narrower definition: the square is someone who has an alcohol dependency; those who use nothing at all aren't even classified. The boozers do bad things, they get drunk and lose control and hurt themselves and other people. They contaminate their tubes, and whenever they get really far out, they don't even remember it the next day. The pillhead's disdain is sometimes rather excessive. One girl, for example, was living with a fellow who, like her, was taking over 500 milligrams of amphetamine a day. They were getting on well. One night the two were at a party, and instead of chewing pills, her man had a few beers; the girl was furious, betrayed, outraged. Another time, at a large party that sprawled through a sprawling apartment, a girl had been on scotch and grass and she went to sleep. There were three men in the room, none of them interested in her sexually, yet they jeered and wisecracked as she nodded off. It was 4 or 5 A.M. of a Sunday, not too unreasonable a time to be drowsy. When they saw she was really asleep—breaking the double taboo by having drunk too much scotch and been put to sleep by it—they muttered a goddamn and went into another room; she was too depressing to have around.

There is an important difference in the drug-use patterns of the pillhead and opiate dependent: the latter is interested only in getting his drug and avoiding withdrawal; the former is also interested in perceiving his drugs' effects. I remember one occasion attended by someone who had obtained a fairly large mixed bag. In such a situation a junkie would have shot himself insensible; this fellow gave most of his away to his friends. With each gift he said something about a particular aspect of the drug which he found interesting. The heroin-user is far less social. His stuff is too hard to get, too expensive, his withdrawal too agonizing. But the pillhead is an experimenter. Often he seems to be interested as much in observing himself experiencing reactions as he is in having the reactions.

A large part of the attractiveness may be the ritual associated with this kind of group drug abuse: the *PDR* (a holy book), the Source (the medicine man whose preparations promise a polychromatic world of sensory and mystical experiences), the sharing of proscribed materials in a closed community, the sawing and grinding, the being privy to the Pythian secrets of colors and milligrams and trade names and contraindications and optimum dosages. And, of course, using drugs is something of a fad.

But there are costs. Kicks are rarely free in this world, and drugs are no exception. One risks dysfunction; one can go out of one's head; one may get into trouble with the police. Though the users are from a socioeconomic class that can most likely beat a first offense at almost anything, there is the problem that legal involvement of any kind, whether successfully prosecuted or not, can cause considerable embarrassment; an arrest for taking drugs may be negligible to a slum dweller in New York, but it is quite something else for a lawyer or reporter. And there is always the most tempting danger of all: getting habituated to drugs to such a degree that the drugs are no longer something extra in life but are instead a major goal.

One user wrote me, "Lately I find myself wishing not that I might kick the lunatic habit—but simply that our drug firms would soon develop something NEW which might refresh the memory of the flash and glow of that first voom-voom pill." I had asked him why take them at all, and he wrote, "I don't know. Really. Why smoke, drink, drive recklessly, sunbathe, fornicate, shoot tigers, climb mountains, gamble, lie, steal, cheat, kill, make war—and blame it all largely on our parents. Possibly to make oneself more acceptable to oneself."

Many of the pillheads are taking drugs not *only* to escape but also to have an experience that is entirely one's own. There is no one else to be propitiated, there are no explanations or excuses needed for what happens inside one's own head when one is turned on; words won't do, and that is as much a benefit as a disadvantage, because if you cannot describe, then neither can you discuss or question or submit to evaluation. The benefit and the risk are entirely one's own. Indiana University sociologist John Gagnon pointed out at a drug symposium held at Antioch College last year, "I'd like to argue that possibly in our attempt to protect people, we have underrepresented the real payoff for drug-taking as an experience, as a risk people want to run."

You select your own risks—that's what living is all about. For some of these drug-users, the risks currently being marketed do not have very much sales appeal: going South for the summer with SNCC is out because they feel that they are too old and that ofays aren't much wanted anyhow; going to Vietnam for Lyndon is absurd. So they go inside. A scarier place, but no one else can muddle around with it.

There is nothing *wrong* with using chemicals to help cope with life. That is one of the things science is supposed to do, help us cope, and the business of living can be rough at times. And we have the requisite faith: I am sure that far more Americans believe in the efficacy of a pill than believe in God. The problem arises when one's concern shifts so that life becomes an exercise in coping with the chemicals.

I think there has been an unfortunate imbalance in the negative publicity. For years the press has printed marvelous tales about all the robberies and rapes performed by evil beings whose brain tissue had been jellied by heroin. But it has rarely printed stories that point out that opiates make even the randiest impotent, or that alcohol, which has five hundred times as many addicts, is an important factor in sex offenses and murders.

Lately, attention has been focused on drug abuse and experimentation among college students. Yet all the college students and all the junkies account for only a small portion of American drug abuse. The adults, the respectable grown-ups, the nice people who cannot or will not make it without depending on a variety of drugs, present a far more serious problem. For them the drug experience threatens to disrupt or even destroy life patterns and human relationships that required many years to establish.

And the problem is not a minor one. Worse, it seems to be accelerating. As Ed advised one night, "You better research the hell our of it because I'm convinced that the next ruling generation is going to be all pillheads. I'm convinced of it. If they haven't dysfunctioned completely to the point where they can't stand for office. It's getting to be unbelievable. I've never seen such a transformation in just four or five years. . . . "

The Runaway Girl:
A Reaction to Family Stress

AMES ROBEY, RICHARD J. ROSENWALD, JOHN E.
SNELL, AND RITA E. LEE

Running away and its associated behavior is one of the few ways in which an adolescent girl may act out. In a treatment-oriented Court Clinic, a study was made of runaway girls from an essentially middle-class area. The suggested dynamics revolved around family interaction, in which there was a threatened unconscious incestuous relationship with the father incited by the mother. Subsequent acting out of the unresolved Oedipal conflict through running away represents an attempted solution.

Running away from home is one of the most common forms of serious acting out in the adolescent girl. Despite its frequency, it has received little attention in the psychiatric literature. Most papers deal primarily with boys' running away and are predominantly statistical, although several discuss some of the pathogenic elements involved.[1-4,7,11,12,14-16,20-22] Rosenheim[16] in 1940 was the first to postulate the importance of the unresolved Oedipal conflict as a cause of running away in boys. Other studies have since shown that the Oedipal conflict and the threat of an incestuous relationship also play an important role in the etiology of running away in girls.[4,22]

Legally a form of delinquency, the act of running away itself is often treated lightly by the parents, the police and even the courts, unless it becomes chronic or appears in conjunction with severe stubbornness and disobedience at home, sexual acting out, unauthorized use of motor vehicles or other associated delinquent behavior. It should be emphasized, however, that running away, far from being a childish escapade, is almost always in-

From *American Journal of Orthopsychiatry* 34:762–766, No. 4, July, 1964. Copyright ©1964, the American Orthopsychiatric Association, Inc. Reproduced by Permission of the publisher and authors. Presented at the 1963 Annual Meeting; accepted for publication by the *American Journal of Orthopsychiatry*, March 9, 1964.

dicative of some severe individual or family pathology and may result from a wide variety of intolerable home situations. The cause most frequently observed in this study was the unconscious threat of an incestuous relationship with the father, the fear of the resultant dissolution of the family and the concurrent depression.

This study was made at the Framingham Court Clinic, which serves an essentially middle-class suburban population. The primary function of the Court Clinics is to provide a threefold service in supplying direct and immediate psychiatric evaluations for the Court, advice and assistance to Probation Officers in their handling of offenders, and psychotherapy for appropriate cases within the setting of the Court, where judicial controls and authority are readily available.[17,19]

Of the entire caseload of 293 adolescent girls brought before the Court during the past ten years, 162 or 55 percent, had run away. Forty-two of these girls and their families were referred to the Clinic for more study and treatment. The girls' ages ranged from 13 to 17 years and 6 months, with a mean of 15 years and 3 months. We have included only those girls who were living with both parents or one parent and a step-parent. Our definition of running away excludes those who had not stayed away overnight and those who denied the intent to run away. When a case was seen in the Clinic, an attempt was made to interview the parents and the girl at least three times, and some cases continued in treatment for as long as two years. Close co-operation between the Probation Department and the Clinic staff was invaluable in setting up and carrying out treatment programs. Frequently the father refused to be interviewed by a psychiatrist, and we had to rely on the Probation Officer for an evaluation of him, as well as for other information not readily obtainable by the Clinic staff.

In evaluating and treating these 42 runaway girls, we saw a consistent pattern of family interaction that we feel is basic to the etiology of running away. This pattern includes a disturbed marital relationship, inadequate control by the parents over their own and the girl's impulses, deprivation of love of the mother and subtle pressure by her on the girl to take over the maternal role.

This role is managed well in most cases by the girl prior to the onset of adolescence. At this time, however, with the breakdown of the prepubescent defenses, the girl becomes involved in an increasingly bitter attitude of rebellion against her role and finally runs away. The superficial conflict from which the girl runs is between herself and her father. What is perhaps not so clear is the disturbed mother-daughter relationship and the role it plays in this conflict. Kaufman,[10] in his paper on overt father-daughter incestuous relationships, described the strong dependent wishes of both parents and their search for a mother figure. It was his feeling that the girl reacted to the mother's wish to place her in the maternal role by developing a pseudo maturity and then, under pressure from mother, by getting involved in an incestuous relationship with the father in search of oral gratification. According to Kaufman, the lack of parental controls and of assistance by the parents in reality testing and superego development was essential to the development of the situation. In our series, we noted a striking similarity to his cases, although we failed to see the depth of pathology in any member of the family. There were only three instances of alleged incest in the entire group of 145 cases. Indeed, it is our contention that it is because of the girl's strength that, when she is given the choice of taking over the mother's role or running away, she chooses the latter as a method of fighting off the incestuous wishes unconsciously shared by all members of the family.

In reviewing the family histories, we found the fathers usually do well at work but outside their jobs tend to be rather passive and inadequate. They show poor control over their aggressive and sexual instincts and are given to violent temper outbursts, usually when drinking. In many cases, they indulge in extramarital affairs. The mothers are usually better educated and clearly the dominant force in the family structure; underlying this however, one finds a significant level of depression, verbalized feelings of rejection by their own mothers, often a history of running away or early marriage, and feelings of maternal inadequacy. Though they are frequently seductive toward their husbands, a history of long-term unsatisfactory sexual adjustment is usually found.

We see difficulties arising quite early in the parent-child relationships. The mother does not provide her daughter with sufficient warmth and affection. Instead, by offering material incentives, she tends to force the girl into a position of increased responsibility and gradual assumption of the maternal role. In addition to rejecting her husband sexually, the mother also encourages a warm, close, eroticized father-daughter relationship from which all three derive considerable satisfaction. In this setting, the girl develops into what appears superficially as a hypermature individual, in her struggle to meet her mother's demands. With only material rewards for her efforts, she turns to her father to meet her needs for love, and quite early learns to use seductiveness to gain her ends. Men become objects to be controlled and used, but, as with the mother, the goal is oral gratification.

The family balance achieved during the girl's latency is disturbed by the onset of her physical maturation. The mother pushes her daughter into premature dating and sexual sophistication in an attempt to work out her own poorly resolved Oedipal conflicts. At the same time, she not only rejects her husband further, but continues to foster the close relationship between him and the daughter. With few effective controls demonstrated by either parent, the fear of overt incest comes uncomfortably close to consciousness, and the intimate relationship between the father and the daughter now becomes extremely threatening to both. The father reacts by becoming angry and restrictive. He projects his own sexual feelings onto the girl and accuses her of sexual misbehavior, thereby justifying his extreme restrictiveness. The girl, angry and rebellious, flouts her father's authority and, with mother's encouragement, attempts to solve her Oedipal conflicts by seeking outside objects. Because of her underlying feelings of worthlessness, she chooses boys who are themselves degraded or emotionally disturbed. The mother now finds herself caught in the middle, wanting unconsciously to continue encouraging her daughter's behavior, but aware of the realistic dangers. The father, upon seeing these boys, becomes more restrictive, the girl more rebellious, and finally, with the increasing tension in the home, the girl begins to fear that she will cause family dissolution. At this point she sees no alternative to impulsive running away.

It is clear from this brief presentation that the family dynamics are extremely complex and in some cases may be sufficiently subtle to escape the notice of the casual observer. It could hardly be considered abnormal for a father to wish to protect his daughter from the clutches of an emotionally disturbed, poorly educated, delinquent boy, nor can it be considered unusual for the girl to rebel against a large number of restrictions. Contemporary society encourages early dating and sexual maturity. It is not unreasonable for the mother to expect help from her daughter with the household duties and care of the younger children. Yet all these factors take on a more sinister significance in a setting of oral deprivation and misdirected, inadequate controls. For the girl to run away under these circumstances becomes not only comprehensible but almost predictable.

Without treatment, the girls tend to leave school, frequently continue to run away, and occasionally become involved in prostitution.[15] More often, however, they contrive to get married either by falsifying their age or by becoming pregnant. From the mothers' histories, we have some indication that, if the girl's marriage endures, her daughter will in turn repeat the runaway pattern. Placement in a foster home or institution, frequently the only solution available to the Court, is usually inadequate to control the girl's behavior unless it is combined with treatment or includes a carefully tailored program that takes into consideration the dynamics and needs of the girl.[9] Severe acting out in terms of further runaway attempts, flouting of authority despite disciplinary action and occasionally homosexual activity may occur in an institutional setting,[8] or acute depression, often with suicidal gestures, may be seen. Where placement does result in improvement, a return home will almost invariably reactivate the previous situation. Even with treatment, the prognosis for successful adult adjustment is guarded. When attempted by a private psychiatrist or a clinic not affiliated with the Court, treatment may be completely impossible due to lack of adequate controls and inability to enforce attendance. Even in a Court Clinic setting, with the Probation Officers and the Judge immediately available to supply the necessary control and authority, treatment may fail because a relationship cannot be established. Invaluable in this connection is a female probation officer who can provide the warmth and control not supplied by the mother.

It should be emphasized that successful treatment of the girl necessarily includes simultaneous treatment of the mother. Here the major goal is an improvement in her relationship with her daughter, which can frequently be effected quite rapidly by extremely direct interpretation of the girl's underlying dynamics.[22]

The girl, when first seen, is usually hostile and uncommunicative. Gradually she begins to talk more freely and, as she does, her depression becomes quite apparent. In an attempt to control the treatment situation, she then becomes seductive.[6] This behavior requires interpretation, with tacit reassurance that she does not need to be seductive to be cared for. It is at this point in treatment that we usually find rapid and striking improvement. Maintenance of this improvement, however, is dependent upon a continuing therapeutic relationship with both the mother and the daughter. Too often we found that, with improvement in the girl, probation would be terminated, and she would then refuse to attend the Clinic any longer. This usually resulted in prompt deterioration of the home situation.

We seldom found the fathers willing to come regularly to the Clinic, but our results so far support our feeling that they are not essential in the treatment process.

In conclusion, we feel that running away is the result of a complex neurotic interaction between the parents and the daughter in a "triangle" situation, and its seriousness as a symptom calls for far greater concern than is presently given by most parents and law enforcement officials.

Because the material on which this study is based consists of only 42 cases, or about one-fourth of the total number of girls who had run away in the ten years covered by this study, we feel strongly that more complete understanding of the runaway girl and the underlying dynamics warrants further study in this and other clinics.

REFERENCES

1. Armstrong, C. P.: "A Psychoneurotic Reaction of Deliquent Boys and girls." *J. Abnorm. Psychol.* 32:329, 1937.
2. —— :*660 Runaway Boys.* Boston: R. G. Badger, 1937.
3. Balser, B. H.: "A Behavior Problem: Runaways." *Psychiat. Quart.* 13:539, 1939.

4. Counts, R.; Leventhal, T.; Weinreb, J.; and Shore, M.: "Running Away as an Attempted Solution to a Family Problem." Unpublished manuscript.

5. Deutsch, H.: *Psychology of Women,* Vol. 1. New York: Grune & Stratton, 1944, Chs. 2 and 3.

6. Eisner, E. A.: "Relationships Formed by a Sexually Delinquent Adolescent Girl." *Amer. J. Orthopsychiat.* 15:301, No. 2, 1945.

7. Foster, R.: "Intrapsychic and Environmental Factors in Running Away From Home. "*Amer. J. Orthopsychiat.* 32:486, No. 3, 1962.

8. Halleck, S., and Hersko, M.: "Homosexual Behavior in a Training School for Girls." *Amer. J. Orthopsychiat.* 32:911, No. 5, 1962.

9. Hersko, M.; Halleck, S.; Rosenberg, M.; and Pacht, A.: "Incest: a Three-way Process." *J. Soc. Therapy* 7:22, No. 1, 1961.

10. Kaufman, I.; Peck, A. L.; and Taguiri, C. K.: "The Family Constellation and Overt Incestuous Relations Between Father and Daughter." *Amer. J. Orthopsychiat.* 24:266, No. 2, 1954.

11. Leventhal, T.; Gridley, A. M.; Counts, R. M.; and Gluck, M.: "Preliminary Report on the Seriousness of Running Away in Childhood and Adolescence." Presented at the Annual Meeting of the American Orthopsychiatric Association, New York, March, 1958.

12. Lowrey, L. G.: "Runaways and Nomads." *Amer. J. Orthopsychiat.* 11:775, No. 4, 1941.

13. O'Kelly, E.: "Some Observations on Relations Between Delinquent Girls and Their Parents." *Brit. J. Med. Psychol.* 28:59, No. 1, 1955.

14. Riemer, M. D.: "Runaway Children." *Amer. J. Orthopsychiat.* 10:522, No. 3, 1940.

15. Robins, L. N., and O'Neal, P.: "The Adult Prognosis for Runaway Children." *Amer. J. Orthopsychiat.* 29:752, No. 4, 1959.

16. Rosenheim, F.: "Techniques of Therapy." *Amer. J. Orthopsychiat.* 29:651, No. 4, 1940.

17. Russell, D. H., and Devlin, J.: "The Massachusetts Court Clinic Program." *Juvenile Court Judges J.* 13, No. 3, 1962.

18. Sloane, P., and Karpinski, E.: "Effects of Incest on the Participants." *Amer. J. Orthopsychiat.* 12:666, No. 4, 1942.

19. Special Massachusetts Court Clinic Issue. *J. Assn. Psychiatric Treatment of Offenders.* 4, No. 2, 1960.

20. Staub, H.: "A Runaway From Home." *Psychoanal. Quart.* 12:1, No. 1, 1943.

21. Stengel, E.: "Studies on the Psychopathology of Compulsive Wandering." *Brit. J. Med. Psychol.* 18:250, 1939.

22. Wylie, D. C., and Weinreb, J.: "The Treatment of a Runaway Adolescent Girl Through Treatment of the Mother." *Amer. J. Orthopsychiat.* 28:188, No. 1, 1958.

AFFILIATIONS AND ACKNOWLEDGMENTS

1. Ames Roby, M. D., Medical Director, Bridgewater State Hospital, Bridgewater, Massachusetts.
2. Richard J. Rosenwald, M. D., Director, Framingham Court Clinic, Framingham, Massachusetts.
3. John E. Snell, M. D., Assistant Professor of Psychiatry, Emory University, Atlanta, Georgia.
4. Rita E. Lee, Formerly Probation Officer, Middlesex Juvenile Probation District.

Family and Differential Involvement
With Marihuana:
A Study of Suburban Teenagers

NECHAMA TEC

This paper examines the relationship between some aspects of family life and differential involvement with marihuana. Data are based on a survey of 1704 youths, aged 15 to 18, who live in an affluent suburban community and who attend the local public high school. Results point to a negative association between degree of involvement with marihuana and: (1) availability and quality of parental models for behavior, (2) high evaluation and amount of recognition received within the family, (3) perceptions of the family as warm and not simply rigidly controlling and/ or indifferent, (4) subjective feelings of satisfaction and involvement with as well as the ability to rely upon the family as a unit.

Despite the general interest in and numerous publications about illicit drug use by the younger generation, there is a lack of systematic knowledge in this area of behavior. Indeed, the many disagreements and contradictory views which permeate most current discussions on the subject only emphasize the need for systematic analysis based on empirical research (Blum and Associates, 1969). The present study, by relying on systematically collected empirical data, is an attempt to increase the knowledge of illicit drug use by the younger generation. As such, it is guided by two broad assumptions.

First, illicit drug use by the younger generation constitutes a complex area of behavior for which no simple explanations are readily available. It is imperative therefore, that any systematic study should consider a multiplicity of variables as possible explanations. Secondly, in view of the complexity and

From Journal of Marriage and the Family 32:656–664, No. 4, Nov., 1970. Reprinted by permission of the author and the National Council on Family Relations. An enlarged version of this paper is to appear as a part of a book to be published by Markham Press.

relatively little clarity surrounding the subject, any systematic analysis should carefully specify the dependent and independent variables involved. Such specification should apply both at the empirical and theoretical levels.

SAMPLE AND METHOD

Empirical data for the present study are based on a social survey conducted in February 1969 in a well-to-do-Eastern suburban community. The sample consisted of 1704 teenage boys and girls, all enrolled in high school. This is over 90 percent of the community's population between the ages of 15 and 18, with 52 percent females and 48 percent males. Only five percent of the sample reported father's occupation as blue-collar.

A self-administered questionnaire was handed out to students on the school premises. This questionnaire was answered in the presence of a teacher. Prior to the actual data collection it was made clear that the sponsors of the study had no affiliation with the school. The anonymity of each respondent was emphasized, and students were asked not to sign their names. Since the questions were precoded a respondent had only to place a check mark next to the most appropriate answer. Once completed the schedule was placed on a pile in any order desired by the subject. These precautionary measures might have had an effect, for despite the fact that participation in the project was voluntary, approximately 94 percent present completed the questionnaires.

Information collected included answers to 75 items covering a variety of areas. A large proportion of these concerned the degree of involvement with various drugs: marihuana, LSD, "speed," heroin, and glue sniffing. Space limitations, plus the complexity of the information obtained, dictated that only a selected number of variables be analyzed.

Differential Involvement with Drugs

Turning to the dependent variables—differential involvement with illegal drugs—the present analysis is confined to involvement with marihuana alone. This decision was prompted by the fact that of all the illegal drugs used, marihuana is most popular, both among American youths and among the sample studied. Indeed, while almost a third of the sample had direct experience with marihuana, only about 10 percent of them had direct experiences with any other drug.

To ascertain the extent of marihuana use, three distinct questions were asked, each yielding essentially similar information. These questions were dispersed in the schedule as a precautionary measure to assure greater reliability of responses. Subsequently, an index of exposure to marihuana was constructed which combined responses to all three questions.

The specific procedure was as follows: when answers to a given question were close, for example: "took it once" and "use it occasionally," this respondent was defined in terms of the higher degree of involvement stated. In cases where responses skipped a degree of involvement, for example, "never took it" to "take it with regularity," to "never took it," this particular questionnaire was set aside.

There was an extremely high consistency of answers. Of the 1704 questionnaires, only four had contradictory responses. According to the index of marihuana use, the following distribution was derived: regular users —12 percent, occasional users—12 percent, tried it once—eight percent, never tried it but would like to—eight percent, never wanted to and never did try it—60 percent. The usefulness of this categorization varies with the specific questions studied. In the present context, it was found that the extreme categories rather than the moderate ones followed a definite pattern. For the sake of simplicity, some categories were collapsed. Subsequently the following groupings were set up.

1. Non users or abstainers. This includes both those who never tried marihuana but would like to try it and those who never did and never want to try it.

2. Moderate users include those who tried marihuana once and those who use it occasionally.

3. Regular users consisted of those who used marihuana once a week (30 percent), more often than once a week (49 percent), once or more a day (18 percent), miscellaneous use (3 percent).

Legitimacy of Norms Regarding Marihuana

Marihuana for the youths studied constitutes a tolerated type of activity. That is, while not prescribed, neither does marihuana refer to behavior to which they themselves or their peers would apply strong negative sanctions. Specifically, it was found that slightly over 10 percent of the sample believed that they or their friends would discontinue a friendship because of marihuana use. In addition, a majority of non-marihuana users consistently expressed tolerant attitudes towards this drug.

In contrast, it is known that such tolerant views are neither reflected in the societal laws, nor in the opinions of the older generation with whom the young come into direct contact. Indeed, the possession and use of marihuana is prohibited on the state and federal level and is defined by representatives of the older generation, school authorities and parents, as deviant behavior. According to a recent national poll of parents, 85 percent of them said that they would apply severe negative sanctions if their children used marihuana. The remaining 15 percent said they would disapprove but in a less severe fashion (Philadelphia Inquirer, 1968). In the present sample, only two percent believed that their parents would not care if they smoked marihuana, while 98 percent anticipated a variety of negative sanctions.

However, knowledge about the existence of a given norm does not necessarily lead to its legitimation and/or conformity. Indeed, theoretically as well as empirically, the legitimacy attributed to a given norm and behavior which corresponds to the same norm may vary independently. Logically four types of relationships obtain between these two variables:

1. One may define a norm as legitimate and behave in a way which conforms to it.

2. One may define a norm as legitimate but still for many reasons fail to conform to it.

3. One many define a norm as illegitimate and nevertheless engage in behavior which conforms to the given norm.

4. Finally, one may define a norm as illegitimate and engage in behavior which constitutes a deviation from the norm.

The overall tolerance towards marihuana among the young suggests an area of behavior in which the definitions of the older and younger generation diverge. Thus, the legitimacy of the norms, particularly as these apply to marihuana, are being questioned by the young. In effect the attitude of the adolescents studied can be summarized as follows: "You may smoke marihuana if you want to, there is nothing wrong with it." In contrast, the position of the older generation is: "You ought not to smoke marihuana, if you do you will be punished." From the point of view of society and its representatives, marihuana use is defined as deviant behavior. Although some members of the older generation are opposed to the severe marihuana laws, this definition is still appropriate (Cholst, 1968; Kurtz, 1969; Leary, 1968, McGlothin, 1968; Taylor, 1966; New York Times, 1969a, 1969b, 1969c; American Medical News, 1969).

Given this conceptualization, the rather broad question to be examined is under what conditions those who question the legitimacy of a given norm will or will not deviate from it.

Differential Involvement with Family

The independent variables must be clarified, variables capable of explaining the variations in the level of this deviant behavior. The basic interactions of an adolescent revolve around the family, school, and peer group. It is primarily through role relationships in each of these units that the teenager is attached to society at large. All three spheres of activity are interdependent, and all have an impact upon an adolescent's attitudes, values and behaviors. To the extent that family, school and peer group are the most important interaction systems, the appropriate strategy for explanations of adolescent behavioral patterns should be sought in terms of all three statuses. Since simultaneous analysis of all of these statuses constituted a formidable task, each of them will be focused upon separately.

In comparing the saliency of these three spheres of behavior, the familial status and roles emerged as the most important. Despite the possible conflicts and problems which an adolescent may experience as a member of his family, the fact still remains that the kind of family he comes from and the decisions reached by it will mold and modify his life. It is indeed the family which determines the geographic and social location, the schools attended and in large measure the kind of peers.

Viewing the family of orientation as a social unit, it is important to know what kind of properties and/or conditions of this unit are associated with what levels of deviancy (Eisenstadt 1956: 305–210; Nye, 1958). To reiterate, the family of orientation is the independent variable which may be expected to explain differential involvement with marihuana. It is thus hypothesized that differential involvement with marihuana will vary with:

1. Availability of parental models for behavior, parental behaviors, controls and pressures, evaluations and attitudes.

2. Subjectively derived statisfactions and meanings from the family as a unit.

A methodological note about the independent variables—those referring to different aspects of family life is in order here. Prior to any actual examination of their impact upon the dependent variables, all questions referring to family life were cross tabulated. Results of these cross tabulations showed consistent associations in the direction expected. For example, those who reported that their families demanded the impossible were less likely to feel that the family was the most important unit in their lives, and those who did not enjoy being with the family were less likely to turn to the family when in trouble. However, while the direction of these associations was consistently predictable, none of them were sufficiently strong to warrant the conclusion that these variables measured the same aspects of reality. Although related, each of them seemed to reflect a distinct aspect of family life. Also, it should be pointed out that whatever the consistent patterns found, they refer mainly to extreme categories of marihuana involvement or non-involvement. That is, the relationships seem to be most consistent for those who abstain from marihuana use, the regular users, and less frequently the moderate users.

Chi-square tests of significance were performed on all associations with the level of significance for each being .001. This is true for tables included in the text as well as—with one exception—other findings discussed but not appearing in table form. The exception refers to the two questions which dealt with mothers' and fathers' use of a number of legal drugs. In both cases the criteria necessary for significance were not fulfilled.

FINDINGS AND DISCUSSION

The importance of both parents as behavioral models for their children has been recognized by sociologists and psychologists. Accordingly, the absence of one parent is said to impede the process of identification, resulting in problems of adjustment. Sociological, as well as psychological literature, provides many examples of the detrimental effects of broken homes. With respect to illegal drug use, specifically hard drugs such as heroin, a high positive correlation between broken homes and heroin use has been demonstrated (Charen and Perelman, 1948; Chein et al., 1964; Gerard et al., 1964; Clausen, 1957; Hill, 1962). With respect to marihuana use, however, this association has not as yet been sufficiently explored.

Turning to the sample studied, it was found that there was a significantly higher proportion of marihuana users among these from broken families than among those from unbroken families (see Table 1). Interesting here are the 19 adoptive youths (one percent of the sample) who do not appear in Table 1 because of the small number. Among them there were 16 percent regular marihuana users and 65 percent non-users. In terms of regular marihuana use, they seem to resemble those who come from broken homes. The problem of adopted adolescents in general and those within the area studied in particular, are discussed in Tec and Gordon (1967) and Tec (1969).

TABLE 1. LIVING ARRANGEMENT BY DEGREE OF INVOLVEMENT WITH MARIHUANA[a]

	Living Arrangement	
Involvement with Marihuana	Living with Both Parents %	Do not Live With Both Parents %
Non users	71	54
Moderate users	19	29
Regular users	10	17
N[b]	1425	251
$x^2 = 27.67$ d.f. $= 2$		p $<$ .001

[a]19 individuals are adopted and live with both adoptive parents. Because of their small number they are not included in this table.

[b]In this and the rest of the tables the total number of cases is less than 1700, because the "no answer" respondents are not included. In none of the tables the "no answer" exceed one percent.

Drug Use and Drinking Among Parents

The point is sometimes made that ours is a drug consuming culture. This is reflected in the staggering amounts of drugs produced and consumed, as well as the attitude that every ill can be solved through a pill. Indeed, some argue that the difference between the consumption of drugs by the older and younger generation lies only in the type of drugs used. Drugs favored by the older generation are alcohol, tranquilizers, barbiturates and other (DeRopp, 1961; Eddy *et al.,* 1965). The source of supply is legal for adults and illegal for the young (Goddard and Barnard, 1969: 124; Nowlis, 1969:24; Parry, 1968).

Those interested in this problem further assert that a positive association may exist between parental involvement with legal drugs and their children's involvement with illegal drugs. With the present data, however, this assumption can only partially be tested. Thus, the subjects were presented with a list of behaviors and were required to place check marks next to those which applied to mother and father separately. Among the behaviors were: use of tranquilizers, sleeping pills, and hard liquor, the last refers to "drinking more than just cocktails." An individual could place as many checks as he wished. Unfortunately, however, those who failed to check any answers might have been those whose parents do not engage in any of the behaviors, or those who simply refused to answer, for no provisions were made for the distinction between "no answer" and "does not apply." Clearly this is a methological shortcoming, since a large number of subjects left this question unanswered, 17 percent in the case of the father and 14 percent in the case of the mother.

Despite this shortcoming, when answers from the preceding two questions are related to involvement with marihuana the results are most suggestive. Thus, focusing on the answers referring to the mother, among those whose mothers take sleeping pills there were 18 percent regular users of marihuana, 20 percent among those whose mothers took tranquilizers and 23 percent among those whose mothers "drink more than just cocktails." In contrast, among respondents who left the question unanswered only eight percent were regular marihuana users. Results from responses referring to these behaviors as they are exhibited by the father point in the same direction. Briefly, then, it can be tentatively concluded that children whose parents use legal drugs show a higher level of involvement with an illegal drug such as marihuana.

Parental Acceptance/Rejection

It was anticipated that there would be a negative association between positive evaluations and attitudes of the family and involvement with marihuana. It must be emphasized that the data collected about parental pressures, controls and evaluations as well as the respondents satisfaction with and meaning of the family, are all based on subjective reports. The extent to which these reports reflect reality can not be ascertained. In a sense, then, the data at hand represent reality as perceived by these youths. This brings to mind the famous theorem of W. I. Thomas: "If men define situations as real, they are real in their consequences." If the marginals in all but the first table are observed, it can be noted that responses to questions concerning positive evaluations and attitudes of the family are neither extreme nor stereo-typed. Indeed, there was a great deal of variation with overall moderate and rather positive views of the family. The last point is especially interesting because of the general ideas about rebelliousness of the young and the exist-ence of a generation gap. These marginals point out that despite the existence of a generation gap, the family not only objectively is a salient unit for teen-agers but is even subjectively perceived and evaluated as such by a substantial proportion of these young people

Probing into this problem, subjects were asked if their family was proud and pleased, disappointed and displeased, or indifferent of them as a per-son. Relating these responses to marihuana use, it was found that young people who felt that their family was proud and pleased with them were less likely to smoke marihuana. Some interesting differences emerged from a com-parison of the "disappointed and displeased" and "indifferent" groups (see Table 2). Those whose parents were displeased and disappointed comprised a higher proportion of marihuana users than those whose parents were merely indifferent.

TABLE 2. FAMILY'S ATTITUDE TOWARD RESPONDENT BY DEGREE OF INVOLVEMENT WITH MARIHUANA

Involvement with Marihuana	Family's Attitude		
	Proud and Pleased %	Disappointed and Displeased %	Indifferent to you as a Person %
Non users	75	42	49
Moderate users	18	26	31
Regular users	7	32	20
N	1295	232	139
	$x^2 = 169.44$	d.f. $= 4$	P $<$ .001

	Amount of Recognition and Respect Received from Family			
	Definitely Enough %	On the Whole Enough %	Some but Not Enough %	No, not at all %
Non users	78	70	57	49
Moderate users	16	20	24	21
Regular users	6	10	19	30
N	482	768	346	99
		$x^2 = 85.86$	d.f. $= 6$	P $<$ .001

Subjects were asked if they "get enough recognition" from their families. Implied here is not only the evaluative aspect, but also degree of fairness.

As in the preceding case, a consistently negative association between the amount of recognition received from parents and the degree of involvement with marihuana emerged (see Table 2).

A strategic variable affecting adolescent behavior is the amount and type of control or pressure applied by parents. Although this variable is thought to be of significance, very little about its specific direction is known. Indeed, one could argue with equal plausibility that parental control is conducive to conformist as well as deviant behavior. The problem is by no means simple depending on kind of control, strength, and a variety of other conditions and circumstances under which it is employed. Clearly then, the variable is complex, requiring a great deal of refinement (Cohen, 1966; Ney, 1958; Parsons, 1951).

In describing their families the respondents were provided with the following choices: "easy going and warm," "demanding but warm," "demanding and cold," and "indifferent." In Table 3 which relates responses from this question to marihuana use, it can be observed that among those who said that their family was warm, and regardless of whether it was also said to be demanding or easy going, the proportion of marihuana users was the same. Since "easy going" and "demanding" have the same percentage of marihuana users, this tentatively suggests that to be demanding seems to have no effect on the degree of involvement with marihuana, when accompanied by warmth.

TABLE 3. DESCRIPTION AND EVALUATION OF FAMILY BY DEGREE OF INVOLVEMENT WITH MARIHUANA

| Involvement with Marihuana | Type of Family | | | |
	Easy going and Warm %	Demanding but Warm %	Demanding and Cold %	Indifferent %
Non users	71	71	53	54
Moderate users	19	19	20	27
Regular users	10	10	27	19
N	752	683	113	134
	$x^2 = 42.70$	d.f. $= 6$		P $<$ .001

| Parents Ask The Impossible as Far as School Work Is Concerned | | | | |
	Yes Definitely %	Yes Sometimes %	No, they never demand too much %	No, they don't really care how I do in school %
Non users	52	67	72	41
Moderate users	22	20	20	26
Regular users	26	13	8	33
N	89	683	896	27
	$x^2 = 45.03$	d.f. $= 6$		P $<$ .001

The groups whose families are "demanding and cold" and those whose families are "indifferent" contain a higher proportion of marihuana users. Thus, in contrasting these two groups with the preceding two, the level of marihuana use differs rather substantially. The difference, however, does not seem to be related to presence or absence of demands but rather to presence or absence of "warmth."

Finally, a certain similarity with the results obtained can be noted in Tables 2 and 3. That is, the indifferent parents contain a smaller percentage of regular users than parents who exhibited a purely negative attitude— parents who were "demanding and cold."

Another indicator of parental pressure was sought through the following query: "Do you feel that your parents ask the impossible as far as your school grades are concerned"? As in the preceding case, it was found that the more "impossible" parental demands, the greater the likelihood to use marihuana with regularity (see Table 3).

An exception are those who said that their parents did not care how they do in school. Unlike the data in Tables 2 and 3, the "indifferent" parents contained the highest percentage of regular marihuana users. Thus contradiction, or lack of consistency, is rather intriguing, suggesting at least tentatively that both extremes, total indifference and rigid controls bear a similarly positive association to marihuana use, particularly when compared to warm and involved parents.

With respect to the variable of social control, as operationally defined here, it does not by itself result in conformist behavior involving the use of an illegal drug such as marihuana. For the young, pressures—particularly those emanating from parents —might have a negative connotation. It is possible when pressures are applied in subtle ways, they may produce the desired effects.

Having dealt with the ways in which adolescents perceive their families' reactions and evaluations toward themselves and how these are related to marihuana use, their own reactions to the family and how these are related to involvement with marihuana will be examined.

Significance and Enjoyment of Family

An earlier assumption may be recalled that in the life of a teenager the most strategic status is the familial one. While in reality the family is the most salient group; a teenager may not agree with this. Actually this very dependence upon the family unit may create resentment and opposition in an adolescent. A certain amount of opposition and rebellion during adolescence is a universal and expected pattern. Because of this potentiality for rebellion, when an adolescent says that he derives a great deal of satisfaction from family life, such a response suggests not only an appreciation of the family but also involvement.

The question was asked: "do you enjoy being with your family?" Responses ranged from "yes, definitely" to "no, definitely not." Comparing these answers in terms of involvement with marihuana, it was found that the more the subjects enjoyed being with the family the less likely they were to indulge in marihuana use (see Table 4).

TABLE 4. EXTENT TO WHICH ENJOY BEING WITH FAMILY BY DEGREE OF INVOLVEMENT WITH MARIHUANA

Involvement with Marihuana	Enjoy Being with Family			
	Yes Definitely	Sometimes	No Hardly Ever	No Definitely Not
	%	%	%	%
Non users	85	67	45	38
Moderate Users	11	23	27	24
Regular users	4	10	28	38
N	440	1000	193	58
	$x^2 = 168.54$		d.f. $= 6$	p $<$ .001

Another question reflecting involvement plus relative importance of the family was included. Here an individual was asked to rate the most important aspect of his life, the family, friends, themselves, school, or nothing. In relating these answers to marihuana use, it was found that among those who said that the family was most important, five percent were regular marihuana users as compared to 16 percent among those who said that friends were most important, and 19 percent among those who said that they themselves were most important.

Another significant aspect of the relation to one's family is the extent to which a person can talk to any or all of the family members when in trouble, for the ability to talk to a family when faced with problems implies a feeling of trust and security as well as involvement. Among those who said that they would turn to the entire family when in trouble, eight percent were regular users, as compared to 21 percent regular users among those who would turn to only friends when in trouble. Recalling the overall tolerance among teenagers towards marihuana, this finding is not surprising. Far from applying negative sanctions, the tolerant views about this activity may even encourage direct experimentation. Furthermore, the percentage of regular marihuana users remains the lowest for those who rely on the family when in trouble compared to those who rely on no one and those who rely on siblings only.

SUMMARY AND CONCLUSIONS

It has been shown that the likelihood of conformity to the norm studied (prohibitions against use of marihuana) varies directly with:

1. The presence and quality of parental models for behavior. Youths who come from broken homes and/or do not live with both parents are more likely to use marihuana than youths who come from intact families. It has also been tentatively concluded that adolescents whose parents, particularly mothers, drink hard liquor or use tranquilizers and sleeping pills, are more likely to be involved with marihuana than those who do not report such parental behaviors.

2. The extent to which associations within the family unit are defined as rewarding and meaningful by its members. Thus, the more rewarding the family is in terms of recognition and respect obtained within it, and the more personally satisfactory the relationships are within it, the lesser the likelihood to smoke marihuana. Similarly, the likelihood of turning to the family when in trouble, and the subjective definition of the family as the most important unit both show a negative association to regular involvement with marihuana.

3. The presence of parental controls and/or indifference. That is, the likelihood of marihuana use increases when demands made by the family are perceived as unfair and excessive and are not accompanied by "warmth." Similarly, those who perceive their families as indifferent are also more likely to use marihuana than those who see it as undemanding and/or warm. Thus, sheer strong control and/or complete indifference as measured by the questionnaire bear a positive association to marihuana use. According to broad sociological thinking, conformity within a given unit is achieved by its system of rewards as well as direct controls.

The unit under scrutiny, the family, is by definition a primary group. Therefore, in terms of the cultural expectations as they pertain to this unit the associations are seen as typically of an intimate and personally satisfactory nature. Where those expectations are not fulfilled lack of compliance with some of its norms might be the outcome. In a sense then, rigid controls which are experienced as reality by members of such a unit might be less tolerated than within a less intimate and more formal environment. Furthermore, the age of the sample implies a certain resistance and even resentment toward parental controls.

To what extent this association would have appeared in other units is hard to determine. Many studies conducted in the field of formal organization have shown that the level of personal satisfaction as experienced by its members, rather than rigid controls, is indeed positively associated with a high level of conformity. The present findings, therefore, should be viewed as a mere beginning in what promises to be a complicated but fascinating task.

NOTES AND REFERENCES

1. *American Medical News:* "Marijuana Law Challenged." Sept. 15, 1969, p. 3.
2. Blum, Richard H., and Associates: *Drugs and Society.* San Francisco: Jossey and Bass Inc., 1969.
3. Charen, Sol, and Perelman, Luis: "Personality Studies of Marihuana Addicts." *American Journal of Psychiatry* 102: 674–682, March, 1946.
4. Chein, Isidor; Gerard, Donald L.; Lee, Robert S.; and Rosenfeld, Eva: *The Road to H.* New York: Basic Books, 1964.
5. Cholst, Sheldon: "Notes on the Use of Hashish," in Solomon, David (ed.): *The Marihuana Papers.* New York: Signet Books, 1968, pp. 266–274.
6. Clausen, John A.: "Social Patterns Personality and Adolescent Drug Use," in Leighton, A. (ed.): *Explorations in Social Psychiatry.* New York: Basic Books, 1957, 230–277.
7. Cohen, Albert K.: *Deviancy and Control.* Englewood Cliffs: Prentice Hall, Inc., 1966.
8. DeRopp, Robert: *Drugs and the Mind.* New York: Grove Press, 1961.
9. Eddy, Nathan B.; Halbach, H.; Isabell, Harris; and Seevers, Maurice H.: "Drug Dependence Its Significance and Characteristics." *Bulletin World Health Organization* 32:721–733, 1965.
10. Eisenstadt, S. N.: *From Generation to Generation.* Glencoe, Ill.: The Free Press, 1956.
11. Goddard, James L., and Barnard, Alfred: "The High School Drug Problem," in Goode, Erich (ed.): *Marijuana.* New York: Atherton Press, 1969, pp. 121–129.
12. Hill, Harris: "The Social Deviant and Initial Addiction to Narcotics and Alcohol." *Quarterly Journal of Studies on Alcohol* 23: 562–582, 1962.
13. Kurtz, Ronald S.: "Marijuana and LSD on the Campus," in Goode, Erich (ed.): *Marijuana.* New York: Atherton Press, 1969, pp. 113–120.
14. Leary, Timothy: "The Politics, Ethics, and Meaning of Marijuana, in Solomon, David (ed.): *The Marijuana Papers.* New York: Signet Books, 1968, pp. 121–142.
15. McGlothlin, William H.: "Cannabis a Reference," in Solomon, David (ed.): *The Marijuana Papers.* New York: Signet Books, 1968, pp. 455–471.
16. *New York Times:* "Administration Asks Softer Penalty for Drug Abuse." October 20, 1969, p. 24.
17. *New York Times:* "Marijuana Curbs Endorsed in Poll." October 23, 1969, p. 56.

18. *New York Times:* "Dr. Mead Calls Marihuana Ban Worse than Drug."
October 28, 1969, p. 35.
19. Nowlis, Helen H.: *Drugs on the College Campus.* New York: Doubleday
and Co., Inc., 1969.
20. Nye, F. Ivan: *Family Relationships and Deliquent Behavior.* New York:
John Wiley & Sons, Inc., 1958.
21. Parry, Hugh J.: "Use of Psychotropic Drugs by U.S. Adults." *Public
Health Reports* 83:799–810, 1968.
22. Parsons: *The Social System.* Glencoe, Ill.: The Free Press, 1951.
23. *Philadelphia Inquirer:* "Parents Draw Line on Teenagers Using Drugs."
March 4, 1968.
24. Taylor, Norman: *Narcotics: Nature's Dangerous Gifts.* New York: Dell
Publishing Co., 1966.
25. Tec, Leon: "On Adoption." Paper presented at the Argentine Psychiatric Society Meeting, Buenos Aires, 1969.
26. Tec, Leon and Gordon, Susanne: "The Adopted Child's Adaptation to
Adolescence." Paper presented at the 44th Annual Meeting of the American Orthopsychiatric Association, Washington, D.C., 1967.

AFFILIATIONS AND ACKNOWLEDGMENTS

1. I am very grateful to Herbert H. Hyman for his continuous and extensive help so generously extended at all stages of this study. I also wish to
thank Esther Mallach, Executive Director Mental Health Association of
Westchester County for enabling us to conduct a small pilot study in a
separate high school. My thanks go to the Mid-Fairfield Child Guidance
Center, Norwalk, Connecticut for financing and sponsoring this study.
2. Nechama Tec, Ph. D. is Lecturer, Department of Sociology, Columbia
University, New York, N. Y., and Research Director, Mid-Fairfield
Child Guidance Center, Norwalk, Connecticut.

The Interrelatedness of Alcoholism
and Marital Conflict

SAMUEL C. BULLOCK AND
EMILY H. MUDD

There has been an increasing interest recently in the study of alcoholism from a multidisciplinary approach, with the fields of medicine, psychiatry, psychology, sociology, and anthropology making contributions to understanding the etiology and treatment of chronic alcoholism. Important areas of study have been the pathology in the psychological and social backgrounds of individuals categorized as chronic alcoholics, and their marked difficulties in interpersonal relationships.

Psychiatric studies indicate that alcoholics show a high incidence of personality problems. Sherfey[1] presents a study of 161 cases, approximately one third of the population women; 42.8 per cent of this group fit into well-defined psychiatric diagnostic categories and 59.6 per cent demonstrated serious personality defects and fitted the category of character disorder. The drinking in these cases was a symptom of several different diseases and alcohol was used in a variety of neurotic ways. A study by Manfred Bleuler[2] of a group of alcoholics shows a high incidence of morbid and borderline personality characteristics. The home conditions of the alcoholic cases during childhood were very poor, and a high percentage of cases had been under the influence of morbid personalities before the age of 20.

Psychoanalytic studies, which have been based on the treatment of individual alcoholics, have been the basis of psychological theories on the

From *American Journal of Orthopsychiatry* 29:519–527, No.1, Jan., 1959. Copyright ⓒ, the American Orthopsychiatric Association, Inc. Reproduced by permission of the publisher and authors. This study is part of a larger research project on "The Interrelatedness of Alcoholism and Marital Conflict" financed by funds from the Division of Addictive Diseases, Alcoholic Studies and Rehabilitation, Department of Health, Commonwealth of Pennsylvania. Reprinted with permission of the authors and publisher.

genesis and dynamics of alcoholic addiction. These studies present formulations of the deep unconscious conflict of the alcoholic. Rado[3] presents a view of the ego development of the addict. Narcissistic gratification is originally given to the infant effortlessly; later this must be obtained through handling the environment and, with this, achievement becomes the basis for self-esteem. Because of difficult life experiences an individual may become uncertain that gratification can be obtained by his efforts and there is a longing for infantile gratification, which is passively experienced. When the need is great and the timing of the first experience appropriate, the discovery is made that a self-administered magical substance can dispel the pain of reality and the state of infantile gratification is regained.

Knight's formulation of the etiology of alcohol addiction[4] is based on the study of 30 male alcoholics. He points out that alcohol addiction is a symptom, with excessive drinking as the outstanding presenting complaint and an underlying personality disorder always present. In the symptom there is a regressive acting out of unconscious drives, with alcohol being used as a means of obtaining forbidden gratification, of carrying out repressed hostilities, and of dissolving inhibitions and anxieties. The typical parental constellation seen in this series of cases from well-to-do families was that of an over-indulgent, overprotective mother and a father who was aggressive and dominating in the business world, cold, unaffectionate and dominating to his family, and inconsistently severe and indulgent to his sons. A pattern of oral dependence and oral demanding, with suppressed rage at frustration and a feeling of being rejected by both parents, with an intense desire for indulgence and affection, is built into the personality. There is a sense of guilt for the hatred and a feeling of inferiority for the dependence and passivity. In puberty the feelings of inferiority and envy of masculine potency are intensified, and in the early twenties, on coming in contact with liquor, not to drink is sissified and to drink is a proof of manliness. Drinking enables the individual to feel potent, to restore injured self-esteem, and to regain the sense of infantile omnipotence. It is pointed out that in severe cases there may be an X factor that determines the specificity of drinking and that the parental attitudes may vary a great deal in their expression and effect.

A more general hypothesis of the etiology of alcohol addiction is presented by Higgins.[5] A predisposed individual is confronted with a difficult life situation; anxiety is aroused with an attempt to resolve this by drinking. Predisposition represents fixation at various levels of development. Drinking serves as a defense through diminished awareness of internal or external stress, or facilitates defenses which have been inhibited. This formulation does not handle the question of why alcoholism rather than some other clinical picture.

Schilder[6] states that a central social problem of the alcoholic is the struggle for prestige and close attachment to the parent of the same sex, which evokes sexual repercussions. Simmel[7] describes the parents of neurotic drinkers, the father or mother or both, as emotionally immature, unstable people, who attempt to suppress in their children instinctual reactions they are unable to repress in themselves. The parental prototypes help create multiple superegos, which can be opposed to the instinctual demands of the id, but can also be bribed by the demands of the id.

It is evident that there are several areas of general agreement in the psychiatric literature. In the group labeled chronic alcoholic, variation is recognized in the nature and severity of the drinking behavior, in the character of the underlying personality problems, and in the degree of maturity shown in different individuals. These studies describe pathological family constellations leading to disturbances in psychological development, with emphasis on the early infantile deprivations and faulty identifications as important problems. When these individuals are faced with reality situations requiring independence and assertiveness, anxiety is experienced. The emotional forces described as important are lowered feelings of self-esteem, feelings of inferiority stemming from feelings of passivity and dependence, and suppressed rage. Alcoholism induces a state of feeling good and permits feelings and emotional expressions which may show marked distortions.

There also have been several reports recently on the personality characteristics of the wives of alcoholics, which have emphasized the personality problems of the wives.[8] There are similarities reported in the wives in terms of poor personality integration.[9] Price[10] reports a group of 20 wives who showed nervousness in varying degrees, marked hostility and basic feelings of insecurity, which they brought to the marriage. The personality problems of the wives are presented as a factor contributing to the disturbed marital relationships and having importance in the treatment of the alcoholic.

In summarizing the psychiatric literature, it seems clear that there is detailed consideration of the personality pathology of the chronic alcoholic, with formulations of the genesis and etiology of alcoholism, usually in males. Less material has been presented concerning the personalities of the wives of alcoholics. A detailed review of the literature in 1955 showed not more than 10 to 15 studies focused on the impact of chronic alcoholism on marriage and family relationships. In this study, we were interested in systematically looking at the nature of the marital interaction and the interpersonal relationship in marriages in which the husbands were alcoholic and their wives nonalcoholic. This paper will also report observations on the course of counseling in this group.[11]

General Characteristics of the Population

The first 20 couples completing the research requirements for the over-all project will be the basis for this report. Mitchell[12] has presented in his report some of the characteristics of this group, including the mean ages of the husbands and wives (38.5 years for husbands, 37.2 years for wives) and the mean duration of the marriages (10.5 years). Eighty-five per cent of these families had children, varying in numbers from one to five. This was the second marriage for 30 per cent of the husbands, and for 10 per cent of the wives. One couple had been divorced and had remarried, and one wife was in her third marriage.

Seventy per cent of the husbands began drinking in their teens; the others started in their early twenties, before their marriage. Approximately the same percentage had previously sought help from Alcoholics Anonymous, the medical profession, or both, for drinking. Forty-five per cent of the group had stopped drinking for periods varying from several months to ten years. Over 70 per cent of the men described marked unhappiness and conflict in their family backgrounds, with over 50 per cent having a heavy drinker in their immediate family. Consistently this was the father, but in a few cases it was also the mother.

An unhappy family background was described by over 30 per cent of the wives; the same number had lost a parent by divorce or death before 12 years of age. Difficulties in the relationship with mother or father were de-scribed in equal frequency. A heavy drinker was present in the families of over 30 per cent of the wives, the individual usually being the father.

There were significant economic problems in over half the families; 40 per cent of the husbands were not working and 30 per cent of the wives were the sole support of the family.

Types of Marital Interactions Observed

The marriages of these couples were characterized by a high degree of conflict. The wives presented the husbands' drinking as the main difficulty in the relationship. While the husbands presented a variety of complaints, dissatisfaction with the marriage stemming from the attitudes and behavior of their wives was consistently present. Conflict was of long duration, and as retrospectively reported, had existed in the premarital relationship in over half the cases. The personality problems of both partners appeared to be important factors in the marriage selection and the difficulties which develop-ed.

Illustrations of two of the relationships will be presented. These exam-ples were selected because of the fairly clear picture of personality problems in both partners, a condition which was demonstrated in over two thirds of the cases.

One couple had been married for 20 years, with a divorce and remarriage to each other. The wife was apathetic and withdrawn from her husband, feeling that his drinking was an insoluble problem. In her family background she described her mother as a cold, unaffectionate and critical person who demanded early independence of her. Her only affection had come from an alcoholic father who had died when she was 12, following which she had become lonely and withdrawn from others. Her desire for a home was a strong motivation for marriage. The husband's parents had separated before he was 6; his father left, his mother remarried, and he was sent to live with his grandparents. His grandfather, father and stepfather were alcoholics. Difficult school experiences added to his feeling of being isolated and no good. He entered marriage expecting a better home and more satisfying human relationships. Few gratifications with each other, and the responsibilities of a home and children were followed by conflict, alcoholism and unhappiness for both.

In another couple, married for 15 years, the husband, who for 3 years had abstained from drinking and been an active AA member, complained of an empty marriage with little sexual gratification. His parents' marriage was unhappy, with his father's drinking being a problem. He felt close to and spoiled by his mother, but his father was mean and unapproachable. During adolescence he experienced intense shame over having to find his father in taverns, bring him home and put him to bed; at this time he vowed this would never happen to him. He described his marriage as forced because of his girl friend's pregnancy, and the marriage was followed by a separation of several years owing to his being in the service. On returning he experienced anxieties about increasing responsibilities in the business world and the unhappiness of his marriage. At this point his heavy drinking began. The wife described her relationship with her mother as good. Her father was an alcoholic who disliked children, and he was critical of her during childhood and humiliated her. Immediately following marriage she had crying spells for several months, and for several years had anxiety attacks. She denied any problems in the marriage, and when her husband attempted to discuss their difficulties, she would accuse him of being neurotic and alcoholic. She also denied any problems of difficulties premaritally, and presented a picture of an extremely happy courtship period.

Several patterns of interaction are demonstrated in the group studied. The picture of a dependent inadequate alcoholic male married to a dominating woman that is frequently described in the literature was seen clearly in 4 of our 20 cases. Two of these women had had a child by another man before marriage and had considered their husbands as men accepting of this situation. These women supported their husbands, took care of the home and children, and appeared adequate in assuming responsibility in the practical details of family life. One of the women in this group had had two previous marriages, one to an alcoholic husband.

Two of the four husbands with dominating wives had recurrent gastric ulcers leading to gastrectomy. They entered marriage with the wife having an illegitimate child, and following marriage reacted with intense anger to the child and jealousy over the wife's earlier relationship to another man. The third husband was angry over his wife's attention to her children from an earlier marriage, and the fourth was resentful and jealous over his wife's prolonged attempts to care for another male alcoholic.

Two of the wives had approached marriage with the intention of reforming their husbands and with little awareness of their own needs and expectations. When the attempts at reform failed they were preoccupied with how they had been hurt, and reacted with rage.

Severe personality problems were seen in five wives who showed strong dependency needs and feelings of inadequacy as an important part of their clinical picture, and who entered marriage seeking strong emotional support from their husbands. The additional stresses of marriage and the inability of their husbands to gratify the personal needs of these women increased their dissatisfaction and led to decompensation. Feelings of anger over being hurt by their husbands, with the expression of resentment and withdrawal from them, were a response to this. The problem of strong hostility to men stemming from disturbed relationships with their fathers was clearly shown in over half the wives. There was a history of difficulties with other men prior to marriage, and frequent provocative behavior toward the husbands after marriage.

Emotional Disturbances Seen in Partners

Over half of the alcoholic husbands periodically felt and demonstrated feelings of depression and varying degrees of tension and anxiety. Lowered feelings of self-esteem, feelings of inadequacy and inferiority were frequent complaints. Disturbance in the handling of anger was also frequent, with variations in the expression of anger and rage. In some instances there was marked suppression of anger with some release in action while drinking; others showed a more continuous expression of anger in the marriage. Strong passive and dependent needs were expressed verbally, and lived out in the marriage relationship. Economic dependency on the wives, resentment over the attention given to children, and anger and jealousy over relationships of the wives with their parental families and friends were seen.

Overt symptoms of emotional disturbance were seen in a slightly smaller frequency in the wives than in the husbands. Complaints of feelings of depression and anxiety with somatic complaints were most frequently evident. Feelings of anger were frequently suppressed or expressed indirectly in the marriage, but several of the wives were explosive and combative with their husbands. There was a history of a previous psychotic episode in two wives.

Vogel[13] describes the defense mechanisms of denial, projection and rationalization as commonly used by alcoholics. These defense mechanisms were also striking in this group of alcoholics as methods of handling conflict and anxiety.

Obviously this is too small a population to draw definitive conclusions. However, it is of interest to see that in these couples there is evidence of varying personality difficulties both in the wives and husbands which are important in their marital choice and are significant causes of conflict between the partners.

Results of Counseling

The results of counseling were evaluated in terms of the adjustment in the marital relationship and the drinking behavior of the husbands. This evaluation was based on intensive study by the psychiatrist in the research group of the individual records of counseling contacts, which included direct statements from the clients and, in half of the cases, conferences by the psychiatrist with the counselor who worked with the case. In eight of these marriages (40%), it was judged that both spouses felt improvement; in two of the marriages one spouse felt there was improvement and the other did not. In another 40 per cent it was believed that neither spouse felt any improvement, and in the remaining two marriages it was felt that both the marriages had deteriorated and the individuals concerned showed increased personal disorganization.

As might be expected in these complicated situations, in the cases showing improvement, where greater progress was seen in one partner than the other (either the husband or the wife) and an improved relationship resulted, there ensued an awareness of new areas in which adjustments would have to be made. More marked behavioral changes were seen in the husbands who showed improvement. There was expression of resentment by wives over behavior that was more assertive and independent. There was also in some cases the seeming paradox of the wife's resenting her husband's participation in AA groups because of the time he had to spend away from home, or stating her own dislike for group activity as a reason for her not participating.

It is perhaps not surprising that these 20 couples showed a less favorable response to marital counseling than did a group of couples, none of whom were alcoholics, who sought assistance with their marital conflicts from this same clinic. In this earlier study,[14] up to 66 per cent of the cases showed improvement at the end of their counseling experience, up to 29 per cent showed no apparent change, and 5 per cent showed retrogression. A partial explanation of these differences in the results of counseling may be found in the degree of personal pathology of both spouses, in addition to the extremes of pathology reported about the parental families in which both these alcoholics and their wives were reared. Poor motivation for counseling was also evident on the part of the couples in our study who were found to apply because of referral from legal sources.

The motivation of each partner for help was an important factor in counseling. In the marriages where the total responsibility for the difficulties was placed on the partner, as had been found in earlier studies from Marriage Council of Philadelphia, Inc.,[15] there was little change. In the cases with forced referral it was difficult to get beyond descriptions of the marital conflict.

Consequences of Marital Conflict for Family Living

In the marriages reported on, there were dissatisfaction and unhappiness for both partners. Other individuals were affected by the marital difficulties. Eighty-five per cent of these couples had children, and the significance of the family difficulties for their development cannot be minimized. In this series, when there were several children, one child appeared to be more involved in the parental conflict, and to receive greater hostility from one parent.

However, the family disorganization is important for all the children. The alcoholic fathers had grown up in unhappy family situations, with conflict and frequently an alcoholic parent present, and some of the wives had experienced severe problems with their parents. A similar situation was created in the marriages of the couples studied, with the fathers and mothers presenting poor figures for identification. On the basis of evidence in the literature and here, it seems reasonable to predict that these children represent a population that has an enhanced chance of developing personality problems, and of becoming alcoholics themselves or marrying an alcoholic spouse.

Data are not yet available on the nature of the marital interactions in couples presumed to be "happily married." We recognize that the nature of the interpersonal relationship in such marriages, and the personality and background factors of the partners, would serve as control data for an evaluation of the group reported upon in this paper, and should add to our understanding of the conflicted marriages. It is our hope that sometime in the future this additional study may be undertaken.

Conclusions

Both partners, the alcoholic husband and his nonalcoholic wife, present pictures of difficult family backgrounds and emotional problems. The emotional needs of each partner are important factors in the marital choice. The demands of marriage, with failure to gratify the over-determined needs in the partner, are important in leading to further emotional disturbance in each partner and greater conflict in the marriage. On the basis of this and former evidence it appears essential that in the treatment of alcoholics the possibility of personality difficulties in the marriage partner be recognized and an active attempt be made to offer help to the spouse.

At present it is not accepted procedure for health authorities to consider implementing placement in foster homes of children who are exposed chronically to severe pathology in their parental homes. However, it seems not unreasonable, on the basis of previous and current studies, to suggest that health authorities consider the advisability of placement in foster homes for the children of families chronically disrupted by the alcoholism of one or both spouses, when this is combined with a severe degree of psychiatric disorder in the partner—and if the parents refuse to utilize available community resources for treatment.

NOTES AND REFERENCES

1. Sherfey, M. D.: "Psychopathology and Character Structure in Chronic Alcoholism," in Diethelm, O. (ed.): *Etiology of Chronic Alcoholism.* Springfield, Ill.: Charles C Thomas, 1955, pp. 16–42.
2. Bleuler, M.: "Familial and Personal Backgrounds of Chronic Alcoholics," in Diethelm, O. (ed.): *Etiology of Chronic Alcoholism.* Springfield, Ill.: Charles C Thomas, 1955, pp. 110–166.
3. Rado, S.: "Psychoanalysis of Pharmacothymia (Drug Addiction)." *Psychoanal. Quart.* 2:1–23, 1933.
4. Knight, R. P.: "Dynamics and Treatment of Chronic Alcohol Addiction." *Bull. Menninger Clin.* 1:233–250, 1937.
5. Higgins, J. W.: "Psychodynamics in Excessive Drinking of Alcohol." *A.M.A. Arch. Neurol. Psychiat.* 69:713–726, 1953.
6. Schilder, P.: "Psychogenesis of Alcoholism. " *Quart. J. Stud. Alc.* 2:277–299, 1941.
7. Simmel, E. :"Alcoholism and Addiction." *Psychoanal. Quart.* 17:No. 1, 1948.
8. Futterman, S.: "Personality Trends in Wives of Alcoholics." *J. Psychiat. Soc. Work* 23:37–41, 1953.
9. Whalen, T.: "Wives of Alcoholics. Four Types Observed in a Family Service Agency." *Quart. J. Stud. Alc.* 14:632–641, 1953.

10. Price, G. M.: "Study of Wives of 20 Alcoholics." *Quart. J. Stud. Alc.* 5:620–627, 1945.
11. The authors were participants in a research seminar, 1955–56, on the relatedness of alcoholism and marital conflict. This report is based on a study of the recordings of counselor interviews with these couples, material on schedules checked by the alcoholics and their wives, and conferences with the counselors by the psychiatrist writer.
12. Mitchell, H. E.: "Interpersonal Perception Theory Applied to Conflicted Marriages in Which Alcoholism Is and Is Not a Problem." *American Journal of Orthopsychiatry* 29, No. 1, Jan. 1959.
13. Vogel, S.: "Psychiatric Treatment of Alcoholism." *Ann. Am. Acad. Polit. Soc. Sci.* 12:99–107, 1958.
14. Preston, M. G.; Mudd, E. H; and Froscher, H. B: "Factors Affecting Movement in Casework." *Soc. Casework* 34:103–111, 1953.
15. Mitchell, H.; Preston, M. G.; and Mudd, E. H.: "Anticipated Development of the Case from the Content of the First Interview Record." *Marriage Fam. Living* 15:226–231, 1953.

AFFILIATIONS AND ACKNOWLEDGMENTS

1. The authors wish to acknowledge with appreciation the important assistance in the formulation of this manuscript which was furnished by Dr. Fritz Freyhan, Director of the Delaware State Psychiatric Hospital, and Adjunct Associate Professor of Psychiatry, School of Medicine, University of Pennsylvania. Dr. Freyhan served as consultant to this project.
2. Samuel C. Bullock, M. D., Associate in Psychiatry.
3. Emily H. Mudd, Ph. D., Professor of Family Study in Psychiatry and Director of Division of Family Study.

Family Conflicts
and Criminal Behaviour

BRUNO M. CORMIER, MIRIAM KENNEDY,
JADWIGA SANGOWICZ, MICHEL TROTTIER

Crime is by nature and definition antisocial, infringing as it does on the security and rights of others. When, however, we look at offenders themselves apart from their offence, they are by no means all antisocial citizens. Furthermore, the motivation behind an actual offence may or may not be antisocial.

Certain patterns of criminality can be partially explained by early defect in the process of socialization. This social deficiency is an important factor in habitual criminality, which is indeed one of our most difficult problems. It remains, however, that the majority of offenders appearing in our courts are not basically antisocial, if we examine the total personality of an offender rather than a single or repeated symptomatic act. Many may be described as deeply disturbed and perhaps insufficiently responsible individuals.

We have been studying a group of 176 latecomers to crime, that is, offenders who appear before the court and are sentenced for the first time in their 20's, 30's, 40's and on, with no previous criminal involvement or fixed pattern of delinquency.[1] In our study we found that many of these men bore no grudge against society at the commission of their first offence, though they sometimes developed one to a certain degree following harsh or excessive punishment. This was most evident in the case of married offenders when the sentence, instead of aiming at rehabilitation and restoration of family, only further disorganized and dislocated it.

The study we are presenting will refer to a particular group of offenders

Reprinted from the *Canadian Journal of Corrections*, Volume 3, 1, (January 1961) published by the Canadian Corrections Association, 55 Parkdale, Ottawa, Canada. By permission of publisher and authors.

within the 176 latecomers to crime, that is, to men who have committed a first offence some time after marriage. In the large number of cases, criminality resulted from a conflict of relationship between husband and wife and children, a conflict which was acted out in a variety of offences within or outside the family.[2]

Many delinquent acts of children can be understood in the context of an unfavourable family situation. There has been little serious study given to the fact that these same family conflicts may also result in adult criminality. While there is a great deal of literature on what we call the "problem family", including the problems created by the incarceration of a husband, too little attention has been given to the dynamics within the marital relationship that created sufficient disorder to send a man to prison. The adult offender as part of a family constellation merits as much consideration as the study of the delinquent child within his family group. We do not mean to imply here that every individual who commits an offence after marriage should be called a family offender; but the fact that as many as 102 of our latecomers came to court only after marriage was sufficiently striking to make us attempt to assess to what degree the family situation itself had contributed to criminality

Of our 176 offenders, 115 were married and 102 committed their first offence after marriage. We have divided these 102 offenders into five groups, though we are aware that not every case is clear cut and that some of the offenders fit into more than one category.

Our first group is of offences committed entirely within the framework of the family itself, for which the offender was charged, tried and sentenced. In his history there is no other type of offence whatever. The offences themselves include incest and homicide restricted within the family. The majority of charges, however, consist of assault on wife or children, alcoholism, failure to provide and abusive conduct in the home. We have thirty-four offenders in this group.

There is a second group where criminal acting out takes place both within the family and also outside. That is, an offender will show on his police record a charge for non-support or assault in the home, followed perhaps by one of drunken driving or forging a cheque. These offences outside the home whether slight or serious, however, took place only after the marriage. There are seventeen in this group.

In the third group, contrary to the two first, there is no serious acting out within the family, but criminal breakdown occurs outside. The offences appear, however, to be directly related to a crisis occurring in the family. The problems are displaced outside, resulting in an offence. There are eighteen in this group.

The fourth is a group of husbands who may or may not have severe marital problems, but who have a sufficiently severe personality problem where an additional family stress ends in crime. In this group we have twenty-three offenders.

There remains a group of men who, though they committed their first offence after marriage, show no meaningful connection that we could discover between the marriage and the criminal acting out. They may have a bad marriage, which seems a continuation of previous poor personality relationships, or they show marginal acting out which later becomes frankly delinquent. There are ten offenders in this group.

In our *first group* of offenders, that is, those whose criminality lies entirely within the family, the most obvious offence is the one of incest. This is intrinsically an intra-family situation and all concerned are family members. We have studied a group of incestuous fathers.[3] We can here only say briefly that in incest there is a deep-seated pathology of interpersonal relationships, which goes far back in the early history of the husband. Another striking offence is the murder of one family member by another. Here too we have studied a group of husbands who have killed their wives and which we have reported on.[4] One of our conclusions is that this kind of murder results from a deeply rooted disturbance between husband and wife, where the husband finds himself in an untenable position from which he cannot extricate himself. Finally the only solution apparent to him is to destroy the object he is unable to separate himself from.

Most of the offences, however, in this group are by no means so severe. These are the "family problem" cases, the chronic burdens of social agencies, involving frequent court appearances for non-support, assault, abusive behaviour in the home and often resulting in delinquent behaviour in the children. Except in severe cases, they are seldom referred to penitentiary, but are usually given suspended sentences, fines and short prison terms. This type of problem often appears under the Juvenile Court Act, but is more frequently seen in the magistrate's court.

The most conspicuous factor in the marriage is the interlocking relationship between husband and wife; there is frequently an interplay of sado-masochistic features on the part of both. Even in marriages where the wife appears passive and martyr-like, there is usually much latent hostility which displays itself in frigidity, in withdrawal, or in a sudden about turn of role. The wife, previously submissive, will become very punishing, will lay a charge against her husband or leave him briefly. It would seem that the wife in such cases cannot tolerate a stable and orderly marriage, any more than the husband, despite her protestations. Interestingly enough, in cases when the husband has developed some insight, perhaps following treatment, and is prepared to undertake a more responsible part, the wife may respond by being quite vindictive or she may break down herself. The children in such marriages suffer greatly, because neither parent is primarily concerned with their well being. The wife complains about her husband's alcoholism, his aggression, his misconduct to the children, but, locked herself in the conflicted relationship, she too sacrifices them. The following are examples of this kind of situation.

G. is a man in his middle thirties, the father of six children, five daughters and a son, the last child, the result of an extra-marital affair. Following a quite severe beating which he inflicted on his wife, he was sentenced to two years in the penitentiary. This was his first offence.

G. came to Canada to enlist in 1939, when he was 17 and remained here. Born outside Canada, he was an only and adopted child. His childhood was quite favourable, but he was loved by the mother rather than the father. On her early death, the father remarried, and his interest then centred on his new family and his other relatives. He was disappointed in his adopted son who was rather spoiled and high tempered, but was never in trouble with the law as an adolescent. His army record was good and after discharge he settled down to employment. He had some difficulty becoming established occupationally as he had no trade, but he was strong, quite intelligent, and eventually became a foreman in a factory. He was a good, conscientious worker. At 24 he married a woman a year younger than himself. She had had an illegitimate baby which was adopted by a family member. Moreover, the marriage was precipitated by her pregnancy. G. was fully aware of her history and this was no overt problem at the start of the marriage. Both husband and wife claim that they had four or five good years. The babies came very rapidly, but G. loved children and was a good father. There were stresses in the marriage, however, which told particularly on the wife. The children were frequently ill which created financial problems. After the fifth child, the wife herself became ill and underwent a hysterectomy. The marriage which had already begun to deteriorate grew from this point increasingly bad. Sexually the wife became cold. Their relationship had previously been good and he felt the difference keenly. She became very nagging and scolding. She also insisted on buying household appliances on credit; when payments were not met, the articles were repossessed and this resulted in his losing a good job, as his company had a rule against this practice.

G. claimed that it was due only to her withdrawal that he started to drink, and also became involved with another woman who bore him a son. It happened that he badly wanted the son. By coincidence, the children born to both partners out of wedlock were sons.

The wife, on her part, while admitting that she had become cold to her husband, claimed that his temper was dangerous and that he no longer supported the home adequately. She blamed him for everything and accepted no responsibility for his loss of job due to her buying on credit. They were forced to move to much poorer quarters, the quarreling grew more violent and on one occasion he hurt her quite severely. She laid a charge of assault and misconduct in the home and he was given a two year sentence.

In prison G. underwent considerable change. Free from the turmoil and confusion of the past few years, he could see his situation more clearly, and assess his responsibility. Though resentful of his wife's action, he wanted badly to re-establish a sound marriage. He longed for his children. The wife was at first rather vindictive and also afraid, as she had been instrumental in sending him to prison. However, left alone to handle her many difficulties, she began to realize not only that he was in some ways a good father and husband, but that the children were miserable without him. She knew that she had contributed her share to the accumulating crisis. She even went so far as to say that sometimes she had deserved it when he had struck her. She admitted that she still loved him. She therefore tried hard to secure his release on parole and was successful. The marriage was re-established on a sounder basis.

Following is the case of a 38-year-old man B., sentenced to two and a half years for violence and drunkenness in the home and physical attack on the wife.

B. comes from a small rural community, is the third born of a family of ten. His childhood was not unhappy; though his father was a small farmer, there was no want. He was fond of his parents and on good terms with his siblings. B. is of below average intelligence, and this has to some extent handicapped him, but not occupationally. He is really proud of his good work record which gives him satisfaction and a sense of status.

One of his problems has been drinking which began at age 21, and which he has continued off and on since, perhaps to make up for feelings of inadequacy.

At age 35 he married a young woman of 22 after a two month acquaintance. This marriage followed the breaking of a four year friendship with a girl he liked, but who was of a different religion. According to B. there was one good year in the marriage, but after that difficulties piled up. His wife, an outstandingly poor homemaker, could not manage money and ran him seriously into debt. She was sexually very demanding, and soon became unfaithful. There were many fights and sometimes B. lost control and struck her. She retaliated by laying a charge for which he received a two and a half year penitentiary sentence.

The wife remained in the home with the two children aged 3 and 2, but her behaviour was flagrantly bad and she openly used money provided by Social Service for drunken parties. The social agency eventually intervened, and she was in her turn sentenced to prison and the children were placed. Once in prison, she became superficially quite penitent, and wrote her husband frequently with the hope of a reconciliation. An interesting reversal of feeling now took place in B. He softened in his attitude and began to debate taking her back, and determined not to exclude her from any future plans, because of her infidelity, her accusations which had resulted in his imprisonment, and the fact that she had broken the home.

Shortly after his release, there was therefore a reconciliation and the family was re-established. At first, things went fairly well, perhaps because both partners disliked the interference of agencies and were in a sense banded together. However, the old pattern reasserted itself with the additional problem that B. could not find a job. The family not only had to live on relief, but B. no longer had the pride and satisfaction of work, and accordingly was even less able to cope with his wife. Aggressive and primitive as she was, she could stand frustration no better than he and she did not have his strong conventional morality and love of family to act as controls. The result was that, after a few months, she left with a lover. There is sufficient weakness in both husband and wife to make it doubtful whether the marriage could have succeeded even with the kind of help it needed and did not get. One can also say that his choice of wife is no accident; in a relationship of this kind, he will always be the victim. The fact remains that B. was not delinquent before marriage, never antisocial at any time and that, of the two partners, the wife was the more overtly delinquent. From his last failure he seems to have learnt to accept the loss of his wife, and has re-established a home for his children with one of his sisters.

When we look at these families who have in common that the husband was sentenced to prison as a result of an acute familial crisis, what is apparent is that, though in both cases the husband was legally guilty, the wives also have their share of guilt. In the case of B. the wife's delinquency was sufficiently evident that she too was imprisoned. In the other, the wife recognized that she was herself partly to blame.

The problem in these relationships is that husband and wife mutually act out their conflicts on one another so that, for an outsider, it is difficult to see who provokes whom. By the same token, it is not easy to pick the victim (except for the children, who are always victims).

There is a struggle for predominance in this type of marriage, often taking the form of a fantasy that, if sufficiently punished, the other partner will submit. We see husband and wife alternating in this role. What is also significant is that the conflict remains within the family, the partner always being the significant adversary. They seem to have no need and no room for other objects of hostility. This is especially true of the husbands in this group as most of them have exceptionally good work records and often a good potential for social relationships. We have observed in prison how easy it is for them to establish good social rapport outside the family. For the wife this is equally true, though in some cases when the husband is imprisoned she tends to find another and perhaps similar relationship that leads to the same acting out. This time, as it is extra-marital, it is regarded as delinquent. Most wives, however, do not enter into this delinquent category, but respond rather by drawing sympathy, pity and attention to their plight. Also characteristic of this group is that when a separation occurs, the marital partners are unable to be uncomfortable alone. The relationship is usually resumed, both promising to improve and change. Once together again, the same pathology recurs, the same interplay of forces resulting in continued criminality within the family.

The *second group* which shows criminality both within the family and outside reveals essentially the same pathology as the first. These cases should not be confused with those of criminals, habituals or otherwise, who have a pattern of criminality and who also may have conflicted and difficult marriages. What is important here is that the problem of criminality did not exist before the marriage; the stresses of the marital relationship were at least a factor in breakdown. We are here dealing with severely disturbed personalities, but it remains that the individual was able to function in a non-criminal way till marriage. The problems within the marriage were so acute that, whether the offence was theft, bank robbery or other apparently unrelated acting out, it cannot be seen apart from the family situation. The following cases illustrate this.

R's ongoing problem is alcoholism. He has been a heavy drinker, with short periods of abstinence, since age 17. He managed, however, to make a good work adjustment and, on the whole, continued to be a good worker and provider for his family for the first twelve years of his marriage. R. has five children ranging in age from 16 to 8. He was involved in no criminal behaviour before marriage.

R., now 44 years old, comes from a working class family, living in an area where a certain amount of drinking is the way of life. (This drinking, however, has created no very serious problem for the other members of his family). He went to work at 14 and managed to pick up a semi-skilled trade as a mechanic. He worked in one job for fourteen years, interrupted only by the war.

R. married at age 26, quite impulsively, shortly after he enlisted. The wife states that she too married on the spur of the moment, perhaps because she was trying to get over a broken engagement of her own. She knew that he drank to much, and she claims that neither was in love.

The marriage has been a battle ground, the protagonists being husband and wife. They are quite evenly matched, giving as much punishment as they take. There have been separations, usually instigated by the wife, when she found her husband's conduct unbearable, or his earnings dropped through drink and he no longer supported the marriage. The separations were brief as she invariably tired of these relatively quiet periods and took her husband back. Once R. spent a few months in prison for theft committed during an alcoholic period when he was particularly short of funds. He and his wife were separated and on very bad terms prior to this crisis, but he nevertheless returned to the home. The situation continued from crisis to crisis with various charges of non-support. Eventually the wife laid a charge under the Juvenile Delinquent Act for which he was given a two year sentence.

R's attitude to his wife is a curious mixture of cynicism and some contempt (he calls her an accomplished liar and manipulator), need to establish mastery, and affection, in spite of all. He has no intention of leaving the marriage. In her turn, the wife has expressed fear of his retaliation and anger, as she in fact laid the charge for which he served a prison term. She claimed she would get a legal separation and a divorce. This avowal was somewhat discounted by her continuing to visit him in prison, taking care to make herself as attractive as possible. In the course of this protracted struggle, neither parent showed a consistent interest and concern for the children. The eldest boy, aged 14, became delinquent, and the girl of 16 planned to leave home as soon as possible.

A change in R's pattern took place in the course of his last prison sentence. With enforced abstinence from alcohol, he not only recovered his health, but for the first time in many years was able to think clearly about his life. He was in group therapy for several months. To some extent he began to see his own role, and to understand his wife. He still wanted to return to the marriage, but under different circumstances, and he was unhappy because his wife took the attitude that she was faultless and that he was the one who had to do all the changing. On his release, she veered between a desire to re-establish the marriage and a continuing need to punish, which was evident when she assured him that the judge promised her that if he did not find work, he would be re-arrested. R. accordingly has not yet returned to the home, realizing that, without a mutual understanding, the marriage will break down again.

Another example of a highly conflicted marriage, with criminality outside, is of Mr. V., now 38 years old, the father of two daughters, aged 4 and 2. He suffered from severe personal problems, but no fixated delinquent pattern till after his marriage at age 33.

V. was born in Central Europe of a poor farming family, came to Canada with his parents when he was 4. He was a most unhappy child, overtly hostile to his father, who was a punishing and unprotecting figure. As for his mother, she was outwardly kinder, but she would get other people to punish him if he offended her. His childhood and adolescence could be characterized by a failure to identify with any important family member, a feeling of estrangement, and difficulties in attaching himself.

As a young man, V. drifted from job to job, suffered periods of depression for which he was twice hospitalized and became involved in some unhappy love affairs. He drank periodically when unhappy.

At age 33 he married a younger women who was pregnant by him. The marriage was outstandingly difficult from the start, though the wife was both long suffering and protective. V. was not only an unsteady and unreliable worker, but he often moved his family from town to town, sometimes leaving them stranded without means. V. was fond of his wife and children, and wanted to provide for them, but he became despondent and restless when jobs did not turn out as he hoped. In emergencies, he forged small cheques, and though his wife managed to intercede for him several times, he was in the end charged and served a sentence of one year.

On his release, V. was again very severely depressed and hospitalized. This time he made what appeared a rather good recovery, showed some insight into his problems and began to plan constructively for his family. He wanted a better home for them and a steady job with some training. Most important, he showed real understanding of the effects of the poor marriage on his little girls who were suffering physical and emotional stress.

At this point, the wife, who had previously showed herself extremely sympathetic, made an abrupt about face. She began to complain very bitterly about her husband's misdeeds and his interference in her management of the home. The wife was an outwardly gentle, but very tense, woman, with many somatic complaints and a cancer phobia. She seemed to feel that too much attention was being paid to her husband, and she now made her own claims. Most of all, she did not want him in any way leading the family. V., who had meantime left the hospital, found a job and succeeded in moving his family to a better home, was at first outwardly submissive in the face of her attacks, but rapidly grew depressed under the onslaught. Many of his wife's accusations were well founded since V. had certainly been a delinquent husband, but her view was that only he was to blame and that there was no need for her to change as she was the innocent victim. In fact, she wanted him punished. Accordingly, V. not only left his job, but used household money for drink, sold furniture not yet paid for, and again forged a cheque. He was then both frightened and contrite; in this crisis, the wife forgave him, helped him evade the consequence of his forgery and restored him to his former position of dependent child.

The dynamics of these two cases show all the characteristics of the first group. Why the husband becomes antisocial outside the family is difficult to understand, except that in our particular example the wife appears to be stronger and more dominating. This may prove too frustrating for the husband. When he cannot retaliate sufficiently in the marriage itself, he displaces the problem outside. Husbands tend to blame the wives directly for the offence and punish them by committing misdeeds outside the home, which may hurt them, but they seem to feel that it will hurt the wife more. This is followed by contrition and a desire for forgiveness. Many of the wives under great provocation may entertain ideas of leaving the marriage, but even if they leave, they usually return at the slightest sign of repentance and regret. Both partners frequently claim that they resume only because of the children, not realizing how injurious their retaliatory relationship is.

The *third group* we have isolated is perhaps more difficult to delineate because the offence takes place outside the family itself. It may therefore appear unrelated to family conflict. The sequence of cause and effect, however is striking. What occurs in these cases is that the husband is faced with a loss, or the fear of a loss, of a marriage on which he is very dependent. This may be a good or a bad marriage. Sometimes there may be a severe loss outside the marriage, like unemployment, which brings out inherent weaknesses in the marriage and creates a crisis. The husband is unable to accept the situation, to find a satisfactory solution, and he goes into a depression. In the course of this depression, he will commit a criminal offence, sometimes a serious one. Very frequently this offence is committed in the hope of re-establishing a broken marriage, occasionally in retaliation or revenge against a wife. It may even be committed as a means of restoring a lost sense of security.

An example of this kind of situation is the case of Mr. C., a man in his late forties with a middle class background, who did quite well occupationally and made what appeared at least to him a good marriage.

His childhood was not a happy one. There was a great deal of constraint in the home as his father was an unreasonable, difficult man, and his mother was not overly affectionate. Great demands were made on him with regard to behaviour, scholastic attainment, and choice of friends. There was also open rivalry between himself and the only other child, a younger sister. She was considered the brighter, outstripped him at school, and perhaps as a result, he refused a university education. He took commercial courses, however, and did quite well, eventually holding a well paid and responsible position. He was timid with girls and was sexually very inexperienced.

At age 30 he married a girl ten years younger, but did not establish a home till some years later, when he left the Army. His wife was a good looking, extremely bright young woman with a large circle of friends.

The marriage went well from C.'s point of view, with some reservations. There were no children and the wife refused to consider adoption. She also insisted on continuing to work though he earned enough to support the marriage. She was very houseproud, wanted money for the home and to maintain her position in her social group. The good opinion of her friends and associates mattered a great deal to her.

Things, however, went well for about fifteen years till C. lost his job. Due to a conflict of loyalties, he did not report some irregularities on the part of his immediate superiors. The result was that all involved were dismissed, but there was no question of legal proceedings, as no loss was sustained. He was very distressed over the affair, questioning his own ethics, but there was no problem in finding other work. The wife reacted very sharply, however; she felt ashamed and humiliated at his loss of a job. She insisted on leaving their home and moved by herself to another neighbourhood. She did not at first actually refuse to return to the marriage, but kept putting off forgiveness.

From then on C. had an increasingly difficult life. He moved to another city where he earned more money, but spent it keeping in touch with his wife. As she continued to live and work on her own and established herself as a separated woman, he became very disconsolate. He struck up a friendship with a waitress in a cafe, and having no experience with clubs and night life, found himself disillusioned and angry at what he considered her immorality. In trying to regain some of the property he claims he lent her, he was accused of theft and ended by spending a short term in prison. On his release, he was hospitalized with an osteomyelitis of the jaw. Still in a state of resentment, he visited the waitress to get back some of his books and was beaten up by two of her friends to the point where again he had to be hospitalized. By this time, he had, in his own estimation, sunk far below his previous irreproachable position. He had lost his wife, his social standing, and occupationally he was now at a very low level.

At this point he found a temporary job, and was overjoyed when he was told after a short time that it would be permanent. The work, though inferior, was in his field, and for the first time in many years, the future held some promise. He began to feel that perhaps he could rebuild his life, and eventually even convince his wife to return to the marriage. When therefore he was let off a few days later because the former employee returned, his disappointment was extreme. He now felt that he must hit back at something. Quite impulsively he walked off with the company payroll, left town the same day, and moved to another city. In the course of the next two weeks, he gave away most of the money to charity, and to a needy friend, and spent the rest. He then returned and gave himself up to the police, and was given a four year sentence. His wife told him that, as he was a thief and a jail bird, he could not expect her to return to the marriage.

In trying to understand the sources of C.'s problem, it is evident that he had serious conflicts in early family life, especially with the younger sister. He felt intellectually inferior with no cause, and this impaired his achievements. He refused a university education, which would have meant exposing himself to further competition with his sister. Nevertheless, he managed his life reasonably well, though he operated below his potentialities. By lowering his aspirations, he could deal with what was for him too painful competition.

He was faced with the problem again when he married a woman with many of his sister's qualities, her dominance and her drive. Unlike the sister, however, he could not escape this problem with the wife, because she demanded a good deal. She wanted him to live up to her standards, which were, for him, impossible. He responded by giving in, instead of asserting himself. His way of meeting her attack was to withdraw and become detached, but he remained badly in need of her, and would not on his own have let her go. The wife, however, was increasingly disappointed and eventually left. It was the refusal of the wife to carry on which triggered the series of events that led to criminality.

Criminality in this case, as in others, cannot be understood only in terms of family life, but what is notable is that the major conflict that contributed to the criminality lay in the marriage itself, though it was eventually acted out in an antisocial way outside the marriage.

Another example of criminality outside marriage, precipitated by a loss, but closely related to the marriage itself, is the case of Mr. A., a 28-year-old French Canadian coming from a remote rural area, married, the father of two children.

As the youngest son and one of the last born of a family of ten, A. considers his childhood on the whole happy, in spite of the fact that his mother died when he was only 7. The father did not remarry, the eldest sister took her place and there was a close-knit family group. A.'s father was a poor farmer and, while the family did not go hungry, there was little schooling as the children had to work early. A. was a good scholar and regretted leaving school at 13, but he did not at all object to work, especially outdoors. Though rather a gentle personality, he liked sports, particularly hunting.

To better himself, he came to Montreal and lived with an older sister; then moved to a family where he married one of the daughters. He made a good work adjustment and became a garage mechanic and auto repairman. He was able to establish a comfortable home and he thought of himself as well off. His marriage was a happy one.

The first major crisis in his life came three years after marriage, when he lost his job due to a business recession, and could not find sufficient work to maintain his standard of living. The family was forced to move into one room, giving up their furniture which they prized, and he went through a difficult period of work hunting that went on for several months. A second child was born to them at this time. Eventually he found work, but he had to move his family to an outlying suburb; they were therefore isolated.

One day he went out for a walk taking his gun, for no particular reason that he now remembers, but on the way the idea occurred to him to rob a bank. He went into a small suburban bank, demanded money, which he got and then ran aimlessly into some woods nearby. He threw away his gun and did not know what to do with himself. After a while, he walked out and was arrested. He received a five year sentence for this offence.

When seen in prison shortly after he first arrived, he was in a state of grief. He wept a great deal, and he was very unhappy over his family's poor situation and his own behaviour which he could not understand. He explained that it was as if someone else had done it, that it happened to him suddenly "like a blow". His depression began to clear up when he discovered that his wife had forgiven him, and also that she was not, as he feared, abandoned and destitute. Social agencies had helped the wife to move back into town and were assisting her. Once assured about the safety and continuity of the family group which mattered so much to him, he adapted fairly well to prison. He looked forward, however, only to rejoining his family.

This type of offender, whose delinquency is precipitated by family crisis, is the nearest we can come to what is sometimes referred to as "the normal offender". This man was completely non-delinquent before, and the probability is that he will return to a non-delinquent pattern for the rest of his life unless he is too damaged by over-harsh punishment. The dynamics in this case can be seen originating in his family of origin. Certain early unresolved conflicts were passed on to the family he later established himself. In spite of the loss of the mother, the father and siblings re-established a cohesive group, where all helped one another. Undoubtedly the home grew to symbolize the lost mother. His continuing need of a family is shown in the fact that he remained with them until he came to Montreal, lived in Montreal in his sister's family and then moved to a friend's family, where he looked for the same close-knit integration and protection. This was positive, as it gave him the sense of security he needed, but the negative aspect lay in the fact that, without the family, he felt lost, at an age when he should no longer have been so dependent.

In spite of this latent insecurity, given normal conditions he was able to establish his ideal, a family similar to the one he came from, which he could now head. Along with the warmth and protection towards his wife was a great deal of dependence on her, and an underlying fear that something might destroy the good. The loss of his job recalled the loss of his own mother. When he could not re-establish himself as an earner, he saw himself losing everything, and the birth of another child added to his sense of loss and increasing panic.

As his depression grew deeper, his own family became increasingly a burden rather than a help. This is an example par excellence where, even in a good marriage with no serious psychopathology and no social problem, a crisis may lead to breakdown, here expressed in a criminal acting out.

In the *fourth group* the criminality, though occurring for the first time after the marriage, seems remote from the marital situation, and in fact the relationship to the offence is not direct. When we study the history, however, we see an individual with a severe and ongoing personality problem. The man functions fairly well in the marriage, but the pressures even in a satisfactory relationship, added to a prevalent feeling of inadequacy, may end in a criminal act. He may seek to preserve status in a marriage where he feels himself inferior, or cannot give enough. Thus the marriage, whether in itself good or the reverse, will create stress for an inadequate personality. An example of this kind of situation follows.

Mr. Y., in his early thirties, is serving a very long sentence for a series of bank hold-ups he carried out with two associates, some five years ago. He is married and has one son now 9 years old.

He was not delinquent either as a child or adolescent, and was in no trouble with the law till this very serious offence; his marriage appears an unusually good one. His offence can be seen as an outcome of his continuing problem, which his marriage in one sense relieved, but in another aggravated.

In his childhood, he was cut out of his father's affection by the latter's preference for his older sister and an exceptionally intelligent but invalid brother, who died young. The father was a man who gave little to the home and was much involved in outside activities. He was also given to petty pilfering, for which he was never caught, was an unfaithful husband who eventually left the marriage. In contrast, the mother was gentle and over-protective, but was also highly religious with a rather inflexible moral code.

Y. responded adversely to this difficult family situation, even as a child. At school he was unable to learn to read and write, and his I.Q. was assessed at below 70. Interestingly enough, in prison he has learned to read and write quite adequately, and his intelligence is manifestly normal. Y. had a hard time at school, felt himself humiliated, and responded by fighting his way out. At the same time he avoided trouble as he was very much under his mother's protection and influence. As a young man, he developed a rather devil-may-care attitude, but felt deeply and consciously insecure and inferior, due to his lack of attainment. He was nevertheless socially acceptable and made out well occupationally in a semi-skilled job as a machinist's helper. In his estimation he had little chance of achieving a rather high aspiration level.

He wanted to succeed in order to please and support in style his mother, who still dominated him, and more important, his wife. He loved his wife who was pretty, competent and evidently his superior, and he badly needed to establish himself as head of the home. In spite of a nagging sense of frustration and his inability to bestow all he wanted on his family, the marriage went very well and at no time has there been marital discord. However, after five years, he met a fellow worker, much more knowledgeable and intelligent than he, who offered him a chance to participate in get rich quick bank robberies. Y. was tempted and became involved, along with a third partner who, interestingly enough, has much the same history of a good marriage in a man with a basic longstanding emotional problem.

The robberies were successful at first and Y. spent money freely on his wife and mother. The wife soon discovered the source of his gains, but by then it was too late to prevent his continuing. The three partners were caught and given an exemplary sentence.

Fortunately for Y. both his wife and mother have stood by him, and though he has his bouts of jealousy and fear of abandonment, he is increasingly aware that he can re-establish his personal relationships on a sounder basis. Most important, he is no longer handicapped by his inability to read, and has overcome his acute social embarrassment on this account. Feeling now more adequate, able to maintain his family by his own strictly legal efforts, he will probably do well, if he is released reasonably soon on parole. Should he remain too long, and in particular if his wife cannot tolerate the separation, the prognosis is poor both for his adjustment inside the penitentiary and after.

In this case, the problem lies in Y.'s feeling of inferiority in relation to his wife and mother. Though the wife is dominant by character and attainment, she did not use this against her husband. However, his own sense of inadequacy, despite his good showing, came to mean something he must overcome by almost any means. Money and material assets symbolized for him a better picture of himself. Though there was a desire to achieve social status, the main need was to establish himself as the protector and recognized head of the household. This is shown by the fact that he used the money not for himself, but to give his wife what he felt a good husband should. He saw the criminality as the only way to overcome his financial inferiority and his personal deficiency.

In the *fifth group* we were unable to trace a significant relationship between the marriage and the offence. In some instances the marriage appeared a good one; more often it was not. Usually antisocial behaviour on a marginal level existed before the marriage, and this continued till eventual breakdown in an indictable offence.

An example is a man who in his 20's developed a pattern of black market activity, due to his need to make quick money. His dealings were sometimes within the law, usually on the fringes, gut he managed to stay out of trouble. He was promiscuous besides and did a certain amount of drinking. He met a girl, thought he was in love, and married her. She made him a good wife, but he did not even try to change his way of life following the marriage. He continued to have affairs, to spend freely in nightclubs, and to be mixed up in shady deals. In the process of this marginal activity, he was involved in a fight which resulted in manslaughter. He had meantime maintained the marriage more or less as a separate part of his life. In other words the marital relationship did not affect his man's pattern of behaviour, which eventually got him into trouble and resulted in a penitentiary sentence.

Prevention and Treatment

Having described the family offenders and some of the psychodynamics involved in their conflicted and difficult relationships, we are faced with the all-important question of prevention and treatment. Almost all offenders bring sorrow and distress to those close to them, but most especially is this true of family offenders, involving as they do every member, both in the commitment of the offence and in its consequences.

Let us say at once that in our family cases, treatment, to be successful and to avoid recidivism, must generally include the family as a whole. We cannot separate a family offender from his sphere of activity, the family itself. Needless to say, treatment for this kind of family should occur before the situation becomes so critical as to warrant a charge, or, if a charge is laid, treatment should, if possible, replace imprisonment. These cases are difficult to handle, because of overt hostility, bitterness and recrimination. Frequent recourse to courts further intensifies animosity on both sides. Agencies dealing with these families find themselves faced with a character disorder on the part of the husband, a vindictive and reproachful or a martyred wife and disturbed or delinquent children. It is understandable that these families are often classed as almost untreatable.

But many display considerable potential strength along with the only too obvious disorganization. A surprising number of husbands, for instance, are well regarded outside the home, and are good workers, taking considerable and justified pride in their capacity. This ablity to work is often one of the assets that can help restore a marriage. One should not underestimate the fact that many of our delinquent fathers feel financially and morally responsible for their families. If they evade this responsibility it is often due to a need for retaliation, or a reluctance to give to a wife with whom they are in conflict.

An even more important element is that, in these severely neurotic marriages, husband and wife have a great need of one another, whether for good or ill. Faced with prison or separation, both may be motivated for treatment. It must be stressed, however, that it is essential that the wife accepts that she, too, needs some help, otherwise a plan to restore the family generally breaks down. Unless she recognizes that she had certain needs that drove her into this kind of a marriage, and unless she also involves herself instead of only blaming the husband, the outcome is poor. On the other hand, where husband and wife both accept some responsibility, the outcome is often good. We have treated some cases successfully, where imprisonment was avoided and the family restored to better functioning. We hasten to say that treatment does not solve all problems, nor does it always result in a hoped-for establishment of a sound marriage. Though this is desirable, a well-planned separation may sometimes be the better solution. Even though the father is out of the home, the pattern of criminality may cease; there may be greater responsibility on the part of both parents, resulting in more security for the children.

In attempting to treat those offenders who have committed their offences outside the marriage, we often find that a separation has already taken place and has, in fact, been the precipitating cause of the criminal acting out. Unlike those whose offences occur within the family, the husband in this group tends to avoid a quarrel in the home because he is exceedingly dependent on the wife. It is only after he has been sometimes literally abandoned by her that he may become revengeful. Even then, the acting out has often as its aim the return to the family. We find this man in prison, having had no news from his wife for years, still living in fantasy, refusing to accept the hard realities of his situation. He continues to mourn her loss, and he is determined to restore a no longer existing marriage. This man must be helped to face the fact that his wife has left him, to pass through normal grief and mourning, difficult though it may be, and to see his wife and their relationship as it really was, assessing his own responsibility in the unhealthy marriage as much as hers. He is then able to plan, to re-establish himself and build a better life.

Where there is an ongoing personality problem, we are faced not so much with the treatment of a family, as one of helping an individual from the perspective of his own life-long inadequacy. However, though the husband needs highly individualized attention, the role of the wife cannot be overlooked. She must be aware both of her husband's problem and the resulting stresses created by his sense of deficiency and frustration even in a good marriage.

In conclusion, let us emphasize again how large is the group of late offenders who come to commit crimes as a result, direct or indirect, of a pathologic marriage, or a marital crisis. Let us remember that these are not usually habitual criminals, but people who break under the continuing stress of a highly conflicting and damaging family relationship; or they may be faced with an external situation which is too much for them. In law, an offence is described and an individual who commits it is sentenced. Many husbands and fathers who commit offences are thus sentenced. The tragedy is that so frequently by this means we evade the main problem, and we risk a repetition of an offence. In prison, the father not only fails to understand what has happened to him, and why, but he continues to fail even to support his family for whom he is responsible and who are usually on relief. The mother, in her turn, fails to maintain a stable and sound family and there is often conspicuous breakdown in the children. Everyone is punished, victim and aggressor. To continue to deal with these family offenders by punishment alone, after a law has been broken, only tends to deepen and prolong the crisis. Children of such families grow up to produce similar disorder in their turn. We do not say that people who commit these offences should be allowed to go their way, as in fact they would usually only continue their destructive pattern. But what is essential is a sound rehabilitation program, based on an evaluation of all the many sided interlocking factors, in the personality of the man, in the marriage and in the social environment. Such a program, whether the offender is in or out of prison, depends for its success on the treatment of the family as an organic whole and not with a single deviant member. This may be a complicated and difficult task, but here is where our efforts should be directed.

NOTES AND REFERENCES

1. Cormier, Bruno M.; Kennedy, Miriam; Sangowicz, Jadwiga; and Trottier, Michel: "The Latecomer to Crime." *Canadian Journal of Corrections,* Vol. 3, No. 1, Jan. 1961.
2. Kennedy, Miriam: "Dynamics Involved in Family Offences Appearing before the Court." *Canadian Journal of Corrections,* 1:50–55, No. 4, 1959.
3. _____ : "A Clinical Study of a Group of Incest Offenders." Unpublished paper given at the Second Annual Research Conference on Criminology and Delinquency, Montreal, 1960.
4. Cormier, Bruno M.: "Pathological Mourning as a Component of Murder." Unpublished paper given at the Canadian Psychoanalytic Society, Montreal, 1960.

Complementary Pathology in Families of Male Heroin Addicts

ROSLYN GANGER AND GEORGE SHUGART

As a result of a therapeutic focus on family interaction, caseworkers have increased their knowledge of the dynamics of family pathology and adaptations to stress within the family unit. This article is concerned with familial forces affecting male heroin addicts and the obvious and subtle ways in which family members, in their defensive systems, use the addict as a scapegoat. It is based on a study of more than a hundred male heroin addicts and various members of their families.[1]

THE MOTHERS OF MALE HEROIN ADDICTS

The symbiotic nature of the relationship between mothers and their addict sons has been noted and discussed by many workers in the addiction field. In her investigation of the symbiotic aspects in the mother-child relationship of drug-addicted adolescent sons, Nellie Attardo found that male adolescent addicts had had a significantly greater symbiotic tie with their mothers during latency than had schizophrenics, that the addicts' mothers had held them in a symbiotic relationship through the period when most mothers, including the mothers of schizophrenics, resolve the symbiosis.[2]

The ambivalences and the mutually dependent and destructive interactions characteristic of the mother-son relationships under study were traced in the addicts' life histories. The mothers' need to maintain their sons in a dependent position fostered their faulty development by obstructing their normal, positive aggressive drives and later interfered with whatever effort they might make—or others might make in their behalf—to achieve some degree of autonomy. The mothers bore striking resemblance to each other.

From *Social Casework* 49: 345–361, No. 6, June, 1968. Reprinted by permission of publisher.

They tended to be domineering, compulsive, anxious, and self-pitying women who seemed interested in little more than their sons' addiction problem. Although they and some addicts said that their preoccupation with the sons began as a result of the drug problem, the addicts' histories revealed that special attention had been given to them long before the addiction had begun. From their earliest days emphasis had been placed on punctuality, neatness, and what the mothers termed "respect." The sons' eating habits, social activities, and day-to-day life had also been a matter of overconcern. In a large number of instances the mothers viewed the family unit as the only appropriate social group for the son and obstructed his attempts to form close relationships with persons outside the family.

There was sufficient evidence in our experience to suggest that many of the mothers had suffered emotional deprivation at an early age. Also, their histories revealed that they had been unable to express anger toward parent figures. As mothers, they curtailed their sons' expression of rage as their own had once been curtailed. One mother said, "I felt like slapping my mother many times and that is why I would never let my son slap me." Frequently the mothers adopted a self-pitying attitude to control their sons, to make them feel too guilty to express anger toward a suffering mother. Many mothers said they attempted to make their sons less "rough and tumble," and they acknowledged a disparity between their own attitudes and others'. They quoted neighbors, for example, as saying, "Leave him alone, he's all boy"— thus testifying to their own inability to tolerate normal assertive behavior.

The mothers' lives were also circumscribed, both before and after the addiction problem emerged. Rarely had any of them formed close and meaningful relationships outside their immediate families. Their social contacts were generally limited to visiting relatives, more from a sense of obligation than for pleasure. Marital separations were common, and in instances in which marriages remained intact, husband and wife seldom shared common interests. Many mothers said that their sons had been their major source of companionship and emotional gratification.

Several mothers gave the impression of struggling to defend themselves against overwhelming feelings of anxiety. Some presented multiple psychosomatic symptoms. Frequently one heard mothers speak of "going crazy." Some projected this feeling onto their sons, saying, "I know he is out of his mind," despite the fact that they could not identify any bizarre or psychotic behavior on the son's part. Some mothers became obsessively overprotective of their sons as a result of their wish to be protected against their own impulses; one mother said, "I don't care if I get sick as long as he gets well."

The existence of unconscious fantasies and urges of a sexual nature in both the mothers and the sons was apparent and, possibly, was a contributing factor to the obvious emotional distance between mother and father. The mothers often assumed a clinging, seductive manner with their sons and had a proclivity for inappropriate physical contact with them. Some mothers were known to sleep in the same bed with an addict son. When the discussion in a mothers' and sons' therapy group turned to the sons' needs for heterosexual social life, several of the boys said they thought shyness held them back. During such a discussion, one mother snuggled close to her son and asked, "Do you want to go dancing with me?"

Some of the mothers still tucked their sons into bed, and many reported they did not go to sleep until they knew their sons had arrived home. The administrator of a halfway treatment center has reported the case of an addict who shares a bedroom with his mother while his wife and two children sleep in other bedrooms. Although the addict is twenty-six years of age, his mother still bathes him.[3] At Riverside Hospital, Percy Mason had the opportunity to read the letters mothers had written to their sons and was struck by the abundance of such words of endearment as "dearest," "darling," and "sweetheart."[4] George Vaillant, in a twelve-year follow-up study, found 72 per cent of the addicts still living with their mothers after the age of twenty-two, and 47 per cent living with a female relative as late as the age of thirty. Vaillant concludes that "adult addicts remain unusually dependent on their family of origin."[5]

Despite the fact that heroin is known to inhibit sexual desire, many mothers believed heroin increased their sons' sexual interests. Several mothers insisted, despite repeated denials by the addicts, that their sons had been introduced to drugs during a sexual orgy. Most mothers interfered with their sons' heterosexual activities. As one addict commented, "No matter what girl I brought home, my mother always had something critical to say. The girl was either too dark or too light. She even tried to break me and my wife up. If I had a fight with my wife, she'd say, 'Forget her, there are other girls.'" If the addict had a girl friend who knew nothing of his problem, the mothers were apt to inform the girl of the addiction, supposedly for the girl's benefit. One mother said, "I wouldn't wish my son on any girl."

THE FATHERS OF MALE HEROIN ADDICTS

In many instances the fathers of the addicts who were known to us had been either totally or relatively absent from the home for a large part of the addict's life. The addicts who had such fathers rarely, if at all, remembered them as emotionally responsive persons. The addicts believed that the absent fathers had left the mothers for other women, or because of alcoholism. If there had been a divorce or separation, it was rare that the addict saw his father again on any but a chance basis. Few of the fathers who had left the home made a continuing effort to maintain contact.

Fathers who remained in the home generally played an indifferent role in the dynamic structure of the family. In general, they were characterized by the addicts and mothers as nonassertive and obedient to the mothers' orders. Most addicts admitted that it was the mother who was the disciplinarian and "ruled the roost." In those instances in which the father appeared to be more outwardly assertive, his behavior seemed to be an aggressive overreaction to the mother's subtle, though real, control.

In many instances the fathers of addicts were good providers, and their sons readily acknowledged their positive attributes as hard workers. But the addicts were seldom able to recall having had any meaningful positive relationship with their fathers. Some said they recalled some closeness with their fathers at an earlier age, but it appeared that their memories were more of a fantasy than of a reality. Some addicts recalled having "done things" with their fathers, but they did not recall having confided in them or having been close to them. Most addicts, on the other hand, had confided in their mothers.

Some fathers never assumed a disciplinary role with the addict—though they might with other children. It can be speculated that they kept their feelings in control for fear that, if they released them, they might inflict severe physical damage on their sons. One father said, "I'm afraid I'd cripple or strangle him if I let go." One father said he had never been able to hit his addict son, even though he had frequently struck his daughter. Many fathers took disciplinary action upon the mothers' request, but not at the times when they themselves felt it might be in order. Some fathers were overtly and consistently punitive. One mother said: "I always had to protect my son from his father. I have a special feeling for this child. He's the only one my husband hits. Maybe he beats him because he's jealous of the special attention I give him." In the families in which the fathers were more overtly aggressive, their behavior was not experienced as constructive parental discipline; rather, the sons considered them quick-tempered, dictatorial, and punitive. Manifest hostility on the part of fathers was common, but the fathers who were not openly punitive probably had as much hostility toward the addict son as those who were overtly punitive.

The father-mother relationships in the addicts' families were characterized either by open conflict or by emotional distance, with the relationship in either case maintained on the mother's terms. The mothers sought to ensure that the addict's major relationship would be with them and usually undermined the father's position. One addict said: "My mother would send me to my father to ask what time I should be home. It was very confusing because my father would tell me eleven o'clock and my mother would then insist on ten-thirty. Why did she send me to him in the first place if she was the one who was going to make the decision?" Another son commented: "When I was talking with my father, she always cut in. I once approached my father to go out and play pool. You know, I wanted it to be like father and son. My mother came in and said, 'What do you want to go out for?' "

The behavior of the fathers of male heroin addicts is not to be explained solely by the mothers' effect on them. They performed their roles as fathers and husbands in keeping with their long-standing personality patterns. One addict said: "My mother assumed the dominant role because my father was not able to."

The father were like their own fathers, who had either left them when they were very young or maintained nonaffective relationships with them. The major familial relationships of the addicts' fathers were with their own mothers, who were generally domineering, compulsive, anxious, and self-pitying. These men seemed to marry women who were, or became, very much like their own mothers. Many of the fathers also appeared to have had a rivalous relationship with one of their own brothers. They tended to view themselves as the unsuccessful son and to feel blocked by circumstances from doing what they wanted to do or achieve. Although those who were hard workers and faithful providers might present a facade of satisfaction, they eventually revealed dissatisfaction with the nature and routine of their work. Few took advantage of opportunities for promotion, and most of them had compromised their youthful aspirations, becoming involved in jobs that did not allow full utilization of their potentialities.

The fathers directly or indirectly discouraged their sons from making full use of their work capacities, thus obstructing the rehabilitation process. They sometimes suggested that their sons take up the same occupation as theirs, a suggestion that often created anxiety in the addict fearful of competing with his father. The addicts who followed such suggestions had to maintain their accomplishments at a level lower than their fathers had achieved. Addicts generally appear to avoid surpassing their fathers in occupational and educational areas.

THE SIBLINGS OF ADDICTS

One addict's sister summed up the plight of the nonaddicted sibling in the home, commenting, "My brother has always been the center of *attraction* in the home." A fourteen-year-old male sibling said: "They care about my brother. They don't worry about me so much. When he gets into the hospital, maybe it will be different. But when he comes home, it will be the same way." The dominant preoccupation of the siblings was the addict's monopoly of parental attention and concern. They were envious of his important position in the family, the hold he exerted on the parents through the problems he created, and the parents' involvement in the minutiae of his daily life. The siblings expressed feelings of hurt and bitterness that the addict brother profited at their expense; some experienced a sense of social shame, but most deplored the material deprivation caused by the addict's financial drain on the family.

Siblings, generally, viewed the addict as the child favored by the mother, and they said that they had perceived the mother's intense concentration on the addict long before his addiction. They did not blame the mother for her overinvolvement with the addict, but displaced the blame onto the addict.

The nonaddicted siblings were, either covertly or overtly, hostile toward the addict. Some addicts reported that their siblings had been physically cruel to them during childhood. One addict revealed that his brother, two years older, had beaten him and stamped on him with no interference from either parent. Another addict revealed that his twin brother had attacked him with razors and knives. Not all the sibling rivalry was expressed in such overt hostility. In the main, the siblings argued and fought at home and went their own ways socially.

Whereas the siblings' aggression toward the addict appeared to be based on rivalry for the mother's attention and a displacement of blame for her overinvolvement with him, the addict's hostility toward his siblings appeared to be a displacement of the hostility that he was inhibited from expressing directly toward his parents. It is significant that although all the nonaddicted siblings recognized that the preaddict was the child with whom the mother was most involved, both the addict and his siblings agreed that the mother usually sided with the nonaddicted sibling when arguments and fights occurred between them. Perhaps the addict received the message that assertiveness was forbidden him generally; because of the displacement involved, the mother's taboo on the addict's aggression against his siblings was also a taboo on fantasied or actual aggression by him against her.

At the onset of addiction, the siblings generally either rejected the addict totally or became overtly involved as part of the family task force to fight the problem, though they sometimes vacillated between the two attitudes. Many of the siblings imitated the attitudes of the parents toward the addict: they gave advice and became moralistic, punitive, watchful, and pessimistic. Some of them, in effect, became mother's helper in planning and regulating the addict's life, perhaps to gain her coveted favor. In their over-involvement with the addict, they also denied his autonomy.

Many of the nonaddicted siblings tended to be successful, in striking contrast to the addict. They were good students and diligent workers and often achieved a standard of living superior to that of their parents. Many from lower-class backgrounds found ways to complete a college education and obtained good jobs. Despite their good performance, the mothers continued to center their attention on the addict son. It is possible that the very fact of the mother's over-involvement with the addict allowed the nonaddicted sibling the freedom to develop his potentials and capacities and thus prove himself more worthy of love, although he might continue to feel that he had not received it. An addict with a nonidentical twin brother reported that he and his twin brother had always fought constantly: "I don't know whether he envied me or I envied him. He always got away with more. He was always allowed to stay out, whereas I was whipped if I came home late. He could always talk back to my mother and get away with it."

Often nonaddicted siblings voluntarily tried to help the addict. Many of them offered to send the addict away from home or provided him with money to buy drugs. From our experience we learned that it was important to evaluate the kind of help offered for a potentially destructive quality. Many siblings lorded their successes over the addicts and simultaneously felt guilty for surpassing them. Though some siblings achieved more than the addicts, it is likely that their strong drive to succeed represented aggressiveness against both their mothers and their addict brothers.

DISCUSSION

It is our opinion that the complementary pathology of his family instills in the addict an inability to assert himself by obstructing his expression of normal aggressive drives. We have postulated that the addict is particularly inhibited in the areas of successful productive work and fulfilling affectional relationships and that heroin, enabling him to express anger toward a suppressive mother, may be considered to have a liberating effect. Only a few addicts are able to permit themselves constructive self-assertive behavior, and our experience indicates that their blocked assertive energy is discharged in a variety of symptomatic acting-out behaviors that, instead of evoking approval, evoke disdain.

The mother's determination to keep her son enmeshed in a close tie to her suggests that a core problem in addiction is the maternally induced block to the resolution of the oedipal conflict. In addition to the anxieties that are ordinarily aroused during the oedipal phase, which can be intensified by the maneuvers of an unwittingly seductive mother, the determination and aggressiveness with which the mothers under study pursued their designs resulted in the terrorization of the pre-addict. Since the meaning of the mother's behavior is not understood by the child, he feels her love to be both desirable and dangerous. Under such circumstances the normal urge toward independence carries with it the penalty of castration. To survive, therefore, the child suppresses and subverts normal sexual and aggressive drives; the pathological dependence that ensues is not a desired and acceptable dependence, but a survival maneuver—a defense against anticipated destruction. Behind the shield of dependence lies fear and anger and feelings of guilt arising from the child's inability to distinguish the mother's appropriately maternal feelings from her sexualized feelings. Moreover, the mother who surrounds her child with an aura of anxiety or overconcern for reasons incomprehensible to the child arouses in him a complementary anxiety that he is in some way inferior, inadequate, or unworthy.

A family environment that stifles assertiveness during the important developmental years and instills guilt-laden feelings toward assertiveness continues to be operant after the son becomes addicted. We must keep in mind that the addict has already incorporated early family attitudes into his personality structure. Anxiety stemming from a son's conflicted feelings toward his mother may be transformed into panheterosexual anxiety and hamper his relationship with wife or girl friend. Also, a tendency to re-enact the original mother-son relationship may be observed in the addict's choice of a wife or girl friend. Anxiety related to job performance may persist in relation to authority-supervisory figures, whether male or female. In addition, the addict's internalized prohibitions against work assertiveness hamper him in any potentially successful work situation.[6] We have observed that many addicts become addicted a year or two before graduation from high school, and that, if indeed they are graduated, their grades have dropped markedly prior to graduation. We have also observed their inability to hold jobs or to persevere in activities in which they express an interest or show a talent. We have often observed that, soon after receiving a job promotion, some become re-addicted or admit themselves to a hospital for detoxification if still using heroin—and this action should not be mistaken for a desire to be detoxified in order to hold the job. The addict's inability to maintain positive relationships with an employer is demonstrated by a frequent tendency, when he leaves a job, to give an inept excuse that makes his employer turn against him; it is as if he has lost his usual ability to lie his way shrewdly out of dilemmas. The same phenomenon may be observed in relation to retraining programs; he frequently completes a course and then fails to utilize his new skill.

CONCLUSION

Rehabilitative approaches to addicts that emphasize vocational training, job-finding, rehousing, and medication will not be successful with such addicts as we have described unless they are psychologically prepared to make constructive and productive use of these necessary rehabilitative aids. The addict must be prepared for the anxieties attendant upon his entry into constructive living, and he must receive continuous and unflagging support through the many crises that arise along the way. If a separation from the family is to be effected and effective, the addict must be prepared to accept this separation by being helped to give up the neurotic counterparts of his personality that lead to the inhibition of normal self-assertion. Guilt and anxiety accompanying normal assertive acts must be worked through, for such addicts carry anxiety about assertiveness with them, regardless of where or with whom they live or work.

NOTES AND REFERENCES

1. Ganger, Roslyn, and Shugart, George: "The Heroin Addict's Pseudoassertive Behavior and Family Dynamics." *Social Casework* 47:643–649, Dec. 1966.
2. Attardo, Nellie: "Symbiotic Factors in Adolescent Addiction." *Journal of the Long Island Consultation Center* 4:37–38, Fall, 1965.
3. Personal communication from Father W. L. Damian Pitcaithy, Administrator, Samaritan Halfway Society, Jamaica, New York.
4. Mason, Percy: "The Mother of the Addict." *The Psychiatric Quarterly Supplement* 32: 191, Part 2, 1958.
5. Vaillant, George E.: "A Twelve-Year Follow-Up of New York Narcotic Addicts: I. The Relation of Treatment to Outcome." *American Journal of Psychiatry* 122:733, Jan. 1966.
6. See Bieber, Irving: "Pathological Boredom and Inertia." *American Journal of Psychotherapy* 5: 215–222, April, 1951.

PART 6

FAMILIAL ADAPTIVE PATTERNS TO DEVIANCY

Although deviancy tends to have disaffective and disintegrative effects upon most families, some are able to make adjustments or adaptations which enable them to continue their existence as a viable social unit. There is wide variation, however, in the patterns or modes of adaptation utilized by families, several of which are illustrated in this section.

Insights into these family adjustment configurations are offered in light of some of the theoretical perspectives outlined in the introductory essay. These theoretical perspectives suggest several mechanisms by which families might better adjust to a deviancy crisis; they also have explanatory value with regard to the various ongoing processes concomitant to family adjustment. Many of the specific patterns which have been articulated and illustrated in previous articles, as well as some of those illustrated in this section, may be better explained and understood in terms of the theoretical perspectives presented earlier.

Several adaptive patterns, for example, may easily be couched in terms of role theory. Just as a crisis might be precipitated by the removal or loss of a family member and his specific role duties and responsibilities, the adaptive process may also be viewed as either the adjustment of the family to the disequilibrium associated with the vacated role or the subsequent addition of a new member to assume the role or both. In the former situation, the family might simply reorganize itself to reassign and thus redistribute the particular role duties and responsiblities of the lost member. In the absence of the father due to death or imprisonment, for example, there may be an older son who can effectively assume some segments of the father's role such as economic support or discipline of the younger children. Additionally, the wife/mother might take employment to help support the family.

Given this same situation, the vacated role might be allocated to a new member of the household, rather than distributed among the existing members. This might be effected through the mother's remarriage, or by having a relative or inlaw join the household, or perhaps by transferring the household unit to an entirely new location such as the home of relatives or parents. If the family must reallocate the role duties to the remaining members, the ensuing period of reorganization may be more stressful and demanding of the members than if a replacement were found to fill the vacated role.

Still another problem may occur with respect to the role needs of the family should deviancy dictate the absence of one of the members for only a temporary period. Here the family may be faced with an especially difficult dilemma—the decision of whether to seek a temporary replacement for the vacated status, or to seek a permanent replacement, thus abandoning the deviant member. Still another alternative would be to temporarily suspend the normal family role configurations by means of a short-term reorganization designed to sustain the family in such a manner that the deviant might later return to take up his former role. Of course, the choice exercised by a given family from among these alternatives will depend initially upon the nature and seriousness of the deviancy, second, upon the importance of the role to the family, third, upon the adequacy of the deviant's prior performance of this role, and finally, in the overall level of integration and organization of the family unit.

Familial adaptive patterns might also be viewed from the perspective of their functional reactions to both intergroup and intragroup conflict.[1] This theoretical orientation is helpful in understanding the adaptations and adjustments to deviancy crises which result, not in the removal or loss of a family member, but in some sort of conflict within the family or between the family and the neighborhood or community. As indicated in the introductory essay, conflict may be either integrative or disruptive, depending again upon the nature of prior family integration and the nature of the conflict-producing situation. Thus, a family member's deviancy might effect greater family cohesion or the outcome of the crisis might be further disintegration of the family.

An additional analytical approach to the adaptive processes of families affected by deviancy utilizes some of the basic social process concepts delineated by Park and Burgess, and based upon the writings of Simmel.[2] Among these various social processes which they articulate, perhaps the one most useful here is accommodation. Accommodation refers to the process by which two or more parties, either overtly or covertly, bring about an arrangement whereby conflict is avoided either through some form of compromise or through limiting interaction to only those areas in which no conflict exists. Thus, a family might learn to live with a member's deviant behavior either by arranging a compromise with the deviant, reorganizing the family so that the deviant's behavior does not interfere with family functioning, or by simply ignoring the deviant member's errant behavior. Again, the type of accommodation reached would depend on the family involved and the nature of the deviancy.

There is one final possibility regarding families adapting to deviancy. This is the situation in which the individual's deviancy has very little impact upon the family initially, because either the normative structure of the family itself is such that socially deviant behavior does not stand in clear violation of the family norms, or because the family itself is enmeshed in a deviant subculture. This type of adaptation, if it really qualifies for the label, might more likely be found among families living at a poverty level and particularly those located in social ghettos. For example, illegitimacy within the slum family, and especially within the very poor black family, is so endemic as to be considered normal. Thus, this behavior, defined by the larger society as deviant, would not necessarily be such from the standpoint of the family.

A number of the articles in this collection, although included to illustrate other aspects of the relationship between deviancy and the family, have demonstrated some of the adaptive processes and techniques which families might employ to cope with the impact of deviancy. The best examples of adaptation and adjustment are illustrated by those cases involving deviancy of the children in the family. Illustrations include the case of the pregnant daughter and the instance of the homosexual son. Apparently, more efficacious adjustments are possible when the deviancy involves children than when it involves parents because of the gravity of adult role responsibilities in the family structure.

The selection treating wifebeating and the one concerning father-daughter incest both illustrate special types of accommodation, although in these cases the accommodations reached were themselves deviant in nature. Also, the reading about abandoned children deals with the adjustment not of the deviant but of the victim of the deviant behavior, namely the child who has been abandoned. Another pattern of adjustment, also somewhat deviant itself, is the focus of the article on mate-swapping, in which this unconventional behavior is viewed as an accommodative device to cope with possible marital problems or frustrations.

The articles in this final section illustrate a variety of adjustment patterns and adaptation to a number of different forms of deviant behavior.

MAINTENANCE

Clark Vincent, a leading authority on the subject of illegitimacy, discusses a little known type of illegitimacy in his article, "Illicit Pregnancies Among Married and Divorced Females." Such pregnancies have received relatively little attention because most studies of illegitimacy are concerned with the teenaged unwed mother. Postmarital and extramarital pregnancies occur less frequently than unwed pregnancies, and society is less likely to display the same moral indignation with such deviancy as it does with the unwed pregnancy. Furthermore, not only is the existence of this type of pregnancy less well known, but the attendant circumstances are also less well documented, since married women can often successfully assign paternity to their husbands or are better able to seek an abortion, illegal or otherwise.

This selection represents a departure from the previous articles because Vincent directs his remarks to physicians who are likely to have such women as patients. Thus, the thrust of the article is instructional and intended to provide the physician with insight into counseling his patient for the purpose of maintaining the marital relationship, if possible, in light of an adulterous pregnancy. In the case of the divorced pregnant woman, the doctor is instructed on the maintenance of her self-image and life style, with an aim toward minimizing the disruption to her life. This article is included as an illustrative discussion of the circumstances surrounding this particular type of deviancy and some means of adjustment to it.

There is no way to determine the statistical frequency of these types of illegitimate pregnancies, but some indication may be gained from the general statistics on illegitimacy for women over the age of 25 years, where there has been a notable increase. Such a trend is also supported by the statistics from a study done earlier by Vincent. The overall indication is that this type of pregnancy may be more prevalent than many would suspect.

The article also examines some of the contributive factors involved for both the pregnant divorcee and the illicitly pregnant married woman. In many cases the divorcee retains the relaxed attitude toward the use of contraception developed during her married years. This attitude is reinforced by the fact that in many cases the father of the illegitimate child is her former husband, who may occasionally visit for their mutual sexual gratification. Where the father is not her former husband, the woman's coital activity may result from the need for continued sexual gratification, the need to feel desired and needed as a woman, or from an attempt to remarry.

In the instance of married women pregnant by someone other than the husband, the causal situation is almost always an extramarital affair. Accordingly, Vincent discusses some of the situational factors which are related to such an affair, along with some of the difficulties involved in ending one. Affairs, according to the author, usually progress sequentially in such a fashion that the participants themselves are often relatively unaware of the outcome and its consequences. The article also suggests that the affairs ended gradually usually offer the most successful results. Great emphasis is placed upon the patient's understanding of the context in which the affair occurred in order that she may assuage some of the guilt resulting from her illicit pregnancy.

Although this article addresses itself to the illegitimate pregnancy and the subsequent treatment of the woman patient, it would also be interesting to know what happens to the children of such pregnancies. It is implied that many of these pregnancies are now aborted, but in fact there must be a significant number which are carried to term.

CONCEALMENT

Perhaps the most bizarre type of adaptation or adjustment of a family to the deviant behavior of one of its members is the family's concealment of the deviant behavior. This concealment might take on a number of forms, according to the nature and extent or seriousness of the behavior involved. For example, the family as a unit may desire to conceal the deviant behavior of one or more of its members from the surrounding community of friends and neighbors. In other cases one or a combination of members of the family might wish to conceal the deviancy from other members of the family both within and outside the household. More than likely, the degree of effort made to conceal a deviant act is directly related to the amount of stigma attached to the act as well as the degree of perceived success in the concealment.

Concealment actually represents a type of accommodation. This is due to the fact that the members of the family who are privy to the knowledge of the deviancy must come to some mutual agreement with respect to shielding the deviant member. The success of the arrangement depends upon everyone's participation in the deception, no matter how distasteful the entire matter might be to some of the members.

In Clifton Bryant's article, "The Concealment of Stigma and Deviancy as a Family Function," the author points out a number of possibilities wherein individual members, parts of families, or entire family units might desire to conceal not only deviant acts but also a variety of other situations which might bring stigma and shame to the family. The lengths to which a family might go to hide their problem range from simply not telling anyone about the problem, in the case of a problem of low visibility, to the family's changing its name and moving to a new community in an attempt to completely renew its identity.

REDEFINITION

As an adaptive pattern to deviancy in the family, redefinition as dealt with in this section is an unusual as well as relatively infrequent variation of adaptation and adjustment. Redefinition is unusual because it does not require a radical change in the deviant behavior of the individual; rather, it alleviates many of the problems generated by the deviancy through a process of redefining the deviant behavior as normative. That is, rather than the deviant having to modify his behavior, the social or public definition of his behavior is altered in such a manner that he is no longer labeled or treated as deviant. Thus he is able to enjoy a more normal existence relatively free from the handicap of social and legal incriminations.

That this type of adaptation to deviancy is relatively rare is evidenced by the fact that the public has demonstrated considerable reluctance to change its definitional posture in regard to some types of behavior, especially those forms considered sinful or indicative of moral weakness. For example, only recently has a public redefinition of mental illness occurred which permits these persons to be treated as patients rather than as outcasts possessed of the devil. The same was true for alcoholism, as well as for a number of organic diseases, such as epilepsy or diabetes, which carried pejorative social definitions.

The next article, "Wives, Families and Junk: Drug Abuse and Family Life," illustrates redefinition as an adaptive process. It is basically a study of the wives of drug addicts, some of whom are themselves addicted, but the process of redefinition is introduced because all of the addicts in the study are participants in a methadone maintenance program. Through participation in the program, the addicts come to be redefined, not only by society, but more importantly, by themselves, as patients rather than dope fiends.

The study compares three groups of wives on a number of emotional, psychological, and interactional variables. The groups were divided among the non-addicted wives of male addicts, those wives of addicts who were also addicted, and a comparative group of non-addict wives of non-addict husbands. Although the study is more directly concerned with comparing these groups of wives, the underlying thrust of the findings relates to the renewed stability and strengthened organization of the families of the addicts due to the redefinition of their situations via the methadone program. It was found, for example, that the husbands and fathers reassumed their major roles in a significant fashion after entering the program. They took an increased responsibility in the discipline of the children and generally participated in family activities to a greater extent. This was probably the result of their not having to spend so much of their time out trying to secure their drug needs in the manner of the street addict.

Further evidence of increased family adjustment was seen in their improved sexual adjustment with their wives, their better sleeping habits, their tendency to spend more time at home, and their increased ability to hold better and more stable jobs. Obviously, the redefinitional process serves a useful purpose with respect to improving the family situation of the addict, although the individual deviant still maintains his addiction.

REORGANIZATION

That family life can be greatly disrupted by a deviancy crisis has been amply demonstrated by several of the previous articles. However, some families are better able to adjust to crises by going through a reorganizational process either by ejecting the deviant and learning to get along without him or by restructuring the family situation in such a way that the deviant plays no role vital to the family organization. These reorganization processes are described in "The Adjustment of the Family to Alcoholism."

As in the preceding article, the data for this study were gained from the wives of the deviants, in this instance, alcoholics. Some of the wives were members of Alcoholics Anonymous Auxiliary, an organization for the spouses of alcoholics, and some were the wives of hospitalized alcoholics to which the researcher had access. The approach of the article is to treat alcoholism as a family crisis as it goes through its various stages—crisis, disorganization, recovery, and reorganization—as delineated by Hill and discussed in the introductory essay.[3] The author also introduces the concepts of both primary and secondary crises: primary crisis applies to the drinking behavior of the husband/father, and the secondary crisis refers to the various consequences which result from the drinking problem such as nonsupport, desertion, and so forth.

The process of redefinition also plays an important part in determining the manner in which the family responds or reacts to the alcoholic crisis. If the deviant behavior is defined as weakness or sinfulness, then the deviant member is likely to be rejected, whereas if his behavior is defined as illness, he is more likely to receive moral support and encouragement from his family. The most significant part of the discussion, however, is that concerned with the final stages of the crisis, in which the various modes of reorganization of the family occur, if in fact the family is able to hold itself together. These modes of reorganization may occur either with or without the deviant member, depending upon his own response to available treatment.

INNOVATION

The introduction of new and perhaps radical techniques for the rehabilitation and adjustment of deviants and their families frequently generates a variety of problems, many of which are related to acceptance by the public. The significance of the public definition of a situation involving social deviancy has already been illustrated. The success of such programs as that described in the article, "Conjugal Visiting at the Mississippi State Penitentiary," will depend largely upon the public's willingness to allow such programs to be developed and instituted. Actually, the unique conjugal visitation arrangements described in the article are not new; the program has been in existence for four or five decades. However, it is innovative in the sense that it has been publicly recognized only recently and is now being used in only a small number of prisons throughout the country. Also, it constitutes a radical departure from the traditional visitation regulations at most prisons.

Conjugal visitation allows the married prisoner to visit with his wife in private and to engage in coitus if they so desire. However, the visitation program described here is actually more comprehensive because the entire family may participate in the visits. There is an additional aspect of the program which allows the prisoner to go home on a leave-of-absence under special circumstances. The entire program, which operates almost entirely on an informal basis, is justified on the grounds that it helps to maintain family stability and unity while the husband/father is incarcerated.

The physical arrangement of the prison allows for a casual and private atmosphere in which the inmate may visit with his family. The penitentiary consists of a number of widely scattered camps, each of which houses about 100 inmates. The families are allowed to drive into the prison proper, which is a large plantation, and then to proceed the several miles on to the particular camp. There is an abundance of open space in which the prisoners may visit with their wives and children, and while another inmate looks after the children, the husband and wife may avail themselves of the little houses which have been constructed specifically for the conjugal visits.

There is strong agreement among inmates, camp guards, and officials that the conjugal visitation program does play a major role in the maintenance of a stable family situation until the inmate is paroled.

REHABILITATION

Probably the most often stated purpose of any correctional institution is the rehabilitation of those committed to its custody. This is especially the case with the institutions whose clients are young delinquents, and it is at these institutions that more actual rehabilitative activity takes place. Most prisons, for example, cite rehabilitation as their primary purpose, but actually are able to demonstrate very little effort or success in this regard.

Among those concerned with the treatment of juvenile offenders, it has long been an accepted fact that very little could be accomplished if the delinquent were returned to the same home and family environment from which he came, and which in a sense produced the problem initially. Thus, there has been a great deal of interest in developing techniques by which the whole family might be rehabilitated to some extent, or at least some change effected in the juvenile's home environment. The article, "Families Come to the Institution: A 5-Day Experience in Rehabilitation," describes an experiment in which an institution for juvenile offenders attempted to involve the entire families of its inmates in a comprehensive and concentrated period of therapy and interaction.

A number of sporadic attempts to involve the families led up to the experiment as it finally evolved. In addition to conferring with parents on visiting days, the staff personnel had also tried making visits to the homes of the boys with the boys themselves. The results of these attempts were somewhat limited, but were productive enough to encourage the staff to try a more controlled family therapy experiment. The plan for a "Family Camp" emerged out of the staff discussions, the basic idea being that selected families would be invited to spend an entire week at the institution with their sons. The purpose of the visit was to both submit the families to some limited forms of therapy as well as to seek to involve the families in the treatment of their sons. The activities of the week centered around therapy and conference sessions along with recreation designed to involve the entire family.

The writer is very cautious in his assessment of the benefits of the program, although he indicates that the staff were all highly enthusiastic about the future possibilities for such a program of total family rehabilitation.

REINTEGRATION

The last article of this collection, "A Parolee Tells Her Story," was written under a pseudonym and is a first person account of one family's reunification and reintegration after both the writer and her husband were sent to prison for writing bad checks. Although the account is overly sentimental, several aspects of the reintegration process emerge, and it is clear that if some circumstances of their situation had been different, reintegration might not have been possible.

Among the factors contributing to the successful outcome of this case was the healthy prison experience of the writer, the understanding of her employer about her past criminal record, her apparently strong relationship with her husband, and certainly her own personal fortitude. The account briefly demonstrates that some ex-convicts can be rehabilitated and their families reintegrated, given the proper response and treatment by the social world to which they return.

NOTES AND REFERENCES

1. See, Coser, Lewis: *The Functions of Social Conflict*. New York: The Free Press, 1956, especially Chap. 4 and 5.
2. Park, Robert E.; and Burgess, Ernest W.: *Introduction to the Science of Sociology*. Chicago: University of Chicago Press, 1921, Chap. 10.
3. Waller, Willard: *The Family* (rev. by Reuben Hill). New York: The Dryden Press, 1951, pp. 464–468.

Illicit Pregnancies Among Married and Divorced Females

CLARK E. VINCENT

Physicians, more than any other professional group, have long been aware of the problems posed by *postmarital* pregnancies (those occurring in divorced women) and by *extramarital* pregnancies (those occurring in married women impregnated by men other than their husbands). Although the incidence of such pregnancies is impossible to ascertain, the limited and highly selective information which is available suggests that, during the past three decades, postmarital and extramarital pregnancies in this country have either increased in incidence or have been more openly admitted. . . .

The information and impressions presented in this chapter were derived from the author's research in cooperation with more than five hundred physicians.[1]

EXTENT OF THE PROBLEM

Data on illegitimacy available from the National Center for Health Statistics do not specify whether the mothers are married, divorced, or never married. Therefore we have no way of knowing how many of the estimated 300,000 illicit births in the United States during 1966 were to divorced women or to married women impregnated by men other than their husbands. Nor do we have any way of ascertaining how many of the approximately 4,000,000 live births occurring in this country annually result from postmarital and extramarital coition but are not reported as illicit.

We do know, on the bases of data reported from thirty-five states and estimates projected for the fifteen states not reporting illegitimacy, that

From Vincent, Clark: "Illicit Pregnancies Among Married and Divorced Females," in Vincent, Clark E.: *Human Sexuality in Medical Education and Practice*. 1968, pp. 472–484. Courtesy of Charles C Thomas, Publisher, Springfield, Illinois. By permission of the publisher and author.

between 1938 and 1965 the increase in the illegitimacy rate was much greater among women aged twenty-five and above than among those aged fifteen to nineteen (more than five times as great in the 25- to 34-year age group, and more than three times as great in women 35 to 39 years of age). These figures (shown in Table 1) suggest that extramarital and postmarital conceptions may be responsible for a greater proportion of illicit births than is commonly assumed.

TABLE 1. RATE OF ILLEGITIMATE BIRTHS IN THE U.S. FOR 1938 AND 1965*

(By age of mother)

Year	Under 15	15–19	20–24	25–29	30–34	35–39	40 and over
	Age of Mother						
Rate of Illegitimacy (Illicit Births Per 1,000 Unmarried Females)							
1938	0.3	7.5	9.2	6.8	4.8	3.4	1.1
1965	0.7	16.7	38.8	50.4	37.1	17.0	4.4
Increase from 1938 to 1965 (%)	133	123	322	641	673	400	300

*Adapted from the following sources: Schacter, Joseph, and McCarthy, Mary: Illegitimate births: United States, 1938–57. *Vital Statistics—Special Reports, Selected Studies, 47* (No. 8), Washington, U.S. Government Printing Office, 1960; and *Vital Statistics of the United States, 1965.* Washington, U.S. Department of Health, Education and Welfare, 1967, vol. I (Natality), Tables 1–26 and 1–27.

Only a few studies have differentiated among pre-, extra-, and postmarital pregnancies. One study,[2] conducted in a metropolitan county in California and involving 736 illegitimate births during one year, disclosed that 137 women (19%) were married (Table 2). This study also indicated that postmarital and extramarital pregnancies are more often attended by physicians in private practice. The fact that very few studies are made of unwed mothers who are attended by physicians in private practice has helped to maintain the emphasis on the young, never-married mothers who go to maternity homes or county hospitals where they are more easily studied. Projecting the figures from the California study to the national scene, we might expect that the 300,000 illicit births estimated annually involve about 15,000 married women and about 54,000 divorced women.

The minimum attention given to extramarital and postmarital pregnancies is consistent with society's tendency to emphasize only selected aspects of a given social problem such as illegitimacy. The emphasis upon 130,000 teen-age unwed mothers in 1965 obscured the 170,000 who were twenty to forty-four years of age and ignored the fact that there were an estimated 45,000 to 75,000 divorced and married women who were illegitimately pregnant and potentially in need of counseling. Most of these women will, at some time, consult a physician, and some of them will seek counseling help concerning either their illicit pregnancies or their extramarital affairs. I hope that the following discussion will be of some help to physicians confronted by such patients. It is based on my general impressions derived from (1) data obtained from questionnaires answered by more than three hundred divorced and married women who were illegitimately pregnant, (2) counseling sessions with more than two hundred such women, and (3) available literature and discussions with physicians attending such women.

TABLE 2. DISTRIBUTION OF 736 ILLEGITIMATE BIRTHS DURING ONE YEAR IN ALAMEDA COUNTY, CALIFORNIA*

(By marital status of mother and by situation in which attended)

	Situation in Which Attended			
Marital Status of the Mother	Private Practice No. %	Booth Memorial Hospital No. %	Alameda County Hospital No. %	Alameda County Totals No. %
Single, never married	(106) 60	(153) 81	(280) 75	(539) 73
Divorced or separated 9 mos. or more	(47) 27	(21) 11	(69) 18	(137) 19
Married, but not to baby's father	(18) 10	(8) 4	(2)	(28) 4
Marital status not given	(4) 2	(7) 4	(21) 6	(32) 4
Total	(175) 99	(189) 100	(372) 99	(736) 100

*Adapted from Vincent, Clark E.: *Unmarried Mothers*. New York, Free Press, 1961, p. 56, Table 1.

A basic premise underlying the discussion is that physicians who seek to give counsel as well as medical care to such women will rarely be involved in psychotherapy but will be education-consultant oriented—an orientation consistent with the physician's time limitations and with the patient's need to be heard and to be given information.

THE PREGNANT DIVORCEE[3]

For at least two reasons, the physician who is consulted by a pregnant divorcee needs to be aware of some of the social and psychologic factors involved in postmarital pregnancies: (1) Such an awareness will increase his own understanding of the problem; and (2) the patient needs to know that her physician understands some of the contributing factors. In most cases the patient does not seek the physician's approval so much as she seeks and needs one person's understanding of how an out-of-wedlock pregnancy could happen to a woman who regards herself as normal and moral. The physician who has read William Goode's book, *After Divorce*,[4] will have better empathy with the pregnant divorcee and hence will be better able to help her gain perspective concerning the circumstances and factors involved in her illicit conception.

One of the factors contributing to postmarital pregnancies is the *reduced sexual caution of divorced women*. This is due in part to a desire to escape the socially stigmatized category of the divorcee as soon as possible, and in part to habits of heterosexual interaction acquired during marriage. Most divorcees and some widows discover very quickly that readjustments have to be made in their relationships with other men after the loss of a husband. Many men perceive the divorcee as easy sex prey since they assume she is accustomed to sexual intercourse, misses it, and therefore will welcome their advances as a favor. The divorcee herself may inadvertently foster such a view. While married and accompanied by her husband, she may have become accustomed to fairly open and frank discussions of sex in mixed groups; now, however, she has to relearn some of the coyness that traditionally accompanies courtship. Without such coyness and under the implicit pressure of society to prove, by means of a successful marriage, that it was not *she* who failed in the first marriage, she may permit her involvement with men after divorce to progress much more rapidly than she means to—until she finds that she is pregnant and the man has lost interest.

A second contributing factor is that *an unknown proportion of divorces involve a period of continued, sporadic coition between the ex-partners*. In cases of "friendly" divorce, many couples report that the continuation of coition, with no love or family obligations expected, is mutually enjoyable. If pregnancy occurs, it is terminated by abortion in an unknown number of cases. When abortion is either unavailable or unacceptable to the woman, however, she is very reluctant to name her former husband as the father. Understandably, she feels that others would think her foolish for having continued coition with her husband after divorcing him.

In cases where the divorce was not mutually desired, the wife may view intercourse, and even pregnancy, as a potential means of reclaiming her husband. Pregnancy may also be desired by divorcees who, as one stated, "want a memory of him. . . . I hope it's a boy that looks just like him . . . that way a part of him will always be with me." There are also ex-husbands who desire a reconciliation and who finally succeed in persuading their ex-wives to engage in intercourse "for old times' sake"—only to find that the resulting pregnancy makes reconciliation even more impossible.

The physician's awareness of such background factors will make it possible for him to communicate to the patient his understanding of the problems she shares with many other divorced women. Some physicians save time by suggesting that the pregnant divorcee read *After Divorce* before her second appointment. With the assurance that her physician understands some of the web of circumstances leading to her predicament, the patient will be more receptive to his medical guidance and will be better able to maintain the context in which her illicit conception occurred.

EXTRAMARITAL PREGNANCIES AND AFFAIRS

Why does she tell?

Perhaps the most puzzling question concerning the extramarital pregnancy is why a married woman ever reveals that it was not her husband who impregnated her. The answers provided by physicians fall into two categories. The first category includes cases in which the wife seeks counseling help from the physician because the husband knows he is not the father and the marriage is threatened, and cases in which the wife seeks help in resolving her own feelings and planning her course of action without telling her husband of her problem. Answers in the second category mention the woman's need for at least one confidant and her fear that she will reveal the information inadvertently while under the influence of anesthesia during delivery.

The physician's feeling about this responsibility concerning the feelings, attitudes, and wishes which the mother may express under the stress or anesthesia of delivery will depend on his view of the professional ethics involved. Some physicians report that they ignore, or compartmentalize, such information as being unrelated and irrelevant to their medical role. Others state that they always discuss with the patient any "confidences" revealed during delivery if it seems likely that the attitudes expressed at that time will jeopardize her marital and mental health. Still others call in a consulting psychiatrist. The professional ethic concerning the patient's confidences is of long standing; but subsequent discussions with the patient about "confidences" uttered during periods of extreme stress or while partially anesthetized may involve considerations of the future welfare of both the mother and the child. The procedure followed will obviously depend upon a number of factors peculiar to each case and to each physician. More open discussion of the professional ethics involved and of the results that might be expected from each method of handling such problems is needed to provide guidelines for medical students and young physicians.

Since almost all extramarital pregnancies are the result of extramarital liaisons, it seems appropriate to discuss at this point some of the factors both inside and outside marriage that are responsible for development of such liaisons, and to consider ways in which the physician can help married couples to mend the damage done to their relationship by the involvement of either partner in an extramarital affair.

Arthur Miller's play, *The Seven-Year Itch,* contains many insights concerning the almost imperceptible manner in which the marital relationship becomes sufficiently dull, boring, and unrewarding as to set the stage for an affair. "The itch" for a relationship more vital, romantic, and meaningful than the current marriage is not limited, however, to the seventh year. It can as easily come in the fourth, fourteenth, twentieth, or thirtieth year.

Occupational Propinquity as a Factor

If and when the itch does occur, an extramarital liaison is facilitated in today's society by occupational settings which encourage the development of heterosexual intimacy. Eyebrows would quickly rise if the husband were to have coffee or lunch with the wife of his neighbor several times a week; but within the work situation it is possible for male-female relationships to develop during coffee breaks, lunch periods, and shared "business projects," without any raised eyebrows. The role of occupational propinquity in extramarital involvement may be illustrated (not proven) by data from a study which included the occupations of 316 women illegitimately pregnant and *their reports* concerning the occupations of the men who impregnated them.[5] To give only a few examples, five nurses were impregnated by five physicians; nine teachers were impregnated by nine teachers; five legal secretaries were impregnated by five lawyers; five executive secretaries were impregnated by five executives; four medical receptionists were impregnated by two dentists, one intern, and one lab technician; a bookkeeper was impregnated by an accountant; and two bus drivers were impregnated by two bus drivers.

Although occupational propinquity is obviously not the only factor involved, it is one important characteristic of modern society which facilitates the slow, almost imperceptible development of heterosexual intimacy outside of marriage.

Imperceptible Development of Affairs

It is my impression that the vast majority of "affairs" develop in such a way that the parties involved are only belatedly aware of how far the relationship has progressed. Relatively few married people deliberately set out to become involved in an affair (by an affair I mean emotional involvement and not a one-night-stand or roll-in-the-hay). More typically, it is as if there were a scale from 1 to 10, with point 1 representing perhaps a cup of coffee or a drink with a member of the opposite sex and point 10 representing coition. Few people move in one giant stride from step 1 to step 10. More frequently, they take one step at a time; but once they have arrived at step 9, then step 10 is no further away than step 2 was from step 1.

Emphasizing the "imperceptible" pace at which affairs may develop can be both reassuring and disquieting for the female patient who asks her physician to help her be more sexually responsive and attractive "to keep my husband from looking elsewhere." As one wife states this ambivalence, "It helps knowing that it doesn't happen with the drop of a hat; but if it happens so slowly, how will I know about it in time to stop it?" Such ambivalence, however, can provide high motivation for both husband and wife to work at improving the overall marital relationship, rather than fuming at the itch or symptom of marital disease. Also, it can help the couple realize that very few things of real value can safely be taken for granted.

What Kind of Adultery?

The physician confronted by the patient who is castigating his or her spouse for committing adultery may provide the patient with perspective by asking, "What kind of adultery?" In response to the patient's look of puzzlement, he can then point out that it is possible to commit *religious, recreational, or ideologic* adultery, and so forth. This statement will require the further explanation that many individuals who never commit sexual adultery have far more religious, recreational, or ideologic intercourse with other persons of the opposite sex than with their own spouses. The total exclusion of the wife from some of these areas is sometimes associated with more hurt and humiliation for her than is sexual adultery, since the latter is usually less public and does not exclude her entirely. Curiously enough, those who appear to be most traumatized by sexual adultery are frequently the ones who avow that sex is of minor importance; yet they are far more upset by sharing in this area than in other more "important" areas.

By asking "What kind of adultery?" the physician can stimulate the patient to reexamine his or her hierarchy of values and the degree of consistency between belief and practice. Some patients regain confidence when they perceive how many marital areas are still shared and unadulterated. Others may acknowledge for the first time that sex is a far more important aspect of marriage than they had previously admitted; these patients then begin to develop a more meaningful sexual relationship with their spouse in order to preclude outside competition. Still others discover that few, if any, areas of their marriage involve any meaningful intercourse and that the sexual adultery is symptomatic of lack of development in several areas; they may then resolve to enrich the total marital relationship.

Closure of an Affair

If it is the husband who is involved in the affair and the wife who has sought counseling or supportive understanding from the physician, she may need help in understanding that there is a need for dignity and finesse in the closure of an affair. If the relationship with the other woman has developed gradually and has been a meaningful one, the husband will find it difficult to terminate the affair abruptly—and in many cases too abrupt termination will exact a price from the marriage. If the husband is to maintain his respect and dignity, as well as his image as a male, he will not wish to hurt the other woman unduly. This reluctance is particularly strong if the period leading up to actual physical involvement included the sharing of ideas, problems, values, and so forth. If he terminates the relationship too rapidly and hates himself for doing so, he will subsequently redirect this hostility toward his wife. The physician-counselor can sometimes help the wife to appreciate that one of the reasons she loves her husband is because he is compassionate and dislikes hurting other people; she may then have more patience during the closure period and may not misinterpret the time taken to bring the affair to an end as meaning that her husband loves the other woman more than he loves her.

Our double standard, of course, makes it somewhat easier for the wife to understand and endure the extramarital involvement of her husband than for the husband to understand and endure a similar involvement on the part of his wife. In the latter case the husband will need considerable help in understanding the very gradual and almost imperceptible manner in which affairs develop. He can also be helped to appreciate and accept, if not understand, the woman's need for a reaffirmation of her ability to attract males. Quite frequently, the wife is not motivated by sexual desire but rather becomes involved in a meaningful relationship as an end result of having sought reaffirmation that she is still feminine, lovely, and lovable. The need for such reaffirmation results from her indoctrination as a young girl, as a teen-ager, and during courtship with her own husband when it was emphasized implicitly and explicitly that her worth as a female was measured by her success in attracting males. If her husband has denied her this affirmation over a period of years, she inevitably feels the need to obtain it from another man, even though she may not realize precisely what she is seeking.

Maintaining the Context

As indicated in the preceding chapter, one of the counseling needs common to a variety of cases involving illicit pregnancies before, during, and after marriage is the need of the female to maintain a historic and contextual perspective concerning her sexual experience. Adult women may condemn themselves too harshly by imposing adult judgments upon their adolescent sexual experiences during adolescence. Married women may judge too harshly in retrospect their earlier "love" affairs involving coition with other men. Knowing at age thirty-five, for example, the depth and quality of love they have for their husbands, they may continually reinforce guilt feelings about earlier sex unions with other men before marriage. Certainly it is not easy to maintain the context within which a given event or experience took place ten, twenty, or thirty years previously, but it is important to try to do so. I do not mean to imply that all prior or even current sexual experience outside of marriage should be lightly excused. I do mean to say that the mature woman should not judge an experience she had at eighteen as if she then had the wisdom, judgment, and values she has at forty-five. In the case of the extramarital affair, the couple who have resolved some of their marital difficulties a year after involvement in an affair for one of them should try to remember the situation as it was when the affair developed. The married woman impregnated during an affair will need considerable help in maintaining the total context within which her affair took place. Otherwise, her guilt and self-condemnation may result in her placing so much blame on herself or her husband that the chances for subsequent strengthening of the marriage are greatly reduced.

Guilt or Sorrow?

The wise physician will attempt to help the couple recognize the difference between guilt and sorrow concerning an extramarital affair. The former can become quite destructive by necessitating an ongoing effort to justify one's own actions and to blame others. Sorrow more often reflects recognition of a mistake, genuine regret for the hurt imposed on others, and a determination to avoid hurting others in the future.

Frequently the sorrow is expressed with reference to "what might have been (in the existing marriage) if I had only known better." Sometimes it is expressed "if I had only met the other person first" (before meeting my spouse). This latter thought frequently reflects a romantic myth still perpetuated by our society—that for every individual there is one and only one right mate to be found and married. Thus husbands and wives too quickly reject the possibility that they could love two persons of the opposite sex at the same time—though perhaps in quite different ways. Unprepared for the possibility that perhaps there are ten women with whom he could have had a very satisfactory marriage, the husband who finds himself attracted to another woman begins to think this means he no longer loves his wife. Believing he can only love one woman at a time, he consciously or unconsciously begins accentuating the negatives in his wife and the positives in the other woman to help himself determine which one he "really loves."

The physician can provide primary prevention of much marital dis-ease by making the foregoing explicit and by emphasizing such points as the following: (1) Today's mobile society means that after marriage we have far greater opportunities than did our parents and grandparents for meeting one or more of the six to ten other persons we might have married. (2) The demands upon marriage are constantly increasing, yet education for marriage—the most complex relationship of adult life—receives less attention than education for the relatively simple task of driving a car. (3) Successful marriages do not "just happen naturally" but require as much work, creative thought, time, and dedicated effort as any other successful venture involving two or more people. (4) The embers of the marriage may indeed be quite cold; but this does not *ipso facto* answer the questions of whether these embers might be rekindled into flame and whether the new love with the other person might be of even shorter duration were it to receive no more creative thought, time, and energy than was given the existing marriage. (5) There are and always will be some cases of sexual infidelity which are symptomatic of the wrong union—two people who are individually worthwhile and good potential for a successful marriage but simply do not belong together. We recognize this in chemistry—that each element is worthwhile and some combinations result in something even more worthy, while other combinations produce an explosion or gradual destruction. In such cases we fault the combination, not the individual elements.

Time Scabs or Heals

Whichever partner is involved in an extramarital liaison, the physician can reassure both husband and wife who desire to strengthen their marriage that extramarital involvement *can* provide the motivation and stimulus for developing a much deeper marital relationship than existed previously. This statement is not to be interpreted as condoning extramarital affairs; it is analogous to reassuring the businessman who has already suffered bankruptcy that others in similar circumstances have benefited from the lesson and have subsequently established highly successful businesses. Such a businessman is well aware that there are easier ways to learn.

Such reassurance will be needed desperately during the ensuing months which seem to be years for the married couple trying to resolve the aftermaths of an affair in which one of them has been involved. The physician can help them to accept, as inevitable but nondefeating, the recurrent flare-ups when a word, a look, or a memory will evoke fresh pain from a wound that has crusted over but not healed. Both parties will need reiterated reassurance that healing takes time, that flare-ups will become less frequent, and that other couples have eventually found the wound no longer tender to the touch.

NOTES AND REFERENCES

1. Vincent, Clark E.: *Unmarried Mothers*. New York: Free Press, 1961.
2. Vincent, Clark E.: *Unmarried Mothers*. New York: Free Press, 1961, Chap. 3.
3. Some of the ideas in this section were included in abbreviated form in Vincent, Clark E.: "Divorced and Married Unwed Mothers." *Sexology* 28:674–679, May 1962.
4. Goode, William J.: *After Divorce*. New York: Free Press, 1956.
5. Vincent, Clark E.: "Ego-involvement in Sexual Relations. Implications for Research on Illegitimacy. "*Amer. J. Sociol.* 65:287–295, Nov. 1959.

The Concealment of Stigma and Deviancy as a Family Function

CLIFTON D. BRYANT

Every family has "skeletons in the closet." Because a major and universal function of the family is that of status conferring, it is not surprising that the family fulfills, as a corollary function, the role of status protection. Every individual is first introduced to and elicits an appropriate response from the community or larger society through the family. The newborn infant, whatever his status, legitimates his claim, or lack of it, for deference from his family of orientation. The family as a social unit depends for its very survival on its status relationship with other family units in the community or society. Effective cooperation in the social enterprise may depend upon mutual respect and confidence, not to mention cooperation in the more mundane processes of mate exchange, trade systems, neighborhood and kinship obligations, and mutual participation in communal endeavors. It is, therefore, incumbent upon the family to support, shield, and, if possible, to enhance the family status and its reputation as a viable and contributory element in the social organism. Any assault on its social worth or any erosion of its internal cohesion and functionality as a result of defamatory or derisive information, therefore, is to be avoided at all costs as a possible threat to survival as a social unit and to the well being of the individual member.

A wide variety of information and knowledge must, accordingly, be concealed both from a potentially critical or hostile community and often from individual family members or different combinations of members. In a society which attaches special social import to assigned statuses, one's ancestral heritage in terms of race, caste, religion, occupational history, or endogamous kinship may well be vulnerable to social criticism, sanction, or consequence. The concealment of ethnic background is often accomplished by a change of individual or family name. Cleveland Amory in his *The Pro-*

Prepared especially for this volume.

per Bostonians tells the humorous story of a Polish family who attempted to legally Anglicize their native family name, Cabotsky.[1] The local Cabots legally objected but to no avail. Local wags, however, improvised on the old limerick, "Here's to Boston, the land of the bean and the cod, where the Lodges speak only to the Cabots and the Cabots speak only to God," to instead rhyme, "Here's to Boston, the land of the bean and the cod, where the Lodges speak only to the Cabots, but the Cabots speak Yiddish, by God!" (It is interesting to note the large number of entertainers who saw fit to change their names to seem more consistent with the WASP cultural orientation.) As Sinclair Lewis so well articulated in his novel *Kingsblood Royal,* public knowledge of even minute Negro heritage may well precipitate public wrath in a bigoted community. The fact of close ancestral kinship, the marriage of first cousins, for example, may well elicit negative community response, if exogamous norms predominate. Among the Boston Brahmin, where generations of statesmen, merchants, and professionals and multi-generational success are common, disclosure of a relatively recent family business or financial success may only categorize one as being *nouveau riche.* Episcopalians may have had fundamentalist forebears, but do not publicly advertise the fact, nor do persons of aristocratic background speak openly of horse thieves or "yard children" as historical antecedents. Furthermore, such secrets must not only be concealed from peers in the community but also from children who might become disloyal or alienated from family in their disillusionment, not to mention potential spouses who might seek marital alternatives.

Physical or mental infirmity is also to be concealed from neighbors and even from kith and kin. Strong in the belief of genetic "weakness" leading to mental deficiency, insanity, and neurological defect, the potential spouse (or family of the spouse) may withdraw proposed conjugal alliance for fear of perpetuating a genetic insult. Interestingly enough, studies have shown that many women are not particularly concerned about the homeliness of their spouses, providing they have reason to believe that their children will not inherit their fathers' ugly looks. The Siberian Chuckchee believe that an individual who throws epileptic fits is divinely endowed and therefore ordained to be a *Shaman* or healer, but in our society such a defect is often an impediment to marriage. In our societal quest for physical and mental perfection parents have been known to withhold knowledge of genetic propensity to disease, disability, and defect from children, as well as from the community. Often such persons only reveal such information to their offspring on the eve of matrimony, leaving their children to confront the awful decision of celibacy and social purity or marriage and the attendant hazard of defective children.

In a similar vein, the presence of physical or mental infirmity may even be disavowed when it involves members of the family. A mentally ill or mentally deficient member may be denied medical or rehabilitative treatment for fear of public reaction or intrafamily response. The older child, for example, upon learning that a younger sibling may be retarded may object to the extra attention which the afflicted child receives and may become increasingly adamant about institutionalization.[2] The overly attentive wife may deny or evade the issue of the mentally or physically retarded offspring, staunchly maintaining that the child is merely a slow learner or lacks coordination.

Deviant behavior as an affront to community social or legal standards as well as a threat to family cohesion is especially to be concealed. The illegitimate offspring may be skillfully concealed with an elaborate fictive account of early marriage and divorce, or death of father, thereby protecting family standing and mother's social reputation. An act of legal deviancy, especially when a prison sentence results, calls for concerted family concealment. The fact of the father's imprisonment may, in some instances, necessitate a new family social identity. For example, several years ago in a large Southern city an upper middle-class individual in his forties was arrested for bank robbery. This man was the son of moderately well-to-do parents. He had married and inherited sufficient wealth to establish a business which ultimately failed. His sister married, however, and became a well known show business celebrity and the social and economic success of her and her husband no doubt generated some sibling rivalry. He tried a succession of jobs and for a time managed to maintain an upper middle class life style and social reputation for his family. Eventually, he failed in all of his enterprises, and as a desperate resort undertook to rob a local bank. He was quickly apprehended, tried, convicted, and sentenced to a long term in federal prison. Faced with the expense of his attorneys and the confiscation of most of his assets, the family was thrown into bankruptcy, and the prospect of his lengthy absence eliminated what possible asset he might have constituted as a breadwinner. The length of his sentence even with possible parole meant that he would be jailed until his late 50s. His oldest daughter was engaged, but the public scandal of his crime prompted the young couple to break their engagement. The family was forced to sell their home and move away from the community and break most of their ties there. To conceal the stigma the members of the family took the mother's maiden name and attempted to reestablish new lives elsewhere. The impact of this individual's deviant act created such social trauma for the family that it had to dissolve its original identity and was effectively dismembered, at least in its former configuration.

Various members of the family may conspire to conceal deviancy from certain other members. Children may conspire to cover up the facts of the father's amorous escapades in order to protect the mother. Parents also may undertake to insulate their offspring from the knowledge of deviancy in the family. In this connection, it is reported that the children of the celebrated Captain Dreyfuss never learned of his imprisonment on Devil's Island until after his vindication and subsequent acquittal. A mother's alcoholism or a father's narcotic addiction may have to be concealed from neighbors, friends, family, and children alike. The impregnated daughter may have to seek abortion alone to conceal her condition from parents, or with only the aid and assistance of her mother to withhold the knowledge from the other family members, or through the collective efforts of family and relatives in order to prevent the information from becoming public knowledge. Public disclosure would both harm the family's image of propriety and comportment as well as injure the daughter's chance for marriage. As a last concealment resort, families may have to permanently exile the deviant member in order to protect the family from the impact of public reaction. A favorite ploy of the family anxious to avoid public scrutiny and reaction is to send the pregnant daughter away to live with relatives, in order to either abort or bear her illegitimate offspring. In this connection, families may have to enjoin for collusion purposes to effect appropriate concealment of scandal and stigma. The story of the exiled "black sheep" is both traditional and universal. For example, Saint Simone, the founding father of sociology, was sent away (with a stipend) from the bosom of the family because of his errant ways.

A variety of persons outside the family may be privy to the family's secrets or stigma and may even be involved in a collusion network of sorts to effect the concealment. The family doctor or family lawyer, for example, may have knowledge of the scandal or stigma and assist in its concealment, or employ the information in some manner functional to the family.[3] It has even been pointed out by some writers that other persons outside the family may also inadvertently be privy to the family secrets. The janitor, for example, is such a person by virtue of his access to the family garbage.[4]

The concealment of deviancy and stigma by the family, however, imposes a considerable strain on the family system itself as it subjects the individual members to frustrating role stresses and discomforts. Concealment may involve elaborate fictive disguises and thus often involves a heavy social investment on the part of the family as a whole as well as individual members. A family may have carefully evaded the fact of a son's absence because of court martial and imprisonment in a naval prison by offering as a fictive device an elaborate story of his honorable military career, perhaps even embellished with occasional bouts of heroism. Such a cover-up may succeed, but if the device fails and the truth becomes known, the social impact on the family may be greater than if no concealment had been attempted, since the efforts may have solicited unwarranted deference and admiration and the community may respond aggressively to having been "taken in."

Concealment often requires difficult role falsifications which are stressful to the individual. It may be painful for the mother, for example, to play the role of affectionate and devoted spouse to her husband while knowing that he is engaged in an extramarital affair. Such role falsification may be necessary if the children are to be sheltered from the knowledge of marital disruption, and the dignity of the family is to be upheld in the community. To forgive and forget may be difficult enough. To pretend that nothing is or has happened, even after the fact, is painful indeed.

Perhaps no more tragic family situations exist, however, than those involving heterosexual role falsification. There may well be thousands of marriages where one or the other partner is homosexual. The values of society are such that homosexuals may feel compelled to deny to even themselves their sexual proclivities and, as a means of legitimating their socially approved sexual identity, may enter into ill advised marriages. Many of these people are able to mask their true sexual inclinations from their spouses and the community. They often lead seemingly normal lives with apparently successful marriages, even raising children. The strain of role falsifications is painful, however, and marital adjustments, particularly sexual adjustment, is difficult and seldom satisfactory. Married homosexuals may ultimately seek fulfillment of their sexual desires and thereby run the risk of public exposure and attendant erosion of their marital and family relationships. As some studies have shown, such married homosexuals often have to resort to sexual contacts with strangers in public places with the ever present danger of arrest and public scandal.[5] In a large Southern city several years ago, the police discovered a homosexual ring operating in a public restroom in one of the municipal buildings. The restroom had become a meeting place for homosexuals who were traveling through town and knew of it by reputation, as well as for homosexual inhabitants of the community. After a surveillance of several days, the police raided the restroom and made multiple arrests, because there were several different groups of homosexuals who were rendezvousing there. In many of the cases the offender was married and had children. In several instances the individuals were of prominent community status. The impact of public disclosure was particularly severe on some families, who, in turn, undertook to move away from town immediately for the benefit of the other family members who would experience humiliation and social reprisals.

In regard to internal family relationships, less is known since families are often successful in concealing the fact of a homosexual member even when the homosexual himself fails to maintain the concealment of his sexual identity from other family members. Unfortunately, little research has been done on the impact of homosexual disclosure on marital and family relationships. From reports of such situations in some of the popular periodicals, it is possible to derive some idea of the trauma involved. In one such account the wife tells of a seemingly normal marriage to a promising, young professional and the subsequent birth of two children over the first few years of their marriage. As time went on, their marital relationships became strained and their sexual life, especially, became non-existent.[6] After several acquaintances are exposed as homosexuals, the husband announces one day that he is being investigated because he is a homosexual also. The wife in her pain and anger considered divorce and even flirted with the idea of suicide. After objective reflection, the wife attempted to maintain the facade of normal marital life. She and her husband covered up his forced resignation with an elaborate story of his "retirement" to write a book. The children were not told, and the family moved to a new community. All attempts at sexual companionship were abandoned, but openly the couple maintained the fiction of happily married life. Later, it appeared that the husband was still actively pursuing a clandestine homosexual life. The children by this time were grown and had married and had children of their own. The couple continued their role falsification for the benefit of children, grandchildren, and community regardless of the pain and hypocrisy which they felt, for they considered the significant goal to be the continued concealment of the husband's deviancy and the protection of the family's status. Even when the wife ultimately published an anonymous account of her family's deviancy crisis, it was not without discomfort. As she put it, "My secret is so painful that through all the years I have never whispered it to a soul. Even now, I can hardly bring myself to write about it anonymously."[7]

In some ways a family may be considered a social collusion system for the maintenance of internal secrets and the concealment of stigma, scandal, and inappropriate behavior on the part of its members. Deviancy and other inappropriate behavior committed by family members must often be concealed from the outside community for the protection of family status and reputation. Similarly, the family may have to withhold knowledge of undesired behavior on the part of one member from other specific members in order to prevent family disruption and the erosion of family loyalties and cohesion. Skeletons in the closets are distinct dangers to family system maintenance, and for their own social protection, families must functionally discharge their responsibility for the concealment of stigma and deviancy.

NOTES AND REFERENCES

1. Amory, Cleveland: *The Proper Bostonians*. New York: E. P. Dutton & Co., Inc., 1947.
2. As a similar case in point, a study of the families of narcotic addicts pointed out that the siblings of addicts are often jealous if not hostile to the

addict because of the addict's "monopoly of parental attention and concern." See, Ganger, Roslyn; and Shugart, George: "Complementary Pathology in Families of Male Heroin Addicts." *Social Casework* 49: 356–361, No. 6, June, 1968. (Published in Part 6 of this book.)

3. Balint, Michael: "The Family Doctor and Patients' Secrets." *Psychiatry in Medicine* 2:98–107, No. 2, 1971.

4. Gold, Ray Lee: "Janitor Versus Tenants: A Status-Income Dilemma." *American Journal of Sociology* 57:486–493, 1952.

5. See Humphreys, Laud: *Tearoom Trade: Impersonal Sex in Public Places.* Chicago: Aldine Publishing Company, 1970.

6. Anonymous: "For Ten Years I have Buried Within Myself the Tragic Secret of My Marriage. Now I Am Going To Tell the Truth!" *Good Housekeeping* 167:36–46, July, 1968.

7. *Ibid.,* p. 38.

Wives, Families and Junk: Drug Abuse and Family Life

WILLIAM C. CAPEL, JUNE S. CLARK, BERNARD M. GOLDSMITH, G.T. STEWART

The effect of deviant behavior on the part of one member of the family on other family members has been amply illustrated in fact and fiction. That the "sins of the father" are visited not only on the children but also on the wives and other family connections has been assumd to be axiomatic. Indeed, in the case of alcoholism, considerable attention is given to therapy directed at members of the alcoholic's family.

Surprisingly little research has been done on the internal relations of drug abusers and their families and what has been done has concentrated on the pathological effects of addiction or the personality characteristics of the wives of addicts. Indeed, for most of the period from the passage of the Harrison Narcotic Act (1914) until the most recent epidemic of drug abuse beginning in the 1960s, the "junkie" became stereotyped as an alienated, anomic man, a retreatist in the sense used by Merton (1957) in his typology of deviance. Such a man cannot maintain normal relations with his peers, and certainly cannot cope with the demands of family life. O'Donnell (1969) studied the marital status of 266 native white Kentuckians treated at the Public Health drug facility at Lexington, Kentucky between 1933 and 1959 and found that some 13 percent of the males had never been married. This would be about twice the rate of nonaddicted males, and support for this data can be found in a study of elderly heroin addicts in New Orleans (Capel et al., 1972). Only one out of a group of 38 white males, age 50 through 73, was presently living with his wife.

Most studies of addict families have concentrated on finding some clue

This research was supported by research grant number MH–18339–01. National Institute of Mental Health. Reprinted by permission of the authors.

as to the addict's behavior from within the family group or within the interpersonal relationships of husband and wife.

A question that is often asked about drug abuse in the United States is "Why should drug abuse be so serious here and not so serious in England and in the rest of Western Europe?" This seems to be due, not to inherent factors in the American psyche but in a peculiar series of historical events, involving, among other factors, cultural diffusion, violent change, and the benign neglect of the uncontrolled capitalism of the late nineteenth century. Morphine, the active ingredient of opium, was isolated and named in Germany in 1806 (Terry and Pellen, 1928), and its use as an analgesic slowly diffused across Europe and to America, so that by Colonial times opium, morphine, and morphine derivatives such as laudanum and paregoric were familiar on all medicine shelves. The first use of the hyperdermic injection of morphine came in 1856, making it possible to use morphine in a water soluble form either intramuscularly, or, for quick effect, intravenously. These two cultural innovations converged just as the United States began its great Civil War, with the largest number of battle casualties ever known. The addicting qualities of morphine were known to a few physicians of the time, but not to very many, and certainly many army medical corpsmen on both sides used it freely (when available) in complete ignorance of its long term effects. As a result of the war thousands of veterans returned home with addictions of varying intensity. So common was the condition that it was known as "the soldier's disease."

After the Civil War, particularly with the great Westward movement, the dependence on home remedies increased, and private formulas for all sorts of elixers, cures, tonics, conditioners, and pain killers were dispensed, sometimes by individual "medicine show doctors" and gradually by national manufacturers. Of the products that were not out-and-out frauds, the vast majority consisted of morphine and alcohol. There was no requirement that any of these remedies disclose their contents, either on the label or in advertising, so addictions of varying degrees became widespread by the early years of the twentieth century, particularly among small-town middle-class women who often relied heavily on these drugged compounds for menstrual and childbirth pain. Increasingly, individual physicians became concerned at this widespread and uncontrolled use of morphine, and it was partly in response to this demand that heroin (diacetylmorphine) was developed and widely hailed as a hero drug with great analgesic qualities but nonaddictive. The illusion as to heroin being nonaddictive was soon dispelled and it never became widely used legally in the United States, although it did in Europe and Great Britain.

The first result of this concern was the Shanghai World Conference on Opium in 1909 at which time it was discovered that the United States was the only major nation with no controls over opiates. To remedy this situation the Harrison Narcotic Act was passed in 1914, and after a series of court decisions, resulted in the laws pertaining to opiates that have remained virtually unchanged. The addition of marijuana to the list of outlawed substances was not made until the late 1930s, and the use of many of the amphetamines and barbiturates are still supervised very laxly.

With such widespread use of opium and its derivatives narcotic abusers would, by their very numbers, have had to be members of functioning families, and, as a matter of fact, there is no way of knowing the number of addicts with varying degrees of addiction; but the number must have been very high. Family histories indicate many addicts went about their daily tasks and occupations completely undetected by friends or relatives (Blair, 1919).

The reasons why we again have a widespread family involvement with drugs are too broad a subject for our discussion, but by the mid-sixties drug abuse was of very serious concern to certain central cities and by the early seventies it has extended to small towns and suburbia, so that it can be considered today a problem of national dimensions.

The present study is concerned with 73 families in the city of New Orleans. All 73 husbands and 22 of the wives are addicted to heroin, or have recently transferred from heroin to a substitute (methadone hydrochloride). They are being maintained on this latter drug as members of one of the outpatient clinics operating in the city as part of an effort to combat drug abuse in general and heroin addiction in particular. Fifty-one wives are nonaddicted.

In this study the focus is on the wife of the addict, and is concerned with the following questions: Are there observable differences in the wives of addicts that would distinguish them from wives of nonaddicts, either in behavior or in demographic or sociopsychological dimensions? Does marriage to an addicted husband increase the chance of the wife becoming addicted? Are normal family activities such as child rearing, work habits, and sex relations seriously disrupted by an addicted spouse and are these disruptions increased when both are addicted? Did the wives know of their husband's addiction at time of marriage? Are differences in age or education between spouses significant in terms of drug abuse? Do wives with addicted husbands show significantly different responses to psychological measures when compared with wives in the same environment with nonaddicted husbands? Does the behavior of families in which the wife is a nonaddict differ greatly from those marriages in which both partners are addicted? Finally, have there been significant changes in family organization and stability in those families in which the drug source has been changed from an uncontrolled drug (heroin) to a controlled drug (methadone)?

METHOD

New Orleans, with the exception of tourists, has a stable population for a large city. Its deviant sub-culture reflects this stability. Ninety percent of all the persons entering narcotic clinics or appearing on police records for drug offenses were born and grew up in New Orleans and an additional 5 percent come from contiguous states (Goldsmith et al., 1972).

In any given city at any given time estimates of the number of addicts will vary widely and wildly, depending on the source, but in New Orleans a careful study by Bloom (1968) places the number of hard core heroin addicts at approximately 3,000. A more recent examination, since the beginning of methadone centers, indicates that the number is probably nearer to 2,500 to 3,000 persistent users in Orleans Parish (the central city), which had a total population of some 600,000 in 1970. Over 1200 users are receiving methadone as a heroin substitute from one or another of the clinics.

No couples under 21 are in the sample studied. Methadone is a highly addictive drug and is a substitute for heroin in persons already firmly committed to narcotic use. Restrictions on its use by persons under 21 are very strict, and only a small number of users come in this category. The interviews were conducted by an experienced social investigator and were all conducted in the homes of the subjects. All couples maintaining a permanent home were assumed to be married and no proof was requested. The structured part of the investigation was made by utilizing a research instrument designed for this study, and standardized for all subjects. In addition to the formal questions asked of all subjects the interviewer made certain judgments as to the response of the respondents, their demeanor, the type of home, the maintenance of household discipline, and other purely subjective observations as were felt might assist in evaluating how these families lived.

All of the husbands in the sample are heroin users now on methadone programs. All of the addicted wives are on the program. This means that we do not have a sample of the so-called street addict who is not in a clinic and is still using heroin or other drugs obtained illegally. Studies of the New Orleans addict population, including detailed comparisons between street samples and clinic samples (Goldsmith et al., 1971) have shown that what differences exist are statistically insignificant on most of the demographic and psychological data obtained from both populations. The sample does, however, contain a larger percentage of Whites than is true of the total addict population in the city. The largest methadone clinic, from which we drew the largest number of families, was begun by a White physician in a White neighborhood and gradually spread to include Blacks. A number of clinics have been opened since the inception of the study that encompass more Black areas, some entirely so. With the exception of the bias toward Whites the sample seems to represent adequately the married addicts in the city.

A comparison group of wives whose husbands were *not* addicted was used in the psychological comparisons only. This group was drawn from wives living in the same general area as the married addicts in the sample. They were selected from the patrons of neighborhood beauty shops and matched, as near as possible, for race and age. An attempt to match approximate income levels was attempted, but the nonaddicted wives of nonaddicted husbands tended to have a higher level of income.

The two factor Eysenck scale measuring introversion-extroversion and neuroticism-stability was employed (Lingoes, 1965). Both the validity and reliability parameters of these scales have been established and these two factors appeared to be the ones most likely to be found in the study group. Since an addict and an addict's wife are under the constant stress of the knowledge of unlawful behavior, it would seem that anxiety would be a product of this stress. The IPAT anxiety scale was utilized to test whether or not this anxiety is really present, and whether or not it varies significantly between the groups (Bending, 1963).

RESULTS

Of the 51 nonaddicted wives, 20 (39 percent) were White and 31 (61 percent) were Black, while of the 22 addicted wives 13 (59 percent) were White and 9 (41 percent) were Black. In the clinic population from which this sample was drawn, 83 percent were males (Black 61 percent, White 22 percent) and 17 percent were female (Black 13 percent, White 4 percent). The over-representation of Whites in the study is evident.

In location and appearance there is little difference between the homes of those families in which the wife is nonaddicted and those in which both are addicts. With only one exception the homes are all rented, and are comparable to the prevailing standards of the city. With no exceptions the homes were neat and clean, and, in the opinion of the investigator, this was not "show" cleaning to impress a visitor but reflected a well organized effort at homemaking activity. Few of the respondents lived near one another, and there was little fraternization. Due to accidents of history New Orleans is largely an integrated city in regard to housing. The respondents were scattered over the city with no particular racial or other distribution patterns.

In appearance all the wives, but particularly those nonaddicted to heroin, are clearly above average in looks and demeanor, and it is evident that they could have easily married men other than their husbands, but they not only chose these men for husbands, but 22 (43 percent) of the nonaddicted wives and all of the addicted wives, save two, knew that their husbands were drug users at the time of the marriage ceremony. Of the nonaddicted group seven (14 percent) were positive their husbands were *not* addicted at marriage. Five strongly suspected drug use and 22 (43 percent) knew nothing of their spouses' drug habits at marriage.

In both the nonaddicted and addicted wives' group there were more wives older than their husbands than would be true for the general population. Ten (19 percent) of the 51 nonaddicted wives were older than their husbands, ranging from one to five years older and six (27 percent) of the 22 addicted wives were older, ranging from one to three years. It is not known how this would compare to the general population of New Orleans, and in a small sample such as this, chance could easily account for the variance. Twelve percent of the nonaddicted and 14 percent of the addicted wives had been married for ten years or more, with both groups showing about the same ranges and the same median ages (28 to 29 years).

In education, the nonaddict wives showed a marked advantage over their husbands in years of schooling. This was much more pronounced for this group, with 55 percent of the nonaddicted wives having more education than their husbands as compared to only 27 percent of the addicted wives having this advantage. Of all wives who knew their husbands were addicted at the time of marriage, 38 percent had more, and 33 percent had less, education than their husbands.

TABLE 1. RELATION OF AGE AND EDUCATION OF WIVES TO KNOWLEDGE OF THEIR HUSBANDS' DRUG HABITS AT MARRIAGE

	NONADDICTED WIVES			ADDICTED WIVES		
	Knew spouse addicted	Knew spouse not addicted	No knowledge	Knew spouse addicted	Knew spouse not addicted	No knowledge
AGE RELATIONSHIP						
Wives older	6 (12%)	3 (6%)	1 (2%)	5 (23%)	1 (5%)	0
Same age as spouse	1 (2%)		1 (2%)	2 (9%)	1 (5%)	0
Wives younger	15 (29%)	4 (8%)	20 (39%)	13 (59%)	0	0
EDUCATION RELATIONSHIP						
Wives more educated	10 (20%)	3 (6%)	15 (29%)	6 (27%)	0	0
Same education	6 (12%)	3 (6%)	5 (10%)	8 (36%)	2 (9%)	0
Wives less educated	6 (12%)	1 (2%)	2 (4%)	6 (27%)	0	0

One of the few demographic abnormalities in family patterns appears in the number of children per family. Twenty-nine percent of the nonaddicted and 32 percent of the addicted wives had no children. This is almost double the national rate. The maximum number of children in any family was eight.

A higher proportion of addicted wives report that they do not belong to or attend church than do the nonaddicted wives. While 24 percent of the nonaddicted wives say that "religion plays a large part in my life and I participate often," none of the addicted wives make such a statement. Twenty-five percent of the nonaddicted wives take (or send) their children to Sunday School or church regularly while only 14 percent of the addicted wives do.

In approximately 45 percent of all families studied both the husband and wife worked, but in the nonaddicted group of wives an additional 20 percent worked while their husbands did not. None of the addicted wives worked if their husbands did not. As might be expected, the percentage of cases in which neither worked was almost twice as high when both were addicted. The men worked mostly as longshoremen or at other river jobs and construction work, generally unskilled. A few were carpenters, plasterers, or painters and made good wages. The women worked as waitresses, bar maids, hostesses, in laundries, as clerks, and in other relatively unskilled jobs. One was a registered nurse and another was a secretary.

It would be supposed that the wives of addicted husbands, especially if they themselves were not addicted, would be quite concerned about the possibility of their children becoming addicts due to exposure to drugs. Indeed, 57 percent of the nonaddicted wives expressed such a fear, but in only nine instances was there an indication that she was "very much afraid." Of the addicted wives 50 percent were afraid and 50 percent indicated they were "not afraid."

Rather than trying to induce their wives to take drugs, 81 percent of the husbands of nonaddicted wives objected, sometimes violently, to the idea of their wives using drugs. Whereas, of those whose wives were addicts, 41 percent approved of their use. There was a wide variation in the reactions of wives to the discovery that their husbands (or future husbands) were users. Nine (41 percent) of the addicted wives said they responded to the knowledge by becoming addicted themselves, but five (24 percent) became addicts after marriage rather than before, so there is nothing conclusive about this evidence. Only three wives said they considered ending the marriage relationship because of the drug habit.

Since there was, in these 73 families, a tendency toward hypogamy ("marrying down") on the part of the women in terms of age and education, especially in the nonaddicted wives, it was thought that we might be seeing evidence of the "castrating female" situation in which women deliberately seek weak and pliant men to satisfy a psychological desire for dominance, and who may, unconsciously or not, encourage their spouses in the type of deviancy that they publicly lament. Of the ten nonaddicted wives (Table 1) who were older than their husbands, six knew that their husbands were addicted at the time of marriage. Three knew their husbands were not addicted and only one knew nothing about her about-to-be-husband's drug behavior. Among the wives, who by the time of the study were also addicted, there were six wives older than their husbands, of whom five knew their husbands were addicted at time of marriage and one knew that he was not. However, among wives *younger* than their husbands the percentages were quite different. Among the nonaddicted wives 29 percent of this category knew their husbands were addicted, 8 percent knew they were not and 39 percent had no knowledge. All the younger addicted wives knew their husbands were addicted. While educational differences were not the same, the direction was similar (Table 1).

To test the hypothesis that prolonged exposure to a deviant way of life would produce differences in personalities, or that persons marrying addicted individuals would differ from "ordinary" people, two types of psychological scales were utilized. One, the Eysenck test, measures the degree of extroversion-introversion and neuroticism-stability. Additionally, the fear of arrest, financial strain, and public censure would be assumed to be higher among addicted individuals and should produce considerable anxiety. The IPAT scale measures this anxiety. There were three groups, the nonaddicted wives, the addicted wives and comparison group of nonaddicted wives with nonaddicted husbands. Both the nonaddicted wives and the comparison group had significantly lower (p < .05) anxiety levels than addicted wives, with the comparison group having the lowest level, but not significantly lower than the nonaddicted wives. Extroversion was significantly *higher* for the comparison group (p < .05). The addicted wives had the greater degree of introversion, but the differences on this dimension were not statistically significant.

While it may be a dubious scale, one measure of the degree of satisfaction can be surmised from the answers to the question: "Do you plan to have any more children?" Twenty-five percent of the nonaddicted wives said "yes," 50 percent said "no," and 13 percent were not sure. The other 12 percent either did not answer, or did not care to respond to the question. The addicted wives were almost the same, and the comparison group showed only a slightly higher percentage (35 percent) who plan more children.

When asked about their opinion of existing drug laws the nonaddicted wives felt most strongly (42 percent) that there should be no laws against drugs. The addicted wives felt (68 percent) that while we need drug laws the present ones are too strict.

Since methadone maintenance substitutes one drug for another, and since methadone is also an addictive drug, the difference in behavior patterns observable after shifting from heroin to methadone must come from a differential regard by society of the two types of drug use. Methadone, of course, is an "approved" drug. It has the property of being long lasting and, at high dosages, "blockades" the action of other opiates and creates a condition in which the heroin user, freed from the short up-and-down cycle of heroin, can take this drug orally and for the next 24 hours function without taking more methadone or any other opiate. In time, so the theory goes, steady habits and rehabilitation with freedom from financial worry over supporting his habit and no necessity to resort to crime will permit the methadone user to taper off his habit altogether and become abstinent.

Certainly there are some marked changes in family performances. One example can be seen in the handling of family discipline. Before the addicted husbands changed from heroin to methadone the far greater burden of maintaining discipline rested with the wives whether they were nonaddicted or addicted. However, with the restoration of a more stable life the reassertion of traditional roles is evident. In the nonaddicted wife group, only 12 percent of the husbands exercised more discipline than the wife when they were on heroin, but the percentage changed to 40 percent after going on the program, while the addicted group doubled. Participation in routine household chores such as grocery shopping, painting, and other tasks increased for the males after entering the programs, but the change was not as marked as in the exercise of discipline. Greatly increased amounts of time were spent with wives and children after the males entered the programs, with 50 percent of the nonaddicted wives and 37 percent of the addicted wives reporting such an increase.

A surprising finding came to light in regard to sex relations. All opiates have a negative effect on the libido, and one of the frequent complaints about methadone is that it causes impotence, yet these wives of addicted husbands report greatly *increased* sexual activity on the part of their husbands after switching from heroin to methadone. Again there was a difference reported between the addicted and nonaddicted wives, a bit surprising in that it is the *husband's* performance that appears affected. Seventy-one percent of the nonaddicted and 50 percent of the addicted wives report increased sexual activity. Fourteen percent and 19 percent of the respective nonaddicted and addicted groups reported some decrease in activity, with the rest reporting no change. The modal frequency of three relationships per week for the nonaddicted group compares to a little less than once a week for the group in which both are addicted. Six (21 percent) of the nonaddicted and 18 percent of the addicted wives report intercourse only twice monthly rather than weekly.

Police relationships are an important part of the life of an addict. While he is "on the street" he engages in activity such as buying and selling drugs, panhandling, hustling money in a variety of ways, including crime, which he sums up as "ripping and running." When he enters the methadone program he no longer requires this type of life as he has no habit to support. Some addicts experience a change in their perceptions of how the police regard them, but others retain the same suspicion as in their street days. The wives appear to make a much greater change in their perceptions of the treatment they, as families, and their husbands, as individuals, receive after they enter the programs. While the nonaddicted wives perceive "no harrassment" as being greatly increased, even the addicted wives felt a lessening of the police pressure.

One difference between the two groups studied came to light in terms of the sleep habits of husbands and wives after methadone began. The usual side effects of methadone, myclonic jerks, weight gain (particularly irksome for women) and constipation are noted, but the nonaddicted wives, by 71 percent, feel that their husbands sleep more and are more relaxed after beginning methadone, while the addicted wives feel that while their husbands sleep *more* their sleep is *less* sound or relaxed. In this case the explanation is probably in the wives' own sleep habits. Since the addicted husbands, after entering the methadone programs, spend more time at home, work more regularly, take a greater part in disciplining of the children and are harrassed much less by the police, the wives are apt to be more relaxed themselves and to sleep more soundly than when they were constantly worried about their husbands, and are projecting their responses onto their husbands. The addicted wife, however, is experiencing the same physiological adjustment to methadone as her husband in changing from heroin and is reporting the problem more objectively and perhaps more realistically. Similarly, it could well be that the presumed increase in sexual activity is due to an increase in propinquity and opportunity. It could even be possible that the male might have a lessened desire but this actual performance might still be higher under the methadone condition. While on heroin he was away from home a great deal and involved in physiologically and psychologically debilitating activity in his effort to maintain his drug supply which left him little time for dalliance, marital or otherwise. With more time at home and a reassertion of traditional male roles in other areas of life it would be surprising if there were not an increase in sexual activity unless the drug had a very powerful negative effect, which it does not. The wide variation of frequencies reported between nonaddicted and addicted wives would indicate that nonaddicted wives, not suffering from any depressive effects from either heroin or methadone, are initiating the activity.

DISCUSSION

What emerges from this welter of comparisons? Looking at the questions posed at the beginning of this study we see that these wives, whether nonaddicted or addicted, are not, by being married to addicts, clearly differentiated in either appearance, behavior, or psychological personality factors from wives of nonaddicts generally. The second question, whether or not being married to an addict increases the chances of ones own addiction, is not determined. Although nine of the addicted wives said they became addicted after they found out their husbands or future husbands were addicted, four did so well before the ceremony, while thirteen said their addiction had nothing to do with their husband's drug behavior. Since the 51 nonaddicted wives had all been married for several years (several more than ten) it is clear that if addiction is contagious it is certainly not virulent. The idea that one addict "infects" another simply does not seem to be true so far as husband and wife are concerned and most addicts married to nonaddicts are vehemently opposed to the idea of their wives becoming addicted. It would seem that the addicts share the common condemnation of addiction and wish to avoid it if possible, but they are practical enough at the same time not to be too frightened that their children will acquire the habit from the father. Indeed, the study of the general addict population in New Orleans showed that parent-offspring addiction is a very rare combination.

While more than would be expected of these wives were older and better educated than their husbands, there is no evidence of conscious or unconscious motivation in this regard. There were just as many of the younger and less educated wives who also knew of their husbands' addiction. There might be an explanation other than the obvious part of chance in a small sample, to explain this difference; that would be the possibility that the marriages in the sample have lasted longer than many marriages of addicts do, and the marriages that have survived the usual strains of addict life have done so because of more stable behavior on the part of the wives. There is no way to prove any of these assertions from the data available, however. The frequency of the report that men, after entering the methadone program, resume a greater degree of traditional male roles would indicate that, since the behavior is reported by the wife, it seems to meet their approval, which would not fit a pattern of female dominance.

While the psychological scales do show some differences they are in directions that would be the result of societal reaction to drugs, rather than to any inherent quality of the drug or its users. The slightly greater degree of introversion in addicted wives and the greater degree of extroversion shown by nonaddicted wives would seem to be nothing more than a reflection of the greater amount of time available to devote to ordinary family affairs on the part of nonaddict families. The increased anxiety, especially of addicted wives, would clearly seem to be associated with the societal effects of drug addiction, rather than with worry about the effect of the drug itself on the family organization.

The clear cut differences occurring when the addicted husband, or husband and wife as the case may be, changes from heroin to methadone, demonstrates again the fact that it is not the *drug* or its use that causes the disruptive behavior in the first place, but the way in which society reacts to the use of the stigmatized substance, as both drugs are almost exactly similar in total effect. Additionally, how does the wife of an addict perceive herself after her husband changes from a "drug fiend" to a clinic "patient"? Are these sometimes dramatic changes as much changes in behavior as in perceptions of behavior and interpretations of who and what one is in society?

This study and others like it raise the question implicit in all these figures and comparisons, what is the *real* cause of the perceived problem in drug abuse? If use of opiates were treated as is the use of alcohol would the result on society be only as if we increased the number of alcoholics by this number? It must be remembered that for a considerable period in American history this was exactly the position of opiates in society. For most of our history, drug addiction, while perhaps a serious matter for an individual and his family, was not a serious societal problem. It is no coincidence that the attempt to control drug abuse by law came at about the same time as the culmination of the legal effort to eliminate alcoholism by the Eighteenth Amendment, and with the efforts to enforce patriotism and Americanism by the Palmer raids and deportations of the 1920s.

The medical profession, after beginning the campaign against opiate use in uncontrolled form, to all intents and purposes abdicated from decisions about drugs after 1920 leaving the matter entirely in the hands of enforcement officials who regarded drug use as a criminal offense.

One cannot but speculate what would have been the course of opiate abuse had the Harrison Narcotic Act been repealed at the time of the repeal of the Eighteenth Amendment and the control of opiates returned to the states for regulation and control.

Nothing in this study indicates that the taking of drugs has any particular effect on family life that would not occur ordinarily *except* for the effect produced by police harrassment, financial strain, and criminal activity.

Certainly it is true enough that many drug addicts are criminals, and it is also true that many become criminals because of the necessity to buy drugs on a black market. It is also true that a disproportionately large number (far exceeding chance) of drug addicts had *already* committed criminal acts before they became addicted to drugs. In some cases their exposure to drugs came in prison, or through associates made in prison, but for whatever reason there is no causal chain and no particular reason to think that drugs, of themselves, had a compelling effect on their behavior.

What emerges here most clearly is evidence that instead of discussions as to the possibility of lessening penalities on marijuana or trying to set legal punishments to fit different types of drugs and different types of behavior with drugs, such as selling versus using, society would be better served to give serious consideration to removing *all* drug behavior from criminal classifications and starting over again with a different approach. However, given the present attitude of the public toward drugs and drug users, such action is highly unlikely. Until such drastic change can occur increased use of euphemistically named "cures" such as drug substitution or drug antagonists offers at least some alleviation from the family strains imposed under our present perceptions.

NOTES AND REFERENCES

1. Bending, A. W.: "The Reliability and Factorial Validity of the IPAT Auxiliary Scale." *Journal of General Psychology* 67:27–33, 1963.
2. Blair, T. S.: "Narcotic Drug Addiction as Regulated by a State Department of Health." *Journal of American Medical Association* 72:1442–44, May, 1919.
3. Bloom, W. A.; and Lewis, R. W.: "Heroin Addiction in New Orleans." *Bulletin of the Tulane University Medical Facility* 27:93–100, 1968.
4. Capel, W. C.; Goldsmith, B.; Waddell, R.; and Stewart, G. T.: "The Aging Narcotic Addict: An Increasing Problem for the Next Decades." *Journal of Gerontology* 27:102–106, No. 1, 1972.
5. Goldsmith, B. M.; Capel, W. C.; and Stewart, G. T.: "The Demography of Drug Addiction in New Orleans." *Sociological Abstracts* 19:340, 1971.
6. Lingoes, J. C.: "The Eysenck Personality Inventory." *Sixth National Mental Health Yearbook* 1965, pp. 93–95.
7. Merton, Robert K.: *Social Theory and Social Structure* (rev. ed.). New York: Free Press of Glencoe, 1968, pp. 357–368.
8. O'Donnell, J. A.: *Narcotic Addicts in Kentucky*. Public Health Service Publication Number 1881, Washington, D. C., 1969.
9. Terry, Chas. E.; and Pellem, Mildred: *The Opium Problem*. New York: Bureau of Social Hygiene, 1928, pp. 66–72.

The Adjustment of the Family
to Alcoholism

JOAN K. JACKSON

There is a sizable literature on alcoholism and on families in crisis. However, there have been few publications dealing with families who are attempting to make an adjustment to the crisis of alcoholism.

Individual members of the families of alcoholics have been studied. Psychologists and social workers have evaluated the personalities of wives of alcoholics. While these studies offer descriptions of some of the characteristic behaviors involved in the crisis, they tend to conceptualize this behavior as arising from the pre-crisis personality pathology of the wives, and to focus on those personality attributes and behaviors which appear to prolong and intensify the crisis.[1-4] Comments have been published on some effects of the alcoholic father on the personality development of children.[1,5]

Sociological studies of families in crisis have[6] concentrated on crises of a rather different nature from that precipitated by alcoholism. Such crises as bereavement and war separation and reunion are socially acceptable and do not tend to involve a sense of shame, which is a major characteristic of the alcoholism-induced crisis. Unemployment and divorce, while less socially acceptable, are known by those affected by them to be crises which are shared by others in the society. The family of an alcoholic rarely knows that the problem is a common one until a relatively late stage in the crisis. The family crises referred to above tend to occur in a more or less pure form. This is very rarely true of the crisis of alcoholism. Uncontrolled drinking may be the important initial precipitant of the crisis; but, by the time the crisis has run its course, unemployment, desertion and return, nonsupport, infidelity, imprisonment, illness and progressive dissension have also occurred. It is,

From *Marriage and Family Living* 18:361–369, No. 4, Nov., 1956. Reprinted by permission of the publisher and author.

therefore, very difficult to separate out the particular aspect of the crisis which leads to any specific adjustive behavior on the part of the family unit.

A family crisis which is similar to that induced by alcoholism arises when a family member becomes mentally ill. A recently published report on the preliminary findings of a study of the impact of mental illness on the family[7] indicates that this crisis is similar in the type of confusion generated, its complexity, and in the way in which shame is felt and dealt with. The report is focussed on the way in which the wife defines the situation, and her resulting behavior from the first signs of bizarre behavior to the end of her husband's hospitalization.

Although the crisis induced by alcoholism is somewhat different from most other family crises which have been investigated, and is more complex, the method and theory of the earlier studies are directly applicable.

METHOD AND SAMPLE

The method of gathering data for the study of family adjustment to alcoholism had elements in common with that used by Koos in his investigation of the incidence and types of problems found in low-income families[8] and that used in the study of the impact of mental illness on the family.[7] The investigator was associated in a friendship relationship with a group of wives of alcoholics over a prolonged period of time. At the time of the first report on this research, this association had been of three years' duration,[9] and at present, of five years'. The women who contributed the data belong to the Alcoholics Anonymous Auxiliary in Seattle. This group is composed partly of women whose husbands are or were members of Alcoholics Anonymous, and partly of women whose husbands are excessive drinkers who have never contacted Alcoholics Anonymous. At a typical meeting one fifth would be the wives of Alcoholics Anonymous members who have been sober for some time; the husbands of another fifth would have recently joined the fellowship; the remainder would be divided between those whose husbands were "on and off" the Alcoholics Anonymous program and those whose husbands had not as yet had any contact with this organization. The meetings of this group, which usually take a form similar to a group psychotherapy session, were recorded verbatim in shorthand. In addition, the frequent informal contacts with past and present members were recorded. This group of approximately seventy-five women provided the largest body of data.

When the initial report was completed, it was read to members of the Auxiliary with a request for correction of errors in fact or interpretation. Corrections could be presented anonymously or from the floor. Only one change was suggested, that the family of the solitary drinker had some problems which were due to the in-the-home, rather than away-from-home locale of the drinking. This suggestion was incorporated. The investigator is certain that her relationship with the group is such that there was no reticence about offering suggestions for change in the formulation.

Additional information on family interactions and responses to the crisis was garnered from interviews with the relatives of hospitalized alcoholics. These data, gathered as one aspect of a larger study of alcoholism, were used to raise questions about the data derived from the Auxiliary group, and to give some indication of the degree to which these findings could be generalized to other samples of families undergoing a similar crisis.

It should be noted, however, that the findings of this research are applicable only to those families which are seeking help for the alcoholism of the husband. Other families are known to have divorced, often without having sought help for the drinking problem. It is known that some families never seek help and never disintegrate. While the wives of the hospitalized alcoholics gave substantially the same picture of the crisis as did the women from the Auxiliary, there is no evidence that the conclusions of this study can be generalized beyond these two groups. In addition, there are good theoretical reasons for believing that where the alcoholic family member is the wife or a child, the process of the crisis is substantially different.

FINDINGS

The crisis induced by alcoholism goes through several stages. When the interactions of family members in respect to the excessive drinking per se are viewed, the crisis starts as a series of acute crises, probably widely spaced in time, passes into a progressive type of crisis in which the emotional involvement and hostility expressed are diminished, and finally, if the family has stayed together, into a habituated crisis. In the latter stage, the family is accustomed to the excessive drinking and the behavior surrounding it, has made its adjustment to it, and is concerned about it but not disrupted by it.[10]

However, a characteristic of the over-all crisis of alcoholism is that secondary crises arise from the very nature of the illness. Many of these crises, too, go through the same stages, beginning as sporadic acute crises, and gradually passing into progressive and finally habituated crises. For example, the nonsupport problem begins as a series of acute crises over the spending of money for drinking rather than for necessities. As time passes, the conflict over diminishing support becomes cumulative and persistent. Finally, the family adjusts by ceasing to expect support and makes other arrangements for subsistence. After this the crisis is of a habituated nature, being one element of a larger area of continued disagreement. At this latter stage the disruptive effects of lack of support have been minimized.

The elements of the crisis of alcoholism, and each of the subsidiary crises, are similar to those of less complex crises. Throughout, all family members behave in a manner which they hope will resolve the crisis and permit a return to stability. Each member's actions are influenced by his previous personality, by his previous role and status in the family group, and by the history of the crisis and its effects on his personality, habit patterns, roles and status up to that point.[6] Action is also influenced by the past effectiveness of that particular action as a means of social control or as an adjustive technique before and during the crisis. The behavior of the members of the family individually and as a unit during each phase of the crisis contributes to the form which the crisis takes in the following stages and sets limits on possibilities of behavior in subsequent stages.

In addition, family members are influenced strongly by the cultural definitions of alcoholism as evidence of weakness, inadequacy, or sinfulness; by the cultural prescriptions for the roles of family members; and by the cultural values of family solidarity, sanctity, and self-sufficiency. Alcoholism in a family poses a situation which the culture defines as shameful, but for the handling of which there are no prescriptions which are effective, or which permit direct action that is not in conflict with other cultural prescriptions. In crises such as physical illness or bereavement the family can draw on cultural definitions of appropriate behavior and on procedures which will terminate the crisis, but this is not the case when there is alcoholism in the family. The cultural view is that alcoholism is shameful and should not occur. Thus, in facing alcoholism, the family is in a socially unstructured situation and must find the techniques for handling it through trial and error. In this respect, there are marked similarities to the crisis of mental illness.[7]

The over-all crises and each of the subsidiary crises go through the stages delineated by Hill,[6] that is, crisis—disorganization—recovery—reorganization. As in other crises, and especially the bereavement crisis, there is an initial denial of the problem, followed by a downward slump in organization during which roles are played with less enthusiasm and there is an increase in tensions and strained relationships. Finally, as some of the adjustive techniques prove successful, an improvement occurs and family organization becomes stabilized at a new level. Characteristics of each stage of the crisis are: reshuffling of roles among family members, changes in status and prestige, changing "self" and "other" images, shifts in family solidarity and self-sufficiency and in the visibility of the problem to outsiders. In the process of the crisis, considerable mental conflict is engendered in all family members, and personality distortion occurs.

In evaluating the following presentation of the stages through which the family passes in adjusting to the alcoholism of the father, it should be kept in mind that we are dealing with the wife's definition of the situation. As most of the families investigated were composed of a wife, husband, and minor children, her definition of the situation was the relevant one.

Hill[6] points out that the way in which a family defines a given situation or event is an important element in whether or not a crisis results. He calls this the "c factor" in the development of a crisis. In the case of alcoholism in the family, it is difficult to envisage the possibility that there could be a family definition of excessive drinking behavior such that a crisis would not occur. In the experience of the investigator, excessive drinking tends to constitute a crisis even in the special case where both spouses are alcoholics.

However, the definition of the crisis and its nature by the family does determine in large measure the action which is taken to cope with it. Some families shorten the crisis by casting the alcoholic member out of their ranks at an early stage of excessive drinking; others prolong the crisis by continuing their attempts to adjust to the alcoholic member. The latter is particularly the case among the families who define the alcoholic as sick, thereby activating the cultural prescriptions for behavior in relation to the chronically and seriously ill.

The extent to which the family's definition of excessive drinking behavior contributes to the development of alcoholism or increases the probability of alcoholism is unknown. That the definition of the excessive drinker by others is an important factor in the process of becoming an alcoholic and in developing a conception of oneself as a problem drinker (a necessary first step towards the termination of alcoholism) is a hypothesis worthy of investigation.

STAGES IN FAMILY ADJUSTMENT TO AN ALCOHOLIC MEMBER

The Beginning of the Marriage

At the time marriage was considered, the drinking of most of the men was within socially acceptable limits. In a few cases the men were already alcoholics but managed to hide this from their fiancees. On dates they drank only moderately or not at all and often avoided friends and relatives who might expose their excessive drinking. Those relatives and friends who were introduced to the fiancee were those who had hoped that "marriage would straighten him out" and thus said nothing about the drinking. In a small number of cases the men spoke about their alcoholism with their fiancees. The women had no conception of what alcoholism meant, other than that it involved more than the usual frequency of drinking. These women began marriage with little more preparation than if they had not been told anything about the drinking problem.

Stage 1: Attempts to Deny the Problem

At some time during the marriage, incidents of excessive drinking begin. Although they are sporadic, these episodes place strains on the husband-wife interaction and pose crises of the acute type. After each drinking episode, the relationships of family members are redefined, usually in a way that minimizes other family problems which are not obviously related to the drinking. Both spouses attempt to explain the drinking episode in a manner which will permit them to regard it as "normal" behavior.[7] Thereafter, as a kind of safety measure, situations or behavior which are thought to be related to the onset of drinking are avoided. During periods of reconciliation when inappropriate drinking does not occur, both husband and wife feel guilty about the thoughts they had had about each other, about their behavior, and about their impact on their mate. Each tries to play "Ideal Spouse" roles in an attempt to deny that strains exist in the marriage.

As inappropriate drinking behavior becomes recurrent, initial explanations of the reasons for this behavior as being within the range of "normal behavior" become unsatisfactory. The wife's definitions of the nature of the problem change from one formulation to another, until gradually she recognizes the behavior as alcoholism. The process by which the wife comes to recognize alcoholism is precisely the same as the process of recognizing mental illness. The report on the Impact of Mental Illness on the Family[7] points out that the problems in accurately and immediately defining the situation are understandable within the framework of perception theory. "Behavior which is unfamiliar and incongruent and unlikely in terms of current expectations and needs will not be readily recognized, and stressful or threatening stimuli will tend to be misperceived or perceived with difficulty or delay." The same study delineates the stages in defining the problems as follows:

1. The wife's threshold for initially discerning a problem depends on the accumulation of various kinds of behavior which are not readily understandable or acceptable to her.

2. This accumulation forces upon the wife the necessity for examining and adjusting expectations for herself and her husband which permit her to account for his behavior.

3. The wife is in an "overlapping" situation, of problem—not problem, or of normal—not normal. Her interpretations shift back and forth.

4. Adaptations to the atypical behavior of the husband occur. There is testing and waiting for additional cues in coming to any given interpretation, as in most problem solving. The wife mobilizes strong defenses against the husband's deviant behavior. These defenses take form in such reactions as denying, attenuating, balancing and normalizing the husband's problems.

5. Eventually there is a threshold point at which the preception breaks,

when the wife comes to the relatively stable conclusion that the problem is a psychiatric one and/or that she cannot alone cope with the husband's behavior.

In this initial stage of the crisis, both the husband and wife are concerned with the social visibility of the drinking behavior. They feel that if the nature and extent of the drinking become widely known, family status will be threatened. The wife tends to be the more concerned. The family's status in the community is dependent on the behavior of the husband, and the wife feels less in control of the situation than he. As a result she attempts to exert some control and is usually blocked in her efforts by the sacredness of drinking behavior to the male. The usual response of the husband to her efforts is to state no problem exists.

Friends contribute to her confusion. If she compares her husband with them, some show parallels to his drinking and others are in marked contrast. Depending on which friends she is comparing him with, her definition of his behavior is "normal" or "not normal." If she consults friends, they tend to discount her concern, thus facilitating her tendency to deny that a problem is emerging. As the report on the Impact of Mentall Illness on the Family points out, "social pressures and expectations not only keep behavior in line, but to a great extent perceptions of behavior as well."[7]

Stage 2: Attempts to Eliminate the Problem

When incidents of excessive drinking multiply, the family becomes socially isolated. The isolation results partly from a voluntary withdrawal from extra-family social interactions, and partly from ostracism by others. The increasing isolation magnifies the importance of intra-family interactions and events. The behavior and thought of the husband and wife become obsessively drinking-centered. Drinking comes to symbolize all conflicts between the spouses, and even mother-child and father-child conflicts are regarded as indirect derivatives of the drinking behavior. Attempts to keep the social visibility of the excessive drinking at the lowest possible level increase. The children are shielded from the knowledge of their father's behavior; lies are told to employers and to others directly affected by the drinking.

During this stage the husband and wife draw further apart; the process of alienation accelerates.[6] Each spouse feels resentful of the other. When resentment is expressed, further drinking occurs. When it is not, tension mounts until another drinking episode is precipitated. Both search frantically for the reasons for the drinking, feeling that if the reason could be discovered, all family members could gear their behavior so as to make the drinking unnecessary. Such husband-wife discussions become increasingly unproductive as the alienation process continues.

In this stage the wife begins to feel increasingly inadequate as a wife, mother, woman, and person. She feels she has failed to meet her husband's needs, and to make a happy and united home for her children. Her husband's frequent comments to the effect that her behavior is the cause of his drinking intensify the process of self-devaluation, and leave her tense and frightened.

During this stage there are sporadic reconciliations. Usually an attempt has been made to maintain the illusion that there has been no change in husband-wife-children roles. As a result, the family organization is disrupted each time the husband drinks excessively.

The maximum level of trial and error efforts to control the drinking occurs during this second stage of the crisis. At times it reaches a frantic level. Despite these efforts, or because of them, no consistency is achieved. All efforts to structure the situation and to stabilize the family appear to fail. No matter what action is taken, drinking occurs. Gradually all family goals, including permanent sobriety for the husband, become secondary to the short-term goal of having him sober today.

Stage 3: Disorganization

During Stage 3, attempts to control the drinking of the husband became sporadic, or are given up entirely. Family behavior is engaged in as a means of relieving tension, rather than as means to an end. Any techniques which diminished tension successfully in earlier stages of the crisis are used increasingly, with no other motive in mind. The wife adopts a "what's the use?" attitude and begins to think of her husband's drinking as a problem which is likely to be permanent. The demoralization of the family is also shown by the discontinuation of efforts to understand the alcoholic, by the cessation of efforts to keep the visibility of the problem at a minimum or to shield the children from a knowledge of their father's behavior. The myth that the alcoholic has his former status in the family is no longer upheld as he fails to support the family, to play husband or father roles, is imprisoned, sporadically disappears and returns, or is caught in infidelity. Although in actuality his roles have been dropped before this, the alcoholic resists the relinquishment of the myth. His efforts to have his importance to the family verbally recognized add to the general dissension. In addition, the sexual relationship between the spouses has been severely disturbed by this time. The family has also resorted to public agencies for aid, thereby further damaging its self-sufficiency and self-respect.

The wife begins to worry about her sanity during this stage, as she finds herself engaging in behavior which she knows to be senseless and random, and as she becomes more tense, anxious, and hostile. She regards her pre-crisis self as "the real me," and is frightened at the extent to which she has deviated from this earlier self.

Stage 4: Attempts to Reorganize in Spite of Problems

Stage 4 usually begins when one of the subsidiary crises occurs and some action must be taken if the family is to survive as a unit. At this point some wives separate from their husbands and the family goes directly into Stage 5. Some families become stabilized at the Stage 4 level.

The major characteristic of this stage is that the wife takes over her husband's roles in action. The alcoholic husband is ignored or is assigned the status of a recalcitrant child by the wife and children. When the wife's obligations to her husband conflict with her obligations to her children, she decides in favor of the latter. As the husband becomes less disruptive to the ongoing family organization and function, hostility toward him diminishes and feelings of pity and protectiveness arise. The husband's response is frequently intense; but sporadic efforts continue to be made to gain recognition as a husband and father, and to re-enter the family ranks which are being progressively closed to exclude him.

The reorganization of the family structure has a stabilizing effect on the children as they find their environment more consistent and predictable. They accept their mother's definition of the drinking as being unrelated to the behavior of family members, and guilt and anxiety diminish.

As the wife assumes more control of the family, she gradually regains her sense of worth and worries less about her sanity. Long-term family goals begin to emerge again, and plans are made to achieve them. Although by this time the family has been helped by innumerable agencies, this help has come to be accepted as necessary and ceases to be a source of shame. If, as a means of helping herself the wife contacts the Alcoholics Anonymous, she gains perspective on her problem, learns that it is one which is extremely common, and thereby loses much of her shame and her motivation for concealment. She also gains a definition of the illness, prescriptions for behavior in the situation, and a definition of the form which the illness can be expected to take. All this makes her feel that the situation has become structured, that the family is now part of a group, rather than alone, and that her behavior is purposeful. She can also renew extra-family social relationships with a group of people who are undisturbed by the drinking behavior and unpredictability of her husband.

Despite the greater stabilization of the family, subsidiary crises multiply. The violence or withdrawal of the alcoholic increases, so income is less certain; periods of unemployment, imprisonment, hospitalization, and other illness increase in frequency and duration. If the alcoholic formerly saw other women in secret, they may now be brought home. Each of these secondary crises is of an acute nature and is disruptive. The symbolization of these events as being caused by alcoholism, however, prevents the complete disruption of the family.

The most disruptive type of crisis during this stage is the husband's recognition of his drinking as a problem and his efforts to get treatment. Hope for his recovery is mobilized, and the family attempts to open its ranks and to reinstate him in his former roles in order to follow the recommendations of treatment agencies and in order to give the alcoholic the maximal chance for recovery. Roles are partially reshuffled, attempts at attitude-changes are made, only to be again disrupted if treatment is unsuccessful.

Stage 5: Efforts to Escape the Problems: The Decision to Separate from the Alcoholic Husband

The decision to separate from the husband is made in a manner similar to the decision to separate for any other reasons. The wife seeks legal separation or divorce actively while the husband is the passive and resistant spouse. They play their roles and interact in substantially the same way as other separating couples.[6] The problems of support, of depriving children of a father, of the attitudes of others toward the action, of conflicting advice by children, relatives, social and treatment agencies are not unique to the alcoholism-induced crisis. However, there are problems which are more concentrated in this type of crisis. For example, in Stage 4 of the crisis the husband has contributed financially to the family from time to time, often as a means of temporarily regaining the favor of the wife, or of manipulating her in a quarrel. This motivation no longer exists to the same extent after a separation. The wife, in deciding to separate from him, cannot count on any money from him. The mental conflict about deserting a sick man must be resolved, as well as the wife's feelings of responsibility for his alcoholism.

By Stage 5, the family has often been threatened with physical violence or has experienced it. The appearance of this symptom of alcoholism is frequently the precipitant of the decision to separate. The possibility that separation may intensify the feelings behind the violence complicates the decision. The wife is afraid that if she goes to work, child-care personnel may be exposed to the violence, or that she may be absent when the children require protection, or that she will be unable to handle this behavior herself.

The previous tendency of family members to use excessive drinking as the symbolization of all other subsidiary crises and the accompanying conflicts also complicates the decision-making process. When the decision to separate is made, the alcoholic often gives up drinking temporarily, thereby removing what appears to be the major reason for the separation. This action tends to leave the wife feeling confused and bewildered.

While the definition of alcoholism as illness alleviates much of the personal involvement of the wife in the alienation process of earlier stages, at this stage it makes for additional difficulties. To separate from a husband who is a continually disruptive element in the family would be ethically possible; to desert an ill man in his hour of greatest need (as he and agencies treating him insist) leads to the mobilization of feelings of guilt. If alcoholism as an illness is defined to include the concept that no one can influence the outcome except the alcoholic himself, the guilt is less.

Events and experiences of Stage 4 have facilitated the decision-making process in many ways. Recurrent absences of the husband (due to desertion, imprisonment, or hospitalization) have indicated how smoothly the family can run without him. Taking over control of the family has bolstered the self-confidence of the wife. The orientation of the wife has switched from inaction to action, and this orientation adds to the pressure to make a decision. That she is now acquainted with public agencies which can provide help and that she has overcome her shame about using them are also helpful.

Stage 6: Reorganization of the Family

The process of family reorganization after the separation or divorce is substantially similar to that experienced by families with other reasons for this action. Hill and Waller[6] describe this process as involving a reshuffling of family roles, changes in the habit patterns of individual family members, and emotional reactions similar to those in the midst of the bereavement process. The experiences of earlier stages of the crisis, in which the family has closed ranks against the alcoholic father, tend to minimize the disorganization following this subsidiary dismemberment crisis.

Stage 7: Reorganization of the Whole Family

Stage 7 is entered if the husband achieves sobriety, whether or not separation has preceded. It was pointed out that in earlier stages of the crisis most of the problems in the marriage were attributed to the alcoholism of the husband. Thus problems in adjustment which were not related directly to the drinking were unrecognized and unmet. The "sober personality" of the husband was thought of as the "real" personality, with a resulting lack of recognition of other factors involved in his sober behavior, for example, remorse and guilt over his actions, which led him to act like "the ideal husband" when sober. Lack of conflict and lack of drinking were defined as indicating a perfect adjustment. For the wife and husband facing a sober marriage after many years of an alcoholic marriage, the expectations of marriage without alcoholism are unrealistic and idealistic. The reality of marriage almost inevitably brings disillusionments.

The sobriety of the husband does not raise hope at first. The family has been through this before. They are, however, willing to stand by him in the new attempt. As the length of sobriety increases, so do the hopes for its permanence and the efforts to be of help.

With the continuation of sobriety, many problems begin to crop up. Mother has for years managed the family, and now father wishes to be reinstated in his former roles. Usually the first role reestablished is that of breadwinner. The economic problems of the family begin to be alleviated as debts are gradually paid and there is enough left over for current needs. With the resumption of this role, the husband feels that the family should reinstate him immediately in all his former roles. Difficulties inevitably ensue. For example, the children are often unable to accept his resumption of his father role. Their mother has played the roles of both parents for so long that it takes time to get used to the idea of consulting their father on problems and asking for his decisions. Often the father tries too hard to manage this change overnight, and the very pressure put upon the children toward this end defeats him.

The wife, who finds it difficult to conceive of her husband as permanently sober, feels an unwillingness to relinquish control, even though she believes that reinstatement of her husband in his family roles is necessary to his sobriety. She remembers events in the past when his failure to handle his responsibilities was catastrophic to the family. Used to avoiding anything which might upset him, the wife often hesitates to discuss problems openly. If she is successful in helping him to regain his roles as father, she sometimes feels resentful of his intrusion into territory she has come to regard as her own. If he makes errors in judgment which affect the family adversely, her former feelings of being superior to him may come to the fore and affect her interaction with him.

Often the husband makes demands for obedience, for consideration, and for pampering which members of the family feel unable to meet. He may become rather euphoric as his sobriety continues. He may feel superior and very virtuous for a time, which are difficult for the family to accept in a former alcoholic.

Gradually, however, the drinking problem sinks into the past and marital adjustment at some level is achieved. Even when this has occurred, the drinking problem crops up occasionally, as when the time comes for a decision about whether the children should be permitted to drink. At parties the wife is concerned about whether her husband will take a drink.

If sobriety has come through Alcoholics Anoymous, the husband frequently throws himself so wholeheartedly into A.A. activities that his wife sees little of him and feels neglected. As she worries less about his drinking, she may press him to cut down on these activities. That this is dangerous, since A.A. activity is highly correlated with success in Alcoholics Anonymous, has been shown by Lahey.[11] The wife also discovers that, though she has a sober husband, she is by no means free of alcoholics. In his Twelfth Step work, he may keep the house filled with men he is helping. In the past her husband has avoided self-searching; and now he may become excessively introspective.

If the husband becomes sober through Alcoholics Anonymous and the wife participates actively in groups open to her, the thoughts of what is happening to her, to her husband, and to her family will be verbalized and interpreted within the framework of the Alcoholics Anonymous philosophy; and the situation will probably be more tolerable and more easily worked out.

SUMMARY

The onset of alcoholism in a family member has been viewed as precipitating a cumulative crisis for the family. Seven critical stages have been delineated. Each stage affects the form which the following one will take. The family finds itself in an unstructured situation which is undefined by the culture. Thus it is forced to evolve techniques of adjustment through trial and error. The unpredictability of the situation, added to its lack of structure, engenders anxiety in family members which gives rise to personality difficulties. Factors in the culture, in the environment, and within the family situation prolong the crisis and deter the working out of permanent adjustment patterns. With the arrest of the alcoholism, the crisis enters its final stage. The family then attempts to reorganize to include the ex-alcoholic and to make adjustments to the changes which have occurred in him.

NOTES AND REFERENCES

1. Baker, S. M.: "Social Case Work with Inebriates." In Alcohol, Science and Society, Lecture 27. *Quarterly Journal of Studies on Alcohol,* 1945.
2. Futterman, S.: "Personality Trends in Wives of Alcoholics." *Journal of Psychiatric Social Work* 23:37–41, 1953.
3. Whalen, T.: "Wives of Alcoholics: Four Types Observed in a Family Service Agency." *Quarterly Journal of Studies on Alchohol* 14:632–641, 1953.
4. Price, G. M.: "A Study of the Wives of Twenty Alcoholics." *Quarterly Journal of Studies on Alcohol* 5:620–627, 1945.
5. Newell, N.: "Alcoholism and the Father Image." *Quarterly Journal of Studies on Alcohol* 11:92–96, 1950.
6. Waller, W. (Revised by Reuben Hill): "The Family: A Dynamic Interpretation." New York: The Dryden Press, 1951, pp. 453–561. For a resume of the major research on families in crisis.
7. "The Impact of Mental Illness on the Family." *Journal of Social Issues* XI:4, 1955.

8. Koos, E. L.: "Families in Trouble." New York: King's Crown Press, 1946.

9. Jackson, J. K.: "The Adjustment of the Family to the Crisis of Alcoholism." *Quarterly Journal of Studies on Alcohol* 15:562–586, 1954.

10. Folsom, J. K.: "The Family and Democratic Society." New York: John Wiley & Sons, 1943, p. 447.

11. Lahey, W. W.: "A Comparison of Social and Personal Factors Identified with Selected Members of Alcoholic Anonymous." Master's Thesis, University of Southern California, 1950.

Conjugal Visiting at the Mississippi State Penitentiary

COLUMBUS B. HOPPER

Since conjugal visiting is a controversial subject, generally disfavored in American penal practice,[1] it is important that penal administrators and others interested in corrections have an understanding of the way the practice developed and operates in Mississippi. The purpose of this article, therefore, is to describe and discuss briefly the unusual practice of conjugal visiting at the Mississippi State Penitentiary. It is based on specific research I carried out at the penitentiary during September 1963 to April 1964.[2]

The Mississippi State Penitentiary consists of 21,000 acres of delta plantation land. The central plantation and the offices of administration are located at Parchman in Sunflower County in the Yazoo-Mississippi Delta. Parchman, as the institution is called, is one of the world's largest penal-farm or plantation systems. Since it is a plantation system, the buildings and other facilities differ from those at most state prisons in the United States. The buildings are of many different types: administrative, hospital, barns, storehouses, cotton gin, equipment sheds, and repair shops. Other large buildings are found in the 16 inmate camps which form the basic organizational structure of the penitentiary.

Each camp at Parchman is a separate community within the plantation, under the supervision of a sergeant responsible for all phases of the camp's operation. An individual camp consists primarily of a large rectangular building for the detention of inmates. The buildings, made of brick, are built and maintained by prison labor. The one-story camp buildings are designed so that on an average 60 inmates may be housed in one wing. In each wing there are no partitions or cells separating the prisoners; they are housed in congreagate quarters with electric lights, running water, showers,

---

From *Federal Probation* 29:39–46, No. 2, June, 1965. Reprinted by permission of the publisher.

and toilet facilities. Some of the camp buildings are surrounded by wire fences; most are not.[3] The inmates sleep in beds arranged in the pattern of a military barracks. Each wing is ventilated by about 10 windows covered by bars. A hall, dividing the wings of each camp building, leads to a central dining room which also serves as an educational and recreational room where movies are shown once every 2 weeks. A kitchen, in which inmates assigned as cooks prepare food under the supervision of the prison dietician, is connected with each dining room. Each camp has a concession stand and each wing a television set which inmates may watch in their spare time. The number of inmates housed in a single camp is never large. While one or two confine 200 inmates, a few have less than 100, and two less than 50. The camps are segregated for the white and Negro races. Generally, a total of approximately 2,100 inmates are confined in all camps combined.

The institution is a productive plantation, not only producing all food and clothing used by inmates, but sometimes also showing a profit on its products. The work of the plantation is allotted by camp and varies somewhat with the season of the year. The work may be planting, gathering, canning, slaughtering beef or hogs, or whatever chore may be most urgently needed at any particular time. Since cotton is the major crop grown, much of the work for most inmates, especially in the fall, centers around the production of this crop. Although cotton is the chief source of income for the institution, income is also derived from the sale of other crops as well as livestock.

During the period from July 1, 1961, to June 30, 1963, the total cash receipts for the penitentiary products were $2,027,619 while the total expenses for the same period were $2,502,642.[4] Although largely self-supporting, the institution is financed by the State and all profits of the penitentiary are turned in to the State treasury.

A distinguishing feature of the penitentiary in Mississippi is its visitation program. Parchman apparently has the most liberal visitation program of any state penitentiary in the United States. The institution not only emphasizes bringing visitors into the prison, but also allows the inmates to keep contact with their families by leaving the prison themselves. In a survey carried out in 1956, for example, Parchman was the only prison among 47 surveyed which permitted inmates to make home leaves for other than reasons of emergency.[5] Under the existing leave program at Parchman, called the "Holiday Suspension Program," each year from December 1 until March 1, selected inmates who have been in the penitentiary at least 3 years with good behavior records may go home for a period of 10 days. During 1963, out of 275 inmates released on holiday suspension, only 3 did not return voluntarily.[6]

All visiting by the inmates' families occurs on Sunday afternoons;

inmates may receive visits from their families each Sunday. Although visiting hours do not begin until 1 o'clock in the afternoon, the visitors usually begin arriving at any time after midmorning. They come mostly in private automobiles, although some come by bus and taxi. The visiting hours are from 1 o'clock until 3 o'clock except on the third Sunday in each month when they are from 1 o'clock until 5 o'clock. The third Sunday is called "Big Sunday" because of the longer visiting hours; this is the time when the largest number of visitors come. On a "Big Sunday" there may be as many as 300 or more visitors.

While waiting until the visiting hours start, the visitors wait in their cars parked on the sides of the highway in front of the administration building. As the visiting hours draw near, they drive in the main entrance and clear themselves with a guard. After a brief inspection of the car, consisting usually of the guard's looking into the car and recording the number of the license plate, the visitors drive by the administration building, past the hospital, and out on the plantation to the camp that houses the inmate they wish to visit.

On arrival at the camp the visitors must undergo another inspection by the camp sergeant or the guard on duty at the entrance of the camp grounds. This inspection is more rigid than the inspection at the main entrance, particularly if it is the first time a visitor has appeared at the camp. The visitors must identify themselves, and if requested, submit to being searched. The guard looks into the car trunk, and records the visitors' names. If the visiting hours have begun, he admits them into the camp area, and informs the inmate concerned that he has a visitor or visitors. The inmate then is allowed to come out of the camp building unguarded, receive his visitors, and visit with them anywhere within the camp area.

The grounds around each camp building are extensive enough to allow inmates and their visitors room enough to be by themselves, considerably removed from other inmates or staff members. The penitentiary provides tables and benches for inmates and their visitors. When the weather is warm, the grounds around a camp building, although less crowded, look somewhat like a city park on a Sunday afternoon. People sit on blankets eating picnic lunches; others sit on benches in the shade of trees, while others walk around. One may even see a boy and his father having a game of catch with a baseball, or children playing by themselves on swings or slides.

The penitentiary allows all members of an inmate's family to visit him, except in the case where a member of the family had one time been incarcerated in Parchman. Since released inmates are not allowed to return for visits to other inmates, a member of one's own family may not visit if the member himself has formerly been an inmate. Otherwise, however, members of an inmate's family are allowed to visit him, every week if they desire. For the married male inmate, the visiting freedom means that he may see his wife in private. He may go with her to a private room in a little building on the camp grounds and have coitus. Parchman is the only penal institution in the United States which has publicly announced such a practice. The conjugal visit is considered to be a part of the family visitation and home visitation programs. The family visit is emphasized at Parchman, and the conjugal visit is believed to be a logical part of the visiting program.

INFORMAL DEVELOPMENT OF CONJUGAL VISITS

The conjugal visiting privilege has developed informally in the Mississippi State Penitentiary, and it is still best described as an informal, unofficial practice. That is to say, the beginning of the practice may not be determined from the existing penitentiary records and that it still does not have legal notice or control. In fact, until the last camp was built,[7] funds were not allocated for the program. Records are still not kept as to whether an inmate uses the privilege, nor does an inmate have to make application for it or hold any particular grade as an inmate.

At the time of this study, no employee at Parchman remembered when the penitentiary did not allow conjugal visits. Most of the employees believed that the practice had been in existence since the penitentiary was first opened in its present location.[8] One man who had been employed intermittently at the penitentiary for over 35 years and who lived near the penitentiary and had knowledge of it even before his employment, said that the privilege was allowed to his own knowledge as long ago as 1918.

While the practice has apparently been in existence for many years, it has only recently developed into a somewhat systematic program, and especially since it has begun to get publicity.[9] In earlier days of conjugal visiting at Parchman the practice was confined largely to the Negro camps. Moreover, there was little or no institutional control over the privilege. A sergeant of a Negro camp said, for example, that when he became sergeant of his camp in 1940, conjugal visiting was being practiced but no facilities were provided. The usual practice, he added, was for an inmate to take his wife or girl friend into the sleeping quarters of the inmates and secure whatever privacy he could by hanging up blankets over beds. Upon gaining control of his camp, the sergeant allowed the inmates to construct a small building for conjugal visits. He has continued to allow the inmates in their spare time to construct such buildings or add to them. At the time of this study, his camp had three separate conjugal visiting houses, each containing several rooms.

The buildings used for conjugal visits are referred to by the inmates and staff as "red houses." No employee contacted at Parchman remembered the origin of this term. Apparently the first building provided for the visits was red in color, and inmates in talking about it spoke of it as the red building or house. Most of the existing red houses are simple frame constructions with about five or six rooms, although some have as many as 10. The rooms are small and sparsely furnished; in each is only a bed, a table, and in some a mirror. A bathroom which the wives may use is located in each building.

Since the red houses have been built in an unsystematic and unplanned manner, through accommodative relationships between the individual camp sergeants and his inmates, they are not standard in appearance. Nor do they have the quality of workmanship found in the other penitentiary buildings. They do not, on the average, present an attractive or even presentable appearance. Their condition, however, has begun to show some improvement in the past few years.

Each camp sergeant usually referred to a feature of the red house in his camp to which he himself had contributed in its development. One mentioned having put a new roof on his red house; others spoke of painting, adding new rooms, or acquiring new furnishings for the rooms.

The only conjugal visiting facilities at Parchman planned and specifically provided by the penitentiary are those at the first offender's camp, opened in 1963. The planning and institutional construction of the conjugal visiting facilities at this camp denote a significant point in the development of conjugal visiting at Parchman; they represent institutional acceptance of the conjugal visit as an important phase of the general visitation program. In this camp the red house was included in the camp plan from the beginning, and it is made of the same brick and other materials as the main camp building itself. The main camp building is joined on one side by a chapel, and a few yards in back of the two is the red house. The rooms in this red house are larger than the ones in the older buildings. They are also more attractively designed, furnished, and decorated.

The conjugal visiting program at Parchman should, in fact, be considered to be still in a developmental stage or process. It is likely that the practice has only begun to take on the pattern that it will take in the future. Although it has been going on for many years, only recently have the staff members begun to speak of it among themselves. Whereas for many years they felt the practice to be something that should not be mentioned, they now speak of it with frankness and even pride.

EVALUATIONS BY CAMP SERGEANTS

In attempting to obtain the most meaningful evaluation of the program by the institutional staff, attention was directed to the camp sergeants. The position of camp sergeant is one which requires the individual to have constant association with inmates. He lives a very short distance from the camp building and is, in fact, on duty 24 hours a day. The average sergeant spends at least 12 hours a day with his inmates. He knows each inmate personally, his hometown or community, and other members of his family. It is the sergeant's duty to censor the mail of each of his inmates, that which he writes as well as that which he receives. All disturbances and problems among his inmates come to the sergeant's attention, and are usually settled by him. If an inmate has a problem he takes it to his sergeant.

Furthermore, when a member of an inmate's family comes to the penitentiary with a problem concerning an inmate, he is referred first to the camp sergeant. Consequently, the camp sergeants come to know the inmates, their problems, and their behavior much more thoroughly than do the other staff members. In the case of conjugal visiting, the camp sergeants are the only employees who know which inmates do and do not have the visits. Inquiries dealing with staff members' evaluations of the influence of the conjugal visiting program were directed, therefore, to the sergeants of the 14 camps which have conjugal visiting privileges.[10]

Each camp sergeant was asked questions relating to the homosexuality, discipline, work, and cooperation of his inmates. Each was also asked what if any problems had developed relating to the conjugal visits, and what changes he would like to see made in the program as it was being practiced. The first question concerned the extent of homosexuality in their camps. While it is impossible for a camp sergeant to have accurate knowledge of the extent of such behavior, the sergeants were asked on the basis of incidents of it coming to their knowledge to rate homosexuality in their camps as a very big problem; definitely a problem; a small problem; or a very small problem. Of the 14 sergeants, one rated homosexuality a very big problem; six considered it definitely a problem; five said it was a small problem, while two considered it to be only a very small problem.

When asked to compare the extent of homosexuality among their inmates who had conjugal visits with that of those who did not, 11 said those receiving conjugal visits engaged in much less. The remaining three said inmates receiving conjugal visits engaged in a little less. All agreed that those receiving the visits engaged in less homosexuality.

In comparing disciplinary problems presented by inmates, six said they could tell no difference in their inmates in this regard. Four said that those having conjugal visits gave them much less trouble, and four said they gave a little less trouble.

When asked to compare the willingness to work of their inmates, five believed those receiving conjugal visits were much better in this respect. An additional five said those receiving conjugal visits were a little better workers, while four said they could tell no difference. When asked about the overall cooperation of those receiving conjugal visits as compared to other inmates, three reported no difference. All the others, however, stated that they could definitely say those receiving conjugal visits were more cooperative.

The sergeants were also asked what they believed to be the most helpful aspect of the conjugal visiting program. One sergeant said the work of the inmates was most importantly influenced in his judgment; four felt the visits were most helpful in producing cooperative attitudes in general among inmates while two others suggested the reduction of homosexual behavior. Seven of the camp sergeants, however, believed the most helpful aspect and the chief purpose of the visits was to keep marriages from breaking up.

When asked if the program caused any extra work for them, 12 of the 14 asserted it did not. They said, rather, that they had to be on the job all of the time anyway. On the other hand, one believed the practice actually saved him work in some instances. The freedom of visiting privileges in general, he added, kept the prisoners' wives and other family members from worrying so much and making inquiries about them. When an inmate and his wife can see each other in private, talk freely, and even have intercourse, he said, they do not have to come to him often for help or information. Speaking of this he said:

Most problems the inmates have are concerned with worry about their families. And most people who come to the penitentiary are concerned about how the inmate is getting along, how his health is and so on. The best thing I can do is to allow them to see each other and judge for themselves. A common thing in prison is for a married man to worry about his wife, whether or not she still loves him and is faithful to him. One visit in private with her is better than a hundred letters because he can judge for himself.

Two sergeants of Negro camps, however, indicated that the program caused them extra work in ascertaining whether a woman was the wife of an inmate. Although the sergeants of the white camps said they did not allow a woman to visit an inmate unless she had official proof of their marriage, the Negro camps still present problems in this respect. Since many Negro inmates in Mississippi have common-law marriages, which the penitentiary wishes to respect, the sergeants have to question the female visitors and try to determine whether the visitor and inmate have actually been living as a married couple. Often, one said, he checked with one or two people in the inmate's home community as additional proof of marriage. While he admitted that several of his inmates probably received visits from women to whom they were not married, even by common law, he did not believe that many of his inmates did so because most of the women who visited also brought their children with them.

The other camp sergeant who spoke of problems involved in screening out the unmarried female visitors said that at least on one occasion to his knowledge, a prostitute had slipped by his screening and spread venereal disease among several inmates. He also mentioned that several wives of inmates had become pregnant. He did not say that the wives becoming pregnant had caused any trouble at the penitentiary, but mentioned it as a problem associated with conjugal visiting.

All of the sergeants of camps having conjugal visits said that the facilities provided for the visits should be improved. Not a single sergeant rated his red house as being in satisfactory condition. Even with neglected facilities, however, all sergeants enthusiastically supported the program as being of basic importance in their camps. Each believed that the program should, in general, be continued as it was being practiced. The changes they felt would be desirable related to the adequacy of the buildings. All said that they needed larger and more attractive red houses which would afford more privacy and a more pleasant atmosphere.

Except for the two who complained of the work and problems involved in screening wives, the sergeants felt that the informal administration would curtail the freedom and privacy of the visits which they believed to be the most important aspects of them.

INMATE OPINION

A question of importance concerning conjugal visiting is: "How do the single inmates feel about married inmates having the conjugal visiting privilege?" Since the program of conjugal visiting is intended only for married inmates, it is a categorical privilege which the majority of inmates do not have. It might be, for example, that the unmarried men in the institution feel that the penitentiary is unfair in its treatment of inmates. If this were the case, then one would expect that a program of conjugal visiting would, as some writers suggest,[11] cause more tension and conflict than it would reduce. To obtain some indication of this problem, a questionnaire was submitted to a total of 1,600 inmates. Of this number, 822 were unmarried and not receiving conjugal visits; 464 were married and receiving conjugal visits, while the remaining 314 were married but were not receiving conjugal visits.[12]

An item in the questionnaire was directed to unmarried inmates and stated as follows: "If you are unmarried, do you resent married inmates having the conjugal visiting privilege?" The possible answers were: "yes," "very much," "yes," "a little," and "no." The response indicated that the great majority of unmarried inmates did *not* feel resentment over the privilege being granted to married men. Of 822 unmarried inmates responding to the question, 737, or 89.6 percent, answered that they felt no resentment; a total of 85 inmates, however, did report resentment, 58 replying "very much" and 27 replying that they felt a little resentment.

The fact that very nearly 9 out of every 10 unmarried inmates did not indicate resentment suggests that for most inmates a pattern of relative deprivation operates within the institution in regard to conjugal visits.[13] Apparently most unmarried inmates identify with other unmarried inmates and view a married inmate and his wife very nearly in the same way unmarried individuals do in a free community. Of several unmarried inmates talked to by the researcher, not one said he felt any resentment toward the staff or other inmates concerning the visits.

Since the embarrassment associated with and the obviousness of sex in conjugal visits have been objections to the practice,[14] two items in the questionnaire were directed toward these aspects. The inmates who received conjugal visits were asked the following question: "If you engage in conjugal visiting, has any other inmate ever acted in any way disrespectful to your wife?" Of 462 inmates answering the question, only 18, or 3.9 percent, replied in the affirmative. When asked if the visits were embarrassing to them, 42, or 9.1 percent, replied in the affirmative. When asked if they believed the conjugal visits were embarrassing to their wives, however, 87, or 18.8 percent, answered that the visits were embarrassing to their wives.

The inmates who received conjugal visits were also asked to choose from among several items the one for which they believed conjugal visits to be most helpful. The items from which they had to choose were as follows: keeping marriages from breaking up; reducing homosexuality; making inmates more cooperative; helping rehabilitate inmates; making inmates easier to control; or making inmates work harder. As a final choice, the inmates could choose to mark that the visits were helpful for all of the above equally. As may be seen in the table on this page, of the 464 inmates responding to the question, 234 believed that conjugal visits were most helpful in keeping marriages from being broken. It is interesting to note that the inmates, as did the sergeants, ranked the preservation of marriages as the most important function of conjugal visiting.

RATING OF THE HELPFULNESS OF CONJUGAL VISITS, BY INMATES RECEIVING CONJUGAL VISITS

For which of the following do you believe conjugal visits to be most helpful?	Number	Percent of Total
Total	464	100.0
Keeping marriages from breaking up	234	50.4
Reducing homosexuality	75	16.2
Making inmates more cooperative	19	4.1
Helping rehabilitate inmates	19	4.1
Making inmates easier to control	39	8.4
Making inmates work harder	10	2.2
Helpful for all equally	68	14.6

The majority of the inmates using the conjugal visiting privilege did not believe that the facilities provided for the visits were in satisfactory condition. When asked to rate the buildings provided for the visits, only 152 out of 464, or 32.7 percent, rated them as being in satisfactory condition. Most of the inmates who were talked to about the red houses complained that the rooms were too small and that the buildings were in need of repairs.

IMPORTANCE OF SMALL CAMPS

The fact that so few inmates reported embarrassment and so few problems have been encountered despite neglected facilities, is perhaps best explained by the small size of the inmate camps and the informality and freedom small numbers allow. In an inmate camp at Parchman housing only 150 men, the number of visitors coming on a single day is never large. It is easier to evolve and maintain a working system of interpersonal relations, generally, when numbers are small. In conjugal visiting, small numbers are basic, for sex activities are the most delicate of human activities.

Although the practice of conjugal visiting at Parchman has begun to be a recognized, institutionally supported program, informality is still stressed in its operation. Inmates are not specifically encouraged or discouraged to use the privilege. They simply use the privilege if they wish to do so. The wives are not informed officially that they are allowed to make conjugal visits. The individual inmate is responsible for answering any questions his wife may have about the privilege.

The penitentiary provides no contraceptive devices for the inmates nor does it require their use. If an inmate and his wife wish to use contraceptives, the wife must provide them.

The freedom and informality of conjugal visiting at Parchman are further revealed by the fact that the inmates themselves are responsible for the orderly operation of the red houses and for cooperation in the use of them. No time limit is imposed by the staff of the institution on the time an inmate and his wife may stay in a red house. The inmates are left to use their own judgment. They know how many inmates have wives visiting on a single day, and know that when there are few visitors they may stay longer in the red house. In camps having a fairly large number of men receiving conjugal visits, systems have been worked out by the inmates to avoid embarrassment in determining whether a room in the red house is being used. The usual procedure is to erect a board in the front of the building that indicates which rooms are and are not empty. Each room is numbered and its number is written on a piece of wood or some other material suitable for a marker. A string or chain is then attached to the marker and it is hung on the board. Before an inmate and his wife go into the building, they select a room, remove the marker from the board, and take it with them into the room. An inmate may thus determine whether the red house has rooms available simply by walking by the board. This procedure helps prevent embarrassment arising over such things as knocking on doors, standing in line, and other such incidents likely to be of concern.

In leaving the inmates alone without formal rules and regulations, the penitentiary has forced the inmates to cooperate with each other if they are to have the conjugal visiting privilege. Thus, the inmates cooperate in several ways. By informal agreement, married inmates whose wives are visiting are left to themselves in one area of the camp grounds. Inmates not having wives or whose wives do not visit, do not go near the areas in which the red houses are located. Inmates often cooperate by watching or attending to the children of a couple in a red house. Above all, the inmates cooperate by being respectful and courteous to each other's wives.

The conjugal visit at Parchman is not a privilege granted specifically for good behavior. The inmates in the maximum security unit do not have the privilege nor do women inmates have it.[15] All married inmates in the other camps, however, have the privilege. While the privilege is not granted for good behavior within an individual camp, inmates whose behavior presents a persistent problem are often removed to the maximum security camp for a few days. If an inmate attempts to escape, refuses to work, or attacks a guard or another inmate, he will generally be placed in a cell in the maximum security unit until he indicates that he is willing to abide by the farm camp rules. Actually, very few inmates are removed from the regular camps for disciplinary reasons. In October 1963, for example, there were only 13 inmates confined in maximum security, and two of these were on "death row" awaiting execution dates.

The attitude of the staff at Parchman toward conjugal visiting privileges is that a man and his wife have the right of sexual intercourse, even though the man is in prison. Inmates are eligible to receive conjugal visits upon commitment as soon as they are assigned to a camp. No special counseling is given to an inmate using the privilege nor is any extra requirement made of him. He is like any other inmate except that he and his wife take part in the conjugal visiting program.

If a married inmate at Parchman does not use the privilege, it is generally because his wife does not live close enough to visit him, he and his wife are not getting along well, or they simply do not choose to use it. Most married inmates not using the privilege or using it rarely fall into the first category. These are the inmates whose wives live at such a distance that visiting is expensive and time-consuming. Since many wives work, if they live two hundred miles or more from the penitentiary, a visit generally means travelling overnight and considerable expense as well as a loss of a day's work.

The second reason why a married inmate may not use the conjugal visiting privilege is because he and his wife were not getting along well before his incarceration. Inmates serving a sentence for nonsupport, for example, are usually in this category. A few inmates also told me that their wives engaged in conjugal visiting on their first incarceration but that on their second commitment they did not.

Other inmates do not use the privilege because they or their wives do not wish to do so. This may be because children, parents, and other members of the family always come with the wife to visit, or it may be because they are embarrassed by the poor facilities generally available. At any rate, when married inmates do not use the conjugal visiting privilege, it is not because they are different in their offenses or general conduct within the prison.

CONCLUSION

The development of conjugal visiting in the Mississippi State Penitentiary has not been due so much to the individuals or officials involved as to the social and physical organization of the penitentiary itself. It is believed there are general and specific features of the structure and organization of the penitentiary in Mississippi especially amenable to its development. The features believed important in its development are: the rural environment in which the penitentiary is located, the plantation life the penitentiary follows, the small semi-isolated camp organization of the institution, the economic motives of the penitentiary, and the segregation of the Negro and white races within the prison.

The conjugal visit in Mississippi seems, above all, a manifestation of the rural emphasis on the stable family. Mississippians are, and always have been, a rural people. Although the percentage of people living in urban places in Mississippi has been increasing, the rate has been slow. The census of the population in 1960 showed that only 37.7 percent of all Mississippians lived in urban places. Until 1950, more than 80.0 percent of the people of Mississippi lived in rural communities.[16] The influence of the rural environment upon marital and familial relationships is well known, and the stability of the rural family is a widely accepted fact.[17] As a union of husband and wife, parents and children, the rural family is much more closely integrated and more permanent than the urban family, and in comparison with other social institutions, the role of the family is much more important in the country than in the city. A prison in a rural culture in which both staff and inmates have a high regard for the stability of marriage is more likely to make efforts to safeguard a marriage even though the husband is imprisoned than a prison in an urban setting.

Not only does the penitentiary allow wives to visit husbands, but it also allows all members of the family to visit and allows the family to visit as a group in private. The high regard in which rural Mississippians hold the family has not only been a factor in the development and operation of conjugal visiting within the prison, but also is important in making the practice acceptable to the general public and officials of the State. The fact that the practice of conjugal visiting is believed to help in keeping marriages and families from breaking up helps the people of Mississippi not only accept the practice but also gives them pride in it.

The small, semi-isolated camp structure was favorable to the development of conjugal visiting in part because it simply increased the probability of its development. Instead of being one big central prison, Parchman is several different prison camps, most of them separated by several miles. More importantly, however, the small number of inmates housed in each camp reduces security precautions a great deal. It also allows a camp sergeant to know his inmates well and to develop primary relationships with them. The fact that a sergeant knows an individual inmate and his wife is very helpful for the conjugal visit for it means less formality in the reception of wives and in security precautions. The small camps present wives with a less rigid and more informal situation than would a large prison. As a result, they are able to relax and are not constantly reminded of the prison setting of the visit. Such an atmosphere allows wives to keep their self-respect and to have the feeling that the visit has been a private one.

Since segregation of the races is a general feature of the social organization of the State of Mississippi, the functioning of the conjugal visiting program at Parchman is also dependent upon the segregation of the Negro and white races within the penitentiary. While this factor might be of no importance in a prison in a state having successful integration of the races generally, there can be little doubt of its significance in Mississippi. Segregation of the Negro and white races in Parchman precludes conflict of the races in the most carefully guarded aspect of their interaction—that of sexual behavior.

The fact that conjugal visiting in Mississippi developed in an unofficial, unplanned manner as an accommodative adjustment does not necessarily mean that it is undesirable; it merely shows the magnitude of the problem of sexual adjustment in penal institutions. It is to be expected that penal institutions will, when the relationships between the inmates and staff become accommodative or cooperative, for whatever motivation, turn attention to sexual problems of inmates. The practice of conjugal visiting at Parchman reveals such relationships. With adequate facilities, careful selection, and appropriate counsel, it is possible that the conjugal visiting program in Mississippi could be developed into one of the most enlightened programs in modern corrections.

NOTES AND REFERENCES

1. See Balogh, Joseph K.: "Conjugal Visitations in Prisons: A Sociological Perspective." *Federal Probation* Sept. 1964, pp. 52–58.
2. The complete report may be seen in Hopper, Columbus B.: "A Study of Conjugal Visiting, Social Organization, and Prisonization in the Mississippi State Penitentiary." Unpublished Ph. D. dissertation. Florida State University, 1964.
3. Whether a camp has a fence around it depends mostly on the location of the camp. Camps located near the highway have fences; those located out on the plantation generally do not have fences.
4. *Biennial Report of the Superintendent and Other Officers of the Mississippi State Penitentiary, July 1, 1961, through June 30, 1963.*
5. Zemans, Eugene S., and Cavan, Ruth S.: "Marital Relationships of Prisoners." *Journal of Criminal Law, Criminology and Police Science* 49: 50–57, 1958.
6. *Biennial Report of the Superintendent and Other Officers of the Mississippi State Penitentiary, July 1, 1961, through June 30, 1963.*
7. The last camp built was the first offender's camp, opened only in the fall of 1963.
8. The Parchman plantation was first used by the state as a penal farm in 1900. For a history of the various periods in the history of penology in Mississippi, see Foreman, Paul B., and Tatum, Julien R.: "A Short History of Mississippi's Penal System." *Mississippi Law Journal* 10:256, 1938.
9. See Knight, C.: "Family Prison: Parchman Penitentiary." *Cosmopolitan* March 1960, p. 62; and Mitler, Ernest A.: "Family Visits Inside a Prison." *Parade* May 17, 1959, p. 8. The first and most significant professional notice of the practice was at the Fourth Southern Conference on Corrections at Florida State University, in 1959. The Superintendent of the Mississippi State Penitentiary at that time appeared on the program and discussed the practice.
10. The maximum security unit does not have the privilege, nor do the female inmates housed in a small camp near the hospital.
11. See Tappan, Paul W.: *Crime, Justice and Correction.* New York: McGraw-Hill Book Co., 1960, p. 680.
12. The sample studied comprised 76.0 percent of the total inmate population.
13. For a discussion of "relative deprivation" see Stouffer, Samuel *et al.: The American Soldier.* Princeton, N. J.: Princeton University Press, 1949, Vol. 1.
14. Zeman and Cavan, *op. cit.*

15. In October 1963, there were 63 women confined in the women's camp.
16. Belcher, John C., and King, Morton B.: *Mississippi's People*. University of Mississippi: Bureau of Public Administration, University of Mississippi, 1950, p. 13.
17. See Landis, Paul H.: *Rural Life in Progress*. New York: McGraw-Hill Book Co., 1948, p. 319.

Families Come to the Institution:
A 5-Day Experience in Rehabilitation

The idea of involving families of delinquent boys as part of a comprehensive effort in rehabilitation is not new. The reports of Robert MacGregor and his associates in Texas[1] and A. P. Travisono[2] and C. F. O'Neil[3] at Iowa have demonstrated the value of such an approach in conjunction with a humanitarian and progressive correctional program. The difficulty comes in the implementation—utilizing available money, staff, and time to add another effective therapeutic tool to the arsenal of the administrator of a juvenile corrective facility. Too often sound additions to existing programs founder on the rocks of inadequate budget, insufficient and untrained staff, and indifference and apathy on the part of the powers that be.

This article is a brief description of an attempt of one institution serving 150 adjudicated delinquents to demonstrate the feasibility and necessity of involving families in the treatment of committed youngsters.

THE SETTING

The Youth Development Center at Loysville, Pennsylvania, is one of 10 state operated institutions serving delinquent youngsters between the ages of 12 and 18. All students are committed for an indefinite term by local juvenile courts and released by court order, usually upon recommendation of the institution. The Center at Loysville is located in a remote, mountainous area of Pennsylvania having no public transportation facilities and limited contact with the "outside world." The institution served as a Lutheran orphanage for over 80 years until purchased by the State and opened in 1964 in its present function. Physically, the Center strikes the visitor as a small, insulated

From *Federal Probation* 34:46–53, No. 3, Sept., 1970. Reprinted by permission of the publisher.

college, with time-honored old buildings, shaded walks and gardens, and an atmosphere of quiet tranquility. Philosophically, the institution is committed to what can best be described as "participatory administration."[4] We attempt to hire the best young professionals available in each behavioral discipline and provide them with as much autonomy and freedom of movement as they can handle. Ideas leading to policy changes usually flow from the bottom up and staff members are encouraged to challenge the status quo whenever and wherever rules and regulations serve the institution rather than the kids. Such a policy has enabled the Center to assemble an aggressive staff of creative individualists eager to explore new departures in treatment modalities.

The 150 students live in seven cottages and attend a full-time school on grounds, with approximately 25 students yearly moving on to attend "outside school" in the local public school systems. Each cottage is administered by a professional (currently three cottage supervisors hold master's degrees) who is responsible for its entire operation.

The lack of modern urban resources is a continuing frustration in the operation of a rural institution, a frustration which is only partially offset by advantages. Parents (in most cases) have difficulty in making the long and tiring trip to visit their sons; hence, every weekend day is "visiting day" with few restrictions concerning visiting procedures. Since the nearest center for public transportation is Harrisburg—40 miles away—many line and supervisory staff have obtained a bus driver's license and use the institution's bus in transporting kids to various activities and events in the "big city." Weekend home visits are frequent and transportation to and from trains and busses is shared equally by cottage staffs.

A full-time volunteer resources coordinator plans and implements programs and activities between area citizens and students. But the problem of how to actively involve families per se as equal partners in treatment continues to be an elusive and shadowy goal.

INITIAL ATTEMPTS TO MEET WITH FAMILIES

The first step toward reaching this goal was taken when each cottage made a commitment to the principle of a home evaluation for each boy as part of the treatment process. Staff members would make an evaluative-type visit with the boy to the home of his family. It was noted during many of these visits that parents were eager for more involvement with the Center and the staff, especially in terms of what they as parents could do to help their son, although oftentimes their motivation seemed to be more like "what can I do to help my son get released." But the realities of institutional life being what they are, the home evaluation of necessity became a lower priority item on the agenda of busy cottage supervisors and their staffs. And followup contact with concerned families too often was handled on a-lick-and-a-promise basis, with guilt feelings eased by strenuous referrals to already overburdened local probation officials.

The second line of attack became the utilization of visiting days for more than cursory interviews and release planning. Staff devoted many hours of weekend time to sitting down with families and exploring how things were going, and how they could go better. Some families were able to involve themselves on a regular basis throughout the entire commitment period of their sons so that treatment became truly a family affair. But again the priorities on staff time made work with more than just a few families virtually impossible, and the few successes obtained only whetted the appetite and increased the frustration. Acting on its frustration, one cottage planned and implemented a family weekend which involved several families visiting their sons, remaining overnight, and participating in an organized program of cottage togetherness. Again, results were satisfying but the satisfaction was only temporary. We were cutting a few trees, but making no dent in the forest.

One aspect of our regular summer program was a 2-week camping experience at a state park for most of the resident population. Kids were divided into small groups, competed with each other in varied sport and recreational activities, shared work experiences such as KP and camp clean-up, and learned to relate to each other and to adult counselors in moonlight bull sessions, fishing expeditions, and campfire cookouts. In 1968, several families were invited to participate in this program on a trial basis. In addition to the organized recreation and "therapeutic work" activities, time was set aside each day for counseling sessions between the families and involved staff. The results, although a mixture of positive and negative, were encouraging and indirectly led to the current project.

INVITING FAMILIES TO THE INSTITUTION

The idea of devoting an entire week to intensive and comprehensive work with several families was first broached at a staff meeting during the winter of 1968–69, following a seemingly casual suggestion by the Center's director. After several weeks of discussion, three staff members were appointed as a committee to work out the details and present a proposal to the full staff for approval. Initially, the committee planned to utilize the state park again, but as overall summer programming became more concrete, a decision was made to host the families on campus during the period when most students would be involved in other programs off grounds. The crucial questions now became: Would families accept an invitation to spend a week with us, and what approach would be the most effective in securing their cooperation?

Although the staff was in a sense exploring uncharted waters in terms of theory and technique in family therapy, several were familiar with the multiple impact concept discussed by MacGregor. Briefly, this approach involves the use of several therapists working with a single family as a therapy team. The duration of treatment is brief, usually 2 to 3 days and the therapists combine joint sessions involving the entire family with individual meetings between a specific family and team member. Borrowing from this model seemed to make sense, and it was decided that staff members would work in teams of two's, one team being assigned to each family. It was hoped that the team concept would help counteract our acknowledged lack of skill and experience in working directly with families, and that staff confidence and performance would be enhanced. Since each of the cottages is encouraged by administrative practice to operate as an independent, autonomous treatment unit, it was proposed that each cottage supervisor would be responsible for inviting one family of a boy from his cottage to participate in the program and that the supervisor would decide upon the most appropriate vehicle for making contact with the family. There was quite a bit of administrative anxiety over this last decision, since it seemed apparent that many more experienced agencies and individual professionals had stubbed their collective toes badly in attempting to accomplish similar objectives.

FAMILY CAMP: PLANS AND GOALS

Meanwhile, the Committee continued to develop an agenda and program. Initially called Family Camp, the project name was changed to Family Week, but ultimately became Family Camp again. Although the main objective of the Camp from the beginning was to work intensively with selected families around their problems, we hoped to demonstrate the feasibility of involving families in the treatment of their sons on campus, and also hoped to unite and involve all the staff in developing a new rehabilitative tool. We would cut a path through the forest, hopefully the first of many.

Following the lead of Virginia Satir[5] and others, our assumption, in terms of treatment strategy, was that in many cases a boy's delinquency could best be evaluated by including his immediate family in the picture, and that rehabilitation would be most effective when the entire family, rather than the committed student, was seen as our "patient." However, the committee hoped to incorporate other related but separate elements into the Camp program. Since most of our kids come from low income, if not deprived, families who have had little experience with vacation as most middle-class families know it, Family Camp would provide a 5-day release from the everyday cares and tensions of life. We believe that our rustic, mountainous campus, plus fresh air, sunshine, daily swimming, and an unhurried pace would meet this criterion.

Another objective of the Camp was to help the families realize they were not alone in the world—that other parents and families experience similar problems in living, including the commitment of a son to an institution for delinquent offenders. Toward this end, organized recreation for all families was planned to help the families come together, interact, and share an enjoyable activity. The actual game or activity itself would not be as important as its use as a tool in creating conditions conducive to relaxed communications between families with (hopefully) defenses lowered. A second and more structured project was a series of meetings between staff and parents alone, and staff and kids alone, with emphasis on both family life education and frank, informal discussion of what it was like to be the parent of a teenager, especially a delinquent teenager.

A fourth goal of Family Camp was to increase the knowledge base of families concerning the internal workings of the institution. We suspected that despite visiting days, home evaluations, interpretations by counselors, probation staffs and the like, many families of committed students were woefully ignorant as to what the Center was all about, and that this ignorance contributed to such institutional problems as lack of communication between families and staff, an apparent lack of interest and involvement, and even downright hostility and rejection. If we could demonstrate that the simple act of opening our doors to families, with no strings attached, would in and of itself have a powerful effect on the rehabilitation process, then another useful tool would have been added to our planning arsenal.

A final ingredient which the Committee planned to add to the total mix was an opportunity for families to complete a given task successfully as a family. We reasoned that most, if not all, of our families did not work well together and that many moons had passed since each member had worked toward and achieved a common and mutually satisfying family goal. We would indeed be plowing new ground if each counselor team and family could somehow build in as part of therapy a task or tasks which upon completion would engender a feeling of accomplishment and prowess. If our families could leave us having already reached certain limited goals, perhaps their view of themselves as being unable to cope would undergo change and they could work together more confidently.

THE CAMP SCHEDULE

Early in June, cottage supervisors were asked to begin recruiting families for the project. A tentative daily program was drawn up, distributed to staff, discussed, changed, and finally approved. Beginning at noon on a Monday and terminating after the midday meal on Friday, the program encompassed 11 hours of closed-door sessions between the family and its counselors, 6 hours of "organized recreation," and 4 hours of meetings involving parents as a group. The remaining programmed time covered meals and free time, including swimming, hiking, or just sitting around visiting and relaxing. One evening was reserved for participation in an off-campus activity, such as a movie or the local county fair, with emphasis on family togetherness.

Camp would begin with a welcome from the assistant director of the Center. Following lunch, the families would then meet and become acquainted with their counselors who would help them "check in" at their cottage living quarters, introduce them to other families and counselors, and in general strive to create a relaxed and informal opening day climate. An afternoon swim was to be followed by a picnic supper at the pool area in which families would help with the hot dogs and hamburgers, etc. Throughout the week, 6 hours were set aside for all family counselors to meet together to share problems and concerns and to give each other mutual support and encouragement.

At a final staff meeting on the eve of Family Camp, a few wrinkles were added and a few thrown out. Instant coffee, sugar and cream were available at each cottage. Although breakfast and lunch were to be eaten cafeteria style, the evening meal would be more formal. Each student resident of the Center was to come to the dining hall 15 minutes early, "set up" his family table with tablecloth, silver and linen, and then, after serving each member including himself, act as a waiter at the family table. However, the idea of assigning specific tasks for each family—the "success experience" idea—fell by the wayside, at least in a formal sense, as did a plan for encouraging specific interactions between family members at mealtimes.

CAMP BEGINS !

Monday, August 18, dawned bright and clear and by 10:30 a.m. two families had already arrived. One family was unable to provide its own transportation so its counselors arranged to meet them at the bus in Harrisburg. The first potential crisis of the week came early—a telephone call reporting an automobile breakdown. This particular family, however, had had one previous indepth contact with staff and was determined to display its resourcefulness. Almost bursting with pride, the father led the family into the dining hall only 15 minutes late for luncheon.

The Monday afternoon program seemed to go well and many of the six families (28 family members) enjoyed the swimming pool, the sun, and the fresh air. Many of the counselors brought their own families to the picnic and although a few individuals remained tense and uncomfortable, the ice between client and counselor, family and institution, was thawing swiftly.

After the picnic came the first formal session between family and counselors, followed by a meeting of all staff to discuss the day. The staff was enthused and eager, and so were the families. One family, having examined the program for the week, requested a beginning meeting with its counselors on Monday afternoon instead of a swim, citing the need "to get down to work." The scheduled staff meeting was cut short, as it had been a long day and there apparently were few problems.

On Tuesday morning the counselor teams met with the families again, followed by lunch and a staff meeting from 1 to 2 p.m. prior to the third family counseling session. At the staff meeting it was obvious that all of us were making progress in that we were running into heavy flak from the families. However, each counselor team did not at first realize that his fellow counselors were encountering similar difficulties in building bridges to the families, and for a time no one knew how to begin. Finally, two staff members hesitantly began telling about their "troubles" and soon each team was describing where its family "was at." This set the pattern for the daily counselor meetings which were used most productively. Each team would discuss the day's gains and losses, the particularly difficult hurdles, and then other staff would criticize, offer suggestions, and suggest changes in plans for the next session. In this way we were able to utilize all available expertise and counteract our own lack of experience.

THE SOFTBALL GAME

The first organized recreation session was held on Tuesday evening. It turned out to be a softball game with parents, children, and counselors participating. It was a smashing success—one of the highlights of the entire camp. Men, women, and children lined up to be chosen by two Center students. The players were enthusiastic, if not overly skillful, and with darkness approaching, the final inning saw the trailing team rally to win the game by a single run. Husbands rediscovered long dormant athletic ability; wives swung bats and ran with gusto; children squealed with delight at seeing their parents having so much fun. And the air was full of good-natured bantering and kidding. The last bridge had been crossed; we—staff, students and families—had come together and become a community, at least for a period.

On Wednesday morning the first "Family Life Education" meeting, involving husbands and wives with a counselor especially interested in this area, was held in the chapel. The intent was to present some rather structured material in lecture form followed by general discussion. The content of the lecture, with liberal use of the blackboard, concerned general problems in rearing children. Our expectation was that parents would be able to ease themselves into talking with each other about personal and painful family

problems if the discussion leader began with abstract concepts and impersonal statements. However, as with the family who surprised us on Monday
by wanting to "get on with it," the parents soon turned the meeting into a
down-to-earth exchange of mutual problems with a theme of "what it is like
to be the parents of a teenager, especially a teenager in trouble." Once again
these parents of delinquent kids, rejected for the most part as "unmotivated"
or "resistant to treatment" by the community-at-large, had demonstrated
strength far exceeding our expectations.

The Wednesday afternoon staff meeting saw several counselor teams
give discouraging verbal reports concerning the progress of their families.
The staff seemed to be running out of productive and meaningful subject
material and family resistance to change had hardened. It seemed to us as if
the ice had been broken, some significant and painful feelings had been
shared and discussed, and that a "treatment plateau" had been reached which
left both family and staff team confused and wondering what to do next.
Although no one was ready to give up the ship, it was noted that several
teams had cut short the allotted 2 hours of counseling time with their families.
No concrete answers were forthcoming from the staff meeting, other than
our determination to carry on as best we could.

At the Thursday staff meeting, following another individual family counseling session in the morning, the counselors decided to make a change in the
camp schedule. Since the initial meeting of parents as a group had gone well,
it was decided that the organized recreation scheduled for that afternoon
would be scrapped, and another "family life" meeting held. This time, however, all children would meet in a separate group, hopefully to discuss what
it was like to be children in families experiencing the obvious problem of
having a family member residing in a state institution for delinquents. One
counselor volunteered to lead the children's group. Each team was to split,
one counselor going to the children's meeting and the other to the parents'.

By this time the parents' group had developed some characteristics
common to many groups, with natural leaders emerging as well as spokesmen. Other parents were beginning to express their resentment at the dominance of the spokesmen and it became apparent that still others were playing
a passive, resigned role. The task of the counselors in this meeting became
more one of pointing out patterns of communication, identifying unspoken
and "dodged" problems which nevertheless were being expressed nonverbally
and encouraging the more quiet parents to participate. There was no lack
of subject material as husbands and wives actively discussed their childrens'
problems, questioned their own responses, and groped for solutions.

A most dramatic moment occurred as the time for the scheduled close
of the meeting drew near. With startling suddenness fathers and mothers
came together in realizing the awesome and painful gap in communication

between themselves and their offspring. The realization that they could not talk to their kids and that conversely their kids could not talk to them, and the meaning of this painful fact seemed to come to each parent as a lightning bolt from the middle of nowhere. There was a spontaneous clamor to immediately merge the parents' meeting with the children's. Somewhat taken aback, the group leader and the staff pressed the parents for their reasons— for what they hoped to accomplish through such a meeting. Meanwhile, decisions needed to be made—the evening schedule was open and did the parents want to meet with the kids then as a group or did they want another softball game (which the children were pushing for)? Finally, after the staff stood firm in not making a decision for the parents, the group leader stated that he would open up the room and be available to any parents desiring another meeting, while the recreation director would conduct another softball game for those interested.

THURSDAY BLUES

The staff met again briefly to compare notes regarding the outcome of the parents' and the children's meetings. The meeting with the kids had gone rather poorly; most of the youngsters had resisted involvement, and some were "just tired of going to so many meetings." After a vigorous debate on the merits of an evening session combining parents and children, it was believed that our exhaustion threshold had nearly been reached—both for families and for counselors—and that we would go our separate ways, either to another confrontation with parents and children or to a second softball game. This decision was announced to the families at supper, with each family being given freedom to select its own program for the evening— another meeting, softball, or "nothing."

Two families showed up for the meeting and for a couple of hours continued a not-too-profitable discussion concerning the relationship between parents and kids, and possible solutions which they could apply in their own situations. It was interesting to note that these were the two most verbal and dominant families, who had proved rather adept at "wearing down" the counseling teams during individual meetings. Part of one family chose to engage in neither planned activity while the remaining families and most of the staff enjoyed another softball game. This time the game seemed to drain away the tensions built up through the various confrontations and moments of truth that had occurred the last day or so and again adults and kids enjoyed throwing off the shackles and kicking up their heels, with some "elderly" athletes even unabashedly showing off for their offspring.

The final family sessions held on Friday morning were for all concerned a coming together around the entire week's experience. With some families—

where significant change in patterns of relating had been reached—there was rehashing of old arguments and quarrels, much as if the family, faced with the impending loss of their counselors, sought more comfortable ground on which to return home, thereby reassuring themselves that retreat to the "known" was easily possible if the "unknown" of new interaction proved to be too threatening. For all, it was a time for discussing achievements and formulating goals, including the making of agreements between husband and wife, parent and child. At the final meal, mutual goodbyes were said, temporary promises made, reassurances given, and the big week was at an end.

EVALUATION OF THE PROGRAM

About a month after Family Camp, a brief questionnaire was sent to all participating families. Families were asked to rate, along a five-step continuum from "strongly agree" to "strongly disagree," such statements as "We understand our son better now," "We found out that other parents have problems, too," etc. The total Camp program was broken down into eight areas, such as "the meetings with other parents," "the family meetings with our counselors," "the softball games," and families were asked which activities they liked most, liked least, and which were most valuable and least valuable. On a full, blank page, they were asked to make "any additional comments, complaints, or suggestions which you think would be helpful to us." A final question was: "How was this questionnaire filled out?" with selections including "husband mostly, wife mostly, both, whole family," and "other." The rather hastily written questionnaire was not designed with any scientific purpose in mind, but was intended as a guide in evaluating the entire Camp program. Five of six questionnaires were returned, and of these five, four were emphatically positive, while the other was guarded and relatively noncommittal.

In evaluating the entire program, both subjectively and objectively (where possible), it was evident that our original hopes and goals were reached. First, we were able to persuade six "hard-to-reach," "problem" families to interrupt their normal life routines and share a week with us. There were no last-minute cancellations, abrupt departures, or unmalleable hostility.

Second, we were able to demonstrate that it is possible for a rural state institution, handicapped by the usual bureaucratic problems of lack of money, "inadequate staff," not enough time, etc., to fully involve itself in the application of a modern treatment tool. Given a benign administration which encourages individual autonomy and freedom of decision at the lowest level (and the concomitant freedom to "make your own mistakes"), a dedicated staff willing to give freely of its time and talent without regard to 8:00 a.m.

to 5:00 p.m. routines, and a willingness to "try anything" once (i.e., family therapy) despite lack of knowledge and experience, it seems evident that there is no need for professionals and institutions in the correctional field to lag behind their colleagues who labor in seemingly greener pastures. It is certainly evident that the location of institution and staff away from the action and stimulation of city life need not be an insurmountable handicap in developing and implementing new treatment programs.

Third, our other, more minor goals were also met. Although no attempt was made to qualitatively evaluate the therapy with the families, there seemed little doubt that much positive change took place. Four of the six families indicated via the questionnaire that their closed-door sessions as individual families with their counselors were the most valuable part of Family Camp. The returned questionnaires were replete with comments such as "it helped me a lot," "we understand our son better," "we see things more clearly." Two of the six students involved were released shortly after the conclusion of the Camp and at last report were doing well. Even the family returning a "lukewarm" questionnaire left Camp on a positive note, with problem areas clearly identified, and future planning based on total family rather than individual student need. The "vacation" aspect went well. The weatherman cooperated; implementation of the program went smoothly; the swimming pool, organized games, leisurely mealtimes, and country atmosphere were enjoyed by all. The communication between families, evidenced by "visiting" each other, attending offgrounds activities together, and the sharing of intimate problems during parents' meetings, helped each parent realize that others had similar problems, and that these problems could be licked. Everyone seemed to leave with a more complete understanding of what Loysville was all about and what it was trying to do. One parent's written comment indicated surprise at what he had found: "Most valuable and interesting to us was the realization that these very personable young men (the staff) seemed to really have our son's interest in view."

LONG RANGE BENEFITS OF FAMILY CAMP

Perhaps the most meaningful accomplishment of Family Camp was its impact upon the staff and the institution. Aside from the very obvious fact that the program was successfully completed, the staff, a mixture of talented but often temperamental individualists, had drawn closer together as each shared, worked toward, and reached a common concrete goal. One successful program inevitably generates another, and several new ideas are now in the planning stage—including a "family orientation day" to be held for all families of new students several times a year. Now that work with families has proved to be effective, new ground is being broken in work with groups of students where previously there had been some passive resistance. Following a runaway and subsequent recapture of their son, one family became involved in a 3-hour cottage meeting with the boys and staff from their son's cottage, with discussion focused on the meaning of running away as a solution to problems. Now, other boys participating in the meeting are asking when their families can become so involved. The involvement of "nonprofessional" staff as full members of the counseling teams has helped increase the morale, spirit, and eagerness of lower echelon staff throughout the institution.

Finally, the young professionals, having accepted the challenge of attempting some rather concentrated family therapy with very little preparation by way of training or experience, gained a large measure of confidence in themselves, which will enable them to continue to reach for and achieve other "impossible" goals.

NOTES AND REFERENCES

1. MacGregor, Robert et al.: *Multiple Impact Therapy With Families.* New York: McGraw-Hill, 1964.
2. Travisono, A.P.: "Understanding the Family of the Delinquent Child." Proceedings, Sixty Fourth Annual Meeting, NATSJA, Dallas, Texas (printed by Boys Industrial School, Topeka, Kansas).
3. O'Neil, C.F.: "Reaching Families of Delinquent Boys." *Children,* 16, No. 5, Sept.–Oct. 1969.
4. A term used by the author to describe the administrative practice of encouraging maximum staff involvement in the decision-making process. See *Management by Participation,* by A.J. Marros, et al., New York: Harper and Row, Inc., 1967.
5. Satir, Virginia: *Conjoint Family Therapy.* Palo Alto, Calif.: Science and Behavior Books, Inc., 1961.

AFFILIATIONS AND ACKNOWLEDGMENTS

1. Since writing this article, Mr. Stollery has been named Director of Youth Forestry Camp No. 3, Aitch, Pennsylvania.

A Parolee Tells Her Story

BETTY TYLER

As the great iron doors clanged shut behind me and I walked down the gray stone steps and into the world as a free woman, I was aware of only one emotion—fear.

I had been in county prison, outside Philadelphia, for almost 2 years, and facing me were another 2 years on parole. For 24 months I had looked forward to this day, the day I would be free to go back to being a mother to our four children.

The one thing I hadn't counted on was being afraid! As I walked down the street amid crowds of people on their way to work, it seemed to me that every eye was upon me. Every face seemed ready to shout, "Get back in prison where you belong!"

When I finally reached the tiny furnished room my husband had, I closed the door with tremendous relief, feeling as if I wanted to stay behind that door forever. My husband, a mechanic, was at work and would not be home until dinner time. If only he had been there to help ease the pain of re-entering a strange world! Suddenly, the words of a matron I had grown very fond of in prison came into mind:

"You are going to feel frightened and alone many times when you leave prison. When you do, just pray to God above to give you the strength to go on."

I knelt by the bed and poured out my heart in prayer. As I arose, my glance fell on a picture of our four children, on the bureau. It restored my confidence in myself. It would be a long, hard task, but my husband and I both had set a goal of 1 year before we would be together with our children again. We knew it would be unlikely that we could have the children back with us immediately. We had to prove ourselves first.

From *Philadelphia Sunday Bulletin Magazine.* Copyright © Bulletin Co., 1963. Reprinted by permission of the publisher.

My husband and I had been imprisoned for writing checks which we couldn't cover. My husband had been unemployed for over 6 months before it happened. Our small savings had dwindled to nothing.

I was pregnant with my fourth child and unable to work. We were renting and we got further and further behind. We should have gone to our families for help, but pride held us back.

How immature and stupid we were. We went deeply into debt, writing checks for bills, mainly food, hoping against hope that we'd be able to cover them. We got into a financial hole from which we couldn't climb out. The result was a 2-year prison term for me and a lesser one for my husband, so that he could get out and start to support our family.

Our children were placed in foster homes. I shall never, in all my years on earth, be able to forget that terrible moment when I kissed each of them goodby, knowing I wouldn't see them for at least 2 years!

Prison life was frightening at first, but I slowly adjusted to it. I was not overworked, although I had daily chores to perform. The food was good, right off the prison farm, and I found the matrons to be a great spiritual help. I still correspond with three of those matrons and one of them visits with me and my family regularly as a friend, even does some sewing for me. I never was a good seamstress and she often helps me when I'm stuck on a pattern. I also found the prison chaplain and his wife unbelievably understanding.

I know some of you who are reading this are probably saying, "That's just what is wrong with prison. It isn't hard enough for the prisoners; they have all the comforts of home."

My reply to you is this: They could have wall-to-wall carpeting, personal TV sets, swimming pools and maid service, but all of these are as nothing, without your loved ones to share it with you.

Jail serves one main purpose and this is to separate the prisoner from society. In that society are your loved ones, and you are made painfully aware of how much you love them and miss them, when you lie in bed each night and stare up at the stars through barred windows.

I did not see my children for almost 2 years. I wrote to them regularly and they answered in their childish scrawl. I thank God that they were all small enough at the time to believe that Mommy was very ill in the hospital.

After serving 16 months I was notified I was eligible for parole. It was just cause for celebration among all the inmates. Parole is a highly sought goal. Not everyone automatically goes on state parole. It is a definite privilege extended only to those who the State Parole Board feels are worthy of it.

Several months before a prisoner is eligible, an official from the State Parole Board visits with prison officials and the prisoner. Naturally, the inmate's record, along with recommendations by those in authority, are all taken into consideration.

At the time of the interview, the potential parolee is usually extremely nervous. In my case, I was interviewed for about an hour—60 minutes of reliving my crime again, of stating definite plans for my future, of trying to convince this man I had learned my lesson and that I'd be a good risk once out in society again.

These interviews are trying to any prisoner. After being imprisoned for many, many months or maybe years, a prisoner tends to have pushed his crime into the background. He's tried hard to forget it.

When the State Parole Board officer arrives, he takes him, in memory, right back to the scene of the crime and questions him about it. By doing this he can pretty well determine whether the prisoner is harboring any unhealthy resentments, or whether he is sincere in wanting to make a success of himself.

These are just a few of hundreds of things that go into the final recommendation. For the prisoner, this interview is just the beginning. He must "sweat it out" for weeks or maybe months before he knows whether he has made it. Even then he may have fines and costs to pay or may have to face charges elsewhere if detainers have been lodged against him.

In addition, the would-be parolee must have a sponsor, a home to go to and a job. One can realize the difficulty a prisoner has, sitting in prison and trying to find someone outside who will employ him. Usually, the person who sponsors a prisoner is of great assistance in this. In my case, the prison chaplain's wife was my sponsor.

Knowing my background as a secretarial graduate before my marriage, my parole officer suggested that I search the Help Wanted columns and check with employment agencies for a job. Because my husband was again employed as a mechanic, it was not necessary for me to have a job at once.

However, I was expected to look for employment immediately. I was also expected to report to my sponsor and the State Parole Board within 24 hours after release from prison, and I had to meet with my sponsor and my parole officer once a month.

In addition, it was my responsibility to send in a written report of my activities, wages, savings, etc. Failure to comply with any one of these regulations meant one thing—back to prison!

I was free, but with many, many restrictions. I was not permitted to go into any bar or night club where alcoholic beverages were sold. This did not bother me too much, as I didn't drink.

I was not permitted to visit with any person who had been an inmate in any prison at any time. I was not allowed to go out of the county or state without permission. These are just a few of many rules a parolee must obey.

A parolee does not immediately have to tell a future employer that he has served time in prison, but if he is hired, he is expected to let his employer know shortly thereafter.

I went to many offices and applied for many jobs. It was hard for me, as I had not worked for 10 years. Finally, I was offered two jobs the same day. One was in a large corporation, the other in a small branch sales office. I chose the latter, as I felt I would feel less conspicuous. There were only two other girls and I liked them instantly.

After I had worked there for 3 months, starting at $200 a month with a raise to $240, my parole officer advised me to tell my boss about my past. I was really frightened at the prospect of doing this, but knew it was a rule I had to obey.

One noon when the other two girls were out to lunch, I asked my boss if I might come into his office and speak to him about a personal matter.

I hurried in, saying a small prayer that he would be understanding. I pulled no punches. I stated the facts. When I finished, there was a minute of silence.

A faint smile crossed his face as he said, "You know, that took courage to tell me that. As for the past, forget it. We've all made mistakes. Some of us just were lucky enough not to get caught. We will consider the matter closed and no one else in this organization will ever know about this."

He praised me for the good job that I was doing and as I walked out of his office I said a small prayer again—this time of thanks.

While on parole, my husband and I were given the privilege of visiting our children. Our first meeting after 2 years was the most wonderful day of all. They were brought from their foster homes to a local school where we met them. To actually see their little faces and embrace them was the real life ending of a long, long dream.

After a few months, we were permitted to take the children out by ourselves for a whole day. When a year had gone by and we had saved some money, we rented a house and furnished it with used furniture.

A social worker came and thoroughly investigated the house, even making sure we had sheets on the beds! Two weeks later we were notified we could have our children back.

That night I said a fervent prayer to God thanking Him for His merciful goodness to us.

We have been back together as a family for more than 3 years now, and I am no longer on parole. We live in a small suburban community outside Philadelphia, and I suppose we seem to others a rather typical family.

My husband works every day. I am still a secretary with the same wonderful boss. I have had five good raises since I started and I now handle checks and money for our office. This really frightened me at first. For him to show such confidence in me still overwhelms me at times.

My husband and I can't erase our past but we are trying our best to make up for it by living maturely within our means.

I can only hope that if any of you who are reading this come in contact with a parolee, you will lend him a helping hand. This can mean the difference between a constant repeater and a successfully rehabilitated person.

If I hadn't had a mother who could forgive and forget, or an employer who graciously told me we all make mistakes, what might have happened to me? Without encouragement from society and from those I love, no doubt I would have ended up a repeater.

The majority of parolees want only one chance to prove themselves. Without that chance, they are doomed before they walk out of jail.

I thank God I was given that chance.

Alternate Contents
(Deviancy Perspective)

Index